INDOOR PLANTS
Comprehensive Care and Culture

Doris F. Hirsch

INDOOR
Comprehensive

PLANTS
Care and Culture

CHILTON BOOK COMPANY   Radnor, Pennsylvania

Copyright © 1977 by Doris F. Hirsch
All Rights Reserved
Published in Radnor, Pa., by Chilton Book Company
and simultaneously in Don Mills, Ontario, Canada,
by Thomas Nelson & Sons, Ltd.
Manufactured in the United States of America

Library of Congress Cataloging in Publication Data
Hirsch, Doris F.
Indoor plants.

Bibliography: p. 217
Includes index.
1. House plants.   I. Title.
SB419.H64   635.9′65   76-57249
ISBN 0-8019-6489-X

Designed by Adrianne Onderdonk Dudden

Line drawings by Marina L. Hankinson, William J. Hankinson, and
Sally Wickham Mollomo

Photography by John T. Chew, Jr.

Special thanks to E. R. Squibb & Sons, Inc.,
for making their world headquarters
at Princeton, N.J. available for photography

2 3 4 5 6 7 8 9 0   5 4 3 2 1 0 9 8 7

In total love to Susie Kline,
my grandmother,
the soul of our family,
the ever blooming rose.

Preface

Self-discipline. That's really what it's all about. The questioning words *imperative? superfluous?* controlled my decisions on data to be included. *Enough* of the book published for the professional, or the popular manual on house plant "how to" in three paragraphs.

Here you have a single source of reference; uncomplicated yet complete in the essentials for successfully maintaining your plant. Everything you, as an experienced or inexperienced plant owner, need to know in plant care is presented in a direct, simple manner. Included are 212 genera with species and varieties, totally describing 1136 plants. Popular demand determined the collection/selection for the majority of plants. However, it would be remiss not to include some seldom seen greens which are naturals for cultivation and appreciation within an interior environment.

When the author's research into the vast arena of horticulture produced discrepancies in cultural approaches, decisions were based on personal experience.

At a very early age, I was made aware of nature's wonders, and as I emerged into the role of adulthood, I applied my hands to the soil. The pleasure derived from my success in plant parenthood provided much peace of mind. But more. These things of beauty provided a new challenge. Much of the plant care to which I had been exposed as a child was no longer relative. I was now dealing with a totally new environment. Glass walls, air conditioning, air convectors. The red flag was slowly but persistently rising. Telltale signs of increased struggle for existence among my charges forced the issue. Obviously, my plants could not meet the challenge of these alien aspects of their new environment unless aided in their adjustment. And so began my delightful treasure hunt.

Every moment of my leisure time not spent in tending to my plants was spent in researching. An area of my home was set up into a sizable intensive care unit for the plant friends of many people friends. My telephone rang with frequency, the caller requesting plant care or cure information. Circumstances or curiosity seemed to demand constant questing, leading me down many unfamiliar paths. As I floundered along, repeatedly I stumbled onto yet another new species. Captivated, I would pursue it until IT captured me.

Inevitably, time, space, and consuming interest dictated the phasing out of my then vocation of some 20 years, commercial interior design. I had planted many atriums and placed proper plants in proper places, but no more did that suffice. Then occurred my nemesis. In reviewing my drafted layout of a public waiting area for a design project, I discovered I had planned and specified a greater quantity of plants than seats. No self-discipline.

Acknowledgments

A long-spun list of people know of my sincere appreciation. Blessings are on many heads for aid in mental challenge and physical endurance as this project evolved.

Beth Errickson, graduate entomologist and plant pathologist from the University of New Hampshire, who kept me abreast of the everchanging plague in the Rx department; Susan Abbott and Elfriede Roth-Poiner, fresh from their horticultural training at Rutgers University, in plying research; Mary Robertson, previously with Time-Life Inc., whose experience and energies were a godsend; John Gellatly, a long-time administrator in publishing; and Lydia M. Driscoll, my Chilton editor, consultant and mediator.

I acknowledge the patience of my Stagandoe family, my homefolk, Ger, Bill, Jackie, and Leslie, who silently bore my emotional levels, sharing my triumphs and honoring my needed solitude. A special thank you.

And, Jack, my husband, whose vital force in our shared years exemplified the strength conceivable, in order that I could grab hold of my boot straps, take up my pen, and turn again to life and smile—in memoriam—my deepest gratitude.

Introduction

This handbook has been developed specifically for the amateur. It is simple yet complete, instructing in the cultural needs of plants in an interior environment. In Section I, plants are listed alphabetically by their botanical names. To have listed them by their common name would have been confusing since many plants have several common names; each plant has only one botanical classification and name. The genus in which a plant is categorized is determined by specific characteristics of cultural needs, usage, and physical features. The nomenclature—most frequently Latin—selected for a plant is in some way descriptive of that plant. Therefore, each botanical name is also conveying information on its character. So that the reader can find individual plants with ease, the common names, followed by the botanical names, form a detailed index.

Following the detailed listings in Section I, general information for plant care and culture is presented in Section II. Thus, in one complete volume, you have a single source of reference for all your plant needs.

Contents

Section I
ENCYCLOPEDIC GUIDE TO PLANTS

ABUTILON MEGAPOTAMICUM (ab-yew'-til-on meg-ap-poh-tam'-ik-um) Flowering Maple.
Your Abutilon may be aesthetically displayed in a hanging basket that shows off its beautiful cascading stems. Or, the plant can be trained on a slender pole. It will bloom continuously throughout the year, providing pleasure in all seasons.

Family Tree: Malvaceae (mal-vay'-see-ay) Mallow family, a native of Brazil, from the great "Malakos," meaning soft or soothing; thought to be a reference to an ointment made from the seeds. Abutilon is a latinized version of an Arabic name. A member of the hollyhock family, it is related to the Chinese hibiscus and rose of Sharon.

Foliage: deep green leaves supported on long stalks; to 3″ (76 mm) long; shaped to lobed, maple tree-like. The species variegatum has leaves flecked, splashed, or spotted with yellow or gold.

Flower: blooms throughout the year when set in bright light; paper-thin texture, bell-shaped blossom grows singly in the leaf axil; drooping nature; color yellow with red calyx (outer leaflike part).

Size: commonly to 36″ (.90 m), but varieties to 10′ (3 m).

Location: WINTER—full sun; set in southern exposure.
SUMMER—*Inside:* partial shade; at least four hours bright sun; set in east to south morning sun. *Outside:* partial shade; set in eastern exposure or under a protective structure where plant receives strong light, but no direct rays.
FALL: move indoors by mid-September.

Dormancy: none, maintain proper culture throughout year.

Water: keep soil evenly moist.

Mist: daily, in time to dry by dusk.

Humidity: 40%-50%.

Air circulation: helpful condition.

Feed: only when plant shows signs of lack of nutrition; use fertilizer with low nitrogen content.

Soil: standard potting soil.

Temperature: Day—68°-72°F (20°-22°C). Night—55°-60°F (13°-16°C).

Potbound: very unhappy; repot or pot-on in spring.

Mature plants: better bloom if stems pinched back (as they become straggly). Pinch off to point where plant retains compact, uniform shape; pinch center out of young shoots for a wide plant; too tall a plant for standing upright—stake and tie main trunk (leave small amount of slack in ties to eliminate potential injury from tie cutting into fleshy stem).

Propagate: by seeds or stem cutting, latter should be about 4″ (100 mm) long.

Offspring established: when established, pinch out top shoot to aid compactness of growth. Cut back or pinch every three to four months to prevent legginess.

Insect alert: mealybug, whitefly, scale, mites.

Notable: Unfortunately, this plant tends to develop yellow leaves. If they are removed daily, new growth will quickly be replaced on healthy plants; keep in a cool place and pinch back frequently to prevent legginess.

A. x hybridum (hib'-rid-um) meaning hybrid; flower colors: red, pink, purple, white, or yellow; leaves lobed or simple; sometimes flecked.

Variety—Apricot: orange flower.
Variety—Golden Fence: yellow flower.

A. striatum (strye-ay'-tum) meaning channeled or grooved, usually the leaves; flowers: orange veined with crimson; 2″ (50 mm) long; leaves many lobed.

Variety—Thompsonii (tom-soh'-nee-eye): green and yellow variegated leaves.

Abutilon megapotamicum,
Flowering Maple

ACACIA ARMATA (ak-kay'-see-uh ar-ma'-ta) Kangaroo Thorn.

An eye-catching, showy plant when flowering; its name obviously relates to its natural habitat. The Kangaroo Thorn has a growth of an upright, erect nature.

Family Tree: Leguminosae (le-gum'-in-oh-say) Pea family. A native of Australia and other tropics.

Foliage: small thorny, stiff, flattened leaflets borne on leaflike stems called phyllodes.

Flower: yellow, fuzzy clusters (the size of peas) blossoming February into May.

Size: to 10' (3 m); controlled easily by pruning.

Location: WINTER—full sun; set in southern exposure.

SUMMER—*Inside:* partial shade; set in eastern to southern exposure for direct rays of morning sun. *Outside:* partial shade; set in eastern exposure or under a protective structure where plant receives strong light but no direct rays.

FALL: move indoors by mid-September; site in southeastern exposure.

Dormancy: starts mid-October; temperature during the winter months should be kept very low, 35°-40°F (1°-4°C); slowly diminish watering; cease fertilizing.

Water: keep soil evenly moist.

Mist: daily, in time to dry by dusk.

Humidity: 50%-60%.

Air circulation: helpful condition.

Feed: weekly, diluted liquid manure.

Soil: standard potting soil with some sharp sand or perlite; soil should have good drainage.

Temperature: Day—60°-72°F (15°-22°C). Night—50°-60°F (10°-15°C).

Potbound: very happy.

Mature plants: better bloom if stems pinched back (as they become straggly). Pinch off to point where plant retains compact, uniform shape; pinch center out of young shoots for wide plant; too tall a plant for standing upright—stake and tie main trunk (leave small amount of slack in ties to eliminate potential injury from tie cutting into fleshy stem); may be trained into standard form (tree form) or espaliered plant by proper pruning or pinching.

Propagate: by using new shoots as cuttings 3" (76 mm) long, after flowering; put cuttings in mixture of peat moss, sharp sand, or perlite with potting soil; or propagate by seeds (boil seeds in water and soak overnight); germinate seeds in potting mixture under glass.

Offspring established: transplant into larger pots with normal soil standards.

Insect alert: mealybug, scale, whitefly.

A. decurrens (dee-ker'-renz) meaning running down; the leaf blade extends as a wing or ridge down the stem; known as Green Wattle.

　　Variety—Dealbata: silvery green foliage; heads of soft yellow flowers (the florists' Mimosa).

A. farnesiana (far-neez-ee-ay'-nuh) Popinac or Sweet Acacia. A multibranched, thorny shrub; leaflets 1/8" (3 mm) long; heads of fragrant, dark yellow flowers (used for perfume).

A. baileyana (bay-lee-ay'-nuh) graceful, ferny, blue gray foliage; large puffs of yellow flowers; propagation best by seed.

ACALYPHA HISPIDA (ak-al-lye-fuh hiss'-pid-uh) Chenille Plant; nickname: Redhot Cat's Tail.

The Chenille plant's flowers, soft and gentle, are lovely to espy over a long blooming period. This plant has been dubbed the Chenille plant because of the drooping, skinny nature and color of the flower, which resembles the tufts on the bedspread of the same name. Hispida means rough with bristly hair.

Family Tree: Euphorbiaceae (you-for-bi-ay'-see-ay) Spurge family; native of Burma and the East Indies.

Foliage: pointed, oval, coarse, evergreen, hairy, dark green leaves.

Flower: 8"-20" (.25 m-.55 m) pendulous spikes of tiny, crowded red flowers making tassellike inflorescences (flower grouping) of reddish purple; blooms year round profusely in fall and winter.

Size: upright bushy plant, usually 1'-3' (.30 m-.90 m) in cultivation but up to 5' (1.50 m).

Location: WINTER—full sun; set in southern exposure.

SUMMER—*Inside:* partial shade; set in eastern to southern exposure for direct rays of morning sun. *Outside:* partial shade; set in eastern exposure or under a protective structure where plant receives strong light but no direct rays.

FALL: move indoors by mid-September.

Dormancy: none; maintain proper culture throughout year.

Water: keep soil evenly moist.

Mist: twice daily with lukewarm water in time to dry by dusk; when flowering, spray only leaves.

Humidity: above normal, 45%-50%.

Air circulation: helpful condition.

Feed: monthly while plants are growing; with a mild liquid manure in spring through fall.

Soil: standard potting mix; a bit of extra peat moss is helpful.

Acacia decurrens,
Green Wattle

MLH

Temperature: Day—70°F (21°C) or higher, Night—60°-65°F (15°-18°C).
Potbound: happy; pot-on or repot in spring as needed.
Mature plants: better bloom if stems pinched back as they become straggly; pinch off to point where plant retains compact, uniform shape; pinch center out of young shoots for wide plant; to rejuvenate old plants, prune severely in early spring leaving 8″-12″ (.25 m-.30 m) of growth.
Propagate: from 3″ (76 mm) cuttings rooted in a sandy medium or perlite.
Offspring established: plant into larger pots when roots are well established, using specified soil for this genus.
Insect alert: mealybug, scale.
Notable: Good bright light enhances the brilliance of the color of the blossom; needs regular cultural attention for success.

A. wilkesiana (wil-kis-ee-a′-na) Beefsteak Plant; foliage plant with sparse red flowers that bloom only in winter; coppery green leaves, often mottled with yellow or orange.
  Variety—Macrophylla: meaning with large leaves; bronze, copper foliage.
  Variety—Macafeana: coppery leaves; grown for foliage.
A. godseffiana (god-sef-eye-ay′-na) leaves: 2″-3″ (50 mm-76 mm) dark green with white or yellow edges; a foliage plant with green white flowers; 2′-3′ (.60 m-.90 m) upright, bushy plant.
A. hispida (hiss′-pid-uh).
  Variety—Alba: pinkish white flowers.

ACHIMENES HYBRIDS (ak-kim′-in-eez) Magic Flower; nickname, Kimono Plant, Nut Orchid, Widow's Tear, Japanese Pansy, Hot Water Plant, Cupid's Bower.
A beautiful, hanging basket genus, so popular in the Victorian era, that offers many possible color selections for summer flowering. In winter put it in storage, see *Dormancy* section. Some species of the genus are good for cut flowers in fresh bouquets or to dry for showy arrangements.
Family Tree: Gesneriaceae (jes-nare-ee-ay′-see-ay) Gesneriad family, a native to Central America. Related to the African Violet and Gloxinia.
Foliage: glistening, often hairy leaves; 1″-3″ (25 mm-76 mm) long; opposite or whorled leaves supported on upright or trailing stems; pale green to reddish bronze.
Flower: satiny masses in pastel blue, deep pink, pure yellow, deep red with yellow throats, and deep purple; 1″-2″ (25 mm-50 mm) across; open faced; grow from leaf axils; bloom June through October.
Size: 8″-12″ (.25 m-.30 m).
Location: WINTER—full sun; set in southern exposure.
SUMMER—*Inside:* partial shade; set in eastern to southern exposure for direct rays of morning sun. *Outside:* partial shade; set in eastern exposure or under a protective structure where plant receives strong light but no direct rays.
FALL: move indoors by mid-September; site in southern exposure.
Dormancy: starts mid-October; slowly diminish watering; let plant slowly dry out as leaves and flowers fade; cease fertilizing; let plants die to the ground; store dormant rhizomes (modified stems, usually underground) at 60°F

Acalypha hispida,
Chenille Plant

(15°C) over winter in plastic bags with dry peat moss, vermiculite, or perlite; when new growth starts after dormancy (in spring), soil should never be allowed to dry out until dormancy returns otherwise dormancy will be induced during the flowering season.
Water: keep soil evenly moist at roots.
Mist: daily, in time to dry by dusk.
Humidity: 40%-50%.
Air circulation: helpful condition.
Feed: every 2 weeks during growing season, mild liquid manure.
Soil: 2 parts peat, 1 part standard potting soil, 1 part perlite; or humus-rich soil; use a drainage material (preferably broken pieces of clay pottery) to fill bottom half of pot.
Temperature: Day—75°F (23°C) or higher. Night—65°-70°F (18°-21°C).
Potbound: happy.
Mature plants: better bloom if stems pinched back as they become straggly; pinch off to point where plant retains compact, uniform shape; pinch center out of young shoots for wide plant.
Propagate: during dormancy; divide the tiny rhizomes (modified stems) that appear on roots or leaf stems; or propagate from seeds or stem cuttings in the spring.
Offspring established: once germination takes place and two leaves appear, transplant into larger pots, using specified soil.
Notable: the Achimenes is a flowering house plant that is for the shaded exposure; it does very well grown under 14-16 hours of artificial light, or a total of 14-16 hours combination of natural daylight and artificial light; do not allow soil to dry out completely.

A. andrieuxii (an-drews′-ee-eye) small violet flowers with purple-dotted white throat.

A. antirrhina (an-tir-rin'-uh) scarlet and yellow flowers; upright to 20″ (.55 m).

A. candida (kan'-did-uh) meaning the flowers, pure white; flowers white inside, buff, cream, or reddish outside.

A. ehrenbergii (air-en-burg'-ee-eye) flowers orchid with purple-marked white throat.

A. erecta (ee-rek'-tuh) meaning upright; scarlet flowers; formerly known as A. coccinea, meaning bright deep pink.

A. flava (flay'-vuh) meaning pure yellow; basket plant; golden yellow flowers.

A. grandiflora (gran-di-flor'-a) meaning with larger flowers than other species; flowers purple with white throats; upright to 26″ (.65 m).

A. pedunculata (pe-dunk-u-la'-ta) meaning with a distinct stalk; fiery orange flowers; upright to 28″ (.70 m).

A. hybrids meaning hybrid.

  Variety—Charm: compact to 16″ (.40 m); pink flowers.
  Variety—Purple King: compact to 16″ (.40 m); extremely floriferous.

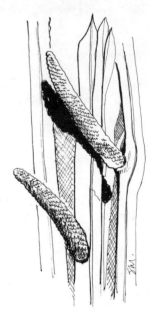

Acorus calamus,
Sweet Flag

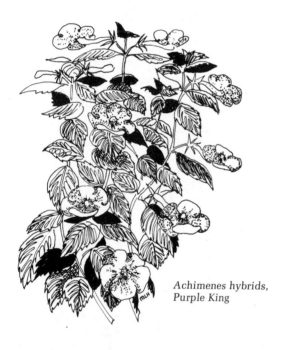

Achimenes hybrids,
Purple King

ACORUS GRAMINEUS (ak'-or-us gram-in'-ee-us)
  Japanese or Chinese Sweet Flag.

A most fragrant foliage plant, this genus imparts a lemony scent. Its rootstock is used commercially for perfume. Actually, it is a flowering genus, producing green to yellow spiked flowers in early summer.

Family Tree: Araceae (air-ay'-see-ay) Arum family; belongs to Jack-in-the-pulpit family; native to boggy areas of the Northern Hemisphere.

Foliage: flat, iris or grasslike, green, stiff, fan-shaped tufts.

Size: 2″-12″ (50 mm-304 mm), depending on species.

Location: WINTER—southern exposure.

SUMMER—*Inside and Outside:* southern exposure.

FALL: move indoors by mid-September; site in southern exposure.

Water: keep soil thoroughly moist.

Mist: daily, twice daily when possible.

Humidity: happiest when very high, 60%-70%.

Feed: mild liquid manure at 6-month intervals; do not feed newly potted or purchased plants for 6 months.

Soil: 1 part each standard potting mix, perlite, sand, and peat moss.

Temperature: Day—70°-80°F (21°-26°C). Night—40°-65°F (4°-18°C).

Potbound: normal; when plant's root system overbalances soil content of pot, pot-on.

Propagate: by division of plant and root; pot-up in soil as specified for this genus; or set in container of water.

Notable: a good plant for artificial light; it will grow well in just water culture; keep on the cooler side of recommended temperatures; drafts and winds are of no concern to Acorus.

A. gramineus (gram-min'-ee-us) meaning grass family; native of Japan; slender, irislike foliage, green; to 12″ (.30 m) high.

  Variety—Variegatus (ver-i-gay'-tus) cream-striped leaves 8″-12″ (.25 m-.30 m) tall.
  Variety—Pusillus (pew-sill'-us) miniature, slender, grasslike leaves, green; 3″-4″ (76 mm-101 mm) tall.

A. calamus (kal'-am-us) known as Sweet Flag; foliage variegated, 3′-6′ (.90 m-1.80 m) high.

ADIANTUM (ad-ee-an'-tum) Maidenhair Fern, American Maidenhair, Delta Maidenhair Fern.

The name of this genus derives from *adiantos*, which means dry. Most of the species have an unusual feature, in that fronds (leaves) can be submerged in water, yet upon removal are dry. Cut fronds provide interesting floral backdrops, no harm is done to plant by this pruning. Maidenhair fern is second to none in adding a graceful, delicate, almost fragile note to an interior site. A few species grow wild in the United States and are on preservation lists of several states.

Family Tree: Polypodiaceae (pol-ee-poh-dee-ay'-see-ay) common Fern family; origin, Brazil.

Foliage: feathery fronds are triangular in shape with wedge-shaped, emerald green leaflets; wiry, black shiny or polished stems; fronds are about 15″ (380 mm) long, 9″ (228 mm) wide.

Size: 1′-4′ (.30 m-1.22 m) high.

Location: WINTER—eastern exposure.

SUMMER—*Inside:* eastern exposure. *Outside:* northern exposure.

FALL: move indoors by mid-September; site in eastern exposure.

Dormancy: none really, but rests lightly through fall and winter.

Water: an extremely important part of the culture of these plants; be guided by the following: ordinarily, water thoroughly, allowing moderate drying between waterings; never allow to dry out completely; be aware of cool weather, when slower evaporation should mean less frequent watering; use room-temperature water only.

Mist: daily, twice a day if possible; use room-temperature water.

Humidity: very high, 60%-70%, especially March through September.

Air circulation: essential for super success but avoid drafts.

Feed: very, very weak solution of mild liquid manure (cut recommendation of manufacturer to 2/3), every 3 weeks.

Soil: 2 parts standard potting mix, 1 part vermiculite, 2 parts peat moss.

Temperature: Day—68°-75°F (20°-23°C). Night—50°-60°F (10°-15°C).

Potbound: very happy; do not pot-on until root system is 80% of pot content (best done in February or March). Roots adhere to interior pot walls, therefore, to avoid excessive injury, gently ease them loose. Rapping pot against end of a table is an aid, as well as running a spatula around inside of pot, pressing against pot wall with tool to avoid slipping into root ball. Wrap fronds of a large fern in newspaper for protection while handling. Set plant on 1½″ (37 mm) layer of gravel, then add soil.

Mature plants: if fern looks sad, cut back to 2″ (50 mm) above soil line; repot and proceed in proper culture. If aerial roots develop, cut them off. Wash foliage at least every 3 weeks. Remove yellowed or withered fronds as they appear.

Propagate: by division of mature plant, best done around March; or by spores (these resemble little brown dots) attached to underside of leaflets.

Insect alert: mealybugs, aphids, thrips, red spider; control with soap and water remedy; repeat every 3 days until eradicated.

Notable: ferns need coolness at their roots, so use pebble and water in tray method for cooler temperature and high humidity; best to grow in clay pots, as their porosity allows evaporation and aids in keeping roots cool; if fronds droop from too dry soil, they cannot be revived; fronds of young plants cannot stand water directly on them; fronds bruise easily so plant should be located where it will not touch or be touched; ferns cannot stand pesticides, which will kill insects and your plant, too.

A. capillus veneris (kap′-il-us ven′-er-iss) means hair of Venus, thus it's known as Venus' hair, though also called Southern Maidenhair fern; slender, erect fronds 8″-18″ (.25 m-.45 m) long, with compound, fan-shaped black leaves; will take warm temperatures but needs high humidity.

Adiantum cuneatum, Delta Maidenhair Fern

A. hispidulum (hiss-pid′-yew-lum) meaning with bristly hairs; known as Rosy Maidenhair; hairy, stiff stalks, fronds 8″-15″ (.25 m-.38 m) long are metallic when young, dark green when mature; native to Australia and New Zealand.

A. pedatum (pe-day′-tum) means with segments, cleft like a bird's foot; known as American Maidenhair fern; wiry, black purple stalk 1′ (.30 m) high, forked at top, with bluish green leaflets; large feathery fronds to 1½′ (.45 m) across; grow in cool shade.

A. tenerum (ten′-er-um) means slender, tender, soft; known as Brittle Maidenhair fern; deeply notched, glossy green fronds on shiny brownish black stems; to 4′ (1.22 m).

A. caudatum (kaw-day′-tum) meaning tailed; known as Trailing Maidenhair; looks much different than other species; dull green or grayish leaflets, short brown hairs on stalks; to 3′ (.90 m).

A. cuneatum (kew-nee-ay′-tum) means wedge shaped; Delta Maidenhair fern; of Brazil; dark stalks with light green leaflets, with short dark hairs (sporangia) on undersides; feathery fronds are 12″ (.30 m) wide, 18″ (.45 m) long.

ADROMISCHUS (ad-roh-misk′-us) Calico Hearts; nickname: Leopard Spots.

The genus Adromischus, previously known as Cotyledron, is small-scaled, and slow growing. All species of this perennial are succulents and of interesting various forms. They work well in terrarium-type planters but must have open tops to avoid rotting to which they are so susceptible in overly wet circumstances. Some flower, but most species' bloom is unimportant. Foliage includes various hues of green, some highlighted with reds or purple blotches or shadings.

Family Tree: Crassulaceae (krass-yew-lay′-see-ay) Stone crop family; native to Cape Province in South Africa.

Foliage: all shades of green; many with red and purple coloring accenting leaves; thick, fleshy leaves, in alternate pattern.

Flower: mostly very small, green tinged, of no aesthetic value.

Size: 2 ″ (50 mm) to 16″ (.40 m).

Location: WINTER—southern exposure.

SUMMER—*Inside and Outside:* southern exposure.

FALL: move inside by mid-September; site in southern exposure.

Dormancy: none; October through February is a resting time; slowly diminish watering; keep soil sufficiently moist to keep leaves from shriveling; cease fertilizing.

Water: March through September allow soil to become quite dry between thorough, even waterings.

Mist: daily, very lightly, around plant but not directly on it.

Humidity: low normal, 20%-25%.

Air circulation: helpful condition.

Feed: mild liquid manure, once a month, April through July.

Soil: 1 part standard potting mix, 2 parts sharp sand.

Temperature: Day—68°-80°F (15°-26°C). Night—50°-70°F (10°-20°C).

Potbound: normal; repot or pot-on when foliage appears crowded, and/or root growth is 50% of pot content; best done in early spring prior to new growth evidence.

Mature plants: frequently, older plants lose bottom leaves; bright light and sun improve richness of colors of foliage.

Propagate: from leaf cuttings or tip cuttings, any time; or by offsets; pot-up in soil as specified for this genus; do not use damp soil and do not water for 5 days after potting.

Insect alert: scale, mealybug.

Disease alert: root rot from overwatering.

Notable: soil must have excellent porosity; do not try to create humid conditions; normal interior air, even a dry site, is most suitable: *Most notable:* plants rot very easily. A good artificial-light plant, up to 16 hours combined natural and artificial light hours; do not allow soil to dry out completely.

A. clavifolius (kla-vi-foh'-lee-us) meaning and nicknamed Pretty pebbles; club-shaped, gray green leaves with tiny reddish flecks.

A. cooperii (ko-pe'-ri-e) Cooper's Adromischus; egg-shaped, blue green leaves, dark green blotches; flowers insignificant; height to 1′ (.30 m).

A. cristatus (kris-tay'-tus) meaning comblike or crested; nickname Sea shells; wedge-shaped, wavy-edged, light green leaves, on tiny reddish stems, covered with fine hairs; greenish flowers, to ½″ (12 mm) long, inconspicuous; slow growing; height to 10″ (254 mm).

A. festivus (fes-ti'-vus) meaning festive, gay, bright; nicknamed Plover eggs; egg-shaped, blue green leaves with reddish brown spots.

A. hemisphaericus (hem-iss-feer'-ik-us) half-round, thick leaves, frosted olive green; spikes of tubular, green-tinged flowers.

A. maculatus (mak-yew-lay'-tus) neat clumps of thick, practically stemless leaves, heart-shaped, gray green spotted with reddish brown; insignificant bell-shaped, erect white or pink flowers; 3″-4″ (76 mm-101 mm) tall.

Adromischus maculatus,
Calico Hearts
W.H.

AESCHYNANTHUS PARVIFOLIUS (esk-in-anth'-us par-vi-foh'-lee-us) Basketvine; nickname: Lipstick Plant, Blushwort, Bugle Plant. Nicknamed Lipstick Plant for its brilliant red tubular flowers.

Parvifolius—of small tubular flowers—was formerly listed as Trichosporum. Basketvines are most aesthetically displayed in hanging containers which show off their graceful trailing or climbing stems. These plants can be ever blooming if cultural conditions are near perfect. The more light (quantity, not intensity) they receive, the more blooms produced.

Family Tree: Gesneriáceae (ges-ner-ee-ay'-see-ay) Gesneriad family; native to East Indies and tropical Asia.

Foliage: dark, glossy, fleshy leaves; 2″ (50 mm) long.

Flower: two lipped, borne on stems 2′-3′ (.60 m-.90 m) long; blooms in spring and flowers throughout year; buds resemble lipsticks; waxy, yellow throated, scarlet flowers with deep purple, leaflike calyx (outer petal-like structures).

Fruit: long, tube-shaped.

Size: 2′ (.60 m) trailing, slender stems.

Location: WINTER—full sun, set in southern exposure.

SUMMER—*Inside:* partial shade; set in eastern to southern exposure for direct rays of morning sun. *Outside:* partial shade, set in eastern exposure or under a protective structure where plant receives strong light but no direct rays.

FALL: move indoors by mid-September.

Dormancy: none; maintain proper culture throughout year.

Water: very thirsty; keep soil evenly moist at all times.

Mist: daily, in time to dry by dusk.

Humidity: high; 70%—moist, moist air.

Air circulation: helpful condition.

Feed: monthly, mild solution of 21-7-7 acid fertilizer.

Soil: humus-rich; mixture of equal parts sphagnum moss and osmunda (root fibers) with a small amount of charcoal added.

Aeschynanthus parvifolius,
Lipstick Plant or Basketvine

Temperature: Day—75°F (23°C) or higher. Night—65°-70°F (18°-21°C).

Potbound: happy, do not pot-on until absolutely so rootbound there is 80% roots, 20% soil.

Mature plants: after plants flower, cut stems back to height of 6″ (152 mm) to produce new growth. If plant isn't making new growth, reduce watering and don't fertilize. Drafts, too much or too little water, and damage to roots may cause lower leaves to drop; if unsightly, cut back longest shoots to 2″ (50 mm) to keep plant shapely. Artificial fluorescent lights above vines will encourage a long blooming season.

Propagate: by seed, layering, and stem cuttings (best done in spring).

Offspring established: transplant into larger pots using soil mixture noted above.

A. marmoratus (mar-moh-ray′-tus) Zebra Basketvine; pointed foliage, 4″ (101 mm) long leaves, mottled green and maroon with yellow netting underneath; olive green, brown striped flowers, 1″ (25 mm) long, appear in leaf axils (angle of leaf stem joining branch).

A. speciosus (spee-see-oh′-sus) meaning showy; sometimes called Trichosporum splendens; 2′ (.60 m) wiry stems; glossy, lanceolate, 4″ (101 mm) leaves; waxy, scarlet-tipped, orange flowers, borne in terminal clusters.

A. Black Pagoda (*A. marmoratus* X *A. speciosus*) easily grown; variegated leaves; pretty green and yellow, brown marked flowers in leaf axils.

A. pulcher (pull′-ker) meaning pretty; Royal Red Bugler; 2″ (50 mm) waxy, ovate leaves borne on down-curved branches; scarlet 2½″ (62 mm) flowers with yellow throats.

A. Publobia (*A. parvifolius* X *A. pulcher*) easy to grow; frequent blooms; calyx (outer petal-like structures) turn from green to dark purple as it opens.

AGAPANTHUS AFRICANUS (ag-ap-panth′-us af-rik-kay′-nus) African Lily; nickname: Blue African Lily, Lily-of-the-Nile.

A large growing, thick-rooted perennial remembered as a tub plant from grandparental days; name derived from the Greek, *agape*—love, *anthos*—flower; long blooming during summer, with very showy blossoms.

Family Tree: Liliaceae (lil-ee-ay′-see-ay) Lily family; a native of Cape Province in South Africa.

Foliage: narrow, thick, 1′-2′ (.30 m-.60 m) long straplike evergreen leaves of leathery texture.

Flower: spherical, shapely clusters of up to 30 1″-5″ (25 mm-127 mm) lilylike blooms ranging from deep violet-blue to white; blossoms throughout April and May.

Size: 18″-36″ (.45 m-.90 m).

Location: WINTER—full sun, set in southern exposure.

SUMMER—*Inside:* partial shade; set in eastern to southern exposure for direct rays of morning sun. *Outside:* partial shade, set in eastern exposure or under a protective structure where plant receives strong light, but no direct rays.

FALL: move indoors by mid-September.

Dormancy: late fall; foliage dies naturally; store plants indoors at 40°-50°F (4°-10°C); water once monthly, just enough to keep leaves from dying; cease fertilizing during dormancy.

Water: do not allow soil to dry out.

Mist: daily, twice a day during growing period—March through October.

Humidity: above normal, 40%-50%.

Air circulation: helpful condition.

Feed: every 2 weeks during growing season, mild liquid manure.

Soil: 2 parts standard potting soil, 1 part peat moss.

Temperature: Day—68°-72°F (20°-22°C). Night—50°-55°F (10°-12°C).

Potbound: yes, to keep happy for profuse bloom.

Agapanthus orientalis,
Lily-of-the-Nile

Mature plants: remove dead flower stems and heads.
Propagate: in February or March, dividing fleshy roots when repotting; or sow seeds.
Insect alert: mealybug, scale, thrips.
Notable: so lovely a plant to possess—a vigorous grower if you can provide a large tub of rich soil in a coolish, spacious area; failure to bloom indicates soil's depletion of nutrients.

A. inapertus (in-a-pert'-us) to 4' (1.20 m) drooping, mid-blue flowers; massive root stock.
A. praecox orientalis (pre'-cox or-ee-en-tay'-liss) *praecox*, developing early or earlier than other species, *orientalis*, from the East; 1'-5' (.30 m-1.50 m) tall; 100 or more blue or white clustered flowers.
> Variety—albus: meaning white.
> Variety—maximus: meaning the greatest or largest; larger leaves and flowers.

A. campanulatus (kam-pan-yew-lay'-tus) describing bell flowers; to 18" (.45 m); sky blue flowers all summer.
A. cavlescens (kaw-less'-senz) meaning with long stems; to 24" (.60 m); narrow leaves; violet blue flowers in June.
A. pendulus (pen'-dew-lus) 2½' (.75 m) high; tender drooping clusters of purple blue tubular flowers blooming all summer.
A. hybrids
> *A. Peter Pan;* dark blue flowers on 12"-18" (.30 m-.45 m) stalks.
> *A. Dwarf White;* white flowers on 18"-24" (.45 m-.60 m) stalks.

AGAVE (ag-gay'-vee) Century plant.
True succulents, most species of this genus are large tub plants that need space and sun, a few are small, good for spot siting. This fantastic foliage plant has been used as a fiber for a juice to be fermented. False rumor has it that the plant must be 100 years old before flowering, if ever it does with interior life, but it does approach a score of years or more before flowering.

Agave americana,
Century Plant

Family Tree: Amaryllidaceae (am-ar-rill-i-da'-see-ay) Amaryllis family; native to Mexico and Central America.
Foliage: fleshy, rigid, lance-shaped leaves in habit of rosettes; some species smooth-edged, others very spiny margined and tipped; bluish-green, some with creamy stripes length of leaf or along edges.
Flower: seldom in indoor culture, generally yellow, petite and clustered around long, erect stems up to 16' (4.8 m).
Size: 10" (.25 m) to 5' (1.50 m), height and spread.
Location: WINTER—southern exposure.
SUMMER—*Inside and Outside:* southern exposure.
FALL: move indoors by mid-September; site in southern exposure.
Dormancy: none, although a resting period from October through February; slowly diminish watering, water only enough to keep leaves from shriveling; cease fertilizing.
Water: allow soil to become quite dry between thorough, even waterings.
Mist: daily, very lightly, around plant but not directly on it.
Humidity: low normal, 20%-25%.
Air circulation: helpful condition.
Feed: once a month, April through July, with normal mild liquid manure.
Soil: 1 part standard potting mix, 2 parts sharp sand.
Temperature: Day—68°-80°F (20°-26°C). Night—50°-70°F (10°-21°C).
Potbound: normal, repot or pot-on when foliage appears crowded or root growth is 50% of pot content; best done in early spring prior to new growth evidence.
Mature plants: flowers appear only on plants generally 10 years or older; frequently, plant dies after flowering.
Propagate: by seed or young shoots (suckers) that grow near base of plant, any time.
Insect alert: scale, mealybug.
Disease alert: brown spots on foliage from excessive heat, not enough sun, or too high winter humidity.
Notable: soil must have excellent porosity; do not try to create humid conditions; normal interior air, even a dry site, is most suitable. *Most notable:* plants rot very easily. A good artificial light plant; up to 16 hours combined natural and artificial light hours; do not allow soil to dry out completely.

A. americana (am-eh-ri-kay'-nuh) native to America; trunkless, gray green leaves, yellow green flowers; to 40' (12 m) in 50 years but to 6' (1.8 m) in tubs.
> Variety—Marginata (mar-ji-nay'-tuh) yellow-edged leaves.

A. filifera (fye-lif'-er-uh) meaning bearing threads; bright olive green leaves 1'-2' (.30 m-.60 m) long; white bristled edges that dry and split to show curled threadlike fibers; 2"-3" (50 mm-76 mm) purplish flowers; trunkless; to 15' (4.50 m) high.
A. picta (pik'-tuh) painted or variegated; blue green leaves with white edges tinged with pink, studded with small blackish brown teeth; to 12" (.30 m) or more.
A. victoriae (vik-toh-ree'-ay) royal or queenly.
> Variety—Reginae (reh-jye'-nay) stiff, tightly compressed leaves, 4"-6" (100 mm = 150 mm) long, white markings and edges; propagate by seed; the crème de la crème.

AGLAONEMA (ag-lay-oh-nee'-muh) Chinese Evergreen. This is an indestructible foliage plant, easily grown by water culture and content in dimly lighted areas. The name is derived from Greek, *aglaos*—bright, *nema*, a thread. Some species resemble the Dieffenbachie, dumb cane, but are considered more durable, not so readily dropping lower leaves.

Family Tree: Araceae (uh-ray'-see-ay) Arum family; native to Indonesia, Malaya, and Africa.

Foliage: dark green to silvery leaves, sometimes blotched and patterned. Lance, heart, or arrow shaped, to 4″ (100 mm) wide and 6″ (150 mm) long, depending on species.

Flower: tiny calla shaped; inconspicuous; does not often bloom in cultivation.

Fruit: showy, inedible berries that last for several months.

Size: to 3′ (.90 m) high, to 3′ (.90 m) across, depending on species.

Location: WINTER—eastern or western exposure.

SUMMER—*Inside:* northeastern or northwestern exposure. *Outside:* northeastern or northwestern exposure; site in shelter to protect foliage.

FALL: move indoors by mid-September; site in eastern or western exposure.

Dormancy: none; but a resting period of slower growth during winter months, generally October through February; slowly diminish watering; plant will indicate needs as determined by environmental conditions; develop sensitivity to feel of soil moisture level; cease fertilizing.

Water: thoroughly and evenly; do not allow soil to dry.

Mist: daily, twice a day when possible.

Humidity: above normal for happiness, 45%-55%.

Air circulation: helpful condition.

Feed: mild liquid manure every 2 weeks.

Soil: standard potting soil.

Aglaonema modestum
Chinese Evergreen

Temperature: Day—70°-80°F (21°-26°C). Night—62°-68°F (16°-20°C).

Potbound: very happy; pot-on only when root growth of plant is 80%, soil 20% of pot content; top- or side-dress yearly; preferably spring.

Mature plants: if plant becomes too tall, cut growing ends (which can be used for propagation); remove dried or withered leaves as they appear; older plant has tendency to drop lower leaves.

Propagate: by stem cuttings in rooting medium; or by air layering; or by divisions; stem cuttings or divisions can be rooted in water.

Insect alert: mealybug, red spider, scale, thrip, aphids.

Notable: do not allow soil to become entirely dry, ever; use pebble, water, and tray method to maintain humidity level; sponge foliage at least every 3 weeks; always use room temperature water; leaf shiners and/or oils are an absolute no-no.

A. commutatum (com-mew-tay'-tum) meaning changing in form or color; native to Ceylon; previously called *A. marantifolium* and *Schismatoglottis commutatum;* lance-shaped, dark green, leathery leaves with silver gray areas, to 9″ (228 mm) long, 3″ (76 mm) wide.

A. costatum (kos-tay'-tum) native to Malaya; a low grower, 10″ (254 mm) tall; shiny green heart-shaped leaves; white central vein, white spots.

A. crispum (krisp'-um) meaning curled; may be referred to by its previous name, *Schismatoglottis roebelinii;* grayish leaves 10″-12″ (254 mm-304 mm) long, to 4″ (101 mm) wide; with soft green edges and ribs; to 3′ (.90 m) tall, with 3′ (.90 m) spread.

A. maculatum (mak-yew-lay'-tum) meaning spotted; green leaves with silvery veins.

A. modestum (moh-des'-tum) slender, leathery, wedge-shaped leaves have tapering points that dip, 6″-8″ (150 mm-200 mm) long; colored solid green; plant grows to 2′ or 3′ (.60 m-.90 m) high.

A. picta (pik'-tuh) meaning painted or variegated; leaves to 6″ (150 mm) long and 3″ (76 mm) wide, have white spots.

A. roebelinii (roh-bel-in'-ee-eye) Silver queen; narrow leaves 6″ (150 mm) long, 1½″ (37 mm) wide, are silver with green edging on main veins; plant to 2″ (5 cm) high).

ALLAMANDA CATHARTICA (al-lam-mand'-uh kath-art-ik-uh) Golden Trumpet.
This species is a rapid growing vine type; one must therefore support its slender rodlike stems. It has a profusion of blooms which resemble the petunia. Its flowers are poisonous, so keep out of reach of children and pets. Consider it a tub plant.

Family Tree: Apocynaceae (a-poss-i-nay'-see-ay) Dogbane family; a native of Brazil.

Foliage: large dark green, glossy, tubular leaves; opposite or whorled arrangement; 6″ (150 mm) long.

Flower: 4″ (100 mm) waxen; golden, shiny yellow; very fragrant; blooms April through September.

Size: 2′-15′ (.60 m-4.50 m).

Location: WINTER—full sun; set in southern exposure.

SUMMER—*Inside:* partial shade; set in eastern to southern

Allamanda cathartica,
Golden Trumpet

exposure for direct rays of morning sun. *Outside:* partial shade; set in eastern exposure or under a protective structure where plant receives strong light but no direct rays.
FALL: move indoors by mid-September.
Dormancy: mid-October through January; prune by cutting back old shoots in February; slowly diminish watering, keeping soil barely moist; cease fertilizing.
Water: keep soil evenly moist.
Mist: twice a day in spring and summer.
Humidity: 30%-50%, especially important before flowers appear.
Air circulation: helpful condition.
Feed: every week. April through September, with a mild liquid manure.

Allophyton mexicanum,
Mexican Foxglove   W.H.

Soil: 1 part peat moss, 2 parts standard potting mix, 1 part vermiculite.
Temperature: Day—70°-80°F (21°-26°C). Night—60°-65°F (15°-18°C).
Potbound: happy; at least 35%-40%.
Mature plants: better bloom if stems pinched back as they become straggly; pinch off to point where plant retains compact, uniform shape; pinch center out of young shoots for wide plant; to retain shape, cut back only the excessively long shoots in spring.
Propagate: from 4″ (100 mm) stem cuttings in spring; put stems in sand or vermiculite and cover with plastic bag; keep in at least 75°F (23°C) temperature while rooting.
Offspring established: when well rooted, pot each cutting in individual pot, using soil specified above.
Insect alert: mealybug, scale, whitefly, red mites.
Notable: soil must have good drainage; keep humidity level up during growing and blooming season.

A. neriifolia (neer-ee-if-foh′-lee-uh) oleander Allamanda; flowers are yellow streaked with orange on inside, yellow-rust striped outside; shrub to 3′ (.90 m).
A. violacea (vye-ohl-lay′-see-uh) meaning violet color; violet Allamanda; flowers, bell-shaped, rose violet color; climbing habit, up to 4′ (1.20 m).
A. cathartica (ka-thar′-ti-ka)
　　Variety—Hendersonii (hen-der-soh-nee-eye) larger, more profuse blooms than other varieties.
　　Variety—Williamsii (will-yams′-ee-eye) double flowers.

ALLOPHYTON MEXICANUM (al-low-phy′-ton mex-i-cane′-um) Mexican Foxglove.
Sold under the name *Tehanema mexicanum,* this perennial, a look-alike to the violet, needs proper culture for good bloom. *A good genus for the terrarium.*
Family Tree: Scrophulariaceae (skroff-u-lar-i-a′-cea) figwort family; a native of Mexico and Guatemala, the Central America regions.
Foliage: a compact rosette of small, dark green, leathery leaves, 4″-5″ (100 mm-127 mm) in length.
Flower: flower stalks rise from the center of leaf rosettes bearing ¼″ (6 mm) pink through purple blossoms in spring and summer.
Size: 6″-8″ (150 mm-200 mm).
Location: WINTER—full sun; set in southern exposure.
SUMMER—*Inside:* partial shade; set in eastern to southern exposure for direct rays of morning sun. *Outside:* partial shade; set in eastern exposure or under a protective structure where plant receives strong light but no direct rays.
FALL: move indoors by mid-September.
Dormancy: none; maintain proper culture throughout year.
Water: keep soil evenly moist.
Mist: daily; twice a day when possible.
Humidity: very happy high; 50%-60%.
Air circulation: helpful condition.
Feed: weekly, mild liquid manure.
Soil: 2 parts standard potting soil, 1 part peat moss.
Temperature: Day—68°-72°F (20°-22°C). Night—60°-65°F (15°-18°C).
Potbound: seldom a problem; not a massive root system.

Mature plants: better bloom if stems pinched back as they become straggly; pinch off to point where plant retains compact, uniform shape; want wide plant—pinch center out of young shoots.

Propagate: any time by dividing old plants, use 4″ (100 mm) pot; or from seeds.

Offspring established: keep in good light but no direct sun; nip out tips one time; pot-up individually.

Insect alert: aphid, mite, scale, mealybug.

Notable: never allow soil to dry out completely; keep on warmer side of recommended temperatures; a very good plant for artificial light culture, placed 12″ (.30 m) from light; in fact, this genus must have more light hours than a winter's day provides if it is to bloom in winter months; a total of 14-16 light hours combining natural and artificial exposure.

ALOE VERA (al-oh′-ee vee′-rah) Unguentine Plant.

This plant is known to have existed in the time of the Roman Empire. The leaf, when cut, exudes a milky, gluelike substance which—applied directly to an injury— is used as a healing balm for cuts and burns. If flowering occurs, as it seldom does in inside culture, it is generally in December through February; flowers are bright, deeply colored, mostly tubular in shape. While A. vera is native to India, this genus has many species, all succulents, from small shrub type to large tub size, all with rigid, fleshy, thick leaves.

Family Tree: Liliaceae (lil-ee-ay′-see-ay) Lily family; native to South Africa.

Foliage: thick, fleshy leaves, growing fan shaped out of soil line, very pale green, soft spines on leaf edges.

Flower: bell shaped, red or yellow, on leafless stems; winter blooming.

Size: up to 20″ (.55 m).

Aloe variegata,
Partridge-breasted Aloe

Location: WINTER—southern exposure.

SUMMER—*Inside and Outside:* southern exposure.

FALL: move indoors by mid-September; site in southern exposure.

Dormancy: none; resting time from October through February; slowly diminish watering; use enough to keep leaves from shriveling; cease fertilizing.

Water: allow soil to become quite dry between thorough, even waterings.

Mist: daily, very lightly, around plant but not directly on it.

Humidity: low, 20%-25%.

Air circulation: helpful condition.

Feed: monthly, April through July, with mild liquid manure.

Soil: 1 part standard potting mix, 2 parts sharp sand.

Temperature: Day—68°-80°F (20°-26°C). Night—50°-70°F (10°-21°C).

Potbound: normal; repot or pot-on when foliage appears overcrowded or root growth is 50% of pot content; best done after flowering in July or August.

Mature plants: older plants frequently lose bottom leaves.

Propagate: by offshoots, division, seeds, or cuttings. Pot-up in dry soil as specified for this genus; do not water for 5 days after potting.

Insect alert: scale, mealybug.

Disease alert: root rot from overwatering.

Notable: soil must have excellent porosity; do not try to create humid conditions; normal interior air, even a dry site, is most suitable; *Most notable:* plants rot very easily; a good artificial light plant, up to 16 hours combined natural and artificial light hours; do not allow soil to dry out completely.

A. arborescens (ar-bor-ess′-senz) Tree aloe; huge blue green leaves to 15′ (4.50 m), flowers between March and July. *Note:* grows in winter months, so alter treatment of dormancy; resting period August through November; feed during growing period only; likes cool temperatures.

A. aristata (ar-iss-tay′-tuh) Lace aloe; 4″-6″ (100 mm-150 mm) wide rosette of many 4″ (100 mm) stemless, slender leaves, with fine tooth edge; gray green studded on back with white dots; reddish yellow flowers, to 1″ (25 mm) long.

A. brevifolia (brev-i-foh′-lee-uh) Short-leaved aloe; pale gray green leaves edged with small teeth, 3″-4″ (76 mm-100 mm) long and wide; red flowers on spike up to 15″ (.38 m) tall.

A. ciliaris (sil-ee-ay′-riss) sword-shaped, soft green leaves, white-toothed, to 5″ (127 mm) long, on sprawling, weak, pencil stems, 2′-3′ (.60 m-.90 m) in length; brilliant red flowers, on 8″ (200 mm) stalks; good for hanging container.

A. globosa (gloh-boh′-suh) Crocodile aloe; gray green leaves, 4″-7″ (100 mm-177 mm).

A. nobilis (noh′-bil-iss) Gold-toothed aloe; 2′-3′ (.60 m-.90 m) long stems, frequently prostrate; with 6″-10″ (150 mm-250 mm) leaves, pale green edged with prickly teeth; red flower clusters.

A. variegata (var-ee-eh-gay′-tuh) Partridge breast, Pheasant wing; to 12″ (.30 m) tall, 6″ (.15 m) across; triangular leaves accented by bands of white prickly edges, tinted with bronze if grown in bright light; large orange red flowers.

AMARYLLIS BELLADONNA (am-ar-rill'-iss bel-luh-don'-nuh) Belladonna Lily; nickname: Naked Lads; Naked Ladies. In the poems of Theocritus and Virgil the shepherdess Amaryllis—of proclaimed loveliness—inspired the naming of this regal genus by taking bright red flowers to Alteo, a namesake horticulturist, more interested in his vocation than *amor.*

Belladonna, meaning pretty lady, is a truly fitting name for this species of the Amaryllis, known as The Pretty Lady. It is so known because many years past, our prima donnas sometimes used an extract from this plant to brighten their eyes.

Family Tree: Amaryllidaceae (am-ar-rill-i-da'-see-ay) Amaryllis family; native to South Africa.

Foliage: dark green, strap-shaped leaves are supported on stout stalks that arise from bulbs.

Flower: smooth textured, open trumpet shaped, lilylike; orange-red, white, pink, salmon pink, deep red, violet; sometimes striped, banded or bordered; 8-10″ (200 mm-250 mm) across; bloom in winter or spring in clusters of 3-4 blossoms.

Size: flower stems reach 1′-3′ (.30 m-.90 m).

Location: WINTER—western location.

SUMMER—*Inside:* partial shade; set in east-to-south exposure for direct rays of morning sun. *Outside:* partial shade; set under a protective structure to protect from water on flowers and foliage and to allow plenty of light but no direct rays.

FALL: move indoors by mid-September.

Dormancy: in early fall; cease fertilizing for 2 months; remove dried or yellowing leaves; remove plant to cool temperature about 70° F (21° C); dark site; in 2-3 months buds will start to sprout through soil; move to bright light.

Water: keep soil evenly but barely moist.

Mist: very lightly, daily; mist only leaves, not flowers.

Humidity: 40%-50%.

Air circulation: helpful condition.

Feed: biweekly, with mild liquid manure until dormancy period.

Soil: 2 parts standard potting soil, 1 part rotted cow manure.

Temperature: Day—70° F (21° C) or higher. Night—60°-65°F (15°-18°C).

Potbound: very happy; flowers best; repot every 3-4 years.

Mature plants: leaves do not appear until after flowering; stake foliage as plant grows in height; prune after blooming; cut flowering stem to 1″ or 2″ (25 mm or 50 mm); when shriveled, remove stem completely.

Propagate: by offshoots of hybrid; these are small bulbs that develop beside the large parent bulb; plant offshoot early in an 8″ (200 mm) pot with ⅔ of bulb above soil level; or, by seeds—which take 3-4 years to reach flowering size.

Offspring established: maintain culture as for adult plant; bulbs commence flowering 6-8 weeks after planting.

Insect alert: mealybugs, red spider, bulb flies.

Notable: keep plants cool and out of direct sun while in bloom; a very easy bulb to grow as an inside plant; stake foliage so it will support the flowers' heavy weight; most bulbs send up a second flower stalk when the first one begins to fade. Please do not overwater.

Amaryllis belladonna,
Belladonna Lily

A. belladonna

Variety—elata (ee-lay'-tah) rosy flowers.

Variety—major (may'-jor) larger in all parts.

The above species and its varieties are the only true Amaryllis. A transition has occurred in which many plants closely resembling the Amaryllis in appearance and culture are now technically placed in the Hippeastrum genus. Because of the general acceptance of the public for the hybrids of this genus to be known as those of the Amaryllis, we include for your reference those better known and more frequently grown as indoor house plants. The following are Hippeastrum (hipp-e-as'-trum):

H. pratense (pra'-tens) meaning growing in meadows; native to South America; flowers: bright scarlet with a yellow base; funnel-shaped up to 3″ (76 mm) across; blooms late spring and early summer; stems 1′; tender, may be grown outdoors.

H. rutilum (roo-til'-um) native to Brazil and Venezuela; spring flowering; small scarlet flowers; more graceful than the hybrids.

H. aulicum (awe-lik'-um) referred to as Lily of the Palace; native to Brazil and Paraguay; crimson colored, 6″ (.15 m) long flowers supported on an 18″ (.45 m) stem; winter flowering.

H. reginae (rej-jye'-nee) lance-shaped leaves to 2′ (.60 m) long; bright red flowers with whitish spot on throat; up to 2″ (50 mm) wide; two to four flowers in cluster on stalk to 2′ (.60 m).

H. vittatum (vit-tay'-tum) bright green, straplike leaves; red and white striped flowers; flower stalk to 3′ (.90 m); flower custer of two to five blooms.

H. x. ackermannii (ak-ker-man'-ee-eye) an early summer blooming hybrid with small, profuse, dark red flowers.

H. x. johnsoni (jon-son'-ee-eye) cross between *H. vittatum* and *H. reginae*; 5″ (127 mm) scarlet flowers with white streaks on petals and a green base.

H. hybrids
Claret; 8″ (203 mm) flowers, crimson on wine with red-black lines.
Grant White; 7″ (177 mm) glistening flowers.
Peppermint; 8″ (203 mm) white- and red-striped blooms.

ANTHURIUM ANDRAEANUM (an-thoor′-i-num an-dree-ay′-num) nickname: Painter's Palette; Flamingo Plant; Lakanthurium; Tail Flower; Pigtail Plant.

The eye-catcher is actually the brilliance of the large, waxy, leaflike sheath, which looks made of patent leather. A favorite plant for Victorian conservatories, you will enjoy the exotic beauty of this plant and find it easy to maintain. It also provides long-lasting cut flowers (2-3 weeks) for the home.

Family Tree: Araceae (ar-ay′-see-ay)—Arum family. Native to Central and South American jungles, particularly Colombia.

Foliage: glossy, dark green, drooping, leathery, lance-shaped leaves up to 8″ (203 mm) long and 5″ (127 mm) across.

Flower: single, straight, or curly spadix (a dense spike of tiny flowers) arising from apex of each leaf; scarlet, pink, or white colored; some varieties have green flowers; spathe (on the anthurium, a leaf or petallike sheath which protects the flower) about 6″ (150 mm) long and 3″ (76 mm) wide.

Size: to 16″ (.40 m); other family members to 3′ (.90 m).

Location: WINTER—partial shade; set in eastern to southern exposure so plant will get some direct rays; when plant is in flower, however, keep out of direct rays.

SUMMER—*Inside*: northeastern exposure. *Outside*: northern exposure.

FALL: move indoors by mid-September; site in eastern exposure.

Dormancy: none; maintain proper culture throughout year.

Water: keep soil evenly moist.

Anthurium andraeanum,
Painter's Palette

Mist: daily, twice a day if possible.
Humidity: happy when very high, around 80%.
Air circulation: helpful condition.
Feed: every 2 weeks, February through July, mild liquid manure.
Soil: 1 part standard potting soil, 1 part fir bark.
Temperature: Day—72°-85°F (22°-29°C). Night—65°-70°F (18°-21°C).
Potbound: very happy; do not pot-on until root system is at least 80% of pot content.
Mature plants: new roots may appear on the surface of soil, if so, place a layer of sphagnum moss over the roots and moisten moss daily; although this sizable plant needs a large pot, it also needs to be kept potbound; ensure good drainage for the necessary moist conditions by having the bottom ⅓ of the pot full of crocks (pieces of broken clay pots); insecticide sprays injure flowers.
Propagate: by seed or by division of young shoots formed at base of plant. These may be removed, complete with roots, and grown in separate pots. Pot in osmunda fiber or fir bark; place in cooler spot for this period.
Offspring established: once established, repot (not pot-on) in fresh soil and return to warmer, proper environment.
Insect alert: red spider, mites, mealybug, whitefly, scale.
Notable: retain high humidity; never allow soil to dry out completely; soil must be well aerated and have good drainage; roots sensitive—easily burned if fertilizer is too strong; eliminate harsh light; do not grow under artificial light.

A. crystallinum (kriss-tal′-in-um) foliage: bronze green when young, later bright olive green, with a velvety sheen, pale silvery gray veins; heart-shaped leaves; flower bract is green, to 6″ (150 mm); size up to 14″ (350 mm); native to Peru.

A. scherzerianum (sher-zer-ee-ay′-num) Flamingo flower. A profuse flowering, evergreen house plant; foliage lance shaped, 8″ (203 mm) long, 2″ (50 mm) across; deep red, orange red, and pink red flower varieties; curly yellow spadix (dense spike of tiny flowers, like a pig's tail); size up to 16″ (400 mm); native to Guatemala.

A. bakeri (bake′-er-eye) 15″ (380 mm) brilliant red blooms.

A. forgetti (fur-get′-eye) oval leaves; similar to A. crystallinum, but smaller plants.

A. scandens (skan′-dens) meaning climbing; climbing to 3′ (.90 m); dark green foliage.

A. warocqueanum (war-ock′-ee-ay-num) native to Colombia; a climber; 30″ (.75 m) rosette, long, velvety leaves with pale green veins.

A. veitchii (veech′-ee-eye) metallic green leaves to 3′ (.90 m) long, 10″ (250 mm) wide; green white spathes (petallike sheaths that protect the flowers) to 3″ (76 mm) long; a florist's foliage plant.

APHELANDRA (a-feh-lan′-druh) Zebra Plant, Tiger Plant. A tropical flowering shrub really exquisite in its spring into summer floral show. Very special culture attention needed. Aphelandra likes and needs much warmth and humidity. Keep it below 15″ (380 mm) high for a controlled pleasing shape.

Aphelandra squarrosa,
Zebra Plant

Family Tree: Acanthaceae (uh-kanth-ay'-see'ay) Acanthus family; native of South America, Mexico, West Indies.
Foliage: leaves large, fleshy, gray green or dark green; oppositely arranged, shiny, attractively veined in white; stout, tough stem.
Flower: shaped as inflorescence (a group arrangement of flowers) nesting and rising pyramidally; usually large 6″ (152 mm) spikes; color range yellow through orange to red in all species; blooming time approximately 6 weeks.
Size: to 3′ (.90 m).
Location: WINTER—full sun; set in southern exposure.
SUMMER—*Inside:* partial shade; set in eastern to southern exposure for direct rays of morning sun. *Outside:* partial shade; set in eastern exposure or under a protective structure where plant receives strong light but no direct rays.
FALL: move indoors by mid-September.
Dormancy: 6 weeks of rest at end of blooming; slowly diminish watering to keep evenly and lightly moist; cease fertilizing in September; resume feeding program along about January or when plants show signs of new growth; maintain warm temperature.
Water: keep thoroughly and evenly moist.
Mist: daily, 2 or 3 times a day when possible.
Humidity: high is essential for survival, 65%-75%.
Air circulation: helpful condition.
Feed: every 2 weeks with mild liquid manure.
Soil: 1 part standard potting mix, 2 parts peat moss, 1 part perlite.
Temperature: Day—70°-75°F (21°-23°C). Night—65°-70°F (18°-21°C).
Potbound: repot in March; best to root, prune, and retain in small pot for control of plant size.
Mature plants: normally pruned to stay 12″-18″ (.30 m-.45 m); prune year old shoots to 1 leaf in February; in March, when repotting, cut back half of previous season's growth; best to prune and propagate when new growth is starting; aerial roots (roots appearing on plant stems or branches) should not be removed.

Propagate: best in spring from new growth, stem cuttings, or seed, but can be any time. Keep humidity level up by using plastic bag culture.
Insect alert: scale, whitefly.
Disease alert: brown spot and rolled leaf edges from too dry air.
Notable: with pebble and water in tray culture to provide an atmosphere as like a hothouse as possible; soil must have good drainage; as much bright light as possible; good to extend light hours to total 14 by combination of natural and artificial; maintain on higher side of recommended temperatures; at temperatures below 65°F (18°C) plant will not flower and leaves will contort, dry, and drop.

A. pectinata (pek-ti-nay'-tuh) meaning obscure; to 3′ (.90 m); scarlet flowers in tight spikes in winter.
A. tetragona (tet-rag'-on-uh) a West Indian species; to 3′ (.90 m); blooms in fall with 8″ (203 mm) spikes of 2″-3″ (50-76 mm) tubular scarlet flowers.
A. aurantiaca (aw-ran-tye'-ak-uh) gray green, leathery leaves; long-lasting terminal flower clusters of orange or yellow take about a month to develop.
A. squarrosa (skwar-roh'-suh) a compact species; large, shiny corrugated leaves, veins and midrib appear coated with white; shaded yellow bracts (modified leaf part of flower head but on stem); yellow flowers.
　　Variety—Leopoldi: yellow or orange blossom.
　　Variety—Dania: several flower stems, compact shape, tolerates temperature to 55°F (12°C) without reducing flowering level; other compact varieties: Brockfeld and Fritz Prinsler, all to 20″ (.55 m) in height.
　　Variety—Louisae: stronger, brighter veining.
A. chamissoniana (ka-miss-oh-nye-aye'-nuh) known as Zebra plant; to 14″ (.35 m); upright thin, shiny leaves with white midrib and veins; bright yellow flower spike.
A. tetragona (tet-rag'-ohn-uh) meaning New Zealand spinach; from West Indies; fall blooming; spikes to 8″ (203 mm); blossom 2″-3″ (50 mm-76 mm) long, deep red.

ARAUCARIA EXCELSA (ar-raw-kay'-ree-uh ex-sel'-suh)
　　Norfolk Island Pine
In Holland, the Norfolk Island pine is traditionally given as a wedding present. In a natural environment, a height to 200′ (60 m) is attained, but when sited within an interior habitat, size to around 6′ (1.80 m) high and breadth about 4′ (1.20 m), provides a very well-scaled evergreen. A. excelsa, looking like a pine tree, displays a delicate, very graceful form. Branches have a rigidity countered by softly drooping needlelike leaves and briefly pendulous branch tips. Site in medium to soft light out of traffic patterns, for the foliage has an aversion to handling. This species is slow growing and long-lived.
Family Tree: Araucariaceae (ar-raw-kay'-ree-ay-see-ay) Araucaria family; native to South America and South Pacific.
Foliage: glossy green, overlapping; covered with ½″ (12.70 mm) rigid, pointed needles on branches of whorling growth habit, 5 branches to a tier; erect; evergreen.
Fruit: cones to 8″ (200 mm)
Size: up to 6′ (1.80 m)
Location: WINTER—southeastern or southwestern exposure.
SUMMER—*Inside:* northeastern or northwestern exposure.

Araucaria excelsa,
Norfolk Island Pine

ing brittle and brown tipped; develop sensitivity to feel of soil moisture level; cease fertilizing.

Water: evenly and thoroughly, allowing soil to dry between waterings.

Mist: daily, twice a day when possible; around plant not directly on foliage.

Humidity: normal, 30%-35%.

Air circulation: essential for good cultural response.

Feed: every 3 weeks, with mild liquid manure throughout growing season, April through August.

Soil: 3 parts standard potting mix, 2 parts peat moss, 1 part perlite.

Temperature: Day—65°-75°F (18°-23°C). Night—40°-64°F (4.4°-18°C).

Potbound: before new growth is evident in late winter, early spring.

Mature plants: pinch off brown tips, if they occur; check plant's culture for good soil drainage, good air movement, proper watering.

Propagate: by seeds or by cutting—top cutting only, side shoots do not develop into proper growth habit. Root cutting in moist sharp sand, preferably under polythene unless rooting site is of high humidity.

Insect alert: aphid, mealybug, mite, scale, leaf miner.

Notable: soil must have porosity; no soggy conditions; keep on lower side of recommended temperatures. Note: good air circulation needed for top performance; do not overpot, use pot only 2″ (50 mm) larger than previous housing.

A. araucana (ar-oh-kay′-nuh) Monkey-puzzle tree; pyramidal shape; flat, stiff, sharp-pointed bright green leaves, overlapping habit; twisted branches; native to Chile.

A. bidwillii (bid-will′-ee-eye) Bunya-bunya; rigid, shiny bright green leaves; native to Australia.

Outside: northeastern or northwestern exposure; site in sheltered area to protect foliage.

FALL: move indoors by mid-September; site in eastern or western exposure.

Dormancy: none, a resting time during winter months, generally September through March; slowly diminish watering; plant will indicate needs by appearance, becom-

ARDISIA CRISPA (ar-diz′-ee-uh kriss′-puh) Coral Berry. Also known as *A. crenulata*, meaning closely curled or crested. A tropical evergreen, of a shrub type; good as a small topiary tree if so pruned. It is lovely and very special with both a summer flowering and separate fruit-bearing cycle beginning in fall. Berries carried through winter make it a good holiday selection.

Family Tree: Myrsinaceae (murr-sin-ay′-see-ay) Myrsine family; from Malaya, China, and the East Indies.

Foliage: wavy, margined, alternate leaves to 3″ (76 mm) long; thick and glossy.

Flower: small, white, fragrant flowers.

Fruit: long-lasting pea-size red berries, fall through spring.

Size: a bushy shrub to 3′ (.90 m); treelike after 18″-24″ (.45 m-.60 m).

Location: WINTER—full sun; set in southern exposure.

SUMMER—*Inside:* set in eastern to southern exposure for direct rays of morning sun. *Outside:* partial shade; set in eastern exposure or under a protective structure where plant receives strong light but no direct rays.

FALL: move indoors by mid-September.

Dormancy: in early spring; cut down to 2″ (50 mm); keep soil dry until new shoots appear; then remove all but 3 strongest shoots; repot in fresh soil or pot-on if necessary;

Ardisia crispa,
Coral Berry

cease fertilizing when period commences; begin new feeding schedule 1 month after repotting or potting-on.

Water: use only tepid water to keep soil evenly moist but never soggy.

Mist: daily; during flowering very lightly around plant (not directly on leaves or flowers).

Humidity: high, at least 50%.

Air circulation: good air movement essential.

Feed: small amount of mild liquid manure weekly, except throughout dormant period.

Soil: standard potting mix.

Temperature: Day—68°-72°F (20°-22°C). Night—50°-55°F (10°-12°C).

Potbound: pot-on when earth ball is 50% roots.

Mature plants: better bloom if stems pinched back as they become straggly; pinch off to point where plant retains compact, uniform shape, pinch center out of young shoots for wide plant; prune lightly when berries have dried up or dropped.

Propagate: by seed (stake straggly seedlings), by cuttings—which make bushier plants—or by air layering (if latter does not take, cut off top anyway, new growth will appear just below cut).

A. japonica (jap-pon'-ik-uh) meaning from Japan; similar but coarser than *A. crispa,* to 18″ (.45 m); leaves bunched at branch buds; white berries.

ASPARAGUS SPRENGERI (uh-spar'-uh-gus spreng'-er-eye) Asparagus Fern.

These species are not ferns but receive the common name from the similarity of certain plants to the airy gracefulness of so many ferns. A genus of vines, herbs, and shrub-type forms, the variety Altilis (alt'-il-iss), of the species *A.*

officinalis (off-fiss-i-nay'-lis) is our cultivated, edible asparagus. The ornamental sprengeri is a feathery foliaged, delicate pleasure for hanging basket or broad shelf. It defies you to destroy it.

Family Tree: Liliaceae (lil-ee-ay'-see-ay) Lily family; native to Africa.

Foliage: deeply arching stems, 18″-24″ (.45 m-.60 m), covered with loose billows of bright green, 1″ (25 mm) long, flat, needlelike leaves.

Flower: pinkish, in loose cluster.

Size: to 2′ (.60 m).

Location: WINTER—southern exposure.

SUMMER—*Inside* and *Outside:* southeastern exposure.

FALL: move indoors by mid-September; site in southern exposure.

Dormancy: none, really, but resting period evident by no new growth, generally October through February; slowly diminish watering, keeping soil barely moist; cease fertilizing.

Water: keep evenly moist.

Mist: daily, twice a day when possible.

Humidity: normal, 30%-35%.

Air circulation: helpful condition.

Asparagus sprengeri,
Asparagus Fern

Feed: weekly, mild liquid manure.

Soil: 1 part each standard potting mix, peat moss, and perlite.

Temperature: Day—68°-72°F (20°-22°C). Night—50°-55°F (10°-12°C).

Potbound: happy; pot-on only when roots are 80%, soil 20% of pot contents. When one sees crowding roots pushing soil surface to top of and, finally, above pot's rim, it is potting-on time.

Mature plants: better bloom if stems pinched back as they become straggly; pinch off to point where plant retains compact, uniform shape; pinch center out of young shoots for wide plant; develop thorns with progressing age; must be pruned hard and frequently for retention of fullness and good health.

Propagate: by seed or by division—divide roots, pot individually, cut stems off at soil level and proceed with normal culture for this species.

Notable: a good genus for artificial light, a total of 14-16 hours, combining natural and artificial time; soil must have good porosity drainage, yet do not allow to dry out completely; *do* place outside in summer months; high humidity not needed.

A. asparagoides (as-par-ag-oy'-deez) Similar asparagus; small oval leaves to 1″ (25 mm) long.

A. falcatus (fal-kay'-tus) leaves 2″-3″ (50 mm-76 mm) long in clusters of 3 to 5 at branch ends, tiny white flowers, brown berries.

A. meyerii (mye-er-ee'-eye) Foxtail asparagus fern; upright or arching stems, 1′-2′ (.60 m) long, covered with needles; furry plumelike appearance.

A. myriocladus (mir-ree-oh-klay'-dus) Many-branched asparagus fern; spiny, arching stems, branching into many zigzag branchlets, covered with ¾″ (19 mm), dark green needles; 4′-6′ (1.20 m-1.80 m) tall.

A. plumosus (ploo-moh'-sus) twining vine of several stems; flat, roughly triangular branchlets extend horizontally from main stem; set with ⅛″ (3 mm), dark green needles; tiny, whitish-pink, fragrant flowers; red or purple berries; 12″-36″ (.30 m-.90 m).

A. retrofractus (reh-troh-frak'-tus) Twisted asparagus fern; similar to *A. myriocladus* except needles are bright green, 1″ (25 mm) long.

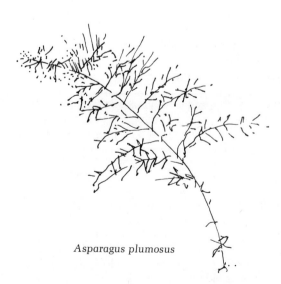

Asparagus plumosus

Aspidistra elatior,
Cast Iron Plant

ASPIDISTRA ELATIOR (ass-pi-dist'-ruh ee-lay'-tee-or) Cast Iron Plant. nickname: Barber Shop Plant.

The Cast iron and snake plants take abuse and neglect equally, more than any other genus. This species will do well in a dimly lit area, even total shade. It derives its common name from its ability to withstand poor cultural conditions.

Family Tree: Liliaceae (lil-ee-ay'-see-ay) Lily family; native of China.

Foliage: lance-shaped, arching green leaves, 15-30″ (.38 m-.76 m) long, 3″-4″ (76 mm-100 mm) wide.

Flower: unattractive purple brown flowers at soil level, seldom produced; when it does flower, blooms generally concealed by the foliage.

Size: up to 3′ (.90 m) tall.

Location: WINTER—southeastern or southwestern exposure. SUMMER—*Inside and Outside:* northeastern or northwestern exposure.
FALL: move in by mid-September, to eastern or western location.

Dormancy: none, but resting period October through February; slowly diminish watering, keeping soil barely moist, allowing to dry between waterings; cease fertilizing.

Water: moderately but evenly.

Mist: daily, twice a day when possible.

Humidity: normal, 30%-35%.

Air circulation: helpful condition.

Feed: every 2 weeks with mild liquid manure.

Soil: standard potting mix.

Temperature: Day—68°-80°F (20°-26°C). Night—50°-65°F (10°-18°C).

Potbound: happy until root growth is 65% of pot content; repot or pot-on in late winter or early spring before new growth is evident.

Mature plants: wash or damp-wipe leaves every 2 weeks.

Propagate: by division. Divide roots in early spring into several pieces of root, each with 2 or 3 leaves, plant separately or together for large plant; carefully split crowns for new plants with sharp sterile knife.

Insect alert: scale.

Notable: a good artificial-light genus, provide a total of 14 hours combined with natural light; although a tough plant that can withstand all conditions, summer sun will bleach leaves; division of plants and potting-on disturbs plant and may curtail flowering.

A. elatior (e-la'-ti-or)
Variety: Variegata leaves with white and green stripes, revert to solid green if given too much fertilizer or too little light.

ASPLENIUM (ass-pleen-ee'-um) Spleenwort, Bird's Nest Fern, Mother Fern.

A fern genus with many species from which to select a size and form to fit determined needs and aesthetic desires. But, be aware, if you are into digging plants in natural areas, what city folk refer to as the "wilds of mother nature," that many species are on preservation lists. Trouble brews if a human is detected "making off" with a specimen from a protected site. Maine protects all native species; Connecticut protects Spleenwort, Asplenium platyneuron, trichomanes, montanum, and pycnocarpon; New Mexico lists trichomanes, resiliens, and septentrionalis as protected species.

Family Tree: Polypodiaceae (pol-i-po'-di-ay-see-ay) Common Fern family; from Asia and Polynesia.

Foliage: evergreen fronds (leaves) vary in features; therefore specific descriptions are detailed under each species.

Size: 4" (100 mm) up to 4' (1.20 m) in height and spread, determined by species.

Location: WINTER—eastern exposure.

SUMMER—*Inside:* eastern exposure. *Outside:* northern exposure.

FALL: move indoors by mid-September; site in eastern exposure.

Dormancy: none really, rests lightly through fall and winter.

Water: an extremely important part of the culture of these plants; ordinarily, water thoroughly, allowing moderate drying between waterings, never allow to dry out completely; be aware of cool weather, when slower evaporation should mean less frequent watering; use room-temperature water only.

Mist: daily, twice a day if possible; use room-temperature water.

Humidity: very high, 60%-70%, especially March through September.

Air circulation: essential for super success but avoid drafts.

Feed: very, very weak solution of mild liquid manure (cut recommendation of manufacturer to 2/3), every 3 weeks.

Soil: 2 parts standard potting mix, 1 part vermiculite, 2 parts peat moss.

Temperature: Day—68°-75°F (20°-23°C). Night—50°-60°F (10°-15°C).

Potbound: very happy; do not pot-on until root system is 80% of pot content, best done in February or March. Roots adhere to interior pot walls, therefore, to avoid excessive injury, work gently, easing them loose. Rapping pot against end of a table is an aid, as is running a spatula around inside of pot, pressing against pot wall with tool to avoid slipping into root ball. Wrap fronds of a large fern in newspaper for protection while handling. Set plant on 1½" (37 mm) layer of gravel, then add soil.

Mature plants: wash foliage at least every 3 weeks; remove yellowed or withered fronds as they appear.

Propagate: by division of mature plant, best done around March; or by spores attached to underside of leaflets (resemble little brown dots); or by plantlets on species so designated.

Insect alert: mealybugs, aphids, thrips, red spider—control with soap and water remedy, repeat every 3 days until eradicated.

Notable: ferns need coolness at their roots, so use pebble and water in tray method for cooler temperature and high humidity; best to grow in clay pots, the porosity of which allows evaporation and aids in keeping roots cool; if fronds droop from too dry soil, they cannot be revived; fronds of young plants cannot stand water directly on them; fronds bruise easily so plant should be located where it will not touch or be touched; ferns cannot stand pesticides, which will kill insects and your plant, too.

Asplenium nidus,
Bird's Nest Fern

A. bulbiferum (bulb-iff'-er-um) meaning bearing bulbs; known as Mother Fern; native to Malaysia and New Zealand; divided feathery fronds, 1'-2' (.30 m-.60 m) long; bright green leaflets; slender dark brown stems; small plantlets, bulbils, are produced on fronds.

A. platyneuron (plat-i-new'-ron) known as Ebony Spleenwort; native to United States; low growing; fronds to 15" (.38 m) long and 3" (76 mm) wide; shiny dark brown stems.

A. trichomanes (trik-oh-man'-eez) known as Maidenhair Spleenwort; native to United States; charming, dainty, small fern, 4"-6" (100 mm-150 mm) high; thickly clustered fronds, to 8" (200 mm) long.

A. nidus (nye-dus') meaning of nest; known as Bird's Nest Fern; from tropical Asia; brilliant green fronds similar to banana leaf, sheathlike with smooth edges; sprout from clustered rosette; fronds to 3' (.90 m) long.

AUCUBA JAPONICA (aw-kew'-buh ja-pon'-ik-uh) Gold-dust Plant, Japanese Aucuba or Laurel.

Aucuba is a latinized version of a Japanese name, japonica means of Japan. The many variations of this attractive evergreen species, with shiny, strikingly colored leaves, all mature to good size, so consider it a tub plant needing a sizable area.

Family Tree: Cornaceae (kor-nay'-see-ay) Dogwood family; native to Japan.

Foliage: waxy green, long, oval with toothed margins; 4"-6" (100 mm-150 mm), arranged opposite on stem; branches heavy, sturdy.

Flower: male and female are separate plants; purple-shaded blooms, small.

Fruit: clusters; to 3" (76 mm) long; scarlet.

Size: up to 15' (4.50 m).

Location: WINTER—southeastern or southwestern exposure.

SUMMER—*Inside:* northeastern or northwestern exposure. *Outside:* northeastern or northwestern exposure; site in sheltered area to protect foliage.

FALL: move indoors by mid-September; site in eastern or western exposure.

Dormancy: none, a resting time during winter months, generally September through March; slowly diminish watering; plant will indicate needs by appearance, becoming limp and droopy; develop sensitivity to feel of soil moisture level; cease fertilizing.

Water: evenly and thoroughly, allowing soil to dry between waterings.

Mist: daily, twice a day when possible.

Humidity: normal, 30%-35%.

Air circulation: essential for good cultural response.

Feed: every 2 weeks with mild liquid manure throughout growing season, April through August.

Soil: 3 parts standard potting mix, 1 part sharp sand or perlite.

Temperature: Day—68°-78°F (20°-25°C). Night—40°-64°F (4°-17°C).

Potbound: slightly for happiness, up to when root growth is approximately 65% of pot content; best repotted or potted-on before new growth develops, in March.

Mature plants: hard pruning should be done in late winter before new growth is evident.

Propagate: by cuttings; in moist sand and/or vermiculite; or by seed.

Insect alert: aphid, mealybug, mite, scale, leaf miner.

Notable: keep on lower side of recommended temperatures; important to wipe or wash foliage every 2 weeks; Note: good air circulation needed for top performance; do not over-pot, use pot only 2" (50 mm) larger than previous housing.

A. japonica
>   Variety—Variegata (var-ee-eh-gay'-tuh) meaning variegated; common name Gold-dust plant; yellow-speckled green leaves.
>   Variety—Picturata (pik-ter-ay'-tuh) leaves have yellow centers, green edges.
>   Variety—Sulphur (sul'-fer) leaves have green centers, yellow edges.

BEAUCARNEA RECURVATA (boh-karn'-ee-uh rek-kur-vay'-tuh) Pony Tail, Elephant Foot Tree.

Beaucarnea recurvata derives its common names from two distinctive characteristics: the crown of long, narrow leaves, rising from trunk and curving back, resembles the tail of a pony; the bulbous, swollen base of the trunk, covered with wrinkled gray bark, is reminiscent of an elephant's foot. This ornamental, evergreen, and extremely durable species is said to be able to store a year's supply of water in its base. Slow growing, it requires many, many years to reach a maximum height of 30' (9 m). *Beaucarnea* may be listed or referred to by previous names, *Nolina recurvata* or *N. tuberculata*.

Family Tree: Liliaceae (lil-ee-ay'-see-ay) Lily family; native to Mexico and South Africa.

Foliage: plume of sturdy leaves, up to 4' (1.20 m) long, ¾" (19 mm) wide; from bulbous base; may have several trunks.

Flower: small, fragrant, whitish flower; lilylike.

Size: up to 30' (9 m).

Location: WINTER—southeastern or southwestern exposure.

SUMMER—*Inside:* northeastern or northwestern exposure. *Outside:* northeastern or northwestern exposure; protect fragile foliage from potentially damaging elements, preferably by overhang.

FALL: move indoors by mid-September; site in eastern or western exposure.

Dormancy: none, but light resting period, October through February; slowly diminish watering, keeping soil barely moist; cut fertilizing program in half.

Water: let soil become moderately dry between thorough waterings.

Mist: daily, twice a day when possible.

Humidity: above normal for happiness, 40%-45%.

Air circulation: helpful condition.

Feed: mild liquid manure every 2 weeks.

Soil: 2 parts standard potting soil, 1 part peat moss, 1 part perlite.

Aucuba japonica
Gold-dust Plant

Beaucarnea recurvata,
Pony Tail or Elephant Foot

Temperature: Day—68°-80°F (20°-26°C). Night—55°-68°F (12°-20°C).

Potbound: repot; or pot-on as needed and indicated by root growth being at least 50% of pot content.

Propagate: by offshoots, remove and plant in equal parts soil as specified for this genus and sharp sand; or by seed.

Insect alert: mealybug, whitefly, mites, scale, slugs.

Notable: good artificial light specimen, a total of 14 hours combined with natural; must have good soil porosity; never allow soil to dry out completely; rinse foliage frequently in room-temperature or tepid water, to prevent dust-clogged pores.

B. recurvata
  Variety—Glauca (glay'-kah) meaning with white or gray bloom; blue gray leaves.

BEGONIA (beg-goh'-nee-uh).

This vast genus—named for a patron of botany, Michel Begon—includes every imaginable size, form, and coloration of both flower and foliage. Flower forms span the gamut of petite clusters through sizable, delicate, large single blooms, each as lovely as the next. Enhancing the flower is a backdrop of leaves, again many forms and sizes. Many species have the foliage featured over the blossom. Cultures, too, are quite different. Some species are birthed from tubers, some from rootstock; both are rhizomatous. The balance are from a fibrous root system. Depending upon species, there is an availability of either ever blooming or seasonal blooming with these perennial plants.

Family Tree: Begoniaceae (beg-goh-nee-aye'-see-ay) Begonia family; native to tropical America and Asia.

Location: WINTER—southeastern or southwestern exposure.
SUMMER—*Inside and Outside:* eastern or western exposure.
FALL: move indoors by mid-September; site in eastern or western exposure.

Dormancy: after flowering; plant indicates dormant or resting period; heavy flowering cycle followed by continuous but very light bloom indicates species does not go into full dormancy; cessation of flowering and, in some cases, withering and dying down of foliage indicate full dormancy; slowly diminish watering, keeping soil barely moist; cease fertilizing until new growth appears.

Water: allow to dry between thorough waterings.

Mist: daily, twice a day when possible; when flowering, spray around plant, not directly on blossoms.

Humidity: normal, 30%-35%.

Air circulation: helpful condition.

Feed: mild liquid manure, weekly.

Soil: tuberous rooted—1 part standard mix, 2 parts peat moss; fibrous rooted—1 part each potting mix, sand, peat moss.

Temperature: Day—60°-75°F (15°-23°C). Night—55°-60°F (12°-15°C).

Potbound: normal; pot-on fibrous-rooted species after blooming, when root system is 50% of pot content.

Mature plants: better bloom if stems pinched back as they become straggly; pinch off to point where plant retains compact, uniform shape; want wide plant, pinch center out of young shoots; remove faded blooms as they occur; remove withered foliage as it may occur.

Propagate: by seed; by division of plant for fibrous-rooted species; by division of tuber and/or rootstock for species of such nature; or by leaf and/or stem cuttings.

Insect alert: mealybugs, slugs, whitefly, scale.

Disease alert: mildew; bud and flower shedding when

Begonia,
Tuberhybrida pendula

soil is too dry or with too high room temperature; mold accumulates on spent flowers.

Notable: soil must have porosity; no soggy feet, causing root or tuber rot; never allow soil to dry out completely; excellent specimen for artificial light, a total of 14 hours combined with natural; use pebble, water and tray method to maintain a good humidity level; syringe foliage every few weeks to avoid dust-clogged pores.

B. argentea-guttata (are-jen-tee-a-gut-tay'-ta) meaning speckled with silver patches; smooth leaves grown from fibrous roots, oval to wing-shaped, toothed edges, up to 5″ (127 mm) long, colored green to bronze with silver marbling; stems lightly hairy; succulent of creeping habit; white to lightly shaded pink flowers, clustered, small blossoms; hanging clusters rising from leaf joints; plant height to 4′ (1.20 m).

B. rexii (rex'-ee-eye) meaning king; creeping rootstock; tall, hairy, stalked, bearing up to 9″ (230 mm) large leaves; undersides hairy; fantastically marked in colorations, patterned striated, banded, marbled, on mottled blotches; leaves greens through red maroons, marking of purples, browns with metallic highlights; flowers up to 1½″ (37 mm) wide, shadings of pink through rose; blooming time depending upon variety; temperature range differs, needing 65°-75°F (18°-23°C); humidity 50%-60%; bright light best for good leaf color but direct sun will bleach leaves; keep soil evenly moist at all times.

B. scharfii (shar'-fee-eye) native to Brazil; previously classified as *B. haageana*; plant up to 4′ (1.20 m) high; fibrous rooted; up to 10″ (250 mm) long, 5″ (127 mm) wide leaves, oval to heart shaped, to pointed at tip, wavy edges; leaf veined red, underside purple; up to 10″ (250 mm) wide drooping clusters, pink through deep rose blossoms.

B. tuberhybrida (too-ber-hib'-ri-da) meaning a hybrid plant of thick tubers; 2 to 3 stemmed; large, slanted leaves; flowers single or double, large, in profusion, all colors except blue; some blossoms camellialike in appearance, others narcissuslike.

BELOPERONE COMOSA (bel-op-er-oh'-nee kom-moh'-suh) Shrimp Plant.
Comosa means "with tufts of hair." Commonly named for having bracts (modified leaves on flower stalk) similar in color, size, and shape to the seafood, shrimp. An interesting genus to add to your collection. It can be kept in bloom throughout the summer by constant pruning.
Family Tree: Acanthaceae (a-kan-tha'-see-e) Acanthus family; native to tropical America.
Foliage: oval, bordered in brick red; hairy.
Flower: tiny, white, tubular resembling shrimp; protruding from 3″-4″ (76 mm-100 mm) long formations of petal-like bracts, colored yellow, yellow and red, or solid red.
Size: 1′-3′ (.30 m-.90 m) stems.
Location: WINTER—full sun; set in southern exposure.
SUMMER—*Inside:* partial shade; set in eastern to southern exposure for direct rays of morning sun. *Outside:* partial shade; set in eastern exposure under a protective structure where plant receives strong light but no direct rays.
FALL: move indoors by mid-September.
Dormancy: none, actually; but there is an obvious resting period at end of blossom cycle; cease fertilizing in October.

Beloperone comosa,
Shrimp Plant

Water: allow to become slightly dry between waterings; water moderately; never allow soil to become completely dry or to be soggy.
Mist: daily.
Humidity: above normal; 45%.
Air circulation: helpful condition.
Feed: February through September; mild liquid manure every two weeks.
Soil: standard potting mix.
Temperature: Day—68°-72°F (20°-22°C). Night—50°-55°F (10°-12°C).
Potbound: repot or pot-on in February; pot-on when soil content is overbalanced by root system.
Mature plants: better bloom if stems pinched back as they become straggly; pinch off to point where plant retains compact, uniform shape; want wide plant, pinch center out of young shoots; pruning back in spring and late summer also encourages repeated blooming.
Propagate: in April, pinched-off tips can be rooted in water.
Insect alert: whitefly, aphids.
Disease alert: if soil becomes too dry, leaves will dry up and drop.
Notable: too high a temperature makes branches long and rangy; recommend keeping stems pinched back to length of 12″-18″ (.30 m-.45 m) to avoid overly weak stems, propagated cuttings will bloom their first year; too much shade makes top leaves pale out.

B. guttata (gut-tay'-tuh) yellow green evergreen herb; the most popular shrimp plant; blooms September through November; flower white with a purple red spot on lower lip; surrounded by hanging red brown bracts (modified leaves on the flower stalk forming part of the flower head).

BLECHNUM (blek'-num) Deer Fern.
One of the more easily maintained ferns, this is a genus that would just as soon have a warm temperature. Mostly large scaled—good as fillers for large voids—they take to

and thrive in interior sites if supplied with adequate humidity and moisture.

Family Tree: Polypodiaceae (pol-i-po'-di-ay-see-ay) Common Fern family; native to Brazil, West Indies, and Australia.

Foliage: solid colored, light to dark green fronds (leaves), feathery, drooping in nature; many species have leathery texture.

Size: 3'-5' (.90 m-1.50 m) in height and spread, depending on species.

Location: WINTER—eastern or western exposure.

SUMMER—*Inside:* eastern or western exposure. *Outside:* eastern or western exposure; sheltered to protect fragile foliage from potentially damaging winds and heavy rains.

FALL: move indoors by mid-September; site in eastern or western exposure.

Dormancy: none, although light resting period in winter months; slowly diminish watering, keeping soil barely moist; cease fertilizing.

Water: thoroughly and evenly, allowing soil to dry between waterings.

Mist: daily, two or more times in warm weather.

Humidity: above normal, 45%-60%.

Air circulation: essential to have good moderate movement for top plant performance.

Feed: very, very mild liquid manure, 1/4 strength of package or manufacturer's recommendations, March through October.

Soil: 2 parts standard potting mix, 1 part peat moss, 1 part vermiculite.

Temperature: Day—68°-75°F (20°-23°C). Night—58°-65°F (14°-18°C).

Potbound: pot-on young plants each year to pot 2" (50 mm) larger; older plants happy when somewhat potbound; side-dress each year, pot-on every 2 or 3 years, when indicated by plant's root growth 80% to 20% soil in pot; this cultural attention to be implemented late winter or early spring, February or March; deep pots are best shape for submerged aerial roots.

Mature plants: in repotting or potting-on, firm soil but do not compact it.

Propagate: by seed or by suckers; or by plantlets on varieties with this habit of reproduction.

Insect alert: mealybug, red spider mite, scale, thrips.

Notable: an excellent genus for artificial light culture, a total of 14-16 hours combined natural and artificial; leaves should be washed or wiped with moist cloth at least once a month to keep pores unclogged; no direct sun, or foliage will burn; remember that most palms are of slow-growing habit.

B. brasiliense (braz-il-ee-en'-suh) meaning of Brazil; native to Brazil and Peru; a vigorous grower; tree-trunklike stem covered in dark brown scales, up to 3' (.90 m) high; solid green fronds to 3' (.90 m) long, 15" (.38 m) wide; lance shaped, leatherlike.

B. fluviatile (flew-vee-at'-il-ee) from Australia and New Zealand; a good hanging basket species, fronds with wavy margins are 30" (.75 m) long, 18" (.45 m) wide.

B. gibbum (jib'-bum) species resembling Tree fern genus; fine serrated fronds 3' (.90 m) long, 1' (.30 m) wide; up to 5' (1.50 m) high trunk.

B. occidentale (ok-sid-en-tay'-luh) meaning western, new world; from Australia; trunkless; fronds rise from base, to 5' (1.50 m) long, 3' (.90 m) wide.

B. spicant (spye'-kant) Deer fern; native to western United States; evergreen plant; leaflets lightly toothed on fronds up to 3½' (1 m) long.

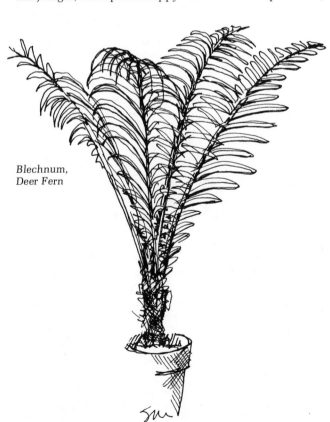

Blechnum,
Deer Fern

BOUGAINVILLEA (boog-in-vill'-ee-uh) nickname: Paper Flower. Bougainvillea commemorates Louis Antoine de Bougainville, a French navigator and commander who explored much of the globe for Louis XV during a circumnavigation in 1766-69. Philbert Commerson, a naturalist on board the voyage, named the genus, which they found on the coast of South America.

A profuse, truly beautiful bloomer of fantastic colors depending on species. This vine-type evergreen shrub spreads vigorously and blossoms almost constantly with proper cultural environment. Consider it a tub plant to be grown on a trellis or handled as any lengthy, heavy vine in need of support or control; lovely when pruned into a standard form.

Family Tree: Nyctaginaceae (nict-tuh-jin-ay'-see-ay) Four o'Clock family; native to Brazil.

Foliage: lance shaped, small, medium green leaves; slightly thorny stems.

Flower: 3 tiny white flowers within 3 bracts (modified leaves on the flower stalk forming part of the flower head) of colors ranging through magenta, purple, red, rose, pink, white, copper, and yellow; bracts are papery and arranged in clusters on the branches; blooms early fall through late spring.

Size: to 15' (4.50 m).

Location: WINTER—southern exposure.

SUMMER—*Inside and Outside: southern exposure.*

Bougainvillea glabra

FALL: move indoors by mid-September; site in southern exposure.

Dormancy: period starts in late fall; a resting period is needed after heavy blooming; move plant to a cool spot, around 50°F (10°C); in a 4-6 week period, plant will drop most of its leaves; allow soil to dry out completely between thorough waterings, cease fertilizing.

Water: keep soil evenly moist.

Mist: daily; 2 times daily while growing after resting period.

Humidity: happy above normal, 45%-50%.

Air circulation: helpful condition.

Feed: weekly, with a mild liquid manure.

Soil: 2 parts standard potting soil, 1 part sand, 1 part peat moss, 2 parts vermiculite.

Temperature: Day—70°-80°F (21°-26°C). Night—60°-65°F (15°-18°C).

Potbound: side-dress in early spring after blooming period; do not disturb roots more than necessary; pot-on only when potbound, indicated by roots 75% to soil 25%.

Mature plants: pinch off dead blooms as they occur to extend blooming period. Trim back after flowering; prune to keep within bounds, can be cut back to 12″ (.30 m) to generate new growth. If overly lengthy shoots have sprouted by repotting, prune these at this time. Pinch tips of new shoots to encourage branching. If a problem of nonblooming occurs, allow plant ball to dry out more between waterings; cut down on fertilizing, and give additional sun length and strength.

Propagate: by 3″-4″ (76 mm-100 mm) tip cuttings of half-ripened wood in spring; dust wood with a rooting hormone and set in equal parts moist sand and peat moss; rooting takes 3-4 months.

Offspring established: maintain proper culture as for adult plants; within a year genus flowers.

Insect alert: mealybug, scale.

Disease alert: avoid too alkaline or too acidic soil.

Notable: high temperatures are needed for bud setting; soil must be light for good drainage; do not allow soil to dry out completely or be soggy; flower and leaf shedding is caused by fluctuating temperatures and roots drying out; in fall and winter this exotic genus benefits from artificial light.

B. glabra (glay′-bruh) meaning smooth or hairless; strong vine with yellow through orange, or peach through purple bracts (a modified leaf on flower stalk at base of flower), that bloom along the slender, shorter side branches.

B. spectabilis (spek-tab′-il-iss) meaning a spectacle; striking; a vigorous grower; large, less pointed, hairy leaves; large red flower panicles (a loose cluster or tuft of flowers borne on several branches), and bracts.

B. hybrids

> *B. Temple Fire:* low and compact; red to cerise bracts.
> *B. Harrisii:* small, variegated green and white leaves; low bushy growth; no flowers but an attractive trailing plant.
> *B. Barbara Karst:* tall, bushy grower with cascading masses of rose red bracts; popular.
> Variety—Sanderiana (san-der-ee-ay′-nuh): heavy flowering; white.

BRASSAIA ACTINOPHYLLA (Brass-say′-ee-uh ak-tin-oh-fill′-uh) Octopus Tree; Australian Umbrella Tree, Queensland Umbrella Tree; nickname: Schefflera.
Schefflera (shef-ler′-a), generally mispronounced as Shef-a-ler′-ia, has its popular name because of a classification error. Now B. actinophylla, the name Octopus tree was derived supposedly from the growth habit relating to the flowering in its natural environment; red flowers blooming on branches of stretching habit resembling the arms of an octopus. This species is a tropical evergreen foliage plant to be sited in a no sun, good light area. It will need space for expansion, for if happily sited with minor cultural attentions properly performed this plant repays with more than moderate growth rate. A sturdy species that will withstand neglect, although it will not be the "apple of your eye" if ignored.

Family Tree: Araliaceae (uh-ray-lee-ay′-see-ay) Aralia or Ginseng family; native to Australia.

Foliage: shiny, dark green, oval, compound leaves of 6 to 8 long leaflets, 3″-12″ (76 mm-304 mm) long, depending on age of plant, form umbrella shape.

Flower: small, red, on armlike branches; rarely bloom under cultivation.

Size: normally 6′-15′ (1.80 m-4.50 m), but to 30′ (9 m) under proper conditions; can be kept smaller by pruning.

Location: WINTER—southeastern or southwestern exposure. SUMMER—*Inside:* eastern or western exposure. *Outside:* eastern or western exposure; site in sheltered area for foliage protection from potentially damaging weather elements.
FALL: move indoors by mid-September; site in eastern or western exposure.

Dormancy: none, but a resting period. Slower growth period during winter months of less intensity, generally October through February; slowly diminish watering; plant will indicate needs as determined by environmental conditions; develop sensitivity to feel of soil moisture level; cease fertilizing.

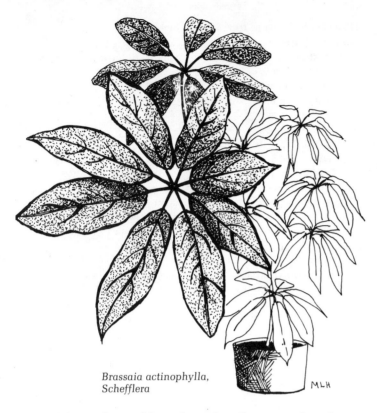

*Brassaia actinophylla,
Schefflera*

MLH

Water: thoroughly and evenly, allowing soil to dry out between waterings.

Mist: daily, twice a day when possible.

Humidity: above normal for happiness, 45%-55%.

Air circulation: helpful condition.

Feed: mild liquid manure every 2 weeks.

Soil: 2 parts standard potting mix, 1 part perlite.

Temperature: Day—70°-80°F (21°-26°C). Night—62°-68°F (16°-20°C).

Potbound: very happy; pot-on only when root growth of plant is 80%, soil 20% of pot content; top- or side-dress yearly; preferably spring.

Mature plants: if plant becomes too tall, cut growing ends (can be started in rooting media). Remove dried or withered leaves as they appear. Overly long and drooping leaf stems are the result of insufficient light.

Propagate: by stem cuttings or air layering.

Insect alert: mealybug, red spider, scales, thrip, aphids.

Notable: good artificial light plant; total of 14-16 hours, combining natural and artificial light; do not allow soil to dry out completely; soil must have porosity, eliminating possibility of soggy conditions; use pebble, water, and tray method to maintain humidity level; sponge foliage at least every 3 weeks; always use room temperature water; leaf shiners and/or oils are an absolute no-no.

BROMELIA FAMILY (bro-mee'-li-uh) Pineapple Family, Bromeliad, Air Plants.

The terminology most frequently heard in reference to this family is Bromeliad and actually refers to any of over 2,100 species listed. In their natural habitat, the plants grow on tree limbs and sometimes on rocks. The air plant reference is not only because of their lofty positions but also because the greater part of their fertilization is through the leaves. The main purpose of their roots is attachment to a host support. Because of the vastly different features in type, size, bloom, color, and culture for each group, I am approaching these plants with a modified general culture and including more information within the specific detailing of eight genera. Many of the plants are stiff-leafed of lovely shaded colors, some muted, others vivid. An interesting array of blooms, some almost abstract in design; berried genera occur. These beauties adjust readily and can be moved to various interior sites for full appreciation, particularly during their flowering periods, which last up to three months. The parent plant may produce up to a dozen offshoots; new plants are easily propagated, which compensates for the fact that the parent in most species flowers but once.

Family Tree: Bromeliaceae (brom-mee'-li-ay-see-ay) Pineapple family; native to tropical America.

Location: WINTER—southern exposure.

SUMMER—*Inside:* southeastern or southwestern site. *Outside:* eastern or western exposure.

FALL: move indoors by mid-September; site in southeastern or southwestern exposure. *Note:* Some species have different requirements; check under culture of specific plant.

Water: keep water in vase-shaped foliage; soil must not be soaked; in filling this cup, allow a bit of water to overflow and trickle down to base of plant and top soil level; for species without this foliage feature, water by spraying entire plant and soil thoroughly at least twice a day.

Mist: daily, twice a day when possible.

Humidity: very happy when high, 50%-60%.

Air circulation: essential to have good circulation for totally successful culture.

Feed: once a month, fish emulsion or a 10-5-5 mild solution, through spring and summer; water soil lightly, then apply very small quantity of very weak solution to dampened soil; also can be sprayed on foliage—the Bromeliads absorb food through the leaf scales.

Soil: referred to as a growing medium; use osmunda, tree fern, or fir bark mixtures, all available packaged at garden supply outlets; also one may find this material designated as orchid potting mix.

Temperature: Day—72°-85°F (22°-29°C). Night—60°-65°F (15°-18°C).

Potbound: very difficult to occur, for root system amounts to almost nothing; if deemed necessary, pot-on to pot no more than 2″ (50 mm) larger.

Mature plants: if plant does not flower when one-year old, set plant in large plastic bag, placing half an apple in bag with plant; secure the bag so that it is airtight; ethylene gas released by the apple activates the lower buds; on fifth day remove bag and apple; blooms should appear in approximately 6 weeks.

Propagate: by division or suckers. Most frequently by offshoots, which generally appear after flowering; when offshoots are 6″-8″ (150 mm-200 mm) tall with 3 good-sized leaves, sever with a sterile knife; dust the exposed new basal and root growth with charcoal; pot in shallow 2″-4″ (50 mm-100 mm) pot; the 4″ (100 mm) pot will hold the largest of any family member, for the root system is meager.

Offspring established: quite on their own when severed from parent, aside from planting process; maintain humidity level at 60%-70%; maintain day temperature, 72°-80°F (22°-29°C); never below 60°F (15°C) at night.

Insect alert: scale, thrips.

Disease alert: yellow leaves caused by too much direct sun or too cool temperatures.

Notable: know that this family blooms only on new growth; use tray, pebble, and water method for constantly high humidity; good under artificial light; do not over-water; soil should be barely moist at time of watering and completely dry between waterings; propagated offshoots will flower in 1-2 years; when the flowering stalk appears, move plant to very bright light to increase intensity of the marvelous coloring; too cool temperatures are a vehicle for rotting; do not use insecticides on any Bromeliads.

Vriesea splendens (vree′-see-ay splen′-denz) Flaming Sword, Painted Feather. Splendens means bright, shining, splendid. It is native to Mexico, South America, West Indies.

Foliage: 3′ (.90 m) long, 1½″-2½″ (37 mm-62 mm) wide, smooth-edged, waxy; dark and light green with mahogany stripes, zebralike stripes in brown to purple with purple underside, or vivid green with brown stripes.

Flower: tall spears of brilliant orange or red overlapping bracts (modified leaf on flower stalk forming part of flower head mistakenly thought to be the flower); sword-shaped spikes of yellowish white.

Size: 1½′-3′ (.45 m-.90 m).

Notable: do not repot; needs bright light but never place in direct sun; keep leaf-cup rosettes filled with water, which must be free of calcium.

Aechmea fasciata (ek-mee′-a fash′-ee-ata) Urn Plant, Living Vase Plant. Meaning broad, flattened stem. Native to primeval forests in Central and South America.

Foliage: rosette of long stiff leaves, toothed edges, up to 20″ (.55 m) high; plant size to 20″ (.55 m) wide; leaves are dark green striated across leaf in silver gray.

Flower: showy spike of pink bracts (modified leaf on flower stalk forming part of flower head mistakenly thought to be the flower), with blue flowers.

Fruit: long lasting scarlet berries.

Size: 1½′-2′ (.45 m-.60 m).

Notable: keep water in leaf-cup rosette; nourishment and water are taken through upper sides of leaves; 3 years old before capable of flowering; when blooming, color retained for up to 5 months; retains foliage well after flowering.

Ananas comosus (a-nan′-as ko-mo′-sus) Pineapple, this is the commercial edible Pineapple plant. Meaning with tufts of hair. Native to Brazil.

Foliage: narrrow, sharp-edged, gray green variegated leaves, up to 3′ (.90 m) long, formed from basal rosette.

Flower: purple blooms with pink, red, and white bracts (modified leaf on flower stalk forming part of flower head mistakenly thought to be the flower), on 2′-4′ (.60 m-1.20 m) stalks.

Fruit: grows in middle of leaf rosette.

Size: 30″-36″ (.75 m-.90 m).

Notable: can take full sun; place 2″ (50 mm) thick cut top portion of fruit in shallow container of water until good root system develops; then pot in soil as specified for this family; takes at least 1½-2 years to fruit.

Billbergia nutans (bil-bur′-jee-uh nu′-tanz) Queen's Tears. Meaning nodding or drooping. Native to Mexico, South America.

Foliage: thick, grasslike tufts of narrow, grooved, leathery, sharp-edged leaves; dark green.

Flower: rose with red bracts (modified leaf on flower stalk forming part of flower head mistakenly thought to be the flower), violet with green-edged petals, or yellow green with blue edges and pink bracts; nodding or drooping on spikes.

Size: 30″ (.75 m) tall.

Notable: has more developed roots than most genera of this family; a fast grower; low to normal humidity; no drafts, please; feed every 3 weeks, very mild liquid fertilizer, only when flowering has ceased; water soil directly; keep evenly moist in summer; use half the normal amount of water in winter.

Cryptanthus zonatus zebrinus (krip-tan′-thus zo-nay′-tus ze-bree′-nus) Earth Stars. Meaning hidden flower, zebra-striped. Native to Brazil.

Foliage: wavy-edged leaves in flat rosette, to 6″ (150 mm) across; leaves zebra-striped, bronze purple with silver gray crossbands.

Flower: small, white, insignificant flowers; rise above leaves.

Size: 1″ (25 mm).

Notable: a stemless, compact plant; does well growing on a piece of bark or hanging on steel wire; if planted, keep in 2″ (50 mm) pot; keep soil very light; do not feed; place in bright light; maintain very high humidity, use tray, pebble, water method, mist frequently; water only in leaf cup.

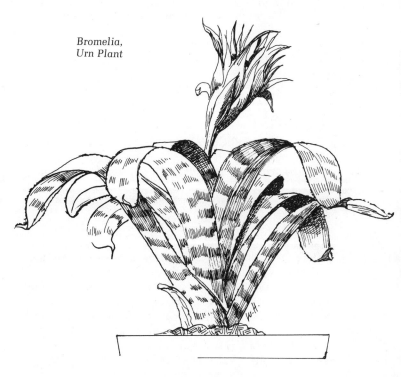

Bromelia,
Urn Plant

Guzmania lingulata (guz-ma'-nee-a ling-u-la'-ta) Meaning tongue-shaped. Native to Andean rain forests.
Foliage: glossy, smooth-edged leaves; apple green, striped with dark red; funnel-shaped leaf rosette.
Flower: star-shaped, densely drooping heads of yellow to orange flowers with bright red bracts (modified leaf on flower stalk forming part of flower head mistakenly thought to be the flower).
Size: 18"-26" (.45 m-.65 m).
Notable: maintain high humidity, use tray, pebble, water method; maintain warm temperatures; color is truly magnificent and long-lasting.

Neoregelia carolinae (nee-oh-rej-ee-li-uh ka-ro-lin'-ay) Painted Fingernail Plant. Native to Guyana and Brazilian rain forests.
Foliage: tongue-shaped, tooth-edged, red-tipped leaves form dense, flat rosette; green striped with yellow, white, and rose; area around vase is rosy red; before blooming inner leaves become shorter and turn carmine.
Flower: orange-red bracts (modified leaf on flower stalk forming part of flower head mistakenly thought to be the flower) surround small white-edged, purple flowers.
Size: 30"-40" (.75 m-.92 m).
Notable: needs warm temperature and high humidity year around; keep water in leaf-cup rosette, grow in northern or eastern exposure.

Tillandsia cyanea (til-land'-zee-a sye-a'-nee-a) Tillandsia refers to Spanish moss, cyanea means dark blue. Native to southeastern United States and Central and South America.
Foliage: dark green rosettes of long, narrow, arching leaves, palmlike, with sharp edges.
Flower: flat, diamond-shaped; light red spike 8" (.25 m) high; large, intensely blue flowers emerge one at a time between bright pink bracts (modified leaf on flower stalk forming part of flower head mistakenly thought to be the flower).
Size: 10"-30" (.27 m-.75 m).
Notable: needs heavy misting; keep water in leaf-cup rosette.

BROWALLIA SPECIOSA (broh-wall'-lee-uh spee-see-oh'-suh) Sapphire Flower.
Speciosa means showy. Pending gracefully for hanging baskets or pots placed on plant stands; this slow growing genus can have tips pinched out for full branching and showy gracefulness.
Family Tree: Solanaceae (sohl-lan-a'-cee-aye) Nightshade family; a native of tropical America.
Foliage: 1½" (37 mm) in length; broad, shaped like a spear or lance; trailing habit.
Flower: 2" (50 mm) wide; violet, blue, or white blossoms with white throat; hybrid, Silver Bells: white flowers; variety, Major, meaning greater or larger; naturally blooms spring or summer but can be made to bloom anytime.
Size: 2' (.60 m), occasionally up to 3' (.90 m).
Location: WINTER—full sun; set in southern exposure.

Browallia speciosa,
Sapphire Flower

SUMMER—*Inside:* partial shade; set in eastern to southern exposure for direct rays of morning sun. *Outside:* partial shade; set in eastern exposure or under a protective structure where plant receives strong light but no direct rays.
FALL: move indoors by mid-September.
Dormancy: none; feed monthly November through February.
Water: keep soil evenly moist.
Mist: daily; hot weather, twice daily.
Humidity: above normal, 45%-50%.
Air circulation: helpful condition.
Feed: diluted liquid manure once weekly, in winter once monthly.
Soil: standard potting mixture.
Temperature: Day—68°-72°F (20°-22°C). Night—55°-60°F (12°-15°C).
Potbound: happy, happy; pot-on only when absolutely essential, root system 80% of pot.
Mature plants: better bloom if stems pinched back as they become straggly. Pinch off to point where plant retains compact, uniform shape; pinch center out of young shoots for wide plant.
Propagate: from seed, March through July, in sandy potting compost 1/16" (1.5 mm) deep; cover, keep in warm room with soil moist; or by stem cuttings in August.
Offspring established: place 3"-4" (76 mm-100 mm) self-supporting transplants into 1" (25 mm) pots or grow pots with standard potting mix; pinch out tops for bushier plants.
Insect alert: whitefly, leaf miners, aphids.
Notable: never allow soil to dry out completely; can be made to flower almost any season of the year by attention

to culture; keep on cooler side of recommended temperatures.

B. americana (am-eh-rik-kay'-nuh) meaning "of America"; sometimes listed as *B. elata*; 1½' (.45 m) tall, medium blue flowers 1" (25 mm) across; slightly hairy foliage.

Variety—alba: white-flowered.

B. viscosa compacta (vis-coh'-sa com-pack'-ta) meaning growing in a compact form; Sapphire, blue-flowered.

BRUNFELSIA CALYCINA (brunn-fel'-zee-uh kal-liss'-in-uh) Yesterday, Today and Tomorrow; nickname: Chameleon plant.

A handsome plant, too seldom possessed. Long-flowering, it is easy to maintain if one sites it in a cool location. Some species have especially handsome, fragrant flowers. Named (by an unknown botanist) after Otto Brunfels, a 16th-century botanist who "turned color"—Catholic monk to Protestant—early in the reformation. Brunfels published the first German herbal, an illustrated study of Rhineland plants, in 1530. He wanted to start his own small reformation of the plant world.

Family Tree: Solanaceae (sohl-lan-nay'-see-ay) Nightshade family; a native of Brazil in tropical America.

Foliage: evergreen, bushy, alternate arrangement; dark, glossy, lance shaped; to 3" (76 mm) long.

Flower: 2" (50 mm), flat-collared, sweet-scented; colors on first day, dark purple with white eyes; second day, lavendar; third day, white; blooming period under right conditions, most of the year except for early winter.

Size: 3'-4' (.90 m-1.20 m).

Location: WINTER—full sun; set in southern exposure.

SUMMER—*Inside:* partial shade; set in eastern to southern exposure for direct rays of morning sun. *Outside:* partial

shade; set in eastern exposure or under a protective structure where plant receives strong light but no direct rays.

FALL: move indoors by mid-September.

Dormancy: period starts late fall; resting period; no true dormancy; slowly diminish watering; cease fertilizing in winter.

Water: keep evenly moist.

Mist: daily, twice daily if possible.

Humidity: high, at least 50%.

Air circulation: helpful condition.

Feed: during active growth period, March through September; mild, liquid manure weekly.

Soil: 2 parts standard potting soil, 1 part vermiculite.

Temperature: Day—68°-72°F (20°-22°C). Night—60°-65°F (15°-18°C).

Potbound: keep slightly so for fuller bloom; if necessary to repot or pot-on, do so in early spring before growth begins.

Mature plants: better bloom if stems pinched back as they become straggly. Pinch off to point where plant retains compact, uniform shape; pinch center out of young shoots for wide plant. Keep pruning light, as plant does not readily form new shoots.

Propagate: grow tip cuttings of half-ripened wood in spring, in moist vermiculite in warm room 80°-85°F (26°-29°C).

Offspring established: pinch back tips of shoots to obtain bushy, well-shaped plant.

Notable: never allow soil to become soggy from overwatering; never allow soil to dry out completely; soil must have good drainage; when working with plant be careful not to injure roots which are tender and have a tendency to grow near surface of soil; do aerate soil once a month.

B. floribunda (floh-rib-bund'-uh) meaning flowering profusely; a dwarf, free-flowering species; blooms are rich violet with small white eyes.

BUXUS SEMPERVIRENS SUFFRUTICOSA (book'-sus sem-per-veer'-enz suf-froo-tik-oh'-suh) Dwarf Boxwood.

Dwarf boxwood, a long-lived, slow-growing plant, is a perfect variety to be trained as a bonsai. Delicate, evergreen foliage is very poisonous, a consideration when exposing plant to potentially curious children and animals. B. s. suffruticosa will adjust readily to all interior environment light exposures except full sun or full shade. With proper minor cultural attentions, it is "a perky" all year round plant.

Family Tree: Buxaceae (book-say'-see-ay) Box family; native to southern Europe, North Africa, Asia.

Foliage: oppositely arranged, shiny, deep green oval leaves, ½" (12 mm); evergreen, on dense branches; whorled growth habit.

Flower: rarely indoors, clustered wee flowers, petalless; in spring.

Size: to 4' (1.20 m).

Location: WINTER—southeastern or southwestern exposure.

SUMMER—*Inside:* northeastern or northwestern exposure. *Outside:* northeastern or northwestern exposure; site in shelter to protect foliage.

FALL: move indoors by mid-September; site in eastern or western exposure.

Brunfelsia calycina,
Yesterday, Today and Tomorrow

Buxus sempervirens suffruticosa,
Dwarf Boxwood

Dormancy: none; but a resting period, slower growth period during winter months of less intensity—generally October through February; slowly diminish watering; plant will indicate needs as determined by environmental conditions; develop sensitivity to feel of soil moisture level; cease fertilizing.

Water: thoroughly and evenly, allowing soil to dry out between waterings.

Mist: daily, twice a day when possible.

Humidity: above normal for happiness, 45%-55%.

Air circulation: helpful condition.

Feed: mild liquid manure monthly.

Soil: standard potting soil.

Temperature: Day—68°-75°F (20°-23°C). Night—50°-65°F (10°-18°C).

Potbound: very happy; pot-on only when root growth of plant is 80%, soil 20% of pot content; top- or side-dress yearly, preferably spring.

Mature plants: after new growth has formed, pinch or cut out centers to increase bushiness. Remove all dead stems and leaves as they appear.

Propagate: by stem cuttings; root in moist vermiculite kept at about 50°-55°F (10°-12°C).

Insect alert: mealybug, red spider, scale, thrip, aphids, leaf miners.

Notable: good artificial light plant; total of 14-16 hours, combining natural and artificial light; do not allow soil to dry out completely; soil must have porosity, eliminating possibility of soggy conditions; use pebble, water, and tray method to maintain humidity level; sponge foliage at least every 3 weeks, always use room-temperature water; leaf shiners and/or oils are an *absolute no-no*; keep on cooler side of recommended temperatures; tolerant of drafts.

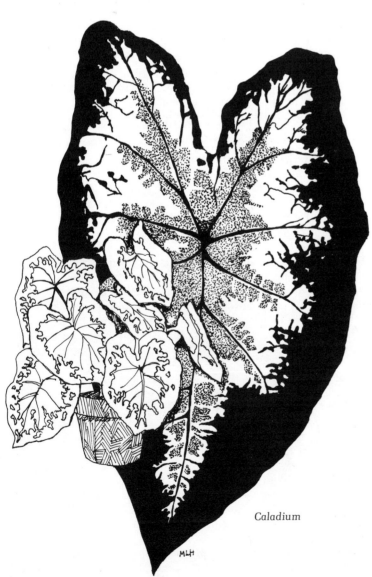

Caladium

CALADIUM (kal-lay′-dee-um) Fancy leaved Caladium.

Delicate, veined and patterned leaves, ranging the color spectrum from green through reds, purples, and whites, are the visual beauty of this tuber plant, which can be forced for either summer or winter bloom. Sited in good, bright light but very little sun is best for most handsome foliage performance. Grown from tubers, the foliage will display well for three to four months prior to plant's recession into dormant state.

Family Tree: Araceae (ar-aye′-see-ay) Arum family; native to South America.

Foliage: heart, lance, or arrow shaped; green, white, pink, red, purple; deeper color accents along ribs; mottled and bordered leaf patterns; all depending on species.

Flower: small; similar to Calla lily; greenish white; generally concealed by foliage.

Size: 2″ (50 mm) to 2′ (.60 m) depending on species.

Location: WINTER—generally dormant; if in leaf, southern exposure.

SUMMER—*Inside and Outside:* eastern to southeastern or western exposure.

FALL: move indoors by mid-September; site in eastern to southeastern or western exposure.

Dormancy: foliage yellows, withers, and dies down around October; store in pots or remove tubers from pot, remove soil from tuber and roots, cut off withered foliage tops and store in shallow box or pan in dry peat moss or sphagnum moss at temperature of 55°-60°F (12°-15°C); slowly diminish watering in October until all foliage has died down, then keep soil barely moist if tuber is stored in soil in pot; cease fertilizing by mid-September.

Water: thoroughly and evenly, keeping soil constantly moist.

Mist: daily, twice a day when possible.

Humidity: high for happiness, 45%-50%.

Air circulation: helpful condition.

Feed: mild liquid manure every 2 weeks, April through mid-September.

Soil: 1 part standard potting mix, 2 parts peat moss, 1 part perlite or sharp sand.

Temperature: Day—72°-80°F (22°-26°C). Night—65°-70°F (18°-21°C).

Potbound: repot tuber between February and April in soil specified for this genus; start full water and feeding culture; keep warm, 75°-80°F (23°-26°C), to promote growth.

Mature plants: as foliage yellows and withers, snip off at soil level. Give pots ¼ turn each watering to retain well-formed plant.

Propagate: by division of tuber clumps in spring when repotting.

Notable: never allow soil to dry out completely; soil must be porous for good drainage; no soggy soil, or tubers will rot; use pebble, water, and tray method for maintaining high humidity level; use only tepid water for misting and watering; bright sun will fade color of foliage, but bright light will increase depth of coloration; tuber planted upside down will produce small foliage in great profusion, proper side up produces normally large leaf in modest numbers.

C. bicolor (bye'-kol-or) meaning two colors; oval leaf; prominently notched at stem; veined and blotched, with shades of green or red and/or white; stems erect; smooth.

    Variety—Candidum (kan'-di-dum) pure white, green-veined leaf.

C. humboldtii (hum-bolt'-ee-eye) miniature caladium; native to Brazil; green leaves, striated and spotted white, 2" (50 mm) long; generally grows year-round without going into dormancy.

CALATHEA MAKOYANA (kal-ath-ee'-uh mak-oy-ay'-nuh) Peacock Plant, Cathedral Window.

The peacock plant was previously classified as Maranta. A genus related to and frequently confused with the Prayer plant, and rightly so; although there is a resemblance in appearance, actions differ, for this species doesn't fold its leaves. Lovely, delicate foliage is multicolored—as beautiful as a peacock's feathers. Great for terrarium growth, if container size is suitable; otherwise, it loves humid air from pebble tray. A very special plant to have in culture to display year round.

Family Tree: Marantaceae (mare-ant-ay'-see-ay) Maranta, or Arrowroot, family; from South America.

Foliage: red stalks, silvery veins, purple undersides; leaves—in tufts—are broad, long, and gently curved to pointed tip; patterned strongly with depth of coloration.

Flower: inconspicuous, seldom in cultivation.

Size: 1'-2' (.30-.60 m).

Location: WINTER—southeastern or southwestern exposure. SUMMER—*Inside:* northeastern or northwestern exposure. *Outside:* northeastern or northwestern exposure; site in shelter to protect foliage.

FALL: move indoors by mid-September; site in eastern or western exposure.

Dormancy: none; a resting period of slower growth during winter months of less intensity, generally October through February; slowly diminish watering; plant will indicate needs as determined by environmental conditions; develop sensitivity to feel of soil moisture level; cease fertilizing.

Water: keep evenly moist but not soggy.

Mist: daily, twice a day when possible, with tepid water.

Humidity: above normal for happiness, 45%-55%.

Air circulation: helpful condition.

Feed: mild liquid manure every 2 weeks.

Soil: 1 part standard potting mix, 1 part peat moss, 1 part perlite.

Temperature: Day—75°-85°F (23°-29°C). Night—60°-70°F (15°-21°C).

Potbound: normal; pot-on when root growth is 50% of pot content.

Mature plants: if plant becomes too tall, cut growing ends; start in rooting media. Remove dried or withered leaves as they appear.

Propagate: by division preferably in very early spring, in shallow pots with soil specified for this genus; or by leaf cuttings, in moist vermiculite.

Insect alert: mealybug, red spider, scale, thrip, aphids.

Notable: good artificial light plant; total of 14-16 hours, combining natural and artificial light; do not allow soil to dry out completely; soil must have porosity, eliminating possibility of soggy conditions; use pebble, water, and tray method to maintain humidity level; sponge foliage at least every three weeks, always use room-temperature water; leaf shiners and/or oils are an *absolute no-no*.

Calathea makoyana,
Peacock Plant

C. bachemiana (bak-em-ee-ay'-nuh) gray green leaves, marked dark green; to 16" (.40 m).

C. concinna (kon-sin'-nuh) dark green leaves, feather design running into deep green, purple underside.

C. illustriss (ill-luss'-triss) shiny olive green leaves, red underneath; to 9" (230 mm).

C. leopardina (lee-oh-par'-din-uh) waxy green with darker green markings; to 12" (.30 m).

C. lietzei (leet'-zee-eye) velvety, light green, purple-red underneath; to 24" (.60 m).

C. picturata (pik-tew-ray'-tuh)
   Variety—Argentea (ar-jen'-tee-uh) dwarf species; silvered leaves, dark green border, maroon underneath.

C. roseo-picta (roh'-zee-oh-pik'-tuh) native to Brazil; dark green, red mid-rib on leaves, edged in red; to 12" (.30 m); good terrarium species.

C. vandenheckei (van-den-hek'-ee-eye) white and dark green foliage; to 30" (.75 m).

C. veitchiana (vite-shee-ay'-nuh) leaves with peacock feather design: brown, chartreuse, green, red; to 4' (1.20 m).

C. zebrina (zeb-rye'-nuh) Zebra plant; native to Brazil; dark green, velvety leaves, chartreuse background; to 3' (.90 m).
   Variety—Binotii (bin-noh'-tee-eye) native to Brazil; larger form; deeper colored foliage; to 3' (.90 m).

CALCEOLARIA MULTIFLORA (kal-see-oh-lay'-ree-uh mult-teh-flor'-uh) Slipperwort, Slipper Flower; nickname: Pocketbook Plant.

At one time a popular rock garden and greenhouse plant, now just as popular for inside culture. This genus is strikingly ornamental in the blooming period March through May. This plant was named from the Latin *calceolus* which means a slipper or little shoe and relates to the strange shape of the flower; multiflora means having many flowers.

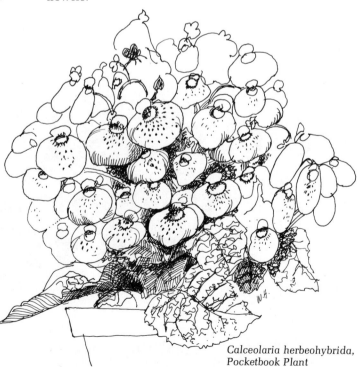

*Calceolaria herbeohybrida,
Pocketbook Plant*

Family Tree: Scrophulariaceae (skrof-u-lare-ee-ay'-see-ay) Snapdragon family; native to Andes mountains of South America, especially Chile and Peru.

Foliage: large, up to 6" (150 mm); soft, pubescent (covered with soft, fine hairs), dark green.

Flower: puffy, pouch-shaped, 2-lipped blossoms up to 2" (50 mm) across; colorful annual interest in yellow, orange, golden brown, and bronze marked with purple or brown spots in a meshlike pattern.

Size: to 2' (.60 m).

Location: WINTER—southeastern exposure.
SUMMER—*Inside*: eastern exposure. *Outside*: northern exposure.
FALL: move indoors by mid-September.

Water: keep soil evenly moist; may have to be watered several times a day in hot conditions; do not allow soil to dry out completely, ever.

Mist: daily, twice daily if possible; do not mist directly on blossoms.

Humidity: above normal, 45%.

Air circulation: helpful condition, but beware of drafts.

Feed: weekly, with mild liquid manure; do not fertilize March through May when plants are blooming.

Soil: standard potting mix.

Temperature: Day—65°-70°F (18°-21°C). Night—50°-55°F (10°-12°C).

Mature plants: better bloom if stems pinched back as they become straggly; pinch off to point where plant retains compact, uniform shape; pinch center out of young shoots for a wide plant.

Propagate: by seed (difficult to germinate in house) in April or August; or by cuttings in spring or late summer in a cool location.

Offspring established: maintain proper culture as for adult plants.

Insect alert: slugs, aphids, red spider mite, and whitefly.

Disease alert: avoid too high temperatures and drying out of plant; gray mould.

Notable: keep on the cooler side of recommended temperatures for best blossoming; flowers spot easily, so do not allow water to drip on blossoms; if set in direct sun, the leaves will wilt or burn. Few people seem to consider it worthwhile to try to carry plants over into another year or blooming season; propagation by cuttings for new plants is much the preferable method.

C. arachnoidea (ar-ack-nay'-dee-uh) meaning appearing to be covered with a spider web; small, pale purple flowers.

C. herbeohybrida (her'-bee-oh-hi-brid-duh) usually yellow or red with spots; bushy, compact; to 24" (.60 m).

C. rugosa (rew-go'-suh) meaning with wrinkled leaves; pink, yellow, and red small flowers; shrubby.

C. multiflora (mult-teh-flor'-uh)
   Variety—Nana: popular dwarf; up to 10" (254 mm).

C. crenatiflora (kren-ay-tif-floh'-ruh) flowers 1" (25 mm); yellow to red to brown with orange or brown spots; blooms April through May.

CALLIANDRA (kal-lee-and'-ruh) Powder Puff.
A most attractive, graceful tub plant with a profusion of lovely, flowering color. Keep this plant warm and be rewarded with a long blooming period.

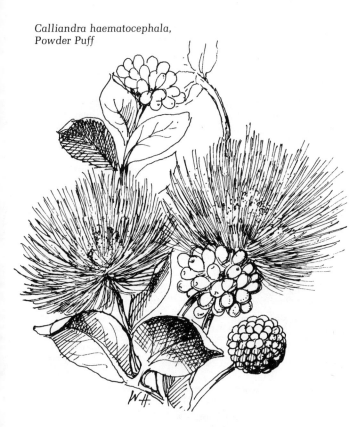

Calliandra haematocephala,
Powder Puff

Family Tree: Leguminosae (leg-goo-min-oh′-say) Pea family; from South America.
Foliage: attractive; many dark green leaflets in compound fernlike arrangement; evergreen; leaflet color, bronzy when new.
Flower: 2″-3″ (50 mm-76 mm) heads formed from a fluff of hundreds of silky, bright red or watermelon pink stamens (male organ, which bears pollen, slender stems with sac), continues for many weeks during winter and spring.
Size: 2′-3′ (.60 m-.90 m).
Location: WINTER—full sun.
SUMMER—*Inside and Outside:* full sun.
FALL: move inside by mid-September.
Dormancy: none, actually; plant will take brief resting period after flowering.
Water: keep soil barely moist.
Mist: daily.
Humidity: above normal, up to 45%.
Air circulation: helpful condition.
Feed: every 2 weeks with mild liquid manure.
Soil: 2 parts standard potting soil, 1 part sand or vermiculite.
Temperature: Day—60°-80°F (15°-26°C). Night—60°-65°F (15°-18°C).
Potbound: repot after flowering; pot-on when rootbound as indicated by plant soil being over 50% root system.
Mature plants: better bloom if stems pinched back as they become straggly; pinch off to point where plant retains compact, uniform shape; pinch center out of young shoots for wide plant. Prune in late spring or early summer, at end of flowering.
Propagate: in spring, from cuttings or newly grown stems; or any time by air layering.
Insect alert: scale.
Notable: as sun exposure changes with the seasons, keep resetting site of plant to capture as much sun as available; do not overwater; must have good soil drainage; use tray, pebble, and water method for good humidity level.

C. Haematocephala (hee-mat-oh-ceph′-uh-luh) previously known as Inga pulcherrima; red powder puff.
C. inequilatera (in-ee-wi-la′-tera) pink powder puff.
C. tweedii (twe′-de-eye) powder puff; Trinidad flame bush; purple flower with 3″ (76 mm) crimson stamens (slender stems with sacs, male organ which bears pollen).

CALLISIA ELEGANS (kal-lees′-ee-uh el′-eh-ganz) Striped Inch Plant.
Striped, green with white foliage ideal for a hanging container, *C. elegans* displays very well in bright light, does not need much space. Hard pruning is essential to keep plant in pleasing visual fullness. It may be listed or referred to by its previous name, Setcreasea striata.
Family Tree: Commelinaceae (kom-el-lye-nay′-see-ay) Spiderwort family; native to Mexico.
Foliage: green and white striped leaves, 1″-1½″ (25-37 mm) long, purple undersides.
Size: up to 3′ (.90 m).
Location: WINTER—southeastern or southwestern exposure.
SUMMER—*Inside:* northeastern or northwestern exposure.
Outside: northeastern or northwestern exposure; protect fragile foliage from potentially damaging elements, preferably by overhang.
FALL: move indoors by mid-September; site in eastern or western exposure.
Dormancy: none, but light resting period October through February; slowly diminish watering, keeping soil barely moist; cut fertilizing program in half.
Water: keep moderately and evenly moist.
Mist: daily, twice a day when possible.
Humidity: above normal for happiness, 40%-45%.
Air circulation: helpful condition.
Feed: mild liquid manure every 2 weeks.
Soil: 2 parts standard potting soil, 1 part peat moss, 1 part perlite.
Temperature: Day—68°-80°F (20°-26°C). Night—55°-68°F (12°-20°C).

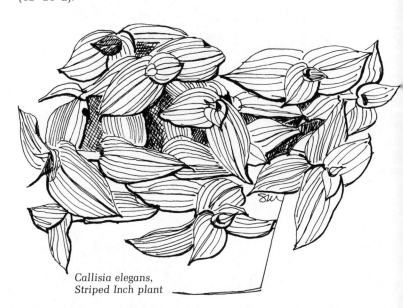

Callisia elegans,
Striped Inch plant

Potbound: repot; or pot-on as needed and indicated by root growth being at least 50% of pot content.

Mature plants: hard pruning to reestablish plant should be done in early spring prior to evidence of new growth. Take cuttings, easily rooted, for fresh replacement.

Propagate: by division or stem cuttings, root latter in water or moist vermiculite.

Insect alert: mealybug, whitefly, mites, scale, slugs.

Notable: good artificial light specimen—a total of 14 hours combined with natural; prune plant often to prevent legginess; do not overwater as plant will rot easily; must have good soil porosity; never allow soil to dry out completely; rinse foliage frequently in room-temperature or tepid water to prevent dust-clogged pores; overfeeding will cause pale leaf color.

CAMELLIA JAPONICA (kam-mell′-ee-uh jap-pon′-ik-uh). In a cool environment and with proper cultural procedure, a handsome year-round genus. It is the official flower of Alabama, a wise choice with its lush evergreen foliage and large, fragrant, perfectly formed blooms.

Family Tree: Theaceae (thee-ay′-see-ay) Tea family; from eastern Asia's mountain forests.

Foliage: oval, dark green, shiny leaves to 4″ (100 mm) long.

Flower: large, waxy double and/or single blooms, very fragrant; color combinations are white to pink to dark red; profuse blooms in winter months.

Size: a mid-size shrub usually pruned to 2½′-3′ (.75-.90 m).

Location: WINTER—eastern exposure.

SUMMER—*Inside:* partial shade; set in eastern to southern exposure for direct rays of morning sun. *Outside:* partial shade; set in eastern exposure or under a protective structure where plant receives strong light but no direct rays. FALL: move indoors by mid-September.

Dormancy: only a slight slowing in early fall; slowly diminish watering to approximately 1/3 less; allow plant to indicate needs; continue fertilizing, same quantity but only monthly.

Water: keep soil constantly moist.

Mist: daily, twice a day if possible; with tepid water.

Humidity: high for happiness, 60%-65%.

Air circulation: helpful condition.

Feed: mild liquid fertilizer every 2 weeks January through July; use fertilizer with acid, 21-7-7 balance.

Soil: 1 part standard potting mix, 1 part humus, 1 part peat moss.

Temperature: Day—64°-68°F (17°-20°C). Night—40°-45°F (4°-7°C).

Potbound: repot only when root growth overbalances (75% to 25%) soil content.

Mature plants: flower buds are set in summer while plant is outdoors; flower size is increased by eliminating all but one bud per cluster. When pruning for bushy plant, do so only after flowering and before new leaf growth. Too tall a plant for standing upright, stake and tie main trunk (leave small amount of slack in ties to eliminate potential of injury by tie cutting into fleshy stem). May be trained into standard form (tree form) or espaliered plant by proper pruning or pinching.

Propagate: by cuttings from half-ripe wood set in damp vermiculite.

Insect alert: scale, mealybug, aphids, mite.

Disease alert: buds drop from incorrect temperature or soil moisture level; or from change in location.

Notable: best culture is to site outside for summer months; soil must have good drainage; do not allow soggy soil conditions; avoid drafts; when repotting or potting-on, firm soil well but do not compact it.

C. reticulata (ret-ik-yew-lay′-tuh) meaning netted, usually the leaf veining; dull green, elliptic leaves on open-

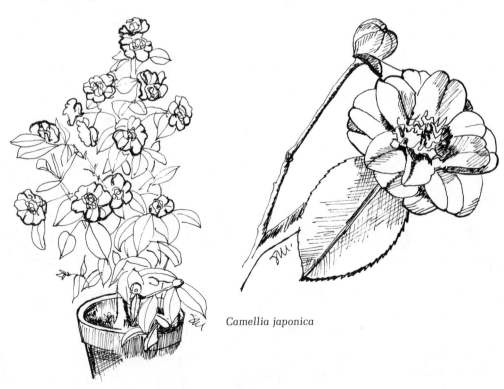

Camellia japonica

branched shrub, to 15′ (3.50 m) high; huge flowers in single and double forms, bloom mid-September until mid-April.

C. sasanqua (sas-an′-kwah) heavy profusion of small flowers, more delicate than Camellia japonica; single, fragrant white, pink, or cherry red blossoms.

C. salvensis (sal-ven′-siss) compact, glossy foliage is darker above than beneath; semisingle flowers, white through pink, rose, and crimson.

CAMPANULA ISOPHYLLA (kam-pan′-yew-luh eye-soff′-ill-uh) Italian Bellflower; nickname: Falling Stars, Star of Bethlehem.

The isophylla member is a natural for hanging in pot or basket. It adds a special charm to any interior with the tidy, graceful and colorful cool blue flowering. Depending on how the culture is timed, its flowering cycle can be had any time of the year for 3-4 months.

Family Tree: Campanulaceae (kam-pan-yew-lace′-see-ay) Bellflower family; from the type of genus, campanula, bellflowers (little bell); native of Europe and Asia.

Foliage: 1″ (25 mm) long gray green, broadly oval leaves borne on fragile, trailing stems.

Flower: short stemmed, shaped like an open cup or star; 1″-1½″ (25 mm-37 mm) violet blue or white blossoms.

Size: to 20″ (.55 m).

Location: WINTER—full sun; set in southern exposure.

SUMMER—*Inside:* partial shade; set in eastern to southern exposure for direct rays of morning sun. *Outside:* partial shade; set in eastern exposure or under a protective structure where plant receives strong light but no direct rays.

FALL: move indoors by mid-September.

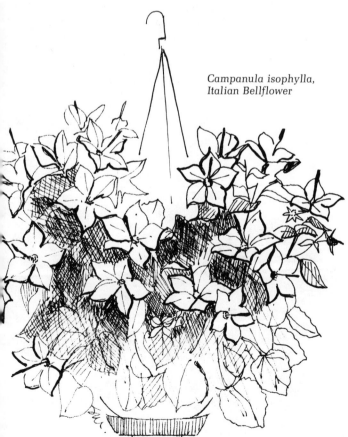

Campanula isophylla, Italian Bellflower

Dormancy: period starts after flowering period (usually November-December); cut stems back to top of pot; site in very cool area; keep barely moist; cease fertilizing.

Water: keep evenly moist March through November.

Mist: daily, lightly.

Humidity: 30%-40%.

Air circulation: helpful condition.

Feed: weekly; mild liquid manure.

Soil: 1 part standard potting soil, 2 parts peat moss, 1 part sand or perlite.

Temperature: Day—68°-72°F (20°-22°C). Night—50°-55°F (10°-12°C).

Potbound: very unhappy; repot each year after flowering.

Mature plants: want wide plant, pinch center out of young shoots; pinch until June if flowering is desired August through November. Remove flowers as they fade. Root prune at time of repotting to keep soil ball within the bounds needed for good handling as a hanging flora.

Propagate: by seed or cuttings, latter in water in spring or August.

Offspring established: pinch out growing tips for bushier plant.

Insect alert: slugs, whitefly, scale, mealybugs.

Notable: soil must be light for good drainage, if soil is allowed to dry out completely this genus will quickly shed all its leaves; must have cool surroundings to be a growing success in interior habitat.

C. elatines (el-at-tye′-neez) 1½″ (37 mm) pale lavender blue to purplish star-shaped flowers with white eyes; trailing stems.

C. fragilis (fraj′-i-lis) flower is purplish blue with white center.

C. poscharskyana (posh-arsk-ee-ay′-nah) Serbian bellflower; deeply cut lilac blue flowers on arching, 12″-18″ (.30 m-.45 m) stems; suitable for window boxes and hanging baskets.

C. alba (al′-bah) the general public's most popular selection; single, snow-white flower.

C. mayii (may′-yee-eye) single, large, intensely blue flowers.

CAPSICUM ANNUUM (kap′-sik-um an-yew-um) Christmas Pepper, Bird Pepper, Chili Pepper.

Annuum, meaning annual, refers to the fact that after dropping fruit it will never reproduce again indoors. A showy plant . . . fun to grow. Fruit is a very hot, edible form of chili. Additional names are Ornamental Pepper and C. frutescens.

Family Tree: Solanaceae (sohl-lan-nay′-see-ay) Nightshade family; from tropical America.

Foliage: oval, rich green, 2″ (50 mm) long.

Flower: tiny white blooms, nondescript in detail yet charming in delicate pureness of color.

Fruit: masses of colorful, pungent 2″-3″ (50 mm-76 mm) long peppers in summer and fall; during ripening many colors, green, white, yellow, red, purple, sometimes appear simultaneously; fruiting begins when plant is 6-8 months old; shapes can be pointed, round, wrinkled, or with basal depressions.

Size: varies with species, 1′-8′ (.30 m-2.45 m) tall.

Location: WINTER—southern exposure for full sun.

Capsicum annuum,
Christmas Pepper

SUMMER—*Inside:* southern exposure for full sun. *Outside:* full sun.

FALL: move indoors mid-September.

Water: keep evenly moist.

Mist: daily.

Humidity: around 35%-40%.

Air circulation: helpful condition.

Feed: do not fertilize.

Soil: standard potting soil.

Temperature: Day—69°-72°F (20.50°-22°C). Night—60°-65°F (15°-18°C).

Mature plants: pruning not necessary.

Propagate: from seed in early spring.

Insect alert: whitefly.

Notable: bathe to keep leaves clean and shiny, discouraging pests; too hot a room will make fruit drop.

> Variety—Acuminatum (uh-cue-min-ay′-tum) meaning long points; 3 flower petals 3″ (76 mm) long; cayenne peppers; plant 2′ (.60 m) tall.
> Variety—Abbreviatum (ub-bree-vee-ay′-tum) a small ornamental.
> Variety—Cerasiforme (see-ras′-if-form) cherry peppers; small, yellow round fruit turns purple red.

CARISSA (kar-riss′-uh) Natal Plum.
A good plant to train as bonsai if Minima variety is used, or as larger, rampant pot or tub plant if Fancy variety is used; handles very well for topiary or espalier; a bonus: the fruit of the hybrid, macrocárpa, cooks down into a super jelly.

Family Tree: Apocynaceae (a-poh-sin-ay′-see-ay) Dogbane family; from Asia and south Africa.

Foliage: 1″-3″ (25-76 mm) long, heart shaped, glossy evergreen leaves; closely set vining and spiny; a heady fragrance.

Flower: fragrant, white 1½″-2″ (37-50 mm) across; star shaped; flowering occurs on and off all year, even during fruiting.

Fruit: 1½″-2″ (37-50 mm), scarlet; looks like plum, tastes like cranberry.

Size: to 7′ (2 m) except for 18″-24″ (.45-.60 m) dwarf varieties.

Location: WINTER—full sun; set in southern exposure.

SUMMER—*Inside:* partial shade; set in eastern to southern exposure for direct rays of morning sun. *Outside:* partial shade; set in eastern exposure or under a protective structure where plant receives strong light but no direct rays.

FALL: move indoors by mid-September.

Water: keep evenly moist.

Mist: daily, twice daily if possible.

Humidity: moist, at least 50%-55%.

Air circulation: helpful condition.

Feed: mild liquid manure monthly.

Soil: standard potting mix.

Temperature: Day—68°-72°F (20°-22°C). Night—50°-65°F (10°-18°C).

Potbound: pot-on when needed; plant indicates need by root system overpowering soil with more than 50% root coverage in soil.

Mature plants: may be trained into bonsai or espaliered plant by proper pruning or pinching; prune at time of minimum flowering.

Propagate: from stem cuttings; also, layering or budding.

Insect alert: aphids, mealybugs, whitefly, scale.

Notable: to maintain handsome plant, keep leaves washed weekly; when plant is trained as bonsai, never allow soil to dry out completely.

C. grandiflora (gran-di-floh′-ruh) has larger flowers than other species.

Carissa grandiflora,
Natal Plum

Caryota mitis,
Tufted Fishtail Palm

CARYOTA MITIS (kar-ee-oh'-tuh mit-tis) Fishtail Palm.
A sturdy addition to a flora collection if a bright sunless
site needs occupying. The Fishtail palm is rather unique
visually, therefore most conversational. Cultural success is
a snap if sited properly and watering, humidity, and temperature aspects are attended to with accuracy.
Family Tree: Palmae (pal-may') Palm family; native to
Asia, Malaysia, and Australia.
Foliage: a number of stems from a central trunk; leathery
wedge-shaped fronds, each resembling a fish tail; deep,
rich green.
Size: to 9' (2.70 m).
Location: WINTER—eastern or western exposure.
SUMMER—*Inside:* eastern or western exposure. *Outside:* east-
ern or western exposure, sheltered to protect fragile foliage
from potentially damaging winds and heavy rains.
FALL: move indoors by mid-September; site in eastern or
western exposure.
Dormancy: none, although light resting period in winter
months; slowly diminish watering, keeping soil barely
moist; cease fertilizing.
Water: thoroughly and evenly, allowing soil to dry be-
tween waterings.
Mist: daily, two or more times in warm weather.
Humidity: above normal, 45%-60%.
Air circulation: essential to have good moderate move-
ment for top plant performance.
Feed: very, very mild liquid manure, 1/4 strength of pack-
age or manufacturer's recommendations, March through
October.
Soil: 2 parts standard potting mix, 1 part peat moss, 1 part
vermiculite.
Temperature: Day—68°-75°F (20°-23°C). Night—58°-65°F
(14°-18°C).
Potbound: pot-on young plants each year to pot 2" (50
mm) larger; older plants happy when somewhat potbound;

side-dress each year, pot-on every 2 or 3 years, when indicated by plant's root growth being 80% to 20% soil in pot;
implement this cultural attention late winter or early
spring, February or March; deep pots are best shape for
submerged aerial roots.
Mature plants: in repotting or potting-on, firm soil well
but do not compact it. Trim browned tips of fronds
(leaves).
Propagate: by seed, suckers, or division.
Insect alert: mealybug, red spider mite, scale, thrips.
Notable: absolutely no drafts; do not allow soil to dry out
completely, but *no soggy soil*; soil must be porous, for
good drainage is essential to successful culture; use pebble, water, and tray method to maintain high humidity;
good in artificial light, needing a total of 16 light-hours,
combining natural and artificial; leaves should be washed
or wiped with moist cloth at least once a month to keep
pores unclogged; no direct sun, or foliage will burn; remember that most palms are of slow growing habit.

CEROPEGIA WOODII (ser-oh-peej'-ee-uh wood'-ee-eye)
    Rosary Vine, Chinese Lantern Plant, String of Hearts;
    nickname: Hearts Entangled.
An unusually charming plant, quite effective trailing
down from a high shelf or stand. Small tubers grow along
the roots and on threadlike stems. Altogether, this species
has a delicate appearance.
Family Tree: Asclepiadaceae (as-klep-ee-uh-day'-see-ay)
Milkweed family; native to Africa and Asia.
Foliage: ¼" (6.30 mm) heart shaped, succulent leaves, silvery mottled green, purplish undersides.

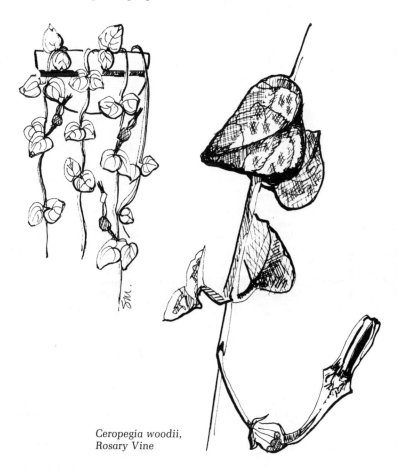

Ceropegia woodii,
Rosary Vine

Flower: slender waxy blossoms about ½" (12.70 mm) long; light purple or pink.

Size: trailing stems to 3' (.90 m) long.

Location: WINTER—full sun; set in southern exposure.

SUMMER—*Inside:* partial shade; set in eastern to southern exposure for direct rays of morning sun. *Outside:* partial shade; set in eastern exposure or under a protective structure where plant receives strong light but no direct rays.

FALL: move indoors by mid-September.

Dormancy: period starts in winter, a rest period; slowly diminish watering, keeping soil barely moist; foliage should not get shriveled appearance; cease fertilizing.

Water: thoroughly and evenly, allowing soil to dry moderately between waterings.

Mist: daily, lightly.

Humidity: normal, around 30%.

Air circulation: helpful condition.

Feed: twice a month with mild liquid manure.

Soil: 1 part standard potting mix, 2 parts sand.

Temperature: Day—68°-72°F (20°-22°C). Night—50°-55°F (10°-12°C).

Potbound: repot in February, keeping in small pots.

Mature plants: pinch stems periodically, near soil line, to encourage new growth.

Propagate: by stem cuttings or tiny tubers from roots or stems, any time; root in moist sand or vermiculite.

Insect alert: mites.

Notable: to avoid a stringy appearance, cut back occasionally; soil must be porous to provide good drainage; this genus benefits from plenty of light.

C. barkleyi (bar'-klee-eye) green leaves with silver markings; to 18" (.45 m) long.

C. caffrorum (caff-roh'-rum) arrowhead-shaped leaves, green veined with red; green and purplish pink flowers; to 20" (.55 m).

C. debilis (dee'-bil-iss) meaning weak, frail; narrow green leaves and red flowers.

C. fusca (fuss'-kuh) meaning grayish brown; brown and yellow blooms.

C. haygarthii (hay-gar'-thee-eye) maroon and cream flowers.

C. radicans (rad'-ee-canz) meaning rooting, especially along stem; green, purple, and white blossoms.

C. sandersonii (san-der-soh'-nee-eye) meaning after proper name; Parachute Plant, to 20" (.55 m); small green leaves and flowers.

C. stapeliaeformis (stap-eel-ee-ay'-for-miss) dark green foliage; white flowers with purple markings; to 26" (.70 m).

CHAMAEDOREA ELEGANS (kam-ee-doh'-ree-uh ell'-eg-anz) Parlor or Neanthe Palm.

This species, at times listed in catalogs as *Collinia elegans,* is a terrarium specimen when young. A variety of *C. elegans,* Bella, at times called Neanthe bella, is an excellent dwarf plant, up to 4' (1.22 m). In natural habitat, there are obvious fruit and flowers, but cultivated plants usually do not produce either; a very slow growing species. It is native to the Yucatan.

Family Tree: Palmae (pal-may') Palm family; from Mexico, Central and South America.

Foliage: up to 3' (.90 m) long, arching, feathery fronds (leaves), on reedlike stems form dense foliage; narrow, deep green leaflets.

Size: up to 8' (2.45 m).

Location: WINTER—eastern or western exposure.

SUMMER—*Inside:* eastern or western exposure. *Outside:* eastern or western exposure, sheltered to protect fragile foliage from potentially damaging winds and heavy rains.

FALL: move indoors by mid-September; site in eastern or western exposure.

Dormancy: none, although light resting period in winter months; slowly diminish watering, keeping soil barely moist; cease fertilizing.

Water: thoroughly and evenly, allowing soil to dry between waterings.

Mist: daily, two or more times in warm weather.

Humidity: above normal, 45%-60%.

Air circulation: essential to have good moderate movement for top plant performance.

Feed: very, very mild liquid manure, ¼ strength of package or manufacturer's recommendations, March through October.

Soil: 2 parts standard potting mix, 1 part peat moss, 1 part vermiculite.

Temperature: Day—68°-75°F (20°-23°C). Night—58°-65°F (14°-18°C).

Potbound: pot-on young plants each year to pot 2" (50 mm) larger; older plants happy when somewhat potbound; top-dress each year, bypassing need for potting-on; with this cultural treatment, plant will be healthy and happy for 10-15 years.

Mature plants: in repotting or potting-on, firm soil well but do not compact it. Trim browned tips of fronds (leaves).

Propagate: by seed or division.

Insect alert: mealybug, red spider mite, scale, thrips.

Notable: absolutely no drafts; do not allow soil to dry out completely, but *no soggy soil;* soil must be porous, for good drainage is essential to successful culture; use peb-

Chamaedorea elegans,
Parlor Palm

ble, water, and tray method to maintain high humidity; good in artificial light, needing a total of 16 light hours, combining natural and artificial; leaves should be washed or wiped with moist cloth at least once a month to keep pores unclogged; no direct sun, or foliage will burn; remember that most palms are of slow growing habit; *C. elegans* adjusts readily to indoor environment, particularly air conditioning and dim corners.

C. erumpens (ehr-um'-penz) known as Bamboo palm; native to Honduras; 20"-30" (.55-.75 m) rosettes of arching, graceful, fanlike fronds; to 8' (2.45 m); on upright stalks of bamboolike stems; older plants have suckers that grow upright from base and conceal the main stem.

C. graminifolia (gram-i-ni-foh'-lee-uh) meaning with foliagelike grass; light green, slender leaflets on delicate, graceful fronds that spread horizontally; to 5' (1.50 m) high.

C. tenella (tee'-nel-luh) meaning delicate, light, or soft; a dwarf, erect plant to 30" (.75 m); with broad fronds.

CHAMAEROPS HUMILIS (kam-ee'-rops hew'-mil-iss) European Fan Palm.

Greek *chamaerops* is for dwarf, *humilis* means of humble growth. Generally, a plant of low spreading habit, multi-trunked from the base of plant, which gives a bushy appearance. Yet, the same species may develop to a taller, more erect plant with less density of foliage. Even leaf color is undependable in this palm.

Family Tree: Palmae (pal-may') Palm family; native to the Mediterranean area.

Foliage: stiff, fan shaped, deeply cut fronds (leaves) up to 2" (50 mm) long and wide; pale gray when young, becoming gray green to blue green with age; leaf stalks rise from rough trunks of black hairlike coverage; plant matures to a bushy clump of several stems, with foliage appearing at different levels.

Size: to 6' (1.83 m).

Location: WINTER—eastern or western exposure.

SUMMER—*Inside:* eastern or western exposure. *Outside:* eastern or western exposure, sheltered to protect fragile foliage from potentially damaging winds and heavy rains.

FALL: move indoors by mid-September; site in eastern or western exposure.

Dormancy: none, although light resting period in winter months. Slowly diminish watering, keeping soil barely moist; cease fertilizing.

Water: thoroughly and evenly, allowing soil to dry between waterings.

Mist: daily, two or more times in warm weather.

Humidity: above normal, 45%-60%.

Air circulation: essential to have good moderate movement for top plant performance.

Feed: very, very mild liquid manure, ¼ strength of package recommendations, March through October.

Soil: 2 parts standard potting mix, 1 part peat moss, 1 part vermiculite.

Temperature: Day—68°-75°F (20°-23°C). Night—58°-65°F (14°-18°C).

Potbound: pot-on young plants each year to 2" (50 mm) larger pot; older plants happy when somewhat potbound; side-dress each year, pot-on every 2 or 3 years, when indi-

*Chamaerops humilis,
European Fan Palm*

cated by plant's root growth being 80% to 20% soil in pot; implement this cultural attention late winter or early spring, February or March; deep pots are best shape for submerged aerial roots.

Mature plants: in repotting or potting-on, firm soil well but do not compact it. Sucker growth of bamboolike shoots develops from base of plant, growing erectly; growth conceals parts of trunk with increasing height and span.

Propagate: by seed or by suckers.

Insect alert: mealybug, red spider mite, scale, thrips.

Notable: absolutely no drafts; do not allow soil to dry out completely, but *no soggy soil*; soil must be porous, for good drainage is essential to successful culture; use pebble, water, and tray method to maintain high humidity; good in artificial light, needing a total of 16 light hours, combining natural and artificial; leaves should be washed or wiped with moist cloth at least once a month to keep pores unclogged; no direct sun, or foliage will burn; remember that most palms are slow growing.

CHIRITA LAVANDULACEA (cheer-ee'-tuh lav-an-dew-lay'-see-uh).

A plant that will flower charmingly for the better part of a year. All species have a lavender shade of blossom. One species grows but 6" (150 mm) tall. A thoughtful hostess gift.

Family Tree: Gesneriaceae (jes-near-ee-ay'-see-ay) Gesneriad family; native to India, China, Java.

Foliage: 8" (203 mm) long, soft, hairy, succulent ovals of bright green; some species have leaves touched with silver.

Flower: 1¼" (32 mm) wide with flaring lobes; reminiscent of gloxinia; throats are white, petals pale blue to lavender; some species have three such flowers in a cluster.

Chirita lavandulacea

Size: 6"-24" (.15 -.60 m) average, some species up to 3' (.90 m).

Location: WINTER—full sun; set in southern exposure.

SUMMER—*Inside:* partial shade; set in eastern to southern exposure for direct rays of morning sun. *Outside:* partial shade; set in eastern exposure or under a protective structure where plant receives strong light but no direct rays.

FALL: move indoors by mid-September.

Water: keep evenly moist.

Mist: daily, twice daily if possible.

Humidity: very high, 60%-70%.

Air circulation: helpful condition.

Feed: mild liquid manure every 2 weeks.

Soil: 2 parts standard potting mix, 1 part peat moss.

Temperature: Day—75°F (23°C) or higher. Night—65°-70°F (18°-21°C).

Mature plants: better bloom if stems pinched back as they become straggly; pinch off to point where plant retains compact, uniform shape; pinch center out of young shoots for a wide plant.

Propagate: in late winter or spring by stem cutting or seed in moist vermiculite.

Offspring established: new seedlings grow to full size in 10 months.

Insect alert: mealybug, whitefly.

Notable: leaf tips will brown if too little humidity—use pebble, water, and tray method to maintain good humidity level; does well under artificial light, therefore can handle 14-16 light hours per day; best to discard plant when flowering cycle is completed. Take stem cuttings to start your new plant.

C. sinensis (sin-nen'-siss) Chinese chirita; tuberous-rooted, summer flowering, with clusters of tiny, lavender blooms; elliptical leaves arranged in rosette, dark green, hairy, blotched with silver; 6" (150 mm) tall.

C. anachoretica (an-nak-or-reh'-tik-kuh) to 2' (.60 m) tall; yellow flowers with white calyx (bractlike growths which protect the bud before it opens).

C. asperifolia (ass-per-if-foh'-lee-uh) 12"-18" (.30-45 m) tall; tubular white and purple flowers.

CHLOROPHYTUM COMOSUM (kloh-roff'-it-um kom-moh'-sum) Spider Plant, Airplane Plant.

Possibly still referred to or listed by its previous names, Anthericum comosum or A. sternbergianum, this is a most effective hanging plant. Its leaves arch and cascade gracefully. Aerial plantlets hang decoratively on long slender stems in profusion if sited in a strong bright area.

Family Tree: Liliaceae (lil-ee-ay'-see-ay) Lily family; from South Africa.

Foliage: long and narrow, grasslike leaves, striped yellow or white; plant sends out long stems with rosettes or plantlets that will root merely by lying on soil.

Flower: very petite, white, clustered in the centers of the rosettes.

Size: up to 36" (.90 m) in length.

Location: WINTER—southeastern exposure.

SUMMER—*Inside:* southeastern exposure. *Outside:* eastern exposure.

FALL: move indoors by mid-September, siting in southeastern exposure.

Dormancy: none, really; a resting period in late fall and winter; slowly diminish watering; cease fertilizing, from November through February.

Water: thoroughly and evenly, allowing soil to dry between waterings.

Mist: daily, twice if possible.

Humidity: normal, 30%-35%.

Air circulation: helpful condition.

Chlorophytum comosum,
Spider Plant

Feed: weekly, with mild liquid manure.

Soil: standard potting mix.

Temperature: Day—68°-75°F (20°-23°C). Night—60°-68°F (15°-20°C).

Potbound: normal; pot-on when root growth is 50% of pot content.

Mature plants: remove yellowed foliage by cutting with sharp scissors close to base. Brown tips always occur unless plant has absolutely perfect cultural conditions; nip periodically to maintain good visual appearance. The most graceful and handsome effect is obtained from a single plant per pot; if multiples develop, separate and pot-up singly.

Propagate: any time, by division of the fleshy roots; by water culture; or by loosely planting the plantlets, still attached to stems, in standard mix.

Offspring established: when plantlets are rooted, sever the stem close to the base of plant; pot-up in 4″ (100 mm) container.

Insect alert: scale.

Notable: good species for artificial light, a total 12-14 hours, combining natural and artificial light; do not allow soil to dry out completely; best in a permanent location where leaves and plantlets are not touched; occasional turning will produce a more symmetrical plant.

C. bichetii (bih-kett′-ee-eye) St. Bernard's lily; grassy green leaves striped with yellowish white form a small tuft; great for bonsai pot.

C. comosum (ko-mus′-um)

> Variety—Mandaianum (man-di-ay′-num) 4″-6″ (100-150 mm), dark leaves with yellowish white center stripe.
>
> Variety—Picturatum (pik-tu-ra′-tum) ribbony leaves striped with yellow.
>
> Variety—Variegatum (vay-ree-eg-gay′-tum) large plant; pale green, white-edged leaves, 10″-16″ (.27-.40 m) long, to 1″ (25 mm) wide.
>
> Variety—Vittatum (vit-tay′-tum) low rosettes, 4″-8″ (100-200 mm). Narrow leaves, pale green with white central stripes.

C. elatum (ee-lay′-tum) dark green leaves, cream striped; small white flowers in airy clusters; 2″-3″ (50-76 mm) high.

CHRYSALIDOCARPUS LUTESCENS (kriss-al-id-oh-karp′-us lew-tess′-enz) Butterfly, Golden Butterfly, Golden Feather, Cane, Areca, Madagascar Palm.

A small, extremely graceful palm with plume-shaped fronds (leaves). This species is an excellent tub plant for bright light and normal house temperature. One may hear it referred to or find it listed as *Areca lutescens, hyophorbe commersoniana*, or *H. indica*.

Family Tree: Palmae (pal-may′) Palm family; from Madagascar.

Foliage: clumps of leatherlike arching fronds, slender leaflets on slender yellow stems; fronds to 3′ (.90 m) or more.

Flower: not very noticeable, but short clusters of flowers do appear near tips of fronds.

Size: up to 5′ (1.50 m).

Location: WINTER—eastern or western exposure.

SUMMER—*Inside:* eastern or western exposure. *Outside:* east-

Chrysalidocarpus lutescens,
Butterfly Palm

ern or western exposure, sheltered to protect fragile foliage from potentially damaging winds and heavy rains.

FALL: move indoors by mid-September; site in eastern or western exposure.

Dormancy: none, although light resting period in winter months; slowly diminish watering, keeping soil barely moist; cease fertilizing.

Water: thoroughly and evenly, allowing soil to dry between waterings.

Mist: daily, two or more times in warm weather.

Humidity: above normal, 45%-60%.

Air circulation: essential to have good moderate movement for top plant performance.

Feed: very, very mild liquid manure, ¼ strength of package or manufacturer's recommendations, March through October.

Soil: 2 parts standard potting mix, 1 part peat moss, 1 part vermiculite.

Temperature: Day—68°-75°F (20°-23°C). Night—58°-65°F (14°-18°C).

Potbound: pot-on young plants each year to pot 2″ (50 mm) larger; older plants happy when somewhat potbound; side-dress each year, pot-on every 2 or 3 years, when indicated by plant's root growth being 80% to 20% soil in pot; this cultural attention to be implemented late winter or early spring, February or March; deep pots are best shape for submerged aerial roots.

Mature plants: in repotting or potting-on, firm soil well but do not compact it.

Propagate: by seed.

Insect alert: mealybug, red spider mite, scale, thrips.

Notable: absolutely no drafts; do not allow soil to dry out completely, but *no soggy soil*; soil must be porous, for good drainage is essential to successful culture; use pebble, water, and tray method to maintain high humidity;

good in artificial light, combine natural and artificial for a total of 16 light hours; leaves should be washed or wiped with moist cloth at least once a month to keep pores unclogged; no direct sun, or foliage will burn; remember that most palms are of slow-growing habit.

CHRYSANTHEMUM FRUTESCENS (kriss-anth'-em-um fru-tes'-enz); nickname: Mum.

The national flower of Japan, where petals are used in salads! Grown in the Eastern countries before the Christian era. There are 60 species, thousands of varieties. You know the chrysanthemums; enjoy the challenge of training one into a standard or cascading plant.

Family Tree: Compositae (kom-poz'-i-tee) Composite family; native to China, Asia, and Europe.

Foliage: dark green tops, grayish undersides, indented or lacy; 3"-6" (76-150 mm) long; growth is vigorous, many stemmed, from a woody base.

Flower: colors range through whole spectrum, depending upon species, excluding blue and violet; shape is daisylike; size 2"-3" (50-76 mm).

Size: 8" (.25 m) to 4' (1.22 m).

Location: WINTER—full sun; set in southern exposure.
SUMMER—*Inside:* partial shade; set in eastern to southern exposure for direct rays of morning sun. *Outside:* partial shade; set in eastern exposure or under a protective structure where plant receives strong light but no direct rays.
FALL: move indoors by mid-September.

Dormancy: period starts after blooming; cut stems back to 3" (76 mm); reduce water to keep soil barely moist; maintain normal temperature so new growth develops quickly to provide stem cuttings for propagation.

Water: keep thoroughly moist.

Mist: daily, twice a day when possible.

Humidity: normal, 35%-40%.

Air circulation: helpful condition.

Feed: do not feed mature plants.

Soil: standard potting mix.

Temperature: Day—68°F (20°C) maximum, 60°F (15°C) ideal. Night—40°-50°F (4.4°-10°C).

Potbound: repot each spring; if not dividing plant, pot-on each spring.

Mature plants: better bloom if stems pinched back as they become straggly; pinch off to point where plant retains compact, uniform shape; pinch center out of young shoots for a wide plant. Too tall a plant to stand upright alone, stake and tie main trunk (leave small amount of slack in ties to eliminate potential of injury by tie cutting into fleshy stem). Pinch for better branching through mid-July. Keep florist's chrysanthemums out of direct sun when flowering.

Propagate: any time by green stem cuttings, or in early spring by division; make 4" (100 mm) cuttings (tips root best), dip ends in hormone powder, and insert in a pan of moist sand, vermiculite, or shredded sphagnum moss; do not allow rooting medium to dry out; no direct sun until roots begin to form (7-10 days).

Offspring established: transplant each seedling into 2"-3" (50-76 mm) pots; standard potting mix; feed every 2 weeks; keep humidity level up (use pebble tray method); quarter-turn pots each watering so plants grow evenly without leaning to light; keep pinching out tips for better

Chrysanthemum frutescens, Mum

branching and bushier plants until mid-July; large varieties however (pompoms) are grown to single stems until proper bud is formed, and then kept disbudded to produce one large flower.

Insect alert: aphids, thrips, whitefly.

Disease alert: yellow leaves caused by soil too cold and/or too wet, or water used too cold.

Notable: do not allow soil to dry out completely; good soil drainage essential; when plant is in flower, keep on cooler side of recommended temperatures; flower buds begin to develop when days are shorter (10-12 daylight hours). To shorten time to flowering, cover the plant gently with black plastic after 10 hours of daylight; remove plastic next morning; do so for about 8-10 weeks; when buds start showing color, stop placing plastic over plant.

C. frutescens (fru-tes'-enz) as above, means "shrubby."
C. parthenium (par-theen'-ee-um) small white double blossoms ¾" (19 mm) across, in thick clusters; native to Europe; grow from seeds, or cuttings of good varieties.
C. maximum (maks'-i-mum) meaning the greatest or largest; Shasta daisy.
C. segetum (sej'-et-um) meaning cornfields; Corn marigold.
C. morifolium (moh-rif-foh'-lee-um) florist's Chrysanthemum: reds, pinks, lavenders, yellows; 2'-5' (.60-1.50 m) tall; blooms for only 2-3 weeks.

CIBOTIUM (sib-oh'-tee-um) Tree Fern.

A slow-growing genus, Cibotium is more coarse than other genera but an interesting contrast in ferns. As with most plants of this family, it is easy to maintain with attention to basic cultural procedures. The softening effect created in a room by the fern genera cannot be duplicated by any other design media.

Cibotium,
Tree Fern

Family Tree: Dicksoniaceae (dik-soh-nee-ay′-see-ay) Dicksonia family; native to the tropics.
Foliage: generally pale green, mainly serrated leaflets or arched, delicate, sometimes almost lacy fronds.
Size: 20″ (.55 m) to 3′ (.90 m) height and spread, depending on species.
Location: WINTER—eastern exposure.
SUMMER—*Inside:* eastern exposure. *Outside:* northern exposure.
FALL: move indoors by mid-September; site in eastern exposure.
Dormancy: none really but rests lightly through fall and winter.
Water: an extremely important part of the culture of these plants; be guided by the following: ordinarily, water thoroughly, allowing moderate drying between waterings; never allow to dry out completely. Be aware of cool weather, when slower evaporation should mean less frequent watering. Use room-temperature water only.
Mist: daily, twice a day if possible; use room-temperature water.
Humidity: very high, 60%-70%, especially March through September.
Air circulation: essential for super success but avoid drafts.
Feed: very, very weak solution of mild liquid manure (cut recommendation of manufacturer to 2/3), every 3 weeks.
Soil: 2 parts standard potting mix, 1 part vermiculite, 2 parts peat moss.
Temperature: Day—68°-75°F (20°-23°C). Night—50°-60°F (10°-15°C).
Potbound: very happy; do not pot-on until root system is 80% of pot content; best done in February or March. Roots adhere to interior pot walls, therefore, to avoid excessive injury, work gently when easing them loose. Rapping pot against end of a table is an aid, as well as running a spatula around inside of pot, pressing against pot wall with tool to avoid slipping into root ball. Wrap fronds of a large fern in newspaper for protection while handling. Set plant on 1½″ (37 mm) layer of gravel, then add soil.
Mature plants: if fern looks sad, cut back to 2″ (50 mm)

above soil line; repot and proceed in proper culture. If aerial roots develop, cut them off. Wash foliage at least every 3 weeks. Remove yellowed or withered fronds as they appear.
Propagate: by division of mature plant, best done around March; or by spores (resemble little brown dots) attached to underside of leaflets.
Insect alert: mealybugs, aphids, thrips, red spider; control with soap and water remedy, repeat every 3 days until eradicated.
Notable: ferns need coolness at their roots, so use pebble and water in tray method for cooler temperature and high humidity; best to grow in clay pots—the porosity allows evaporation and aids in keeping roots cool; if fronds droop from too dry soil, they cannot be revived; fronds of young plants cannot stand water directly on them; fronds bruise easily so plant should be located where it will not touch or be touched; ferns cannot stand pesticides, which will kill insects and your plant, too.

C. chamissoi (kam-iss′-oh-eye) Hawaiian tree fern; fastest growing species; leaflets to 20″ (.55 m) long are spear shaped, serrated, toothed; hairy brown stalks are long and slim.
C. menziesii (men-zee′-see-eye) with fibrous, heavy stem, shorter than most species; triangular-shaped fronds have shiny, mild green, serrated leaflets.
C. schiedei (shee′-dee-eye) Mexican tree fern; native of Mexico and Guatemala; used often in churches; heavy stems on trunks shoot from hair-covered crowns; fronds to 10′ (3 m) long shaped as triangles; leaflets spear shaped, narrow, and pointed.

CISSUS (siss′-us) Grape Ivy, Kangaroo Ivy.
Certain species of Cissus have foliage characteristics similar to ivy and so the common names for this full-foliaged, evergreen genus. Woody vines because the stems are so fibered, and of vining, trailing habit, these ivies are well suited for hanging containers. Best in a bright-light site, Cissus needs no more attention than basic culture. Easy to propagate, for stems will root in water. The previous Vitis classification may be used in listings.
Family Tree: Vitaceae (vye-tay′-see-ay) Grape family; native to Australia, South America, Asia.
Foliage: toothed or smooth-margined, shaped heartlike to oval, leathery texture; dark green to reddish colors; some cling by fine tendrils, small hairlike growths.
Size: to 5′ (1.50 m).
Location: WINTER—southern exposure.
SUMMER—*Inside:* eastern or western exposure. *Outside:* eastern or western exposure; protect fragile foliage from potentially damaging elements, preferably by overhang.
FALL: move indoors by mid-September; site in eastern or western exposure.
Dormancy: none, but light resting period October through February; slowly diminish watering, keeping soil barely moist; cut fertilizing program in half.
Water: keep moderately and evenly moist.
Mist: daily, twice a day when possible.
Humidity: above normal for happiness, 40%-45%.
Air circulation: helpful condition.
Feed: mild liquid manure every 2 weeks.

Soil: standard potting mix.
Temperature: Day—68°-80°F (20°-26°C). Night—55°-68°F (12°-20°C).
Potbound: repot; or pot-on as needed and indicated by root growth being at least 50% of pot content.
Mature plants: hard pruning to reestablish plant should be done in early spring prior to evidence of new growth. Take cuttings, easily rooted, for fresh replacement.
Propagate: by stem cuttings; root in water or moist vermiculite.
Insect alert: mealybug, whitefly, mites, scale.
Disease alert: brown spots on leaves, caused by high light intensity or overwatering.
Notable: good artificial light specimen, a total of 14 light hours combined with natural; prune plant often to prevent legginess; must have good soil porosity; never allow soil to dry out completely; rinse foliage frequently in room-temperature or tepid water, to prevent dust-clogged pores.

C. adenopodus (ad-en-oh-poh´-dus) velvety leaves, trifoliage; red color fades with age.
C. antarctica (an-tark´-tik-uh) meaning of the Antarctic, native to New South Wales; common name, Kangaroo ivy; oval, serrated, shiny leaves, 4″-6″ (100-150 mm) long, dark green; vigorous grower; previously known as *C. glandulosa*.
  Variety: Minima (min´-ih-muh) leaves 3″ (76 mm) long.
C. capensis (ka-pen´-siss) meaning of the Cape of Good Hope; fuzzy new growth; large leaves shaped like grape leaves, to 8″ (.25 m) wide; colored rust underneath.
C. discolor (dis-kol´-or) meaning of many or different colors; common name, Begonia treevine; native to Java; velvet textured, extremely colorful leaves, shaded olive green, similar to Rex begonia; marked with purple and silver variations; reddish undersides, dark red stems; a climber;

Cissus rhombifolia,
Grape Ivy

Cissus,
Begonia Treevine

previously called *C. velutina;* keep humidity very high; provide with very little sun.
C. hypoglauca (hye-poh-glaw´-kuh) native to Australia; leaves of 5 leaflets, 3″ (76 mm) long; leathery texture; plant to 6′ (1.80 m).
C. incisa (in-sye´-suh) meaning cut; common name, Marine ivy; native to North America; heavily toothed leaves, fleshy, thick, to 4″ (100 mm) long; vine to 30′ (9 m).
C. quadrangularis (kwad-ran-gew-lay´-riss) 3-4 winged, shiny green leaves, reddish underneath; fleshy stems; climbs by tendrils; succulent; can take full sun or shade; keep cool; vigorous grower; native to Arabia, Africa, India.
C. rhombifolia (rom-bif-oh´-lee-uh) Grape ivy; fuzzy brown new growth, leaves unfold bronzy, turn shiny deep green; 3-lobed leaf, 4″ (100 mm) long; previously named *Vitis rhombifolia;* native to South America and West Indies.
C. striata (strye-ay´-tuh) meaning striped; common name, Miniature grape ivy; red stems; tiny, 5-fingered, bronze green leaves, to 1″ (25 mm) long; good for terrariums; native to Chile and Japan.

CITRUS (sit-rus).

Semitropical, Citrus includes many species, orange, tangerine, lemon, lime, and grapefruit, to name a few. Interior site important features are the fragrant flowers and crisp evergreen foliage. Growing the fruit is an added bonus for great cocktail conversation. At one time grown by all the "carriage trade" in special conservatories called "orangeries." A super tub plant.
Family Tree: Rutaceae (ru-tay´-see-ay) Rue family; native to the Far East.
Foliage: dark green, shiny, oval; broadleaf (wide) evergreen; some have short, stiff spines.

Flower: fragrant, ½″-2″ (12-50 mm) creamy white; blossoms intermittently through year.
Fruit: ah, yes! Variety depending on species; to assure fruit development indoors, dust pistil (very center, raised) with pollen from immediately around it, using small paint brush.
Size: variable, 2′-15′ (.60-4.50 m), depending on species.
Location: WINTER—southern exposure.
SUMMER—*Inside:* southeastern exposure. *Outside:* eastern exposure.
FALL: move indoors by mid-September; site in southeastern exposure.
Dormancy: none, but resting in nonfruiting and nonblooming periods; slowly diminish watering to approximately half normal amount, allow plant to indicate needs; cease fertilizing when plant is not blooming or with fruit.
Water: very thoroughly, allowing top soil to become almost dry between waterings.
Mist: daily, twice a day when possible.
Humidity: average, 30%-35%.
Air circulation: helpful condition.
Feed: every 2 weeks, mild liquid manure.
Soil: 2 parts standard potting mix, 1 part humus.
Temperature: Day—68°-72°F (20°-22°C). Night—50°-55°F (10°-12°C).
Potbound: side-dress in early spring; pot-on only when root system overbalances soil content by 60%-40%.
Mature plants: better bloom if stems pinched back as they become straggly; pinch off to point where plant retains compact, uniform shape, pinch center out of young shoots for a wide plant. Too tall a plant for standing upright; stake and tie main trunk (leave small amount of slack in ties to eliminate potential of injury from tie cutting into fleshy stem). May be trained into standard form (tree form) or espaliered plant by proper pruning or pinching.
Propagate: from half-ripened stem cuttings or seeds—latter not recommended for amateur.
Insect alert: red spider, scale, mealybug.
Notable: soil must have good drainage; do not allow soil to dry out completely; allow to summer outside, major benefit is natural pollination; keep as cool as possible in winter, 60°F (15°C) or below.

C. aurantium (aw-rant′-ee-um) Sour Orange; tree to 30′ (9 m), but may be kept pruned to tub plant size; leaves to 4″ (100 mm), on winged stems; long blunt spines; large, very fragrant, waxlike flowers; spherical 3″ (76 mm) fruit is good for cooking or marmalade.
C. limonia (li-moh′-nee-uh) Lemon; to 20′ (6 m); short stiff spines, pinkish flowers; egg shaped, very sour fruit, up to 5″ (127 mm) long, is edible; tart for eating; good for marmalade.
C. mitis (mye′-tiss) Calamondin, Panama Orange; small tree, especially hardy; fruit of lemon flavor, up to 1″ (25 mm) diameter; tart for eating; good for marmalade.
C. paradisi (par-a-diss′-eye) large tree that can be kept pruned to tub plant size; smooth leaves and grapefruit in clusters; fruit tart for eating; good for marmalade.
C. sinensis (si-nen′-siss) Sweet Orange; small tree with few blunt spines; oval leaves to 5″ (127 mm) long; fruit to 5″ (127 mm); blossom of this species became official flower of Florida in 1907.

Citrus

C. taitensis (tye-ten′-siss) Otaheite orange, Tahiti orange; small shrub; fragrant, pink-tinged flowers; glossy foliage; orange-colored fruit.

CLERODENDRUM (kleer′-oh-den′-drum) Glory Bower; nickname: Bleeding Heart; Cashmere Bouquet.
This genus is sometimes referred to as Clerodenum. Greek *Clerodendrum* means "chance" and "tree." All species here mentioned are special and unique inside plants; among specific species, one finds some berries; some have a lovely fragrance; some flower only in summer, others all year long. Some are vines, others take a shrub or bush form. Truly handsome flowering displays! It can be developed into a standard by proper pruning.
Family Tree: Verbenaceae (ver-beh-nay′-see-ay) Verbena family; native to tropical West Africa.
Foliage: arranged oppositely or whorled on stems; rich green with brown veins; papery to touch; oval to a point, with plain edges; up to 5″ (127 mm).
Flower: large clusters of 1″-2″ (25-50 mm) pink red; heart shaped with white calyx (bractlike growth which protects bud before it opens); blooms March into July; some species very fragrant.
Fruit: bright, deep red or pale red berries.
Size: 2′-3′ (.60-.90 m) up to 15′ (4.50 m).
Location: WINTER—full sun; set in southern exposure.
SUMMER—*Inside:* partial shade; set in eastern to southern exposure for direct rays of morning sun. *Outside:* partial shade; set in eastern exposure or under a protective structure where plant receives strong light but no direct rays.
FALL: move indoors by mid-September; site in southeastern exposure.
Dormancy: late fall; keep in good light and place in cooler area from September to February; temperature can be as

Clerodendrum fallax,
Glory-Bower

low as 50°F (10°C); slowly diminish watering for all species that have a dormant stage, then allow to remain dry until beginning of February; cease fertilizing.

Water: keep soil evenly moist.

Mist: daily, twice daily if possible (especially in spring).

Humidity: at least 50%.

Air circulation: helpful condition.

Feed: every 2 weeks during March through August with mild liquid manure.

Soil: 1 part standard potting soil, 1 part peat moss, 1 part perlite; needs good drainage.

Temperature: Day—70°-75°F (21°-23°C). Night—60°-65°F (15°-18°C).

Potbound: normal conditions; pot-on when root crowded.

Mature plants: too tall a plant for standing upright—stake and tie main trunk (leave small amount of slack in ties to eliminate potential of injury from tie cutting into fleshy stem). May be trained into standard tree form or espaliered plant by proper pruning or pinching. Prune plants to size desired when repotting. To produce more flowers, which are borne only on new growth, prune the plants after they have stopped blooming.

Propagate: by stem cuttings of half-ripened wood in spring; a minimum of 70% humidity is needed for rooting.

Offspring established: maintain proper culture as for adult plants.

Insect alert: mealybug, red spider.

Notable: rooted, established cuttings will bloom the first year; don't be fearful of hard pruning, for flowers develop only on new growth; plants are well suited for tub growing; a fast grower of several feet a year.

C. thomsoniae (tom-soh'-nee-ee) Bleeding Heart Vine or Glory Bower; trails snow-white flowers, balloonlike at the base, with flaring scarlet petals; blooms in spring and summer, sometimes into winter if given enough warmth, 65°F (18°C) or higher; a vigorous climber; native to West Africa; up to 15' (4.20 m) tall unless pruned back.

C. fragrans (fray'-granz) Cashmere Bouquet; large, hairy leaves; compact, hyacinth-scented, double white, pale pink, and purple blooms in early fall and intermittently throughout year; native to China and Japan; can be pruned to a shrub.

C. fallax (fal'-lax) previously called *C. speciosissimum* (spee-see-oh-siss'-im-mum) meaning exceptionally showy; erect clusters of pink flowers; deciduous; heart-shaped leaves up to 12" (.30 m); up to 3' (.90 m) tall; native to Java.

CLIVIA MINIATA (klye'-vee-uh min-ee-ay'-tuh) Kafir Lily.

Turning full cycle to become once again a favorite as it was two generations past. A relative of the amaryllis. Normally, flowering occurs in spring; yet, if culturally very satisfied, there may be an additional fall display.

Family Tree: Amaryllidaceae (am-mar-rill-ee-day'-see-ay) Amaryllis family; from south Africa.

Foliage: waxy, glossy, deep evergreen; stems strong and rigid; to 2" (50 mm) wide and 18" (.45 m)-24" (.60 m) long; shapes vary among specimens from wide to narrow, blunt to sharp, strap shaped to fanlike.

Flower: heavy clusters of 12-20 blooms, held high over leaves, each up to 3" (76 mm) across; lilylike, fragrant, long lasting; orange or red with yellow throat; blooming time is April, May, and sometimes late fall; hybrids vary in intensity of orange and amount of yellow in the throat.

Fruit: red berries follow flowers.

Size: 30" (.75 m)-3' (.90 m).

Location: WINTER—give bright, diffuse light of eastern exposure.

SUMMER—*Inside:* retain same site as winter location. *Outside:* do not move plant to exterior site for summer vacation; retain normal eastern exposure.

FALL: retain year-round site.

Dormancy: period starts October; keep at moderate heat; slowly diminish watering October through January, keeping soil barely moist; water weekly, except every 2 weeks in cooler room; cease fertilizing.

Water: allow to dry out completely between waterings.

Mist: daily, twice a day during growth period when it has ceased flowering.

Humidity: normal, 30%-40%.

Air circulation: helpful condition.

Feed: weekly, March through August; mild liquid manure.

Soil: standard potting mix.

Temperature: Day—68°-72°F (20°-22°C). Night—60°F (15°C).

Potbound: best for optimum bloom.

Mature plants: subject to root rot if plant remains in same pot for several years; repot and remove very soft, rotten sections after flowering; water carefully to avoid rotting (fleshy roots); to assure flowering, rest period must be observed. Cut off flower stem after blooming.

Propagate: either from young shoots forming at foot of mother plant when repotting, or by root division in late spring at beginning of new leaf growth.

Clivia miniata,
Kafir Lily

Codiaeum variegatum pictum,
Croton

Offspring established: plant each single spread of leaves attached to own root system in a 6″ (150 mm) pot, packing earth solidly; roots are very tender and brittle, so work carefully.

Insect alert: mites, scale.

Disease alert: soggy soil will cause root rot.

Notable: easy to maintain but never move plant; keep in identical position, don't even turn pot; cut off flowers after blooming; plant must be at least 2 years old to bloom; must have good soil drainage but not loose soil; water only after soil has dried out completely.

C. nobilis (no′-bil-liz) meaning of stately or noble appearance; straplike leaves; flowers pendulous in clusters, red and yellow with green tips.

C. x cyrtanthiflora (ser-tanth-if-floh′-ruh) has salmon pink flowers.

CODIAEUM VARIEGATUM PICTUM (koh-dih-ee′-um vay-ree-eh-gay′-tum pik′-tum) Croton; nickname: Copper Leaf.

Legend has this genus so named as a derivative of the Greek word for head, probably referring to use of the leaves as crowns. Dramatic leaf shapes and splashy colors are an exciting and effective display in an interior setting. Colors, shapes, and sizes vary greatly within this genus. Close attention to cultural needs is a must or dropping foliage will clutter the floor. May be incorrectly referred to or listed as *C. tiglium* or *C. eleuteria.*

Family Tree: Euphorbiaceae (yew-forb′-ee-aye′-see-ay) Spurge family; native to Malaysia, islands of South Pacific, East Indies.

Foliage: shapes vary from slender to 18″ (.45 m) long, flat to 6″ (.15 m) wide, lobed, ribbed, twisted or crinkled; colors include yellow, green, copper, red, pink, orange,

brown, and ivory; solid colors or veining, blotches, spots or patterns; smooth edged, alternate leaves on stem.

Flower: insignificant.

Size: up to 5′ (1.50 m).

Location: WINTER—southern exposure.

SUMMER—*Inside:* southeastern or southwestern exposure. *Outside:* southeastern or southwestern exposure; site in shelter to protect foliage.

FALL: move indoors by mid-September; site in southeastern or southwestern exposure.

Dormancy: none, but a resting period with slower growth during winter months of less intensity; generally October through February; slowly diminish watering; plant will indicate needs as determined by environmental conditions; develop sensitivity to feel of soil moisture level; cease fertilizing.

Water: thoroughly and evenly, allowing soil to dry out between waterings.

Mist: daily, twice a day when possible.

Humidity: above normal for happiness, 45%-55%.

Air circulation: helpful condition.

Feed: mild liquid manure every 2 weeks.

Soil: standard potting soil.

Temperature: Day—68°-78°F (20°-25°C). Night—60°-68°F (15°-20°C).

Potbound: slightly for happiness, when root growth is approximately 65% of pot content; best repotted or potted-on before new growth develops, in March.

Mature plants: drop leaves very quickly when not culturally happy; this especially occurs with sudden temperature changes.

Propagate: by cuttings; or by air layering; in moist sand and/or vermiculite.

Insect alert: aphid, mealybug, mite, scale, leaf miner.

Notable: soil must have porosity; no soggy conditions; important to wipe or wash foliage every 2 weeks; Note:

good air circulation needed for top performance; do not overpot, use pot 2″ (50 mm) larger than previous housing; sun enhances fantastic coloring but direct sun, except for winter, may burn leaves; use pebble, water, tray method to maintain humidity level.

C. variegatum
    Variety—Delicatissimum (del-ih-ka-tiss′-ih-mum) green, yellow, and red; narrow leaf.
    Variety—Graciosum (gray-see-oh′-sum) copper to gold; narrow leaf.
    Variety—Harvest Moon yellowish gold and green; broad leaf.

COFFEA ARABICA (koff′-ee-uh ar-rab′-ik-uh) Arabica Coffee.

One needs a sizable spot to enjoy the Coffea arabica. The ripe seeds may be washed, dried, roasted, and ground to make coffee, which makes for topical conversation at low ebbs in tête-à-têtes. The fragrance, heavy, is of the nature of the gardenia to which this genus is related.

Family Tree: Rubiaceae (roob-bee-ay′-see-ay) Madder family; native to Asia, tropical Africa, and South America.

Foliage: 4″-6″ (100-150 mm) long, dark, glossy green oval leaves with wavy margins arranged oppositely.

Flower: fragrant clusters of ¾″ (19 mm) white, star-shaped flowers borne in the leaf axils; blooms heaviest July through September, but will bloom intermittently throughout year.

Fruit: cherrylike; first green, changing to red, and finally to black; ½″ (12 mm) mature berries; within each berry are 2 seeds, the "beans" from which coffee is made.

Size: upright to 4′ (1.20 m), and up to 15′ (4.20 m).

Location: WINTER—eastern to southern exposure.

SUMMER—*Inside:* good shade; set in eastern location. *Out-side:* full shade; set in northern exposure; no direct sun. FALL: move indoors by mid-September.

Dormancy: none, yet a light resting period occurs in winter months; reduce watering by half to keep soil barely moist.

Water: in summer keep evenly and thoroughly wet.

Mist: daily, twice daily if possible.

Humidity: very high for happiness, 60%-70%.

Air circulation: helpful condition.

Feed: every 2 weeks from March to October, monthly the rest of the year.

Soil: 2 parts standard potting mix, 1 part perlite.

Temperature: Day—70°-74°F (21°-23°C); try to keep even temperatures year round. Night—65°-70°F (18°-21°C).

Potbound: repot in February or March, or pot-on as needed.

Mature plants: better bloom if stems pinched back as they become straggly; pinch off to point where plant retains compact, uniform shape; pinch center out of young shoots for a wide plant. Too tall a plant for standing upright, stake and tie main trunk (leave small amount of slack in ties to eliminate potential of injury by tie cutting into fleshy stem). May be trained into standard form (tree form) or espaliered plant by proper pruning or pinching.

Propagate: from seeds—which need bottom heat for satisfactory germination—any time; or by cuttings of upright, growing tips (cuttings of side branches usually grow into poorly shaped plants).

Offspring established: maintain proper culture as for adult plants.

Insect alert: red spider, mealybug, scale, whitefly.

Disease alert: severe drying out of soil will cause the older, lower leaves to fall. Direct sun will cause leaf scorch.

Notable: must have good soil drainage; never allow soil to become soggy; never allow soil to dry out completely; plants must be 3-4 years old to have a true profusion of flowers. *Please*, wash leaves regularly to aid in avoiding pests, but do be extremely gentle, for the leaves are very fragile and bruise easily. This genus is simple to prune, shape, and maintain at desired size.

Coffea arabica,
Arabica Coffee

COLEUS (koh′-lee-us) nickname: Painted leaf plant.

Coleus' variegated foliage of all shapes, colors, and striations is a visual wonder. An evergreen best suited to small, full sun sites—sunlight is conducive to a production of more brilliance of leaf color. Small florets clustered on stems protrude above the foliage. A genus of easy maintenance, if given minor cultural attention, including daily checking for moisture needs and pruning to retain an aesthetic shape.

Family Tree: Labiatae (lay-bee-ay′-tay) Mint family; native to tropical Africa, Asia, Java.

Foliage: striated, bordered; full spectrum of colors; leaf shapes generally oval to a point, serrated edges; succulent stems; erect nature.

Flower: erect stems, tipped by clusters of petite florets; generally bluish or very muted, pale colors.

Size: up to 4′ (1.20 m).

Location: WINTER—southern exposure.

SUMMER—*Inside:* southeastern or southwestern exposure. *Outside:* southeastern or southwestern exposure; protect fragile foliage from potentially damaging elements, preferably by overhang.

FALL: move indoors by mid-September; site in southeastern or southwestern exposure.

Dormancy: none, but light resting period after flowering; slowly diminish watering, plant will indicate needs by appearance, becoming limp and droopy; develop sensitivity to feel of soil moisture level; cut fertilizing program in half.

Water: keep moderately and evenly moist.

Mist: daily, twice a day when possible.

Humidity: above normal for happiness, 40%-45%.

Air circulation: helpful condition.

Feed: mild liquid manure every 2 weeks.

Soil: 2 parts standard potting soil, 1 part peat moss, 1 part perlite.

Temperature: Day—68°-80°F (20°-26°C). Night—55°-68°F (12°-20°C).

Potbound: repot; or pot-on as needed and indicated by root growth being at least 50% of pot content.

Mature plants: pinching of tips must be done on a regular basis in order to maintain bushy shape. Take cuttings, easily rooted, for fresh replacement. If desired, fantastic foliage will be more fantastic if one nips out flower buds as soon as they appear.

Propagate: by seeds or stem cuttings, root latter in water or moist vermiculite.

Insect alert: mealybug, whitefly, mites, scale, slugs.

Disease alert: plants over 1 year old tend to develop root gall; therefore, a failure may not be your fault—easy and better to replace plant.

Notable: good artificial light specimen, a total of 14 light hours combined with natural; prune plant often to prevent legginess; do not overwater as plant will rot easily; must have good soil porosity; never allow soil to dry out completely; rinse foliage frequently in room-temperature or tepid water to prevent dust-clogged pores.

Coleus

C. amboinicus (am-boy'-nik-us) Suganda, Oregano; brittle, variegated green leaves, aromatic; shrubby habit, to 2' (.60 m).

C. blumei (bloom'-ee-eye) leaf to 4" (100 mm); many colors, combinations of red, green, yellow, maroon, pink.

  Variety—Brilliancy red and gold leaves.

  Variety—Firebird orange red leaves, green edges.

  Variety—Sunset salmon rose, moss green markings.

C. rehneltianus (ray-nell-tee-ay'-nus) Rehnelt coleus; native to Ceylon; up to 1½" (37 mm) leaves, with serrated or scalloped edges; trailing habit; good hanging basket plant.

C. thyrsoideus (ther-soy'-dee-us) blue flowers, ½" (12 mm) across; on stems; to 3' (.90 m) high.

COLUMNEA (koh-lum'-nee-uh). The Latin commemorates the name of Fabio Colonna, the botanical star of a talented and noble Roman family of statesmen, generals, and cardinals. Fabio, noted for compiling all botanical data known in 1592, was a member of the exclusive Society of Lynxes which comprised some 30 eminent scientists including Galileo.

A perfect hanging basket plant; very special in its trailing, graceful beauty and colorfully throated blossoms so delicate that the bit of special attention to cultural requirements is rewarded. Columnea is related to Gloxinia. There are recently developed hybrids which bloom off and on throughout the year, and new small-leafed varieties which are fantastic for terrarium growing.

Family Tree: Gesneriaceae (ges-ner-ee-ay'-see-ay) Gesneria family; native to Costa Rica and the jungles of Central and South America, as well as the West Indies.

Foliage: on 4' (1.20 m) trailing stems, evergreen, reddish, often hairy leaves are oppositely arranged; size range is from tiny button to 6" (150 mm); size and color vary with species.

Flower: tubular ½"-4" (12-100 mm) flowers borne in leaf axils through the year; a profusion of scarlet, yellow, orange, pink, red.

Fruit: seasonally attractive red berries.

Size: 36" (.90 m) in length or height.

Location: WINTER—full sun; set in southern exposure.

SUMMER—*Inside:* partial shade; set in eastern to southern exposure for direct rays of morning sun. *Outside:* partial shade; set in eastern exposure or under a protective structure where plant receives strong light but no direct rays.

FALL: move indoors by mid-September, site in southeastern exposure.

Dormancy: taper off watering in September; cease entirely in December; this practice encourages formation of flower buds; for increased flowering, add a month's rest at the height of summer, setting in cool location without water or fertilizer.

Water: keep evenly moist with tepid water January through September.

Mist: daily, twice daily if possible.

Humidity: quite high, 70%; much moist air.

Air circulation: helpful condition.

Feed: mild liquid manure every 2 weeks, January through September.

Soil: 2 parts potting soil, 1 part peat moss.

Temperature: Day—72°-75°F (22°-23°C). Night—65°-70°F (18°-21°C).

Columnea hybrids

CONVALLARIA MAJALIS (kon-val-lay'-ree-uh maj-ay-liss) Lily-of-the-Valley.

Lovely to sight and scent as a special floral arrangement and replacement; site in a cool bright spot or set midst several other flora as a cheery accent during winter doldrums. Buy planted from flower or nursery outlet or order specially treated (they are pre-frozen) and easily plant yourself. The leaves of this genus are used for dyeing. When spring foliage is used, the color of dye is a pale greenish yellow. Fall leaves produce a gold dye color.

Family Tree: Liliaceae (lil-ee-ay'-see-ay) Lily family; from Europe, Asia, and the mountain area of North America.

Foliage: fine-pointed upright leaves 6″-8″ (150-200 mm) long, 1½″ (37 mm) wide, on wiry stems; keep color well after blooming.

Flower: perennial herb; graceful stems covered with a profusion of fragrant white, nodding flowers, each bell-like and 1/3″ (6 mm) across.

Size: 6″-8″ (150-200 mm).

Location: WINTER—eastern or western exposure if forcing. SUMMER—*Inside:* eastern exposure if forcing.

FALL: eastern or western exposure if forcing; when forcing only after the buds have formed, set plant in sight of a bit more direct sun, moving to southeastern and southwestern exposures.

Dormancy: period starts after pips have completed their indoor blooming; remove from fiber or soil growing medium, dry off and place in paper bag in cool, dry place, storing for planting in ground outdoors the following early spring.

Water: keep evenly moist.

Mist: daily, lightly while blooming.

Humidity: above normal, 45%-50%.

Air circulation: helpful condition.

Forcing culture: use 6″ (150 mm) pot 6″ (150 mm) deep,

Potbound: happy; pot-on only when totally root-bound, 80% roots to 20% soil.

Mature plants: to encourage new branches, prune plants after a period of flowering.

Propagate: from seeds or 4″ (100 mm) cuttings of summer-ripened wood immediately after flowering; start in moist sandy or peaty soil (1 part sand or peat, 1 part standard potting mix).

Insect alert: mites, leaf miners, mealybugs.

Disease alert: root rot, crown and stem rot, leaf spots.

Notable: keep temperatures even; needs warm site but direct sun only in winter; thrives in artificial light, requiring a total of 14-16 natural and/or artificial light hours daily; misting directly on leaves will cause brown spots; never allow soil to dry out completely during growing period, January through September; can't stand drafts.

C. affinis (af-feen'-is) meaning allied, close to another species; yellow flowers with orange hairs.

C. hirta (hert'-uh) meaning with small hairs; trailing plant with orange-scarlet flowers.

C. gloriosa (gloh-ree-oh'-suh) blossoms red with yellow throats; leaves dark green ovals with red fuzz.

C. linearis (lin-neh-air'-iz) meaning narrow leaved; rosy pink flowers with white hair.

C. arguta (ar-gew'-tuh) meaning with toothed leaves; these are dainty pointed, shiny and fleshy; flowers large, salmon red.

C. microphylla (my-croh-fil'-luh) meaning small leaved; in this case tiny, downy, and green; trailing habit; flowers are orange red with yellow throats and yellow stripes.

C. hybrids

S. Krishna and S. Pink Imp both are pink; year-round blooming.

C. Pixie small leaved; orange flowered; suited for terrariums.

Convallaria majalis,
Lily-of-the-Valley

sphagnum moss, sand, or pebbles; shorten long roots to depth of container and dampen them before planting; place so tips of crowns protrude from planting medium surface; keep in dim light and under 70°F (21°C) temperature as flower stems develop; as buds start to form, move into permanent site for visual enjoyment.

Notable: never allow soil to dry out completely; plant at least a dozen or more single bulbs or pips close together for a good visual display; can be forced any time of year if one can get the pips, but generally brought into bloom in late fall or winter months; if planting yourself, select the larger, firm pips; bloom about 21 days from planting.

CORDYLINE TERMINALIS (kor-di-lye'-nuh ter-mi-nay'-liss) Hawaiian Ti Plant; nickname: New Zealand cabbage tree.

The Cordyline terminalis is extremely sturdy; a year-round foliage species. In its natural habitat, the shredded leaves are used for grass skirts and thatching. Small "logs," pieces of wood stem, of the Ti plant can be laid on moist sand as a propagation method. This species is native to India.

Family Tree: Liliaceae (lil-ee-ay'-see-ay) Lily family; native to Polynesia.

Foliage: broad, sword shaped, green leaves, palm-type to 18″ (.45 m) long; top-crowning a trunk base.

Flower: insignificant, white flower tufts; late winter, early spring.

Size: to 12′ (3.65 m) tall.

Location: WINTER—southeastern or southwestern exposure.
SUMMER—*Inside:* northeastern or northwestern exposure. *Outside:* northeastern or northwestern exposure; site in shelter to protect foliage.
FALL: move indoors by mid-September; site in eastern or western exposure.

Dormancy: none, but a resting period of slower growth during winter months of less intensity, generally October through February; slowly diminish watering; plant will indicate needs as determined by environmental conditions; develop sensitivity to feel of soil moisture level; cease fertilizing.

Water: thoroughly and evenly, allowing soil to dry out between waterings.

Mist: daily, twice a day when possible.

Humidity: above normal for happiness, 45%-55%.

Air circulation: helpful condition.

Feed: mild liquid manure every 2 weeks.

Soil: standard potting soil.

Temperature: Day—70°-80°F (21°-26°C). Night—62°-68°F (16°-20°C).

Potbound: very happy; pot-on only when root growth of plant is 80%, soil 20% of pot content; top- or side-dress yearly; preferably spring.

Mature plants: if plant becomes too tall, cut growing ends; start in rooting media. Remove dried or withered leaves as they appear.

Propagate: by stem cuttings; or by air layering.

Insect alert: mealybug, red spider, scale, thrip, aphids.

Notable: good artificial-light plant, total of 14-16 hours combining natural and artificial light; do not allow soil to dry out completely; soil must have porosity, eliminating possibility of soggy conditions; use pebble, water, and tray

*Cordyline terminalis,
Hawaiian Ti Plant*

method to maintain humidity level; sponge leaf foliage at least every 3 weeks; always use room-temperature water; shiners and/or oils are an *absolute no-no;* foliage water spots permanently.

C. australis (oss-tray'-liss) meaning southern; native to New Zealand; white tufts of flowers, early spring; central vein light green on leaves, 3′ (.90 m) long, 1½″ (37 mm) wide; needs frequent air layering to maintain size.
   Variety—Veitchii (veech'-ee-eye) leaves colored to red midrib and red base of leaf.
C. banksii (bank'-see-eye) to 3′ (.90 m); dark green, strap leaves, pale yellow midrib; drooping clusters of white flowers.
C. indivisia (in-di-vee'-zee-uh) meaning undivided; thin green leaves, midvein of leaf colored red.
C. marginata (mar-ji-nay'-tuh) meaning margined or striped; tufts of narrow gray green leaves, edged with purple; at ends of bare stems.
C. terminalis
   Variety—Bicolor: dark, metallic green leaves, pink edged.
   Variety—Firebrand: red leaves form compact rosette.
   Variety—Tricolor: pink, red, creamy white leaves; on single stem.

COSTUS (kohs'-tus) Spiral Ginger.

The name Spiral ginger relates to the leaf formation on the stem which resembles steps rising on a spiral staircase. This evergreen herb, a foliage plant, totals to a very attractive ornamental to be sited in a wash of bright light. The bonus, an enhancement by super handsome, large blossoms vividly colored.

Costus igneus

Family Tree: Zingiberaceae (zin-jib-er-ay'-see-ay) Ginger family; native to Central and South America.

Foliage: oval to pointed tip, deeply veined leaves, on ends of stems, in umbrella form.

Flower: ruffle-edged petals, vary in size and form according to species.

Size: up to 5' (1.50 m).

Location: WINTER—southeastern or southwestern exposure.

SUMMER—*Inside:* northeastern or northwestern exposure. *Outside:* northeastern or northwestern exposure; protect fragile foliage from potentially damaging elements, preferably by overhang.

FALL: move indoors by mid-September; site in eastern or western exposure.

Dormancy: none, but light resting period after flowering; slowly diminish watering, keeping soil barely moist; cut fertilizing program in half.

Water: keep moderately and evenly moist.

Mist: daily, twice a day when possible.

Humidity: above normal for happiness, 40%-45%.

Air circulation: helpful condition.

Feed: mild liquid manure every 2 weeks.

Soil: 2 parts standard potting soil, 1 part peat moss, 1 part perlite.

Temperature: Day—68°-80°F (20°-26°C). Night—55°-68°F (12°-20°C).

Potbound: repot; pot-on as needed and indicated by root growth being at least 65% of pot content.

Mature plants: remove withered foliage as it appears. Remove faded blossoms immediately.

Propagate: by division of clumps, preferably in spring before evidence of new growth.

Insect alert: mealybug, whitefly, mites, scale, slugs.

Notable: good artificial light specimen, a total of 14 light hours combined with natural; must have good soil porosity; never allow soil to dry out completely; rinse foliage frequently in room-temperature or tepid water to prevent dust-clogged pores.

C. igneous (ig'-nee-us) meaning fiery or flame colored; native to Brazil; glossy green leaves, red undersides and stems; 3" (76 mm) orange flowers, open flat; to 36" (.90 m) tall.

C. malortieanus (mal-or-tye-ay'-nus) Stepladder Plant; previously *C. elegans* or *C. zebrinus*; hairy, oval leaves, to 12" (.30 m) long; bright green, with dark green lengthwise bands, pale green undersides.

C. sanquineus (san-gwin'-ee-us) meaning bloody or blood red; common name: Spiral flag; blue green leaves, silvery center ribs, reddish undersides and stems.

C. speciosus (spee-si-oh'-sus) meaning showy; common name: Spiral ginger; white flowers with yellow centers and red bracts (leaves attached to stem at base of flowers, generally vivid color, often mistaken for flower).

Costus malortieanus,
Stepladder Plant

Costus sanguineus,
Spiral Flag

CRASSULA ARGENTEA (krass'-yew-luh ar-jen'-tee-uh)
Jade Plant, Chinese Rubber Plant.

As it matures, this plant naturally forms a compact, dignified tree shape, needing just a little help through pruning. The hefty stem gives it a precious, established look in little time. Beautiful and sculptural even when small, it is an undemanding species. It will bloom, however, only when mature and very well lighted. The fleshy foliage indicates Crassula is a succulent.

Family Tree: Crassulaceae (krass-yew-lay'-see-ay) Orpine family; native to South Africa.

Foliage: 1"-2" (25-50 mm) rounded or oval, shiny, fleshy, succulent leaves, often edged with red.

Flower: tiny, star-shaped, pinkish white flowers, on stems reaching just above leaves.

Size: 18"-30" (.45-.75 m).

Location: WINTER—southeastern or southwestern exposure. SUMMER—*Inside:* northeastern or northwestern exposure. *Outside:* northeastern or northwestern exposure; site in shelter to protect foliage.

FALL: move indoors by mid-September; site in eastern or western exposure.

Dormancy: none, but a resting period of slower growth during winter months of less intensity, generally October through February; slowly diminish watering, plant will indicate needs as determined by environmental conditions; develop sensitivity to feel of soil moisture level; cease fertilizing.

Water: essential to let soil become nearly dry between thorough waterings.

Mist: daily, lightly.

Humidity: normal to dry, about 30%-35%.

Air circulation: helpful condition.

Feed: mild liquid manure every 2 weeks.

Soil: standard potting soil but will thrive in poor soil.

Temperature: Day—70°-80°F (21°-26°C). Night—62°-68°F

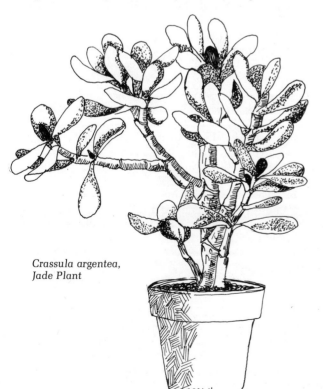

Crassula argentea,
Jade Plant

(16°-20°C) but will tolerate abnormally low house temperatures.

Potbound: very happy; pot-on only when root growth of plant is 80%, soil 20% of pot content; top- or side-dress yearly, preferably spring.

Mature plants: removing growing tips (centers) occasionally makes it branch, bush out and become compact. Remove dried or withered leaves as they appear.

Propagate: any time, from seed or stem or leaf cuttings; plant cuttings in small pot of sandy soil.

Offspring established: when rooted, repot in soil as for mature plant.

Insect alert: mealybug, red spider, scale, thrip, aphids.

Notable: good artificial light plant; total of 14-16 hours, combining natural and artificial light; do not allow soil to dry out completely; soil must have porosity, eliminating possibility of soggy conditions; sponge foliage at least every 3 weeks, always use room temperature water; leaf shiners and/or oils are an *absolute no-no.*

C. arborescens (ar-bor-ess'-enz) previously called *C. cotyledon;* nicknamed Silver dollar plant; gray green leaves with red dots.

C. cooperii (koop'-er-eye) small pointed leaves with dark markings; to 5" (127 mm).

C. cornuta (cor-noo'-tuh) plump, bluish silver leaves.

C. falcata (fal-kay'-tuh) Scarlet paint brush; scarlet flowers in summer; gray green leaves.

C. lycopodioides (lye-cop-od-ee-oy'-deez) nicknamed Shoelace plant; square stems covered with closely packed leaves that overlap like roof tiles; minute yellow white flowers; best in cactus soil.

C. perfossa (per-fos'-suh) symmetrical, necklacelike growth.

C. rupestris (roo-pes'-triss) triangular gray green leaves; to 16" (.40 m).

C. sarcocaulis (sar-ko-kaw'-liss) small, pointed green leaves, small pink flowers; to 1' (.30 m).

C. schmidtii (schmid'-tee-eye) mat-forming shape; clusters of rose red flowers on 2"-3" (50-76 mm) stems.

CRINODONNA CORSII (krye-noh-don'-nuh kor-see-eye)
Amarcrinum (ah-mar-cry'-num).

A rare genus to possess for, interestingly, it is a man-made plant, the result of crossing Crinum moorei with Amaryllis belladonna. Flower and foliage are quite strikingly handsome.

Family Tree: Amaryllidaceae (ah-mar-rill-ee-day'-see-ay).

Foliage: dark evergreen leaves up to 2' (.60 m) long, 1½"-3" (37-76 mm) wide; strap shaped, surround stalks.

Flower: clustered 6-12 on top of stalks; each bloom is up to 4" (100 mm) in diameter, soft pink, trumpet shaped; blooming period late summer and early fall.

Size: 2'-3' (.60-.90 m) high stalks.

Location: WINTER—eastern to southern exposure.

SUMMER—*Inside:* eastern exposure. *Outside:* northern exposure.

FALL: move indoors by mid-September.

Dormancy: period starts October; cool temperatures essential, as close to 50°-55°F (10°-12°C) as possible; slowly diminish watering, keeping soil barely moist.

Water: keep evenly moist.

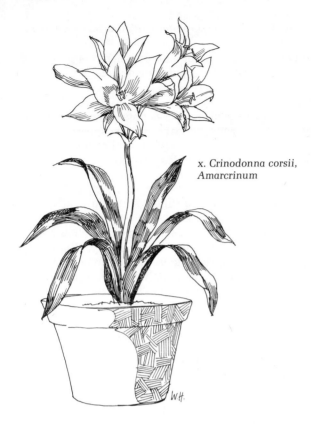

*x. Crinodonna corsii,
Amarcrinum*

Crocus

Mist: daily, very lightly, during growing season—January through October—leaves only, not flowers.
Humidity: above normal, 40%-50%.
Air circulation: helpful condition.
Feed: fertilize monthly during growing season with mild liquid manure.
Soil: 2 parts standard potting mix, 1 part peat moss.
Temperature: Day—65°-70°F (15°-21°C). Night—50°-55°F (10°-12°C).
Potbound: happy! repot only after 3-4 years when container is full to brimming over, don't disturb roots.
Propagate: from the small, 3"-4" (76-100 mm) bulbs developing as offshoots alongside large ones, in late summer or early fall; one bulb per 8"-12" (.25-.30 m) pot or tub, leaving 1/3 of bulb above soil level; use soil mixture specified for culture of this genus.
Offspring established: maintain proper culture as for mature plant.
Insect alert: mealybug, red spider, bulb flies.
Notable: bloom is larger, fuller the less roots are disturbed; if blossoming is extremely heavy, do stake stalks to keep stems erect and keep from injurious bending or breaking; never allow soggy soil conditions.

C. howardii (how-ard'-ee-eye) from California; 3' (.90 m) plant with pink blossoms, large, fragrant.

CROCUS (kroh'-kus).
Brighten a wintery day by forced crocus bulbs charming a corner or two with spots of lively color. Greek *krokos* means saffron.
Family Tree: Iridaceae (eye-rid-ay'-see-ay) Iris family; native to Mediterranean and western Asia.

Foliage: grasslike slender leaves with silver or white streak along midrib.
Flower: showy, colorful, cup-shaped blossoms on 3"-4" (76-100 mm) stems growing from bulbs; vivid colors of white, pink, lavender, purple, yellow, orange, sometimes streaked or mottled.
Size: 2"-5" (50-127 mm).
Interior Site: set in eastern to southern exposure while blooming.
Water: keep soil thoroughly moist as long as foliage is green.
Mist: daily, lightly; not directly on blooms.
Humidity: 35%-40%.
Air circulation: helpful condition.
Feed: not necessary.
Soil: 2 parts standard potting mix, 1 part perlite.
Temperature: Day—68°F (20°C) maximum. Night—40°-50°F (4°-10°C).
Forcing culture: place bulbs (corms) close together but not touching in shallow, 4" (100 mm) pots or bowls; site in cool—around 50°F (10°C)—dark area; keep soil moist but not saturated; when shoots are about 2" (50 mm) long move to slightly warmer—55°-60°F (12°-15°C)—sunny spot, and increase water supply. Or, place corms in trays filled with pebbles; set so bottom of corm is barely below level of pebbles; do not twist bulb to get it into place; fill tray with water so level is just below top of pebble surface line, and keep water level thus; site trays same as soil planting following same culture.
Notable: yellow varieties not recommended for forcing; flower buds just may not open if soil dries out completely; after bloom, remove corms from pots, bowls, or trays and plant in the garden or discard; when temperature during flowering period is too high, flowering period is shortened.

CROSSANDRA INFUNDIBULIFORMIS (kros-san'-dra in-fun-dib-yew-lif-form'-iss) Firecracker Flower.
An attractive almost constantly blooming plant. A different, rather unusual flower color to adorn your inside habitat. Blooming starts when this plant is but 2"-3" (50-76 mm) high. If you have established an artificial light area,

Crossandra infundibuliformis,
Firecracker Flower

you can have superior blooming by placing your Crossandra in this culture.

Family Tree: Acanthaceae (uh-canth-ay'-see-ay) Acanthus family; native to India and Ceylon.

Foliage: very glossy, dark green, lance shaped, arranged on stems in opposite position; size 2"-3" (50-76 mm).

Flower: tubular and overlapping, on short upright spikes; each is 1" (25 mm) across; salmon or orange.

Size: small shrub to 30" (.75 m) but rarely more than 1' (.30 m) tall.

Location: WINTER—full sun; set in southern exposure.

SUMMER—*Inside:* partial shade; set in eastern to southern exposure for direct rays of morning sun. *Outside:* partial shade; set in eastern exposure or under a protective structure where plant receives strong light but no direct rays.

FALL: move indoors by mid-September, site in southeastern exposure.

Dormancy: none actually, yet there is a resting period; slowly diminish watering to half the usual amount in winter.

Water: keep soil evenly moist; use room-temperature water.

Mist: daily, but twice a day if possible; use room-temperature water.

Humidity: above normal, 45%-55%.

Air circulation: helpful condition.

Feed: very mild liquid manure; weekly.

Soil: 1 part standard potting mix, 1 part sand, 1 part peat moss.

Temperature: Day—72°-78°F (22°-25°C). Night—60°-68°F (15°-20°C).

Potbound: repot or pot-on each February; pot-on in normal way only when root-bound.

Mature plants: prune in spring to remove overly long stems and reshape plant; plant may shed some leaves in winter which will be replaced with new spring growth.

Propagate: in spring, root 3" (76 mm) cuttings in sandy soil, in a humid atmosphere to avoid wilting; rooting will occur in 2-3 weeks; germination from seed is slow and erratic.

Offspring established: plant seedlings, each in 4" (100 mm) pot; flowering spike will appear in 4-5 weeks.

Insect alert: red spider, mites, mealybug, scale, whitefly.

Disease alert: too much sun or too low a humidity causes leaves to roll up; using water of too low a temperature will cause brown spots on leaves; overwatering causes lower leaves to yellow and drop off.

Notable: never allow plant to dry out completely; keep out of drafts; needs good drainage, so never soggy soil.

CUPHEA (kew'-fee-uh) Cigar Plant, Elfin Herb.
A perennial plant well known and easily grown in generations past, again coming into its own. A small genus, the Cigar Plant has unusual flowers, quite pretty, and a long blooming season.

Family Tree: Lythraceae (lith-ray'-see-ay) Loosestrife family; native to Mexico and all tropical America.

Foliage: 1" (25 mm) long green oval; in sunny location, edges are red.

Flower: bloom all year with ¾" (19 mm) long cigar-shaped flowers that have ashlike tips; scarlet, lavender, pink, rose, purple, and white; some have tiny, bell-like flowers.

Size: low, bushy, 6"-12" (.15-.30 m).

Location: WINTER—full sun; set in southern exposure.

SUMMER—*Inside:* partial shade; set in eastern to southern exposure for direct rays of morning sun. *Outside:* partial shade; set in eastern exposure or under a protective struc-

Cuphea hyssopifolia,
Cigar Plant or Elfin Herb

ture where plant receives strong light but no direct rays. FALL: move indoors by mid-September.

Dormancy: none; resting period only; maintain normal culture.

Water: keep evenly moist.

Mist: daily.

Humidity: normal, 35%-40%.

Air circulation: helpful condition.

Feed: mild liquid manure every 2 weeks.

Soil: standard potting mix.

Temperature: Day—68°-72°F (20°-22°C). Night—60°-65°F (15°-18°C).

Potbound: normal; repot each spring or pot-on when indicated by plant being overbalanced in root growth against soil content.

Mature plants: better bloom if stems pinched back as they become straggly; pinch off to point where plant retains compact, uniform shape; pinch center out of young shoots for a wide plant.

Propagate: from seed, any time, or from stem cuttings of new shoots in spring.

Offspring established: seedlings are ready to flower when 4-5 months old.

Insect alert: mealybug, scale, mites.

Notable: as plant matures, blossoms increase until plant is literally covered with flowers.

C. hyssopifolia (his-sep-ee-fohl'-ee-uh) elfin herb, 6"-8" (150-200 mm) tall with lavender, bell-like flowers and needlelike leaves.

C. miniata (min-ee-ay'-tuh) meaning cinnabar red; red, bell-like flowers.

C. platycentra (plat-tiss-cent'-ruh) meaning with a broad center; also called *C. ignea* (ig'-nee-uh) meaning fiery, flame-colored; common name, Firefly; best for quick flowering; flower color, red with black tip.

CYCAS (sye'-kus) Fern Palm or Sago Palm.

Cycas, an ancient plant, had forebears flourishing 200 million years past. The Fern palm, slow growing, of shrubby form, is an ornamental evergreen characterized by rigid leaves which grow from and conceal the base of a thick trunk. The most interesting facet of this genus is the handsome, decorative, large cone protruding from top center of the leaves; this, its flower, is different in size and color on male and female plants. Cycas prefers a bright-light site. The common name is derived from the features—some resemble the fern, in spreading habit, others the palm in similarity of foliage.

Family Tree: Cycadaciae (sye-kad-ay'-see-ay) Cycas family; native of many tropical and subtropical areas.

Foliage: stiff leaves in alternate pattern, form rosette from base; spreading habit.

Size: up to 12′ (3.65 m), depending on species.

Location: WINTER—eastern exposure.

SUMMER—*Inside:* eastern exposure. *Outside:* northern exposure.

FALL: site in eastern exposure.

Dormancy: none, really, but rests lightly through fall and winter.

Water: an extremely important part of the culture of these plants; be guided by the following: ordinarily, water thoroughly, allowing moderate drying between waterings; never allow to dry out completely. Be aware of cool weather, when slower evaporation should mean less frequent watering. Use room-temperature water only.

Mist: daily, twice a day if possible; use room-temperature water.

Humidity: very high, 60%-70%, especially March through September.

Air circulation: essential for super success.

Feed: very, very weak solution of mild liquid manure (cut recommendation of manufacturer to 2/3), every 3 weeks.

Soil: 2 parts standard potting mix, 1 part vermiculite, 2 parts peat moss.

Temperature: Day—68°-75°F (20°-23°C). Night—50°-60°F (10°-15°C).

Potbound: very happy; do not pot-on until root system is 80% of pot content; best done in February or March. Roots adhere to interior pot walls, therefore, to avoid excessive injury, ease them gently loose. Rapping pot against end of a table is an aid, as well as running a spatula around inside of pot, pressing against pot wall with tool to avoid slipping into root ball. Set plant on 1½″ (37 mm) layer of gravel, then add soil.

Mature plants: wash foliage at least every 3 weeks. Remove yellowed or withered leaves as they appear.

Propagate: by seed, or by dormant suckers, in late spring, very early summer.

Insect alert: mealybugs, aphids, thrips, red spider. Control with soap and water remedy; repeat every 3 days until eradicated.

Notable: needs coolness at roots; use pebble, water, and tray method for cooler temperature and high humidity; best grown in clay pots (clay porosity allows evaporation, aiding in cooling roots); if leaves droop from too dry soil, they cannot be revived; leaves of young plants cannot stand water on them; leaves bruise easily so plant should

Cycas circinnalis,
Fern Palm

be located where it will not touch or be touched; do not use pesticides, which will kill insects and your plant too.

C. circinnalis (ser-sin-nay′-liss) Fern palm; shiny, leathery, dark green leaves, shaped like fern fronds, but appearance and texture more like palm; leaves 2′ (.60 m) wide, 8′ (2.45 m) long, grow up and out from thick trunk, a few inches high; male has 2′ (.60 m) long red cone at top of trunk, female a 1′ (.30 m), buff-colored cone; faster growing than C. revoluta; to 12′ (3.65 m) tall; native to East and West Indies.

C. revoluta (rev-oh-lew′-tuh) meaning rolled back from the margin (the leaves); common name, Sago palm; crown of leaves to 5′ (1.52 m) long; composed of many shiny, green, narrow, sharp-pointed leaflets 5″ (127 mm) long; male cone 18″-20″ (.45-.55 mm), female a semiglobular head; extremely slow growing, to 10′ (3 m) tall; native to Japan.

CYCLAMEN PERSICUM (sik′-lam-en per′-sik-um) Sowbread, Shooting Star, Poor Man's Orchid.

You may have my African Violet but, please, don't take my Cyclamen; a tuberous plant known for heart-shaped, dark green leaves and waxy, impressive flowers on gracefully statured, upright stems. Historic, it is recorded as far back as 1597. From the Greek *kayklos* "circle," flower stems circle down to soil in some species, for "planting" seeds when blooming is finished. Cool temperatures and watering attention give preservation for months of exquisite blooms. A new variety, Cyclamen Pluck, blooms year-round.

Family Tree: Primulaceae (prim-ew-lay′-see-ay) Primrose family; native to Europe, North Africa, Syria.

Foliage: thick, dark green leaves are heart or kidney shaped; some species have silvery or marbled markings.

Flower: 2″-3″ (50-76 mm) flowers borne singly on long stalks; single, double, and fringed blooms with petals sweeping up like butterfly wings; colors range in pinks, reds, white, purples, and salmons; blooms mid-autumn until spring, depending on species and culture.

Size: 10″-15″ (.27-.38 mm), depending on species.

Location: WINTER—eastern exposure.

SUMMER—*Inside:* eastern exposure. *Outside:* northern exposure.

FALL: move indoors by mid-September; site in eastern exposure.

Dormancy: cessation of flowering in late spring; site in full shade, allow leaves to die back; remove dead stems and leaves by gently pulling, not cutting off; slowly diminish watering, keeping soil barely moist and from drying out completely between waterings; cease fertilizing.

Water: keep evenly moist.

Mist: daily, twice a day if possible.

Humidity: above normal, 50%-60%.

Air circulation: helpful condition.

Feed: mild liquid manure, weekly during growing period, mid-October through March, or when genus has ceased flowering.

Soil: 2 parts standard potting mix, 1 part perlite.

Temperature: Day—65°-78°F (18°-25°C). Night—55°-62°F (12°-16°C).

Potbound: repot after dormancy with fresh mix specified for this genus.

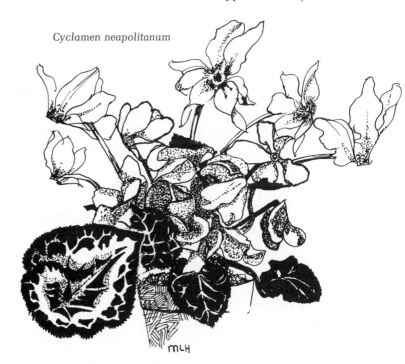

Cyclamen neapolitanum

MLH

Mature plants: pinch center out of young shoots for a wide plant. Too tall a plant for standing upright; stake and tie main trunk (leave small amount of slack in ties to eliminate potential of injury from tie cutting into fleshy stem). May be trained into standard form (tree form) or espaliered plant by proper pruning or pinching. Remove faded blossoms.

Propagate: by seeds.

Insect alert: aphids, mealybug, whitefly, cyclamen mite.

Notable: must have porous soil for good drainage; do not allow soil to dry out completely; can't take drafts; keep on lower side of recommended temperature to allow bud formation; flowers last longer in cooler temperatures; sowing seed to blooming cycle approximately 18 months.

C. europaeum (yew-roh-pee′-um) meaning European; known as European Cyclamen; leaf is kidney shaped, purple underneath, white-marbled top; flower: red or pink, fragrant, on 4″-6″ (100-150 mm) tall stems.

> Variety—Cyclamen Pluck: flowers are pink to rose shades, 2″ (50 mm) wide; blooms year-round.
> Variety—Europeum (yew-roh-pee′-um) rose red flowers on 6″ (150 mm) stem; foliage is heart shaped, white marbled, blooms almost year-round.

C. neapolitanum (nee-ap-ol-it-tay′-num) meaning of Naples; flowers white through all shades of pinks, on stem to 4″ (100 mm) high; leaves ivy shaped, white marbling.

CYPERUS ALTERNIFOLIUS (sye-peer′-us al-ter-ni-foh′-lee-us) Umbrella Plant.

A semiaquatic perennial, C. alternifolius can be grown in water culture; in any case, it must be absolutely and thoroughly wet at all times. It makes a fine tub plant, giving an umbrella effect, delicate and airy. A different species of *Cyperus, C. papyrus,* was utilized by ancient Egyptians for paper-making.

Family Tree: Cyperaceae (sye-peer-aye′-see-ay) Sedge family; native to Madagascar.

Foliage: 20 or more shiny, green leaves, narrow umbrella ribs; rise from tips of slender, base stalks; leaves 4″-8″ (100-200 mm) long.

Flower: small, greenish flowers, from center of leaves.

Size: to 4′ (1.20 m) tall.

Location: WINTER—southeastern or southwestern exposure.

SUMMER—*Inside*: northeastern or northwestern exposure. *Outside*: northeastern or northwestern exposure; protect fragile foliage from potentially damaging elements, preferably by overhang.

FALL: move indoors by mid-September; site in eastern or western exposure.

Dormancy: none, but light resting period October through February; slowly diminish watering, keeping soil barely moist; cut fertilizing program in half.

Water: daily, thoroughly and evenly, keeping constantly moist.

Mist: daily, twice a day when possible.

Humidity: above normal for happiness, 40%-45%.

Air circulation: helpful condition.

Feed: mild liquid manure every 2 weeks.

Soil: 2 parts standard potting soil, 1 part peat moss, 1 part perlite.

Temperature: Day—68°-80°F (20°-26°C). Night—55°-68°F (12°-20°C).

Potbound: repot or pot-on as needed and indicated by root growth being at least 50% of pot content.

Mature plants: remove withered roots, severing at base of plant. Rejuvenate old plants by cutting off all foliage at base.

Propagate: by division or stem cuttings; for latter, cut off leaf with ¼″ (6.3 mm) stem; float in water-filled dish, water at room temperature or about 70°F (21°C). Plantlets, small plants, will sprout; plant each in small pot of moist sharp sand for rooting.

Insect alert: mealybug, whitefly, mites, scale, slugs.

Cyperus alternifolius,
Umbrella Plant

Notable: good artificial light specimen, a total of 14 hours combined with natural; keep on cooler side of recommended temperatures; avoid water with lime.

C. alternifolius
> Variety—Gracilis (gras'-i-liss) meaning graceful, slender; smaller, thinner than *C. alternifolius*, to 2′ (.60 m) tall.
> Variety—Variegatus (var-ee-eh-gay'-tus) meaning variegated; striped green and white foliage.

C. diffusus (dif-few'-sus) meaning spreading; previously known as *C. laxus*; dwarf umbrella plant; native to Mauritius; 8-10 leaves atop each stalk, 4″-15″ (100-376 mm) long, ⅜″ (9 mm) wide; to 12″ (300 mm) tall; a rapid grower.

C. haspan (has'-pan)
> Variety—Viviparous (vi-vi-pa'-rus) Pygmy papyrus; many stiff grasslike leaves atop stalks, 2″-3″ (50-76 mm) long; plant 18″ (450 mm) tall.

C. papyrus (pa-pye'-rus) meaning a sedge used to make paper; Egyptian paper plant; flamboyant leaves; good as tub plant; needs space; native to Egypt; to 8′ (2.45 m) tall.

CYRTOMIUM (ser-toh'-mee-um) Holly Fern.

With fronds (leaves) resembling holly, this small genus really doesn't look like a fern. Cyrtomium is evergreen, a very sturdy plant, that will stand more neglect than other ferns; it will take full northern exposure if necessary.

Family Tree: Polypodiaceae (pol-ee-poh-dee-ay'-see-ay) common fern family; from Asia and Africa.

Foliage: dark green fronds are shiny, stiff, leathery, erect; leaves look like holly; up to 2½′ (.75 m) long, 8″ (.25 m) wide, segmented; young shoots are rolled, resembling what is referred to as a duck's tail.

Size: 1′-2′ (.30-.60 m) high.

Location: WINTER—eastern exposure.

SUMMER—*Inside*: eastern exposure. *Outside*: northern exposure.

FALL: move indoors by mid-September; site in eastern exposure.

Dormancy: none really, but rests lightly through fall and winter.

Water: an extremely important part of the culture of these plants; be guided by the following: ordinarily, water thoroughly, allowing moderate drying between waterings; never allow to dry out completely. Be aware of cool weather, when slower evaporation should mean less frequent watering. Use room-temperature water only.

Mist: daily, twice a day if possible; use room-temperature water.

Humidity: very high, 60%-70%; especially March through September.

Air circulation: essential for super success, but avoid drafts.

Feed: very, very weak solution of mild liquid manure (cut recommendation of manufacturer to 2/3), every 3 weeks.

Soil: 2 parts standard potting mix, 1 part vermiculite, 2 parts peat moss.

Temperature: Day—68°-75°F (20°-23°C). Night—50°-60°F (10°-15°C).

Potbound: very happy; do not pot-on (best done in February or March) until root system is 80% of pot content. Roots adhere to interior pot walls, therefore, to avoid excessive injury, work gently, easing them loose. Rapping pot against end of a table is an aid, as is running a spatula around inside of pot, pressing against pot wall with tool to avoid slipping into root ball. Wrap fronds of a large fern in newspaper for protection while handling. Set plant on 1½″ (37 mm) layer of gravel, then add soil.

Mature plants: if fern looks sad, cut back to 2″ (50 mm) above soil line; repot and proceed in proper culture. If aerial roots develop, cut them off. Wash foliage at least every 3 weeks. Remove yellowed or withered fronds as they appear.

Propagate: by division of mature plant, best done around March; or by spores attached to underside of leaflets (resemble little brown dots).

Insect alert: mealybugs, aphids, thrips, red spider; control with soap and water remedy. Repeat every 3 days until eradicated.

Notable: ferns need coolness at their roots, so use pebble, water, and tray method for cooler temperature and high humidity. Best to grow in clay pots, (porosity allows evaporation and aids in keeping roots cool); if fronds droop from too dry soil, they cannot be revived; fronds of young plants cannot stand water directly on them; fronds bruise easily so plant should be located where it will not touch or be touched. Ferns cannot stand pesticides, which will kill insects and your plant, too.

Cyrotomium falcatum,
Holly Fern

C. falcatum (fal-kay′-tum) meaning like a sickle, known as Japanese holly fern; may be listed or called *Polystichum falcatum*; smooth-edged, pointed leaflets are each 1″ (25 mm) wide; fronds to 2½″ (62 mm) long; plant 1′-2′ (.30-.60 m) high.

   Variety—Rochefordianum (rosh-ford-ee-ay′-num) fronds are sawtoothed, with deeper segments; very deep green, 2″ (50 mm) wide leaflets.

C. caryotideum (ka-ree-oh-tee′-dee-um) previously known as *Aspidium falcatum*; segments larger toothed than other species; fronds more arching.

DAPHNE ODORA (daff′-nee oh-doh′-ruh) Winter Daphne. As indicated by the name of the species, odora is delightfully sweet-smelling and fragrant. A very decorative shrub type genus, some with summer berries of bright red to complement the profusion of delicate blooms through winter. Know that it is poisonous if taken internally. Greek mythology has it that a river nymph, Daphne, prayed for help in escaping Apollo by whom she was being pursued. Her safety was ensured by her transformation into a laurel bush, which in turn became sacred to Apollo.

Family Tree: Thymelaeaceae (thy-mel-ay-ay-see′-ay) Mezereum family; native to China, Japan, and Europe.

Foliage: 2″-3″ (50-76 mm) long, shiny, leathery, green leaves.

Flower: ½″ (12.70 mm) wide, pink to reddish purple, paling to light pink or pink-tinged white in interior habitat.

Size: 1′-4′ (.30-1.20 m).

Location: WINTER—full sun.

SUMMER—*Inside and Outside:* full sun.

FALL: move inside by mid-September; site in full sun.

Dormancy: none, actually; merely a light resting period in late winter and early spring.

Water: thoroughly, after soil has dried out completely.

Mist: daily, lightly, not directly on blossoms.

Humidity: normal, 35%-40%.

Air circulation: helpful condition.

Feed: once each in mid-spring and mid-fall, with liquid acid fertilizer; select a 21-7-7.

Soil: 2 parts standard potting mix, 1 part peat moss, 1 part perlite.

Temperature: Day—62°-68°F (16°-20°C). Night—40°-45°F (4°-7°C).

Potbound: very happy; keep plant in as small a pot as possible.

Mature plants: better bloom if stems pinched back as they become straggly; pinch off to point where plant retains compact, uniform shape. Want wide plant, pinch center out of young shoots.

Propagate: in August or September, root stem cuttings in moist sand or perlite; or air layer; seed propagation is more difficult in the home for this plant.

Insect alert: aphids, mealybug, scale.

Notable: never allow soil to be soggy. Beware with children—all parts of this poisonous plant are fatal if consumed.

D. indica (in′-dick-uh) and *D. sinensis* (sin-nen′-sis) the same species as *D. odora*, but have different origins—as the names indicate: "from India" and "from China" respectively.

D. mezereum (mee-zeer′-ee-um) from old Persian, for deadly or poisonous; native to Europe and Siberia; to 3′ (.90 m) tall; commonly called February Daphne; leaves 3″

*Daphne odora,
Winter Daphne*

(76 mm) long; purple, pink, red, or white flowers in clusters, blooming on after leaves have dropped in fall, on leafless branches; leaves reappear in spring; red berries form in summer.

DAVALLIA (da-val'-lee-uh) Rabbit's Foot or Hare's Foot Fern.

This is an epiphytic or air plant, good for basket culture or can be grown on pieces of bark. A smaller fern genus, it takes its name from the resemblance of fuzzy rhizomes (rootstock) to rabbit feet. The rhizomes creep decoratively over surface and over pot rims.

Davallia fejeensis plumosa

Family Tree: Polypodiaceae (pol-ee-poh-dee-ay'-see-ay) Common fern family; native of tropical Asia and the South Pacific.

Foliage: finely segmented, graceful and feathery; most species green; fronds droop when mature.

Size: 1'-2' (.30-.60 m).

Location: WINTER—eastern exposure.

SUMMER—*Inside:* eastern exposure. *Outside:* northern exposure.

FALL: move indoors by mid-September; site in eastern exposure.

Dormancy: none, really, but rests lightly through fall and winter.

Water: an extremely important part of the culture of these plants; be guided by the following: ordinarily, water thoroughly, allowing moderate drying between waterings; never allow to dry out completely. Be aware of cool weather, when slower evaporation should mean less frequent watering. Use room-temperature water only.

Mist: daily, twice a day if possible; use room-temperature water.

Humidity: very high, 60%-70%, especially March through September.

Air circulation: essential for super success, but avoid drafts.

Feed: very, very weak solution of mild liquid manure (cut recommendation of manufacturer to 2/3), every 3 weeks.

Soil: 2 parts standard potting mix, 2 parts vermiculite, 1 part peat moss.

Temperature: Day—68°-75°F (20°-23°C). Night—50°-60°F (10°-15°C).

Potbound: happy; pot-on when rhizomes become crowded; or divide into several plants and repot; best done in February or March.

Mature plants: if fern looks sad, cut back to 2" (50 mm) above soil line; repot and proceed in proper culture. If aerial roots develop, cut them off. Wash foliage at least every 3 weeks. Remove yellowed or withered fronds as they appear.

Propagate: the use of rhizomes by potting sections is the easiest method; set on soil surface and barely cover with more potting mix; top of rhizome should be elevated above rim of pot.

Insect alert: mealybugs, aphids, thrips, red spider. Control with soap and water remedy, repeat every 3 days until eradicated.

Notable: ferns need coolness at their roots, so use pebble, water, and tray method for cooler temperature and high humidity; best to grow in clay pots (porosity allows evaporation and aids in keeping roots cool). If fronds droop from too dry soil, they cannot be revived; fronds of young plants cannot stand water directly on them; fronds bruise easily so plant should be located where it will not touch or be touched. Ferns cannot stand pesticides, which will kill insects and your plant, too.

D. bullata (bul-lay'-tuh) Squirrel's Foot fern or Ball Fern; from Japan and Java; rhizomes have deep red or brownish scales; gracefully arching fronds have toothed segments, leaflets 8"-12" (.25-.30 m) long, 4"-8" (.12-.25 m) wide, triangle shaped; vivid green; fronds are deciduous.

D. canariensis (ka-ner-ee-en'-siss) Hare's Foot fern; rhizomes are obese, creeping over pot rims; light green fronds 12″ (.30 m) long, up to 12″ (.30 m) wide; coarse, leathery texture.

D. fejeensis plumosa (fee-gee-en′-siss plu-moh′-suh) meaning feathery; from the Fiji Islands; erect stems; vivid green fronds are delicate and lacy, triangular in shape, 6″-9″ (.12-.27 m) long, up to 12″ (.30 m) wide; mature fronds have graceful, gently pending nature; hairy rhizomes ¼″ (6.3 mm) thick are covered with white through tan scales; soil for this species should be 2 parts sharp sand, 1 part each of standard potting mix, peat moss, vermiculite. This species grows very, very large, yet remains handsome in its airy fineness.

D. pentaphylla (pen-ta-fill′-uh) means 5 petaled; from Java; a wiry, miniature fern; fronds usually have 5 segments, are wavy-toothed, up to 6″ (.15 m) long and ½″ (12 mm) wide; young fronds are almost metallic-colored, mature are a deep, rich green.

DIEFFENBACHIA (deef-fen-bak′-ee-uh) Dumbcane; nickname: Mother-in-law plant.

The Dumbcane, an ornamental, evergreen foliage plant, was classified previously as *D. brasiliensis*, and may be listed or referred to by this name. This genus has boldly patterned colorations and designs according to species. A sizable plant, it prefers low light sites. Leaves and stems are toxic, causing temporary swelling of mucous membranes—slaves once were forced to eat the plant as painful punishment.

Family Tree: Araceae (uh-ray′-see-ay) Arum family; from South America and West Indies.

Foliage: large oblong green leaves to 18″ (.45 m), green with yellow, white and gold in various patterns, depending on species; thick stemmed; of erect growing habit.

Flower: rarely blooms in interior environments.

Dieffenbachia picta,
Variable Tuftroot

Size: 2½′-8′ (.75-2.45 m), depending on species.

Location: WINTER—northeastern or northwestern exposure. SUMMER—*Inside:* northern exposure. *Outside:* northern exposure; site in shelter to protect foliage. FALL: move indoors by mid-September; site in northeastern or northwestern exposure.

Dormancy: none, but a resting period of slower growth during winter months of less intensity; generally October through February; slowly diminish watering, plant will indicate needs as determined by environmental conditions; develop sensitivity to feel of soil moisture level; cease fertilizing.

Water: thoroughly and evenly, allowing soil to dry out between waterings.

Mist: daily, twice a day when possible.

Humidity: above normal for happiness, 45%-55%.

Air circulation: helpful condition.

Feed: mild liquid manure every 2 weeks.

Soil: standard potting soil.

Temperature: Day—70°-80°F (21°-26°C). Night—62°-68°F (16°-20°C).

Potbound: very happy; pot-on only when root growth of plant is 80%, soil 20% of pot content; top- or side-dress yearly, preferably in spring.

Mature plants: if plant becomes too tall, cut growing ends; start in rooting media. Remove dried or withered leaves as they appear (tendency to shed bottom leaves).

Propagate: by stem cuttings or air layering.

Insect alert: mealybug, red spider, scale, thrip, aphids.

Notable: do not allow soil to dry out completely; soil must have porosity, eliminating possibility of soggy conditions; use pebble, water, and tray method to maintain humidity level; sponge foliage at least every three weeks, always use room-temperature water; leaf shiners and/or oils are an *absolute no-no.*

D. amoena (ah-mee′-nuh) meaning charming, pleasing; charming dieffenbachia; 18″ (.45 m), blue green leaves with white blotches; height to 5′ (1.50 m); tolerates dim light.

D. bausei (bau′-see-eye) 18″ (.45 m), yellow green leaves with green edges, green and white spots.

D. bowmanii (boh-man′-ee-eye) chartreuse foliage mottled green; to 3′ (.90 m) high.

D. exotica (eg-za′-tik-uh) meaning not native, foreign; a small species, previously named, *D. arvida*; firm, dull green leaves with white blotches.

D. picta (pik′-tuh) meaning painted or variegated; or called by previous name, or *D. brasiliensis*; common name, Variable tuftroot; shiny, green leaves, to 12″ (.30 m); irregular white or yellow markings; to 4′ (1.20 m) high; one of the hardier, more attractive varieties, Rudolph Roehrs.

D. sequine (seg-wye′-nee) Sequin tuftroot; dark brown leaves, to 18″ (.45 m); with transparent white blotches; height to 6′ (1.80 m).

D. splendens (splen′-denz) meaning splendid; leaves with small white spots.

DIZYGOTHECA (dye-zye-goh-theek′-uh) False Aralia; nickname: Thread Leaf False Aralia.

False aralia, an evergreen foliage genus of graceful elegance, thrives in a bright light site. The growth habit is erect, yet visually, it looks very soft with a display of lacy semipendulous foliage. With simple cultural needs attended to, Dizygotheca will be pleasing for years in an interior environment.

Family Tree: Araliaceae (uh-ray-lee-ay′-see-ay) Aralia family; native to the New Hebrides Islands in the Pacific.

Foliage: slender compound leaflets 7″-10″ (177-254 mm) long with leathery texture and jagged edges; dark green with reddish tinge, mottled with white; leaves of alternate pattern.

Flower: small, greenish white; not usual in cultivated plants.

Size: to 5′ (1.50 m).

Location: WINTER—southeastern or southwestern exposure. SUMMER—*Inside:* eastern or western exposure. *Outside:* eastern or western exposure; in sheltered site for foliage protection. FALL: move indoors by mid-September; site in eastern or western exposure.

Dormancy: none, but a resting period of slower growth during winter months of less intensity, generally October through February; slowly diminish watering, plant will indicate needs as determined by environmental conditions; develop sensitivity to feel of soil moisture level; cease fertilizing.

Water: thoroughly and evenly, allowing soil to dry out between waterings.

Mist: daily, twice a day when possible.

Humidity: above normal for happiness, 45%-55%.

Air circulation: helpful condition.

Feed: mild liquid manure every 2 weeks.

Soil: 3 parts standard potting mix, 1 part peat moss, 1 part perlite.

Temperature: Day—70°-80°F (21°-26°C). Night—62°-68°F (16°-20°C).

Dizygotheca elegantissima,
False Aralia

Potbound: very happy; pot-on only when root growth of plant is 80%, soil 20% of pot content; top- or side-dress yearly, preferably in spring.

Mature plants: as plant ages the leaves become quite large and plant has tendency to drop lower leaves. If the plant does flower, it must be several years old prior to bud-setting.

Propagate: by stem cuttings or air layering.

Insect alert: mealybug, red spider, scale, thrip, aphids.

Notable: good artificial-light plant; total of 14-16 hours, combining natural and artificial light; do not allow soil to dry out completely; soil must have porosity, eliminating possibility of soggy conditions; use pebble, water, and tray method to maintain humidity level; sponge foliage at least every 3 weeks, always use room-temperature water; leaf shiners and/or oils are an *absolute no-no.*

D. elegantissima (el-e-gan-tiss′-im-uh) meaning most elegant or beautiful; threadleaf false aralia; slender, finger-like leaves are dark green to reddish with white spots; to 2′ (.60 m) high.

D. veitchii (veech′-ee-eye) native to New Caledonia; leaflets have wavy margins, marked with white and red; leaves slim and narrow.

DRACAENA (dra-seen′-uh).

Many species of the Dracaena genus are known and owned. Form and size vary greatly. These decorative, evergreen foliage plants, especially those with treelike proportions, merit their popularity. They are slow growing and adaptable to adverse conditions and need minor attention. They add nature's warmth to an anterior site for a good span of years.

Family Tree: Liliaceae (lil-ee-ay′-see-ay) Lily family; from tropical Africa.

Foliage: narrow to broad, sword-shaped leaves, usually clustered on stalk, some with stripes and speckled markings; mostly erect in habit of growth but with graceful arching of foliage.

Size: to 20′ (6 m).

Location: WINTER—southeastern or southwestern exposure. SUMMER—*Inside:* northeastern or northwestern exposure. *Outside:* northeastern or northwestern exposure; site in shelter to protect foliage. FALL: move indoors by mid-September; site in eastern or western exposure.

Dormancy: none, but a resting period of slower growth during winter months of less intensity; generally October through February; slowly diminish watering, plant will indicate needs as determined by environmental conditions; develop sensitivity to feel of soil moisture level; cease fertilizing.

Water: thoroughly and evenly, allowing soil to dry out between waterings.

Mist: daily, twice a day when possible.

Humidity: above normal for happiness, 45%-55%.

Air circulation: helpful condition.

Feed: mild liquid manure every 2 weeks.

Soil: standard potting soil.

Temperature: Day—70°-80°F (21°-26°C). Night—62°-68°F (16°-20°C).

Potbound: very happy; pot-on only when root growth of

plant is 80%, soil 20% of pot content; top- or side-dress yearly, preferably in spring.

Mature plants: if plant becomes too tall, cut growing ends and start in rooting media. Remove dried or withered leaves as they appear.

Propagate: by stem cuttings or air layering.

Insect alert: mealybug, red spider, scale, thrip, aphids.

Notable: good artificial-light plant; total of 14-16 hours, combining natural and artificial light; do not allow soil to dry out completely; soil must have porosity, eliminating possibility of soggy conditions; use pebble, water, and tray method to maintain humidity level; sponge leaf foliage at least every three weeks, always use room-temperature water; shiners and/or oils are an *absolute no-no.*

D. deremensis (der-e-men'-siss) rosette of green leaves, 2″ (50 mm) wide, 2′ (.60 m) long; 2′-15′ (.60-4.50 m) high; upright growth.

    Variety—Janet Craig: shiny dark green leaves; strap-like, 12″-18″ (.30-.45 m) long, 2″ (50 mm) wide.

    Variety—Warnecker (war'-nek-ee-eye): stiff, swordlike leaves; gray green with white stripes, 8″-12″ (.25-.30 m) long; good in dim light.

D. draco (dray'-koh) Dragontree; thick, stiff, pointed leaves, 18″-24″ (.45-.60 m) long, 1½″ (37 mm) wide, silvery green; young plant forms rosette, as it matures forms stubby trunk; 3′-4′ (.90-1.20 m) high.

D. fragrans (fray'-granz) lance-shaped, shiny green leaves

Dracaena

in terminal rosette; unbranched young plant becomes tree and branching; to 20′ (6 m) high.

    Variety—Massangeana: slightly arched leaves, 18″-36″ (.45-.90 m) long, 2″-3″ (50-76 mm) wide, broad yellow stripe down center; to 6′ (1.80 m) tall.

D. godseffiana (god-sef-fee-ay'-nuh) Gold dust dracaena; flat oval leaves, dark green, with creamy yellow speckles that fade to white, pairs or whorls of 3 leaves on thin, wiry stems, form horizontal tiers; bushy, branching, to 2½′ (.75 m) high.

    Variety—Florida Beauty: mainly yellow or white leaves.

D. goldieana (gold-ee-ay'-nuh) Goldie dracaena; dark green, white-striped leaves, large, branching; to 3′ (.90 m) high.

D. hookeriana (hook-er-ee-ay'-nuh) thick, glossy, sword-shaped leaves, dark green with translucent white edges, 2′ (.60 m) long, 2″ (50 mm) wide; slow growing; to 6′ (1.80 m) tall.

D. marginata (mar-jin-ay'-tuh) Red-margined dracaena or Spanish dagger; terminal rosettes of red-edged leaves, 12″-15″ (.30-.38 m) long, ½″ (12 mm) wide; slender-branched trunk; to 8′ (2.45 m) high.

D. sanderiana (san-der-ee-ay'-nuh) Sanders dracaena; narrow, lance-shaped, twisted leaves, gray green with broad white edges, 7″-10″ (177-254 mm) long; tall, slender stems; 4′-5′ (1.20-1.50 m) tall.

    Variety—Borinquensis: leaf color reversed, milky center flanked by narrow white stripes, green edges.

ECHEVERIA (ek-eh-veer'-ee-uh).

All succulents, these good looking plants are of very easy culture and maintenance. They prefer full sun and a small-ish site. The many species include wide range of greens, many textures of foliage. Lovely flowers, usually tube-shaped, grouped, clustered, or spiked, bloom spring or summer, depending on species.

Family Tree: Crassulaceae (krass-yew-lay'-see-ay) Orpine family; native to tropical America.

Foliage: fleshy, generally thick, green leaves in rosette form.

Size: up to 2′ (.60 m).

Location: WINTER—southern exposure.

SUMMER—*Inside and Outside:* southern exposure.

FALL: move indoors by mid-September; site in southern exposure.

Dormancy: none, but a resting period October through February; water only enough to keep leaves from shrivelling; cease fertilizing.

Water: allow soil to become quite dry between thorough, even waterings, March through September.

Mist: daily, very lightly, around plant but not directly on it.

Humidity: low, 20%-25%.

Air circulation: helpful condition.

Feed: monthly with mild liquid manure, April through July.

Soil: 1 part standard potting mix, 2 parts sharp sand.

Temperature: Day—68-80°F (20°-26°C). Night—50°-70°F (10°-21°C).

Potbound: normal; repot or pot-on when overcrowded appearance of foliage or root growth is 50% of pot content; best done in early spring prior to new growth.

Mature plants: older plants often lose bottom leaves. Plant frequently develops branching stems.

Propagate: by offshoots, or by leaf or stem cuttings, preferably in September or October.

Insect alert: scale, mealybug.

Disease alert: root rot from overwatering.

Notable: soil must have excellent porosity; do not try to create humid conditions; normal interior air, even a dry site, is most suitable. *Most notable:* plants rot very easily. A good artificial-light plant, up to 16 hours combined natural and artificial light hours; do not allow soil to dry out completely.

*Echeveria Setosa,
Mexican Firecracker*

W.H.

E. affinis (af-fin'-iss) meaning related; dark greenish black foliage, red flowers.

E. amoena (a-meen'-uh) meaning charming, pleasing; lance-shaped bluish leaves ¾" (19 mm) long, coral red flowers rise from center on 8" (200 mm) stalks.

E. brittonii (bri-toh'-nee-eye) green yellow flowers, white leaves, 16" (.40 m) high.

E. candida (kan-did'-uh) meaning pure white, shining; small plant, white leaves, green yellow flowers.

E. derenbergii (der-en-berj'-ee-eye) Painted lady; smooth pale green leaves, red-edged, 1" (25 mm) long; yellow to orange flowers ½" (12 mm) long, bloom late winter, early spring.

E. elegans (ell'-eg-anz) meaning beautiful, elegant; previously known as *Cotyledon elegans*; called Mexican snowball; spoon-shaped, pale green leaves appear white because covered with waxy powder called bloom; pinkish flowers with yellow tips cluster on 8" (.25 m) stems.

E. gibbiflora (jib-ih-floh'-ruh) fringed echeveria; native to Mexico; oblong, blue green leaves with metallic bronze sheen, to 7" (.20 m) long; scarlet flowers last a long time, in late winter; 1'-2' (.30-.60 m) high.

E. glauca (glaw'-kuh) meaning with white or gray bloom, as on blue spruce; roundish leaves ¾" (19 mm), in basal rosettes; flowers pinkish outside and yellow inside; on reddish branches.

E. metallica (meh-tal'-li-kuh) meaning with metallic green; pinkish bronze leaves with white or reddish margins.

E. peacockii (pee-kok-ee'-eye) Peacock echeveria, previously named E. desmetiana; silvery blue leaves, red edges and tips.

E. pilosa (pye-loh'-suh) meaning hairy; softly, hairy green, red-tipped rosettes of leaves; orange flowers.

E. pulverulenta (pull-ver-oo-len'-tuh) meaning powdered or dust-covered; rosette 1'-2' (.30-.60 m) high; clusters of red flowers, covered with powdery white substance.

E. pulvinata (pull-vin-nay'-tuh) Chenille plant; leaf rosette densely covered with white hairs, become reddish at leaf edges when in cool site; older plants may develop irregularly branching stems 12"-18" (.30-.45 m) with rosette at tip; clusters of red flowers in winter; to 7" (.20 m). Direct sun only in winter, eastern or western exposure other times. Propagate this species, in addition to other methods, by rosettes at tips of straggly stems.

E. secunda (sek-kund'-uh) meaning side flowering; oval blue green leaves 1"-2" (25-30 mm) long, in saucer-shaped rosettes; reddish flowers on 15" (.38 m) stems.

E. setosa (seh-toh'-suh) meaning beset with bristles, called Mexican firecracker; stemless, hairy green leaves in single globular rosette; red and yellow flowers.

EPISCIA (ep-piss'-ee-uh) Flame Violet, Peacock Plant. Gracefully cascading runners carry small plants from creeping stems. This relative of the African Violet is grown primarily for its handsome foliage. If given warm humid air, it will produce an abundance of its showy blooms.

Family Tree: Gesneriaceae (jes-ner-ee-ay'-see-ay) Gesneria family; from Colombia and Brazil.

Foliage: 2"-3" (50-76 mm) veined in contrasting colors such as green leaves in silver; somewhat quilted texture; some hairy, some smooth, or glossy; some copper-colored varieties.

Flower: ½"-1½" (12-37 mm) flowers bloom from March through August; colors are brilliant hues of pink, lavender, yellow, red, blue, and white.

Size: 14"-20" (.36-.55 m).

Location: WINTER—western exposure.

SUMMER—*Inside and Outside:* eastern exposure.

FALL: move indoors by mid-September.

Dormancy: period starts fall through late winter; slowly diminish watering to maintain barely moist soil; cease fertilizing; leave in set site.

Water: keep evenly moist.

Mist: daily, twice daily during growing season but not directly on leaves; mist around plant not on plant.

Humidity: high, 65%-75%; very moist.

Air circulation: helpful condition.

Feed: fertilize every 2 weeks, April through August with mild liquid manure.

Soil: 1 part standard potting mix, 2 parts peat moss, 1 part sharp sand or perlite.

Temperature: Day—72°-80°F (22°-26°C). Night—65°-70°F (18°-21°C).

Potbound: normal; pot-on when plant indicates by root system overbalancing soil content of pot.

Mature plants: at end of blooming period pinch out runners and cut back plants to increase bloom and leaf size.

Propagate: from seed or from runners or rooted stem cuttings, latter two any time; also from leaf cuttings (place in moist vermiculite, sand, or water culture).

Insect alert: nematodes, leaf miners, mealybugs, mites.

Disease alert: root rot, crown and stem rot, leaf spot disease—all can be caused by overwatering.

Notable: temperatures below 55°F (12°C) are fatal to this genus, leaves will turn black; keep plant on pebbled tray with water for good humidity; do not allow soil to become soggy or to dry out completely; good artificial light specimen; a total of 14-16 hours of combined natural and artificial light is the best cultural program; good light increases length of flowering period.

E. lilacina (li-las'-i-nuh) meaning lilac colored; dark bronze leaves; lavender flowers.

E. punctata (punk-tay'-tuh) meaning clotted with depressions; spotted, green leaves, purple-spotted white flowers.

E. cupreata (koop-ree-ay'-tuh) meaning copper-colored; copper foliage with white hairs; scarlet flowers.

E. diantiflora (dy-ant-tiff-loh'-ruh) downy green leaves; white flowers.

E. reptans (repp'-tanz) meaning creeping, rooting stems; native to Colombia; ground level rosette of leaves, green and white variegated with roundish teeth; red flowers; needs high humidity.

E. cultivars

    Acajou (ak-kay-yooh) dark brown leaves with veins of silver green; orange red flowers.

    Emerald Queen: emerald leaves with glossy silver bands; red blooms.

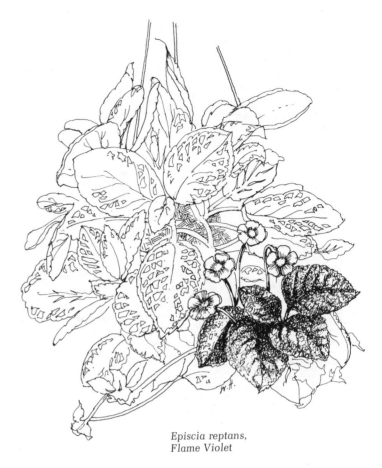

Episcia reptans,
Flame Violet

ERANTHEMUM (eer-anth'-em-mum) Blue Sage.

A lovely, unusual shrub small enough for most sites. Blue Sage will bloom faithfully and vigorously with minor care, adding fresh visual dimensions to wearisome winter days.

Family Tree: Acanthaceae (uh-can-they-see'-ay) Acanthus family; from India.

Foliage: 3″ (76 mm) long, slim, pointed leaves; green with a silvery gloss.

Flower: intensely blue, rose, or purple tubular blossoms 1″ (25 mm) across; arranged on spikes; bloom in winter and early spring.

Size: 12″-36″ (.30-.90 m).

Location: WINTER—full sun; set in southern exposure.

SUMMER—*Inside:* partial shade; set in eastern to southern exposure for direct rays of morning sun. *Outside:* partial shade; set in eastern exposure or under a protective structure where plant receives strong light but no direct rays.

FALL: move indoors by mid-September.

Dormancy: period starts after flowering, continues into March; cut back to 5″ (127 mm) at onset of dormancy; slowly diminish watering until soil is maintained at a barely moist level; cease fertilizing.

Water: keep soil evenly moist throughout flowering period.

Eranthemum nervosum,
Blue Sage

Mist: daily; twice daily during growing time.

Humidity: very high for happiness, 60%-70%.

Air circulation: helpful condition.

Feed: mild liquid manure every 2 weeks during growing season, April through January; or until flowering ceases.

Soil: 2 parts standard potting mix, 1 part dried manure.

Temperature: Day—70°-80°F (21°-26°C). Night—60°-65°F (15°-18°C).

Potbound: normal; pot-on when root system overbalances soil content.

Mature plants: better bloom if stems pinched back as they become straggly; pinch off to point where plant retains compact, uniform shape. Pinch center out of young shoots for wide plant. Too tall a plant for standing upright; stake and tie main trunk (leave small amount of slack in ties to eliminate potential of injury by tie cutting into fleshy stem).

Propagate: from 2″ (50 mm) stem cuttings of new April growth, in moist, sandy peat at 75°-80°F (23°-26°C), or by root cuttings in spring and summer in moist vermiculite.

Offspring established: cuttings will bloom the year after they are started.

Disease alert: overwatering will cause leaf drop.

Notable: a fast grower, keep in large pot; hard pruning essential, otherwise it will become a very leggy eyesore.

E. watti (watt′-ee) purple flowers; 12″-24″ (.30-.60 m) high; green leaves with metallic sheen.

E. nervosum (ner-voh′-sum) meaning having distinct veins or nerves on leaves; 18″-36″ (.45-.90 m) tall; blue or rose flowers 1″ (25 mm) across, in winter and spring; previously known as *E. pulchellum*, meaning "beautiful."

EUCHARIS GRANDIFLORA (yew-kar-is grand-dee-floor′-uh) Amazon Lily.

Grandiflora means that this species has larger flowers than other species of this genus. This continually flowering plant is a favorite of the commercial florist. In this long-lasting flower there is a likeness to the pure white daffodil, but these blooms are clustered at the top of a tall, leafless stem with a heady fragrance to permeate your interior. The special cultural needs of a warm temperature year-round and high humidity are the considerations for questioning success in your inside environment.

Family Tree: Amaryllidaceae (am-ah-rill-ee-day-see′-ay) Amaryllis family; native to the Colombian Andes in South America.

Foliage: 20″ (.55 m) flower stalks are set among shiny broad leaves 8″ (.25 m) up to 1′ (.30 m) long and 6″ (150 mm) wide; leaves are dark, evergreen, in an alternate arrangement.

Flower: fragrant white clusters of 3-6 flowers, each 2″-5″ (50-127 mm) across; appear 2 or 3 times annually; central cup is surrounded by broad spreading, ragged-edged lobes; sometimes slightly tinged with green stripes; strongly scented; blooms mid-spring to early summer.

Size: 18″-24″ (.45-.60 m).

Location: WINTER—southeastern exposure.

SUMMER—*Inside:* eastern exposure. *Outside:* northern exposure.

FALL: move indoors by mid-September.

Dormancy: period starts early winter; plants rest until early spring; then scrape away some top soil and provide with fresh layer of potting mix; throughout dormancy, water only enough to keep leaves from wilting; slowly diminish watering late fall; cease fertilizing early winter.

Water: keep very evenly moist; check frequently for needs.

Mist: daily; leaves only, with room-temperature water; twice a day when possible during growing season of March through October.

Humidity: above normal, 40%-50%.

Air circulation: helpful condition.

Feed: every week during growing season, March through October; mild liquid manure.

Soil: 1 part standard potting mix, 2 parts peat moss, 1 part perlite; add a small amount of bone meal.

Temperature: Day—75°-85°F (23°-29°C). Night—65°-70°F (18°-21°C).

Potbound: happy, does best in this condition; repot or pot-on every 2 years, having bulb tips even with surface of the soil; disturb roots as little as possible.

Propagate: by separating and planting small bulbs that develop beside larger ones and have at least one leaf; place 4 to 6 of them in an 8″ (.25 m) pot and water lightly until growth begins.

Notable: temperature must remain warm, close to 70°F (21°C) year-round; humidity must be kept very high, 70%; never allow soil to dry out completely.

*Eucharis grandiflora,
Amazon Lily*

E. candida (kan'-did-uh) means pure white (the flowers); blooms in autumn; grows to 18″ (.45 m).

E. fosterii (foss-ter-ee'-eye) miniature form having pendulous white flowers; glossy leaves; plant to 8″ (.25 m) high.

E. mastersii (mas'-ter-see-eye) grows to 15″ (.38 m); has white blooms in March.

E. sanderi (sand'-er-ee-eye) same as mastersii.

EUONYMUS (yew-on'-im-us) Spindle Tree, Winter Creeper.

Euonymus species suitable to interior environments are good subjects for pruning to shapes for bonsai. A wealth of selection is available in foliage variation, most all displaying an attractive growth pattern. Culture is of easy maintenance and total attention nonproblematic. A bright site, not sizable, is the main consideration.

Family Tree: Celastraceae (sel-last'-ray-see-ay) Staff-tree family; native to Japan.

Foliage: very small, waxy leaves, colored solid shades of green, or variegated with white through cream shadings of various patterns, all depending on species.

Flower: nondescript, massed, small, white.

Fruit: showy berries, orange to red.

Size: up to 4′ (1.20 m), depending on species.

Location: WINTER—southeastern or southwestern exposure.
SUMMER—*Inside:* northeastern or northwestern exposure.
Outside: northeastern or northwestern exposure; site in sheltered area to protect foliage.
FALL: move indoors by mid-September; site in eastern or western exposure.

Dormancy: none, a resting time during winter months, generally September through March; slowly diminish watering; plant will indicate needs by appearance, becoming yellow or brittle-leafed; develop sensitivity to feel of soil moisture level; cease fertilizing.

Water: evenly and thoroughly, allowing soil to dry between waterings.

Mist: daily, twice a day when possible.

Humidity: normal, 30%-35%.

Euonymus japonicus,
Evergreen Euonymus

Air circulation: essential for good cultural response.

Feed: every 2 weeks with mild liquid manure throughout growing season, April through August.

Soil: 3 parts standard potting mix, 1 part sharp sand or perlite.

Temperature: Day—68°-78°F (20°-25°C). Night—40°-64°F (4°-17°C).

Potbound: slightly for happiness, when root growth is approximately 65% of pot content; best repotted or potted-on before new growth develops, in March.

Mature plants: retain shape by attentive pruning, anytime.

Propagate: by cuttings, best in fall or winter.

Insect alert: aphid, mealybug, mite, scale, leaf miner.

Disease alert: overly high humidity in too cool temperatures can cause mildew.

Notable: soil must have porosity; no soggy conditions; keep on lower side of recommended temperatures; important to wipe or wash foliage every two weeks; good air circulation needed for top performance; do not over-pot, use pot only 2″ (50 mm) larger than previous housing.

E. japonicus (ja-pon'-ik-us) Evergreen euonymus; native to Japan; 1″ (25 mm) bright green leaves; 3′ (.90 m) tall; evergreen; small white flowers.

  Variety—Albo-marginatus (al'-boh-mar-jih-nay'-tus) Pearl-edge euonymus; light green leaves, narrowly edged with white.

  Variety—Argenteo-variegatus (ar-jen'-tee-oh-var-ee-eh-gay'-tus) Silver queen euonymus; green leaves, broad white edges.

  Variety—Aureo-variegatus (aw-ree'-oh-var-ee-eh-gay'-tus) Yellow queen euonymus; yellow-edged leaves.

  Variety—Microphyllus variegatus (my-kroh-fil'-lus var-ee-eh-gay'-tus) small leaves, variegated green and white; dwarf.

EUPHORBIA PULCHERRIMA (yew-forb'-ee-uh pull-ker'-ri-ma) Poinsettia.

The Aztecs cultivated poinsettia as a symbol of purity; crimson dye was made from its colorful bracts (modified leaf attached to the flower stalk being a part of the flower head, frequently referred to, mistakenly, as the flower), as well as a fever medicine from its milky sap. Franciscan priests in the 17th century were first to use it in Christmas festivities, in a Nativity procession. With attention to a minor cultural oddity or two, very easy to understand and handle and requiring little time, poinsettias will bloom yearly, handsomely, so long as properly cared for. Joel Poinsett, first U.S. Minister to Mexico (1825-29) brought home cuttings of two wild plants, Mexican fire plant and what we now call Poinsettia. At first thought to be species of a new genus, they were found later to be of the genus Euphorbia.

Family Tree: Euphorbiaceae (yew-for-bee-ay'-see-ay) Spurge family; native of Mexico.

Foliage: plentiful, dark green leaves, elliptical or lance shaped, lobed, 3″-6″ (76-150 mm) long.

Flower: tiny greenish yellow nublike flowers in the center of large, colorful petallike bracts; colors white or pink, as well as the popular red; flowers and bracts appear in fall and may remain colorful for 3 or more months; bracts up to 1′ (.30 m) across.

Size: 9″ (.27 m) to 4′ (1.20 m) high.

Location: WINTER—full sun; set in southern exposure.

SUMMER—*Inside:* partial shade; set in eastern to southern exposure for direct rays of morning sun. *Outside:* partial shade; set in eastern exposure or under a protective structure where plant receives strong light but no direct rays.

FALL: move indoors by mid-September.

Dormancy: starts after flowering, when bracts have withered and dropped. Put plant in cool, dim frost-free site, keep soil barely moist; cease fertilizing. In May, along about Mother's Day, cut dried stalks back to 2″ (50 mm), shake soil from roots, and repot in soil as specified for this species; site in filtered sun, outside. Or, after flowers and bracts have withered, continue normal culture but cease fertilization; in mid-May, or along about Mother's Day, repot (not pot-on) in potting mix as specified for this species; cut stems back to 6″ (150 mm); site outside in filtered sunlight.

Water: keep thoroughly and evenly moist.

Mist: daily, twice daily if possible.

Humidity: above normal for happiness, 40%-50%.

Air circulation: helpful condition.

Feed: mild liquid manure weekly.

Soil: 2 parts standard potting mix, 1 part vermiculite, 1 part sphagnum moss.

Temperature: Day—65°-75°F (18°-23°C). Night—50°-60°F (10°-15°C).

Potbound: repot each spring, month of May.

Mature plants: keep soil thoroughly and evenly moist while in exterior site; turn ¼ around each week to keep plant in good form; early in September, within a week or two of Labor Day, resite plant indoors in full sun exposure. Resume fertilization program. To assure flowering for December holiday season, place plant in complete darkness for at least 14 hours daily, from late afternoon into following morning; set plant in darkened room or cover plant with an opaque plastic bag to provide dark hours; the 10 daily daylight hours must be exposure to full sun; continue culture for 40 days, beginning 4th week in September. This cultural practice is essential, for this span of total darkness is needed for the Poinsettia species to set buds. Resume normal culture after 40 days, remembering that full sun is now essential.

Propagate: by 6″ (150 m) cuttings in August; dip in rooting hormone, insert in 4″-5″ (100-127 m) pots containing moist mixture of 1 part vermiculite, 1 part standard potting mix; cover pot with plastic bag tied at top to create good humidity level; site in shade to avoid wilting.

Insect alert: red spider mite, aphids, mealybug, scale.

Disease alert: leaf drop (from overwatering or too sharp temperature change).

Notable: soil must be porous for good drainage; never allow overwatering to create soggy conditions; won't take drafts; keep on lower side of recommended temperatures; during flowering, cooler sites mean longer lasting flowers. Caution: do not set on tops of televisions or radiators, or near baseboard heat or air convectors, also avoid siting on windowsills and with line of drafts from open doors. When potted in plastic containers, Poinsettia cannot be watered thoroughly, only moderately and more frequently.

E. fulgens (ful′-jenz) meaning shining or glowing, usually scarlet; previously known as *E. jacquinaeflora* (jak-in-ee-floh′-ruh) scarlet plume; 2′ (.60 m) arching stems with narrow leaves; waxy, orange scarlet bracts, ½″ (12 mm) across; if happy, will produce a profusion of color; winter blooming, generally January through March.

Variety—Mikkeldawn: variegated pink and cream.

Euphorbia pulcherrima
Poinsettia

Euphorbia lactea,
Milk-Striped Euphorbia

Variety—Mikkelpink: clear pink.
Variety—Mikkelwhite: not as strong as others but very pretty.
Variety—Paul Mikkelsen: brilliant red.
   Note these varieties hold foliage and bracts for 3-6 months.

The following species of this family are different in that they are succulents. One finds the majority of these plants native to Africa and Asia. Note that it is the nature of some of these species to contain an acrid sap, milky in appearance, that must be kept out of eyes and open cuts. Of the over 1,600 species and varieties, those more commonly known are listed. Succulents can take higher temperatures: Day—70°-80°F (21°-26°C). Night—55°-65°F (12°-18°C).
Water: as for genus, but in winter months keep barely moist, allowing soil to dry out between waterings.
Feed: as for genus, ceasing fertilization October through February.
Potbound: repot or pot-on when root growth is 60% of pot content.
Soil: 2 parts standard potting mix, 1 part peat moss, 1 part perlite.
Propagate: by seed or stem cuttings.
   Any other cultural differences will be noted within the specific species.

E. lactea (lak'-tee-uh) Milk-Striped Euphorbia; nickname Dragon Bones; to 3' (.90 m); leafless triangular stems, streaked white; thorns; shaped like candelabra.
E. milii (mill'-ee-eye) Crown of Thorns; thorny shrub, 2'-3' (.60-.90 m) tall; ½" (12 mm) bright green leaves; ¼" (6 mm) red blossoms tip branches; may be referred to or listed previously as E. splendens.
E. obesa (oh-bee'-suh) Melon Spurge; nickname Basketball euphorbia; native to Indonesia; globular, to 8" (.25 m) across; 8 spineless ridges, looks like basketball; becomes elongated sphere with age.

EURYA JAPONICA (yew-ree'-uh ja-pon'-ik-uh).
Eurya prefers a growing culture similar to that of the Camellia, a relative; therefore, provide a cool environment and attention to proper cultural needs for success. Most attractive, evergreen foliage will suffice aesthetically while you await the blooming season. This species is native to the Himalayas.
Family Tree: Theaceae (thee-ay'-see-ay) Tea family; native to Asia and South America.
Foliage: alternate, leathery, glossy, roundish, toothed; green, yellow, and creamy white variegated, some red-tinged.
Flower: greenish white; very small; clusters.
Fruit: berrylike; black.
Size: up to 10' (3 m).
Location: WINTER—eastern exposure.
SUMMER—*Inside:* partial shade; set in eastern to southern exposure for direct rays of morning sun. *Outside:* partial shade; set in eastern exposure or under a protective structure where plant receives strong light but no direct rays.
FALL: move indoors mid-September.
Dormancy: only a slight slowing in early fall; slowly diminish watering, to about ⅓ less; allow plant to indicate

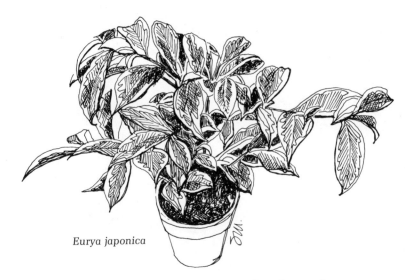

Eurya japonica

needs. Continue fertilizing, same quality but only monthly.
Water: keep soil constantly moist.
Mist: daily, twice a day if possible, with tepid water.
Humidity: high for happiness, 60%-65%.
Air circulation: helpful condition.
Feed: mild liquid fertilizer every 2 weeks, January through July; use acid balance, 21-7-7.
Soil: 1 part standard potting mix, 2 parts peat moss, 1 part perlite.
Temperature: Day—64°-68°F (17°-20°C). Night—45°-55°F (7°-12°C).
Potbound: repot only when root growth overbalances soil content, 75% to 25%.
Mature plants: when pruning for bushy plant, do so only after flowering and before new leaf growth. Plant may not bloom until 2 or 3 years old. Too tall a plant for standing upright, stake and tie main trunk (leave slack in ties to eliminate potential of injury from tie cutting into fleshy stem). Proper pruning or pinching produces standard form (tree form) or espaliered plant.
Propagate: by cuttings from half-ripe wood, set in damp vermiculite (best done in summer).
Insect alert: scale, mealybug, aphid, mite.
Disease alert: buds drop from incorrect temperature or soil moisture level, or from change in location.
Notable: best culture, site outside for summer months; soil must have good drainage; do not allow soggy soil conditions; avoid drafts. When repotting or potting-on, firm soil well, but do not compact it.

E. ochnacea (ok-nay'-ee-uh) native to China and Japan; may be referred to by its previous name, Cleyera japonica; shrub type, smooth-margined leaves; very fragrant, small, cream white flowers; large red berries.

x. FATSHEDERA (fats-hed'-er-uh) Tree Ivy, Aralia Ivy; nickname: Botanical Wonder.
The tree ivy is not of the ivy family, although the leaf resembles that of common ivy foliage. This evergreen foliage plant likes bright light areas, and can be trained as a bush type or vine type plant. Quite an interesting hybrid,

Fatshedera,
Tree Ivy

the result of an accidental crossing of two genera, in France in the early 1900s; the name is a combination of its two parents, Fatsia and Hedera (ivy). And quite unusual in that it is a plant resistant to mealybugs.

Family Tree: Araliaceae (a-ray-li-a'-see-ee) Aralia family; hybrid of France.

Foliage: glossy, dark green, shaped like the common ivy leaves, 3 to 5 lobes; smaller than Fatsia, larger than Ivy foliage; evergreen; upright shrub; eventually develops trailing habit.

Flower: inconspicuous, in autumn.

Fatsia japonica,
Castor Oil Tree

Size: to 15′ (4.50 m).

Location: WINTER—southeastern or southwestern exposure. SUMMER—*Inside:* northeastern or northwestern exposure. *Outside:* northeastern or northwestern exposure; site in shelter to protect foliage.

FALL: move indoors by mid-September; site in eastern or western exposure.

Dormancy: none; but a resting period of slower growth during winter months of less intensity; generally October through February; slowly diminish watering; plant will indicate needs as determined by environmental conditions; develop sensitivity to feel of soil moisture; cease fertilizing.

Water: moderately and evenly.

Mist: daily, twice a day when possible.

Humidity: above normal for happiness, 45%-55%.

Air circulation: helpful condition.

Feed: mild liquid manure every 2 weeks.

Soil: standard potting soil.

Temperature: Day—70°-80°F (21-26°C). Night—62°-68°F (16°-20°C).

Potbound: very happy; pot-on only when root growth of plant is 80%, soil 20% of pot content; top- or side-dress yearly; preferably spring.

Mature plants: if plant becomes too tall, cut growing ends and start in rooting media. Remove dried or withered leaves as they appear. Plant should bloom when several years old.

Propagate: by stem cuttings or air layering.

Insect alert: mealybug, red spider, scale, thrip, aphids.

Notable: good artificial light plant; total of 14-16 hours, combining natural and artificial light; do not allow soil to dry out completely; soil must have porosity, eliminating possibility of soggy conditions; use pebble, water, and tray method to maintain humidity level; sponge foliage at least every three weeks; always use room temperature water; leaf shiners and/or oils are an *absolute no-no.*

FATSIA JAPONICA (fat-see'-uh ja-pon'-ik-uh) Castor Oil Tree, Japan Fatsia; nickname: Fig-leaf Palm.

Previously referred to or listed as Aralia japonica and A. sieboldii, this genus is only one species, with two varieties of this species. Its evergreen foliage needs site of good, bright light. It is a vigorously growing plant of longevity, and a proud plant in its stately, truly handsome green foliage.

Family Tree: Araliaceae (uh-ray-lee-ay'-see-ay) Aralia family; native to Japan.

Foliage: shiny, up to 9 deeply cut lobes, to 16″ (.40 m) wide.

Flower: small, whitish flowers; grouped in long clusters.

Size: up to 4′ (1.20 m).

Location: WINTER—southeastern or southwestern exposure. SUMMER—*Inside:* northeastern or northwestern exposure. *Outside:* northeastern or northwestern exposure; site in shelter to protect foliage.

FALL: move indoors by mid-September; site in eastern or western exposure.

Dormancy: none, but a resting period of slower growth during winter months of less intensity, generally October through February; slowly diminish watering, plant will indicate needs as determined by environmental conditions; develop sensitivity to feel of soil moisture; cease fertilizing.

Water: thoroughly and evenly, allowing soil to dry out between waterings.

Mist: daily, twice a day when possible.

Humidity: above normal for happiness, 45%-55%.

Air circulation: helpful condition.

Feed: mild liquid manure every 2 weeks.

Soil: standard potting soil.

Temperature: Day—70°-80°F (21-26°C). Night—62°-68°F (16°-20°C).

Potbound: very happy; pot-on only when root growth of plant is 80%, soil 20% of pot content; top- or side-dress yearly, preferably spring.

Mature plants: if plant becomes too tall, cut growing ends and start in rooting media. Remove dried or withered leaves as they appear. Prune in late winter, around February, for better, fuller branching.

Propagate: by stem cuttings, air layering, or suckers. Root cuttings or suckers in damp mixture of equal parts of perlite and standard potting mix.

Insect alert: mealybug, red spider, scale, thrip, aphids.

Notable: good artificial-light plant; total of 14-16 hours, combining natural and artificial light; do not allow soil to dry out completely; soil must have porosity, eliminating possibility of soggy conditions; use pebble, water, and tray method to maintain humidity level; sponge foliage at least every three weeks, always use room-temperature water; shiners and/or oils are an *absolute no-no.* Keep on cooler side of recommended temperatures, particularly in winter rest period.

F. japonica
    Variety—Moserii (mos-er-ee'-eye) denser, more prolific foliage.
    Variety—Variegata (ver-i-eh-gay'-ta) medium green leaves, edges irregularly marked creamy white.

FAUCARIA TIGRINA (faw-kay'-ree-uh tig-rye'-nuh)
    Tiger's Jaw.

This genus was known previously as Mesembryanthemum. A small succulent, it is an absolutely almost carefree plant for full sun areas. Leaves have very shapely toothed edges.

Family Tree: Aizoaceae (ay-zoh-ay'-see-ay) Carpetweed family; native to South Africa.

Foliage: fleshy, gray green spotted white, white teeth along inner margins; in pairs of rosettes, to form low clumps.

Flower: yellow flowers, 2″ (50 mm) across bloom at top; in fall.

Size: 3″ (76 mm) high.

Location: WINTER—southern exposure.

SUMMER—*Inside and Outside:* southern exposure.

FALL: move indoors by mid-September; site in southern exposure.

Dormancy: none, although a resting period October through February; slowly diminish watering, just enough to keep leaves from shrivelling.

Water: allow soil to become quite dry between thorough, even waterings, March through September.

Mist: daily, very lightly, around plant, but not directly on it.

Humidity: low normal, 20%-25%.

Air circulation: helpful condition.

Feed: do not fertilize.

Soil: 1 part standard potting mix, 2 parts sharp sand.

Temperature: Day—68°-80°F (20°-26°C). Night—50°-70°F (10°-21°C).

Potbound: please do not disturb; do not repot or pot-on, ever!

Mature plants: growth of plant is determined by the water culture. Never moisten foliage.

Propagate: by seed or division; pot-up in soil as specified for this genus; do not have damp soil and do not water for 5 days after potting.

Insect alert: scale, mealybug.

Disease alert: root rot from overwatering.

Notable: soil must have excellent porosity; do not try to create humid conditions; normal interior air, even a dry site is most suitable. *Most notable:* plants rot very easily. A good artificial-light plant, up to 16 hours combined natural and artificial light hours; do not allow soil to dry out completely.

Faucaria tigrina,
Tiger's Jaw

FELICIA (fel-lish'-ee-uh) Blue Daisy, Blue Felicia, Blue Marguerite, Aster.

A showy genus, mostly full blooming all year; generally blue, always beautiful. Something for the totally sunny exposure; not much special care, a nip or pinch here and there and one delights in the delicate, daisylike profusion of this inside greenery. From the Latin *felix*, cheerful, referring to the vivid blooms.

Family Tree: Compositae (cum-poh'-see-tay) Composite family; from South Africa.

Foliage: knobby texture ½″ (12.70 mm) oval leaves.
Flower: 1″-3″ (25-76 mm) blossoms; yellow-centered daisies of sky blue or white; wiry stems.
Size: 4″ (100 mm) to 3′ (.90 m), depending on species.
Location: WINTER—southern exposure; must have full sun.
SUMMER—*Inside and Outside:* southern exposure.
FALL: move indoors by mid-September and site in southern exposure.
Water: keep soil evenly moist.
Mist: daily, in area around plant but not directly on it.
Humidity: normal, 30%-35%.
Air circulation: helpful condition.
Feed: every 2 weeks with diluted liquid manure.
Soil: 1 part standard potting mix, 1 part sand or perlite.
Temperature: Day—68°-72°F (20°-22°C). Night—50°-55°F (10-12°C).
Mature plants: better bloom if stems pinched back as they become straggly, pinch off to point where plant retains compact, uniform shape. Pinch center out of young shoots for a wide plant. Plant too tall for standing upright, stake and tie main trunk (leave small amount of slack in ties to eliminate potential of injury from tie cutting into fleshy stem).

Felicia,
Blue Marguerite

Propagate: from seeds or stem cuttings, in spring. Temperature of 60°-65°F (15°-18°C) essential for success with seeds; root cuttings in moist potting mix specified for this species.
Offspring established: seeds sown in spring will be flowering plants by winter; when cuttings are well rooted and/or seedlings well established, transplant into 2½″ (62 mm) pots in soil mix as specified for this genus.
Notable: soil must be porous for good drainage; essential to aerate soil at least once a month; consider plant as an annual and replace plant with simple yearly propagation for next year's enjoyment.

F. bergeriana (ber-jer-ee-ay′-nuh) Kingfisher Daisy, 4″-8″ (100-200 mm) tall; slender, grasslike plant; 1½″ (37 mm) bright blue flowers.
F. amelloides (am-el-loy′-deez) meaning like aster; Blue Daisy or Blue Felicia; tends to be bushy; 3′ (.90 m) tall; blue 1½″ (37 mm) flowers; grow from cuttings; this same species also known as F. capensis (ka-pen′-siss) from the Cape of Good Hope.

FICUS (fye′-kus) Rubber Tree, India-rubber Tree, Fig Tree. An extremely popular and durable genus, and with good reason. The species are all of interesting, attractive forms that vary from trailing vines to trees—weeping or erect. All species are evergreen foliage plants most happy in a good light site.
Family Tree: Moraceae (mor-ay′-see-ay) Mulberry family; from tropical and warm temperate regions.
Foliage: evergreen; variable from wavy margined to deeply lobed; lance-shaped leaves to deeply segmented large leaves; pendulous branches or stiff, erect stems, all depending on species; all rich green but some variegated in pattern and color.
Size: up to 20′ (6 m), depending on species.
Location: WINTER—southeastern or southwestern exposure.
SUMMER—*Inside:* northeastern or northwestern exposure.
Outside: northeastern or northwestern exposure; site in shelter to protect foliage.
FALL: move indoors by mid-September; site in eastern or western exposure.
Dormancy: none, but a resting period of slower growth during winter months of less intensity, generally October through February; slowly diminish watering, plant will indicate needs as determined by environmental conditions; develop sensitivity to feel of soil moisture level; cease fertilizing.
Water: thoroughly and evenly, allowing soil to dry out between waterings.
Mist: daily, twice a day when possible.
Humidity: above normal for happiness, 45%-55%.
Air circulation: helpful condition.
Feed: mild liquid manure every 2 weeks.
Soil: standard potting soil.
Temperature: Day—70°-80°F (21°-26°C). Night—62°-68°F (16°-20°C).
Potbound: very happy; pot-on only when root growth of plant is 80%, soil 20% of pot content; top or side-dress yearly, preferably in spring.
Mature plants: if plant becomes too tall, cut growing ends (can start in rooting media). Remove dried or withered leaves as they appear.
Propagate: by stem cuttings or air layering.
Insect alert: mealybug, red spider, scale, thrip, aphids.
Notable: good artificial-light plant, combine natural and artificial light for a total of 14-16 hours; do not allow soil to dry out completely; soil must have porosity to eliminate possibility of soggy conditions. Use pebble, water, and tray method to maintain humidity level. Sponge foliage at least every 3 weeks, always use room-temperature water. Leaf shiners and/or oils are an *absolute no-no.*

F. benjamina (ben-ja-meen′-uh) Weeping Fig, Benjamin fig; shiny, leathery, pointed leaves, 2″-4″ (50-100 mm) long; many twigged, slender branches arch gracefully; 4'-6' (1.20-1.80 m) tall.

F. diversifolia (di-vers-i-foh'-lee-uh) meaning leaves variable; previously called F. lutescens; common name, Mistletoe fig; leathery, dark green leaves, 1"-3" (25-76 mm) across; 8"-24" (.25-.60 m) tall.

F. elastica (el-ast'-ik-uh) meaning rubber producing, elastic; common name, India-rubber tree; dark green, oval leaves, 4"-10" (100-254 mm) long, 2"-3" (50-76 mm) wide; erect in form.

> Variety—Decora: Broad leaved India-rubber tree; leaves to 6" (.15 m) wide, 12" (.30 m) long; prominent central rib, white on top and red on underside.

> Variety—Doescherii: Doescher's India-rubber tree; leaves mottled with gray green, yellow, white; pink central ribs and leaf stems.

F. Lyrata (lye-ray'-tuh) meaning Lyre-shaped; common name, Fiddle-leaved fig; previously called F. pandurata; gleaming, leathery leaves, violin shaped, 12"-18" (.30-.45 m) long; 2'-4' (.60-1.20 m) tall.

F. pumila (pew'-mil-uh) meaning dwarf; common name, Creeping fig; creeper, trailer, climber; heart-shaped leaves, 1" (25 mm) long; aerial roots.

F. radicans (ra'-di-kanz) meaning rooting, especially along stem; climber; aerial roots; oblong pointed leaves 2½" (62 mm) long, 1" (25 mm) across.

F. retusa (re-tew'-suh) meaning notched, common name, Indian laurel fig; previously named *F. nitida*; blunt, oval, dark evergreen leaves, 2"-4" (50-100 mm) long, waxy texture; 4'-6' (1.20-1.80 m) tall.

FITTONIA (fit-toh'-nee-uh) Mosaic plant, Red or Silver-nerved fittonia, named for Elizabeth and Sara May Fitton, authors of *Conversations in Botany*.

Fittonia is an attractive creeping genus. This growth habit, well displayed cascading from a hanging container, is enhanced by the intricately veined oval leaves. Preferable housing is a shallow pot.

Family Tree: Acanthaceae (uh-kanth-ay'-see-ay) Acanthus family; native to South America.

Foliage: oval leaves 2"-4" (50-100 mm), intricately veined in pattern resembling a nerve network; colorations vary according to species and varieties; creeping stems, hairy.

Flower: small, yellow flowers; insignificant.

Size: up to 10" (254 mm) high.

Location: WINTER—southeastern or southwestern exposure. SUMMER—*Inside:* northeastern or northwestern exposure. *Outside:* northeastern or northwestern exposure; site in shelter to protect foliage. FALL: move indoors by mid-September; site in eastern or western exposure.

Dormancy: none, but after flowering a resting period of slower growth during winter months of less intensity; slowly diminish watering, plant will indicate needs as determined by environmental conditions; develop sensitivity to feel of soil moisture level; cease fertilizing.

Water: moderately and evenly, allow soil to dry out between waterings.

Mist: daily, twice a day when possible.

Humidity: above normal for happiness, 45%-55%.

Air circulation: helpful condition.

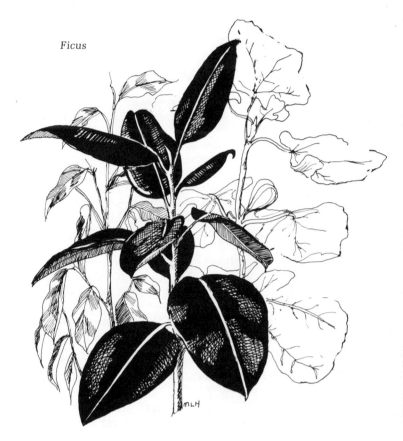

Ficus

Feed: very mild acid fertilizer, weekly; using a 21-7-7 balance.

Soil: 1 part standard potting mix, 2 parts peat moss, 1 part perlite; or packaged African Violet soil.

Temperature: Day—70°-80°F (21°-26°C). Night—62°-68°F (16°-20°C).

Potbound: repot, or top- or side-dress early, early spring prior to evidence of new growth; pot-on when root system is 50% or more of pot's content.

Fittonia verschaffeltii,
Red-Nerved Fittonia

Mature plants: remove dried or withered leaves as they appear. Pinch or prune regularly to retain fullness, remove straggly or unsightly trailers and flower buds as they appear so that nurturing fully benefits foliage.
Propagate: by stem cuttings, in spring.
Insect alert: slugs, mealybug, mites.
Notable: good artificial light plant; total of 14-16 hours, combining natural and artificial light; do not allow soil to dry out completely; soil must have porosity, eliminating possibility of soggy conditions; use pebble, water, and tray method to maintain humidity level.

F. verschaffeltii (ver-shaf-felt'-ee-eye) native to Peru; common name, Red-nerved fittonia; pinkish red veined, oval leaves; up to 8″ (200 mm) high spike of flowers, insignificant; semi-erect form, with trailing stems.
　　Variety—Argyroneura (ar-je-roh-new'-ruh) meaning silvery; common name, Silver-nerved fittonia or Mosaic plant; leaves are silver or white veined.
　　Variety—Pearcei (peer'-see-eye) sized for terrariums; leaves colored olive green with pinkish veins; paper-thin texture.

FORTUNELLA MARGARITA (for-tew-nell'-uh mar-gar-rye'-tuh) Nagami Kumquat, Oval Kumquat.

An easy culture genus, needing little attention, related to citrus fruits but hardier; this small tree makes a handsome tub plant with its white blossoms and long-lasting orange fruit, edible, of course.
Family Tree: Rutaceae (roo-tay-see-ay) Rue family; native of China.
Foliage: shiny dark green, 1½″ (37 mm) long leaves, and usually thornless.
Flower: small white and fragrant, in spring; off and on lightly year-round.
Fruit: in fall, highly decorative oval orange fruit, 1½″ (37 mm) long; remains from October through January; slightly bitter but makes excellent marmalade.
Size: 1'-15' (.30-4.50 m), depending on species.
Location: WINTER—full sun; southern exposure.
SUMMER—*Inside and Outside:* full sun; southern exposure.
FALL: move indoors by mid-September; site in southern exposure.
Dormancy: November starts several months resting period; no actual dormancy; slowly diminish watering to approximately half normal amount, plant will indicate needs; cease fertilizing November through January.
Water: thoroughly, allowing soil to dry out between waterings; check frequently.
Humidity: normal or slightly below, 20%-30%.
Air circulation: helpful condition.
Feed: every 2 weeks February through October, with mild liquid manure.
Soil: 2 parts standard potting mix, 1 part peat moss, 1 part perlite.
Temperature: Day—68°-72°F (20°-22°C). Night—50°-55°F (10°-12'C).
Potbound: keep slightly potbound; pot-on as indicated by plant's root system overbalancing soil content in pot, 60% roots, 40% soil.
Mature plants: prune back top shoots for fuller, bushier plant and to confine plant to site.

Fortunella japonica,
Kumquat

Propagate: from grafting, stem cuttings—in late spring—or from seeds sown any time.
Insect alert: thrips, aphids, mealybug, mites, whitefly.
Notable: cool winter temperatures needed, 55°-60°F (12°-15°C); do not allow totally dried-out soil too long a period, leaves will shrivel and fall off prior, even, to turning yellow; seeds sown from this fruit will germinate into most attractive, small evergreen plants. These plants seldom flower or fruit.

F. japonica (ja-pon'-ik-uh) meaning of Japan; known as Marum Kumquat; flowers almost year round; long lasting, oval, bright orange fruit to 1¼″ (32 mm) in diameter, edible but bitter; plant to 8' (2.45 m) tall.
F. hindsii (hind'-see-eye) decorative cherry sized, scarlet orange, edible fruit; grows to 1' (.30 m).

FRAGARIA INDICA (fra-gay'-ree-uh in'-dik-uh) Strawberry.

A small, low trailing perennial herb, very popular in the 17th century. Fragaria's charming, delicate nature is once more becoming appreciated to accent an interior space washed in the bright light. The strawberry plant will fall into a graceful, pendulous growth habit when planted in a hanging container. The threefold leaves are said to express the holiness of the Trinity.
Family Tree: Rosaceae (roh-say'-see-ay) Rose family; native to Europe and Western Asia.
Foliage: each leaf consists of three small green blades, serrated edges.
Flower: small white blossoms; in spring.
Fruit: inedible red berries in summer or fall.
Size: 3″-6″ (76-150 mm) height and length.
Location: WINTER—full sun; set in southern exposure.
SUMMER—*Inside and Outside:* partial shade; set in eastern to southern exposure for direct rays of morning sun.
FALL: move indoors by mid-September.

Dormancy: none; resting time after blooming and fruiting; keep on lower side of recommended temperature; slowly diminish watering, keeping soil barely moist; cease fertilizing, until plant indicates end of dormancy by showing new growth.

Water: keep thoroughly and evenly moist.

Mist: daily; twice a day when possible.

Humidity: normal, 30%-35%.

Air circulation: helpful condition.

Feed: every 2 weeks, a very, very weak solution of acid fertilizer, 21-7-7 balance.

Soil: 2 parts standard potting mix, 1 part peat moss, 1 part perlite.

Temperature: Day—68°-75°F (20°-23°C). Night—58°-65°F (14°-18°C).

Potbound: repot in early spring in fresh soil as specified for this genus.

Mature plants: when plant blossoms, spray with Blossom Set, a commercial product available at nursery supply outlets; if cultural advice has been followed, one will have delicate, inedible berries within 4 weeks of spraying.

Propagate: by seeds, in early spring, or suckers: in autumn, the plant produces long thin shoots (suckers) which bear little plantlets, these can be removed complete with roots and planted. Use a 7" (177 mm) pot for each plantlet.

Insect alert: aphid, mites, scale, whitefly, thrips, mealybug.

Notable: strawberry plants cannot stand lime; porosity of soil must be maintained; good under artificial light, or a combination of artificial and natural to equal 16 hours daily.

F. vesca (ves'-cuh) Fraises des Bois; European strawberry from the Alps; everbearing; tiny white blossoms, edible fruit, red or white; grows to 8" (203 mm) tall; creeping habit.

FUCHSIA (fook'-see-uh) Lady's Eardrops. Named in honor of Leonhard Fuchs, German physician, professor of medicine, and botanist whose research advanced much knowledge in herbal culture.

Shocking to be told that for these many years you have been mispronouncing the name of your plant as "few-shuh." Be not ashamed, for you were in the good company of many an exposed nurseryman and horticulturist with a degree.

Family Tree: Onagraceae (oh-na-gray'-see-ay) Evening Primrose family. Related to (hybrids of) plant species native to Mexico, Chile, New Zealand, and American tropics.

Foliage: crisp, oval, either rich dark green, soft green, or maroon-tinged (size and color variations determined by species); leaves opposite, alternate, or whorled.

Flower: bloom on new growth; buds are set in spring; again many varieties, single or double flowers of dangling nature; bell-shaped or hoop-shaped on trailer stems for some species, upright stems for yet others; generally 1½"-3" (37-76 mm) in size on stems 1' (.30 m) to 3' (.90 m); red, white, pink, and purple, also combinations of these colors.

Fruit: very small berry—difficult to espy.

Size: up to 3' (.90 m) trailing and upright stems.

Location: WINTER—set in southern exposure; full sun.

Fragaria indica,
Strawberry

SUMMER—*Inside:* set in eastern exposure for strong light but only *morning* sun. *Outside:* set in northeastern location out of strong winds.

FALL: move indoors by mid-September.

Dormancy: period starts mid-October; foliage starts to drop; a few species do not go into dormant state and therefore blossom all winter. (If you are unable to determine the habits of your species, contact the American Fuchsia Society, see *Listing of Botanical Societies.* All you need forward is the botanical name of the variety you own.) Slowly diminish watering; cease fertilizing; can be pruned back (all stems) to 6" (150 mm); can be placed in unheated (frost-free) room until mid-February; keep barely moist. Return to normal culture when new growth (sprouts) appear in March or April.

Water: very thirsty; check your plant for moisture needs every day.

Mist: daily, better yet, twice a day, in time to dry by dusk.

Humidity: high level, 60%—moist air! moist air!

Air circulation: helpful condition.

Feed: weekly, diluted liquid manure.

Soil: 2 parts standard potting soil, 1 part moist peat moss, light sprinkle of bonemeal.

Temperature: Day—happiest around 65°F (18°C). Night—50°-65°F (10°-18°C).

Potbound: very unhappy; pot-on as normally needed.

Mature plants: better bloom if stems pinched back as they become straggly. Pinch off to point where plant retains a compact, uniform shape; pinch center out of young shoots for wide plant; too tall a plant for standing upright, stake and tie main trunk (leave small amount of slack in ties to eliminate potential of injury, by tie cutting into fleshy stem). May be trained into standard form (tree form) or espaliered plant by proper pruning or pinching.

Propagate: by cuttings, 3" (76 mm) young shoots in water, use soft shoots that have not formed flowers or basal suckers (new shoots at bottom of stem) for best results; or

Fuchsia,
Flame Fuchsia

root cuttings in sand or vermiculite. Best time to take cuttings: July. New plants can be started from seed then, too.
Offspring established: after rooted and potted; keep new young plants pinched back to make them bushy; keep flower buds pinched off until plant is large enough to be transplanted into a 4″ (100 mm) pot.

Gardenia jasminoides

Insect alert: watch out for whitefly, red spider and aphids, mealybug, mites, scale, thrips.

Your Fuchsia has been a long-time favorite flowering house plant; lovely to view in its profusion of blossoming, you will receive much satisfaction as it so obviously responds to your tender attention. Soil must have good drainage. Temperature of less than 65°F (18°C) needed during "dark hours" to set flower buds.

There are many species of the Fuchsia family—some cousins of the graceful pendulous variety so suitable for a hanging basket, yet other relatives are upright in form. Some are almost shrub size, others a mere 1′-1½′ (.30-.45 m) high. I shall not attempt full coverage of species and varieties within species, for it would soon be an outdated listing. These are among the more popular available.

F. hybrida (hyb′-rid-uh) meaning of mixed origin, Flame Fuchsia; either single or double flowers; solid color or combination of red, pink, purple, white; 1½″-3′ (37-76 mm) blossoms on 1′-3′ (.30-.90 m) pending stems.
F. fulgens (full′-jenz) 4′-6′ (1.20-1.80 m); Mexican shrub; blossom color yellow red.
F. triphylla (try-fill′-uh) Variety, Gartenmeister Bohstedt or Honeysuckle Fuchsia, will bloom all year if night temperatures are below 60°F (15°C) for bud setting; blossom in clusters; color, orange rose; foliage, maroon toned; stems, 18″ (.45 m) long.
Trailers
  F. brigadoon double purple white or purple red flowers.
  F. swingtime double red white flowers.
  F. tiffany double white flowers.
  F. marenga double red flowers.
Uprights
  F. sleigh bells single white flowers.
  F. Mrs Marshall single pink white flowers.

GARDENIA JASMINOIDES (gar-deen′-ee-uh jas-mi-noy′-deez) Cape Jasmine.
A bushy shrub-type genus with a heavy scent familiar to all. Attention to the adjustment period for settling into a new interior environment is paramount in importance. Provide a cool site and moist conditions for heirloom longevity. Named in 1761 to honor Dr. Alexander Garden, a Scotsman who established a medical practice in South Carolina in the 1750s and contributed much to the knowledge of American flora and fauna. The plant originally was found at the Cape of Good Hope by a sea captain who was captivated by its fragrance, he took two specimens to a friend in London, Richard Warner, who described the new genus in a garden dictionary as "bay leaved jasemins."
Family Tree: Rubiaceae (roo-bee-ay′-see-ay) Madder family; origins in eastern Asia.
Foliage: very glossy, pointed, dark evergreen leaves, 3″-6″ (76-150 mm).
Flower: rich and delicately scented, waxen, creamy white, double, 1″-2″ (25-50 mm) across; blooming time varies with species and culture.
Size: 1′-3′ (.30-.90 m) tall.
Location: WINTER—southern exposure.
SUMMER—*Inside and Outside:* eastern or western exposure.

FALL: move indoors by mid-September; site in eastern or western exposure.

Dormancy: none, actually, but heavy resting period after flowering, November through March; slowly diminish watering, keeping soil evenly damp at all times; cease fertilizing until signs of new vigor appear, along about mid-March, early April.

Water: keep soil evenly moist.

Mist: twice daily with tepid water.

Humidity: high, 50%-60%.

Air circulation: helpful condition.

Feed: March through August, mild liquid solution of 21-7-7, acid fertilizer, every 2 weeks.

Soil: acid potting mix; available packaged at garden supply outlets.

Temperature: Day—60°-75°F (15°-23°C), except when buds are forming. Night—60°-65°F (15°-18°C).

Mature plants: prune back considerably after flowering to conserve plant's strength and foster compactness; too tall a plant for standing upright; stake and tie main trunk (leave small amount of slack in ties to eliminate potential of injury from tie cutting into fleshy stem). May be trained into standard form (tree form) or espaliered plant by proper pruning or pinching. Temperature must be no lower than 60°F (15°C) or higher than 65°F (18°C) for proper and profuse bud formation; below 60°F buds develop malformed, above 65°F leaf growth is profuse and buds shed.

Propagate: from stem cuttings of young wood, in moist vermiculite, March or September; soil must be at least 72°F (22°C) for success.

Insect alert: aphid, mealybug, scale, whitefly.

Disease alert: black leaf tips from dryness or fluctuating temperatures; yellow leaves from calcium in water or water too cold.

Notable: do not allow soil to dry out completely; do not allow soggy conditions; use pebble, water, and tray method to maintain humidity. Gardenia is a natural for double potting, using sphagnum moss between pots to "up" humidity level; removing faded, browned blossoms aids vigor and appearance.

G. stricta nana (strik'-ta na'-na) *stricta,* upright; *nana,* dwarf: free flowering plant, to 30" (.75 m); best for home use because of compact size.
G. radicans florepleno (rad'-i-kanz flo-re-ple'-na) *radicans*—rooting, especially long stem, *florepleno*—double flower; a dwarf, double-flowering specimen.

GASTERIA VERRUCOSA (gas-teer'-ee-uh vehr-roo-koh'-suh) Ox Tongue Plant.
An almost-no-care plant, this succulent from South African deserts. Verrucosa, meaning warty, is one species of a large genus of many different forms and growth habits. Flowers on single stalks rise above the base of the plant in a charming, graceful, and pending habit. Gasteria is quite like the Aloe, though mostly smaller.

Family Tree: Liliaceae (lil-ee-ay'-see-ay) Lily family; native to South Africa.

Foliage: fleshy, lance-shaped, tapering leaves, 6" (150 mm) long, gray green to shades of pink in winter, covered with white warts or tubercles, arranged in opposite pattern.

Gasteria verrucosa,
Ox Tongue Plant

Flower: urn-shaped, orange red, on long stems, in spring and summer.

Size: up to 1' (.30 m).

Location: WINTER—southern exposure.

SUMMER—*Inside and Outside:* southern exposure.

FALL: move indoors by mid-September; site in southern exposure.

Dormancy: none, but a resting time from October through February; slowly diminish watering; just enough to keep leaves from shriveling; cease fertilizing.

Water: allow soil to become quite dry between thorough, even waterings, March through September.

Mist: daily very lightly, around plant but not directly on it.

Humidity: low, 20%-25%.

Air circulation: helpful condition.

Feed: mild liquid manure, once a month, April through July.

Soil: 1 part standard potting mix, 2 parts sharp sand.

Temperature: Day—68°-80°F (20°-26°C). Night—50°-70°F (10°-21°C).

Potbound: normal; repot or pot-on when foliage appears overcrowded or root growth is 50% of pot content; best done in early spring prior to new growth evidence.

Mature plants: older plants frequently lose bottom leaves. Bright light and sun improve richness of colors of foliage.

Propagate: by leaf or tip cuttings, any time; or by offsets; pot-up in soil as specified for this genus; do not have damp soil and do not water for 5 days after potting.

Insect alert: mealybug, scale.

Disease alert: root rot from overwatering.

Notable: Soil must have excellent porosity; do not try to create humid conditions; normal interior air, even a dry site, is most suitable. *Most notable:* plants rot very easily; a good artificial-light plant, up to 16 hours combined natural and artificial light hours; do not allow soil to dry out completely.

G. acinacifolia (ass-in-ay-si-foh'-lee-uh) saber-shaped leaves to 14″ (.35 m) long form rosette, glossy dark green with white spots; loose clusters of red or rose flowers rise from center, on 1′-2′ (.30-.60 m) stems.

G. carinata (kar-i-nay'-tuh) triangular, fleshy leaves, to 6″ (150 mm); flower spike, up to 3′ (.90 m) tall.

G. liliputana (lil-i-pew-tay'-nuh) Lilliput gasteria; shiny, dark green leaves, 2″ (50 mm) long, 1″ (25 mm) wide; plant, 2″ (.60 m) high.

G. lingua (lin'-gwuh) meaning tongue-shaped; 10″ (254 mm), dark green leaves with white spots; flowers on stems, to 36″ (.90 m).

G. maculata (mak-yew-lay'-tuh) meaning spotted; tongue-shaped leaves, 6″-8″ (150-200 mm) long, arranged spirally in 2 opposing ranks around stem; dark green, white spots; bell-shaped, red flowers, on 3′-4′ (.90-1.20 m) stalks.

GAZANIA LONGISCAPA (gaz-zay'-nee-uh lon-jis-kay'-puh).

The genus for sunny windows. A pretty, perfect plant for flowering almost year-round, most profusely in summer. Flowers are large and extremely colorful. Scapes (stalks) are long, therefore "longiscapa." Named in honor of Theodore of Gaza, a Greek-born translator of the 15th century, who translated into Latin *Theoretical Botany* and *History of Plants*, 3rd-century works by Theophrastus, a pupil of Aristotle. These versions, prepared while Gaza was a refugee in Italy from the Turkish invasion, remained the only books on botanical theory for nearly 200 years.

Family Tree: Compositae (kom-pos'-it-aye) Composite family; from South Africa.

Gazania splendens

Foliage: clumps of long, slender leaves with rolled-up edges, irregularly lobed; dark green above, felty, silvery white underneath.

Flower: dark, brown-spotted centers; daisylike petals of yellow, gold, cream, yellow orange, pink, bronze red; 3″-10″ (76-254 mm) diameter; long lasting, blooming year-round though heaviest in summer.

Size: 6″-30″ (.15-.75 m), depending upon species.

Location: WINTER—full sun; southern exposure.

SUMMER—*Inside* and *Outside:* southern exposure.

FALL: move indoors by mid-September; set in site of southern exposure.

Dormancy: none actually, takes resting time October through March; maintain watering program; cease fertilizing.

Water: allow soil to dry out completely between thorough waterings.

Mist: daily, twice daily if possible during growing season, but do not mist directly on flowers.

Humidity: normal, 30%-35%.

Air circulation: helpful condition.

Feed: mild liquid manure, weekly.

Soil: standard potting mix.

Temperature: Day—68°-72°F (20°-22°C). Night—50°-55°F (10°-12°C).

Potbound: normal, repot between February to April; pot-on as plant's needs indicate by root system overpowering soil content.

Mature plants: better bloom if stems pinched back as they become straggly; pinch off to point where plant retains compact, uniform shape. Pinch center out of young shoots for wide plant.

Propagate: from seeds in spring, or division of old plants any time, or cuttings of basal shoots taken in August.

Insect alert: red spider mite, whitefly.

Disease alert: cold, damp soil causes fungus which produces rot.

Notable: blooms close at night and on cloudy days; high temperatures in summer months; maintain humidity on low side; best culture is to start new plants each year at end of blooming cycle.

G. splendens (splen'-denz) meaning bright, shiny, splendid; golden orange spotted with brown or mauve around center.

G. rigens (rye'-jenz) meaning rigid; yellow orange flower with white-dotted black spot near base of each petal; blossom 1½″ (37 mm) across.

G. hybrids

  G. Fire Emerald: emerald center ring with flowers of bronze red, lavender pink, pure pink, rose, or red.

  G. Colorama: white, yellow, cream, orange, or pink flowers.

GEOGENANTHUS UNDATUS (geo-jen-an'-thus un-day'-tus) Seersucker Plant.

G. undatus has a simple culture. The appearance is interesting; the leaf has a textured, puckered pattern similar to seersucker fabric, hence its common name. The only species in cultivation, it is a fast growing plant for small, bright light sites. Extremely colorful evergreen foliage is enhanced by summer flowering of light blue blossoms. Previously known as *Dichorisandra mosaica undata*.

Family Tree: Commelinaceae (kom'-el-lye-nay-see-ay) Spiderwort family; native to Peru and Brazil.
Foliage: leaf oval, pointed, 5″ (127 mm) long, grayish silver banding on olive green, maroon undersides and stems; texture like seersucker.
Flower: light blue; insignificant.
Size: to 10″ (254 mm).
Location: WINTER—southeastern or southwestern exposure.
SUMMER—*Inside:* northeastern or northwestern exposure. *Outside:* northeastern or northwestern exposure; protect fragile foliage from potentially damaging elements, preferably by overhang.
FALL: move indoors by mid-September; site in eastern or western exposure.
Dormancy: none, but light resting period after flowering. Slowly diminish watering, plant will indicate needs by becoming limp and droopy; develop sensitivity to feel of soil moisture; cut fertilizing program in half.
Water: keep moderately and evenly moist.
Mist: daily, twice a day when possible.
Humidity: above normal for happiness, 40%-45%.
Air circulation: helpful condition.
Feed: mild liquid manure every 2 weeks.
Soil: 2 parts standard potting soil, 1 part peat moss, 1 part perlite.
Temperature: Day—68°-80°F (20°-26°C). Night—55°-68°F (12°-20°C).
Potbound: repot or pot-on as needed and indicated by root growth being at least 50% of pot content.
Mature plants: remove flowers as they fade; remove yellow foliage as it appears. Take cuttings, easily rooted, for fresh replacement.
Propagate: by stem cuttings, root in water or moist vermiculite; by division or suckers, remove and plant in specified soil for this genus.
Insect alert: mealybug, whitefly, mites, scale, slugs.
Notable: good artificial light specimen, a total of 14 light hours combined with natural; must have good soil porosity; never allow soil to dry out completely; rinse foliage frequently in room-temperature or tepid water, to prevent dust-clogged pores.

Geogenanthus undatus,
Seersucker Plant

Gloriosa rothschildiana,
Glory Lily

GLORIOSA ROTHSCHILDIANA (gloh-ree-oh'-suh roths-child-ee-ay'-nuh) Glory Lily, Climbing Lily.
The flower, as its common name indicates, closely resembles a lily bloom, yet the convexity of the petal shape gives a charming distinction of its own. A delicate and lovely ornamental vine, definitely for proud possession.
Family Tree: Liliaceae (lil-ee-ay'-see-ay) Lily family; from Africa.
Foliage: lancelike leaves; cling to a support by tendrils at ends of leaves.
Flower: lilylike, slim petals which curve backwards; 3″-4″ (76-100 mm); scarlet or yellow.
Size: to 4′ (1.20 m) vining stems.
Location: WINTER—full sun; set in southern exposure.
SUMMER—*Inside:* partial shade; set in eastern to southern exposure for direct rays of morning sun. *Outside:* partial shade; set in eastern exposure or under a protective structure where plant receives strong light but no direct rays.
FALL: move indoors by mid-September.
Dormancy: allow plant to die down naturally; cease fertilizing and watering; store in same pot (generally October through January), then repot, using potting mixture as specified for this genus; pot as specified for this genus under *Potbound.*
Water: keep evenly moist.
Mist: daily, twice daily during growth and blooming period.
Humidity: above normal, 50%.
Air circulation: helpful condition.
Feed: mild liquid manure every 2 weeks until flowers fade; begin fertilizing when signals of new growth are evident.
Soil: 2 parts standard potting mix, 1 part peat moss.
Temperature: Day—72°-75°F (22°-23°C). Night—60°-65°F (15°-18°C).

Potbound: repot in fresh soil, in early spring; pot-on as needed; keep tubers at same soil level, just below soil surface, as previously planted.

Mature plants: when tying to stake or trellis, leave small amount of slack in ties to eliminate potential injury to stems.

Propagate: by seeds in spring or by dividing tubers after dormancy, usually around March.

Insect alert: mealybugs.

Notable: provide large pot for huge roots; climbing habit makes this a natural for a trellis; in case of heavy blooming, place stakes and loosely tie stems to support flower heads; time of dormancy can be controlled, thus, also the blooming season.

G. simplex (sim'-plex) 2″ (50 mm) yellow to orange bloom; dwarf size plant.

G. superba (soo-perb'-uh) meaning superb; climbs as high as 10′ (3 m); flowers are dwarf, wavy-edged, 3″ (76 mm) long; yellow, turning red as they mature.

x. GLOXINERA (glock-sin-eer'-uh).

A genus produced by cross-breeding gloxinias and rechsteinerias (tuberous plants). This plant looks much like its parental gloxinia but more delicate. Definitely a most unique flowering greenery to possess. This relative blooms longer than the gloxinia.

Family Tree: Gesneriaceae (jes-ner-ee-ay'-see-ay) Gesneria family.

Foliage: heart-shaped or oval glossy leaves; some furry.

Flower: slipper-shaped, ranging in size from ½″-3″ (12-76 mm); blooms at various times of the year according to variety and culture; colors include pink, lavender, and yellow.

Size: 3″-10″ (76-254 mm) tall; depending on variety.

Location: WINTER—eastern exposure.

SUMMER—*Inside:* eastern exposure. *Outside:* northern exposure.

FALL: move indoors by mid-September; can be grown in 14-16 hours artificial and/or natural light per day.

Dormancy: period starts when flowering has ceased; stop feeding; keep soil barely moist until foliage withers; allow soil to dry out completely; leave tubers in warm spot for resting until February; or store tubers in closed plastic bags with tubers wrapped in barely damp peat moss or damp vermiculite; when sprouted in 2-4 months repot in fresh potting mix and cover with ½″-1″ (12-25 mm) soil; when new growth begins gradually resume watering and provide bright light; begin fertilizing when shoots are 1″ (25 mm) tall and foliage has opened fully.

Water: keep evenly moist.

Mist: daily, if possible twice daily, except during dormancy.

Humidity: very high is happiness, 65%-70%.

Air circulation: helpful condition.

Feed: with mild liquid manure every 2 weeks from February until flowering begins.

Soil: 1 part standard potting mix, 2 parts peat moss, 1 part sharp sand or perlite.

Temperature: Day—70°F (21°C) or higher. Night—65°-70°F (18°-21°C).

Mature plants: better bloom if stems pinched back as they become straggly; pinch off to point where plant retains compact, uniform shape; pinch center out of young shoots for wide plant.

Propagate: by leaf cuttings of continuously blooming plants; by stem cuttings of upright plants; or from seed.

Insect alert: aphids, mites, thrips.

Notable: keep warmth and humidity high always; set on tray of pebbles in water; do not allow soil to dry out completely; use only tepid water; know that some miniatures are slow to respond to their cultural attentions; "patience will out."

G. rosea (roh'-zee-uh) meaning rose colored, pink.
   Variety—Rosebells: rosy pink.
   Variety—Alfred K: salmon pink.
   Variety—Laurie: white with yellow throat.
   Variety—Clarice T: salmon red.

GREVILLEA ROBUSTA (grev-vill'-ee-uh roh-bust'-uh) Silk Oak.

The Silk oak displays a feathery, silky, lacelike foliage, yet belies this airy portrayal with a textured feeling of substance and solidity. Clustered gold-toned flowers, not unattractive, are second only to the beauty of the delicate leaf form. G. robusta is totally content in a full sun site, but this results in a slightly bronze-tinged foliage. A bright light setting will aid in the retention of the natural color.

Family Tree: Proteaceae (proh-tee-aye'-see-ay) Protea family; native to Australia.

Foliage: fernlike, lacy leaves, alternate pattern, 6″-18″ (.15-.45 m) long; stems have silver fuzz.

Flower: yellowish orange to reddish orange, in horizontal one-sided racemes (clusters), to 4″ (100 mm) long.

Size: up to 3′ (.90 m).

Location: WINTER—southern exposure.

SUMMER—*Inside:* southeastern or southwestern exposure. *Outside:* southeastern or southwestern; site in sheltered area to protect foliage.

FALL: move indoors by mid-September; site in southeastern or southwestern exposure.

Dormancy: none, a resting time during winter months, after flowering; slowly diminish watering; plant will indicate needs by appearance, becoming limp and droopy; develop sensitivity to feel of soil moisture level; cease fertilizing.

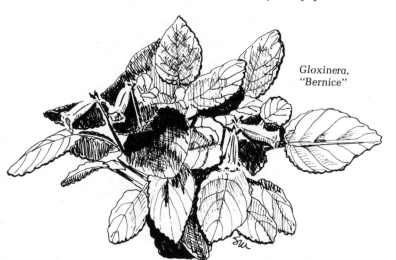

Gloxinera, "Bernice"

Water: evenly and thoroughly, allowing soil to dry between waterings.

Mist: daily; around plant, not directly on foliage.

Humidity: normal, 30%-35%.

Air circulation: essential for good cultural response.

Feed: every 2 weeks, with mild liquid manure, throughout growing season—April through August.

Soil: 3 parts standard potting mix, 1 part sharp sand or perlite.

Temperature: Day—68°-78°F (20°-25°C). Night—60°-68°F (15°-20°C).

Potbound: slightly for happiness, when root growth is approximately 65% of pot content; best repotted or potted-on before new growth develops in March.

Mature plants: remove faded flowers when they are spent. Prune hard in very early spring to retain fullness of plant; can be pruned back to half size.

Propagate: by seed.

Insect alert: red spider, mites, mealybug.

Notable: soil must have porosity; no soggy conditions; keep on lower side of recommended temperatures; good air circulation needed for top performance; do not overpot, use pot only 2″ (50 mm) larger than previous housing; never allow soil to dry out completely; too wet or too dry means potential root damage, and there goes Silk oak.

G. bipinnata lida (bye-pin-nay′-tuh lid′-uh) to 4′ (1.20 m); loose racemes (clusters) of red flowers.

G. rosmarinifolia (rohs-mar-in-if-foh′-lee-uh) narrow, rosemary-like leaves, silky beneath; reddish flowers, in short, dense clusters; shrub natured to 6′ (1.80 m).

G. wilsonii (will-son′-ee-eye) needlelike leaves; red and yellow flowers; to 5′ (1.50 m) tall.

GYNURA AURANTIACA (jye-new′-ruh aw-ran-tye′-ak-uh) Purple Velvet Plant, Purple Passion Vine or Plant. The velvety texture and near iridescence of this species create a soft, lovely facade, the most ornamental asset. Leaves and stems have a soft hairy covering muted to a luscious purple hue. Displayed in a hanging container in a fairly sunny site, the purple passion will glow in good health and merit the appreciation bestowed.

Family Tree: Compositae (kom-pos′-it-aye) Composite family; native to Java.

Foliage: alternate patterned, oval leaves, with serrated margins, pointed tips, 2″-4″ (50-100 mm) long; green with purple hairs; branching habit.

Flower: ¾″ (19 mm); daisylike; orange or yellow.

Size: up to 3′ (.90 m).

Location: WINTER—southern exposure.

SUMMER—*Inside:* southeastern or southwestern exposure. *Outside:* southeastern or southwestern exposure; protect fragile foliage from potentially damaging elements, preferably by overhang.

FALL: move indoors by mid-September; site in southeastern or southwestern exposure.

Dormancy: none, but light resting period, October through February; slowly diminish watering, keeping soil barely moist; cut fertilizing program in half.

Water: keep moderately and evenly moist.

Mist: daily, twice a day when possible.

Humidity: above normal for happiness, 40%-45%.

Grevillea robusta,
Silk Oak

Air circulation: helpful condition.

Feed: mild liquid manure every 2 weeks.

Soil: 2 parts standard potting soil, 1 part peat moss, 1 part perlite.

Temperature: Day—68°-80°F (20°-26°C). Night—55°-68°F (12°-20°C).

Potbound: repot; pot-on as needed and indicated by root growth being at least 50% of pot content.

Mature plants: prune regularly to remove stragglers and help maintain compactness of plant. Take cuttings, easily rooted, for fresh replacement. Remove withered foliage as it occurs.

Gynura aurantiaca,
Purple Passion Plant

Propagate: by stem cuttings, root in water or moist vermiculite.
Insect alert: mealybug, whitefly, mites, scale, slugs.
Notable: good artificial light specimen, a total of 14 light hours combined with natural; prune plant often to prevent legginess; do not overwater, plant will rot easily; must have good soil porosity; never allow soil to dry out completely; rinse foliage frequently in room-temperature or tepid water to prevent dust-clogged pores.

G. sarmentosa (sar-men-toh'-suh) meaning bearing runners; Purple passion vine; more trailing than upright.

HAWORTHIA ATTENUATA (haw-worth'-ee-uh at-ten-ew-ay'-tuh) Aristocrat Plant.
Generally a slow growing genus, very sturdy and of simple culture. Simple, interesting shapes and foliage resemble the Aloe genus. It is one of the most handsome displays of the succulents. The species, H. attenuata, refers to a slender, tapering habit. Most flowers are inconspicuous.
Family Tree: Liliaceae (lil-ee-ay'-see-ay) Lily family; native to South Africa.
Foliage: depth of green with pattern of white dots (tubercles) running bandlike across leaves, which overlap from base rosette.
Flower: inconspicuous, light-shaded clusters on stems.
Size: to 8″ (.25 m).
Location: WINTER—full sun; set in southern exposure.
SUMMER—*Inside:* partial shade; set in eastern to southern exposure for direct rays of morning sun. *Outside:* partial shade; set in eastern exposure or under a protective structure where plant receives strong light but no direct rays.
FALL: move indoors by mid-September.
Dormancy: none, although a resting time from October through February; water only enough to keep leaves from shriveling; cease fertilizing.
Water: allow soil to become quite dry between thorough, even waterings.
Mist: daily, very lightly, around plant but not directly on it.
Humidity: low normal, 20%-25%.
Air circulation: helpful condition.
Feed: mild liquid manure, once a month, April through July.
Soil: 1 part standard potting mix, 2 parts sharp sand.
Temperature: Day—68°-80°F (20°-26°C). Night—50°-70°F (10°-21°C).
Potbound: normal; repot or pot-on when foliage appears overcrowded or root growth is 50% of pot content, best in early spring prior to new growth.
Mature plants: frequently, older plants lose bottom leaves. Bright light and sun improve richness of colors of foliage.
Propagate: by offshoots or by leaf cuttings in spring or summer; pot-up in soil as specified for this genus; do not have damp soil and do not water for 5 days after potting.
Insect alert: scale, mealybug.
Disease alert: root rot from overwatering.
Notable: soil must have excellent porosity; do not try to create humid conditions; normal interior air, even a dry

Haworthia attenuata,
Aristocrat Plant

site, is most suitable, *Most notable:* plants rot very easily. A good artificial-light plant, up to 16 hours combined natural and artificial light hours; do not allow soil to dry out completely.

H. cymbiformis (sim-bih-form'-iss) thick, oval, bluish green leaves, translucent tips, 1½″ (37 mm) long, ¾″ (19 mm) wide; tiny, pale pink flowers striped green, on 1′ (.30 m) stems.
H. fasciata (fas-see-ay'-tuh) Zebra haworthia; small, upward-curving leaves, horizontal bands of tubercles, back surfaces marked with zebra pattern, 2″ (50 mm) long; leaves form rosettes 3″-4″ (76-100 mm) across; clusters of white green flowers.
H. margaritifera (mar-gar-ih-tif'-er-uh) Pearly haworthia; 1½″-3″ (37-76 mm) leaves profusely dotted with tubercles; small flowers in dense clusters on 2′ (.60 m) stems.
H. reinwardtii (ryne-wart'-ee-eye) meaning yellow flap; triangular, dark green leaves to 1½″ (37 mm) long, ½″ (12 mm) wide, overlap and spiral around thick, columnar stem, 6″ (150 mm) high; rows of white tubercles band leaves; 1½′ (.45 m) flower stem.
H. truncata (trun-kay'-tuh) meaning cut off squarely; leaves in 2 ranks rather than rosettes, translucent tips.
H. viscosa (viss-koh'-suh) meaning sticky; dark green pointed leaves in 3 ranks spiral around 6″ (150 mm) stem.

HEDERA (hed'-er-uh) English Ivy, Canary Island Ivy, Algerian Ivy.
The various Ivies, of an evergreen genus, are recognizable by the leaf form and are seen extensively in outdoor and indoor environments. The pendulous or climbing nature of a vine, so faithful in many past generations, has a distinctive charm either from the hanging container or trained on a slab of bark. Site it in a semisunny or good bright light nook. Individual taste should be readily

Author's library. An eastern exposure provides an ideal habitat for the Howea belmoreana and Chlorophytum comosum vittatum. The aspiring palm enhances the 23' ceiling and spider plants soften the contemporary architectural planes.

E. R. Squibb. *Brassaia functioning to dispel sterility of office building in the corporate center in Princeton. Management "works" at creating needed environment.*

Author's home. Summer vacation for the interior flora features a site with plants under a protective overhang. In front, to catch full southern exposure, is a Pelargonium peltatum. The Tradescantia fluminensis variegata on table is somewhat sheltered from direct sun rays. Totally shaded, but with bright light, is an Araucaria heterophylla. Protected from sun at rear, from left to right, hang a Chlorophytum comosum vittatum, a Billbergia nutans (Bromeliad family), a Sedum sieboldii, and a Hoya carnosa. Hanging on shaded side wall is a handsome Platycerium bifurcatum.

E. R. Squibb. Foliage plants are displayed at entrance to and within office of medical center. No exterior exposure means all artificial light, so these plants are kept in portable containers for periodic removal to greenhouses for re-establishment. At entrance, Philodendron selloum and Chamaedorea crumpeus; in office, Brassaia, Dracaena deremensis and Palm genera.

E. R. Squibb. Corporate center dining rooms present good bright light for tropical foliage plants. Aesthetically pleasing tubs of foliage plants add to handsome architectural interiors. Dracaena fragrans with Dieffenbachia leopoldii are in forefront.

Author's home: Intensive care area set aside in laundry room. Proper lighting was installed under hanging wall closets to aid ailing plants at propagating time. Plants from left, front row, are Callisia elegans cuttings, Zebrina pendula quadricolor cuttings, various leaf rootings of Saintpaulia species, and Plectranthus australis cuttings. Plants in back row, from left, are Saintpaulia species, Schlumbergera bridgesii, Cissus rhombifolia cuttings, and several other Saintpaulia species.

Bathroom in author's home. Several Nephrolepsis exaltata bostoniensis, a Chamaedorea elegans, a Chlorophytum comosum vittatum, and a Polystichum aculeatum are robust in a site of high humidity. Through casement drapery they receive filtered light from southeast. The Sedum sieboldii in rear has adjusted to lower light level but would prefer some direct sun.

Author's home. Lower level casual living for people and plants, with full southern exposure and floor to ceiling glass. Casement draperies allow light control throughout day. On table, Saintpaulia hybrid; hanging plants include Zebrina pendula quadricolor, Zebrina pendula discolor, Plectranthus australis, Hedera helix, Columnea arguta, Tolmiea menziesii, Tradescantia albi flora, Asparagus sprengeri; on corner stand, front to back, Saintpaulia hybrid, Philodendron, Zygocactus truncatus; on floor, double-potted in copper container, Episcia cupreata.

E. R. Squibb. Tall Brassaia flourish in this corporate center. Preplanning by architect specified coated glass panels for tropical foliage plant protection. A ground cover of Philodendron cordatum vines softly over planters.

Author's living room. Full southern exposure and high humidity encourage year-round bloom of the Bougainvillea glabra.

satisfied in available selection of the Hedera, for its species and varieties are so many as to fill a tome, by listing sisters and cousins, brothers and nephews.

Family Tree: Araliaceae (ar-ray'-lee-ay'-see-ay) Aralia family; native to North Africa, Europe, Asia.

Foliage: leaves lobed, 3 or 5 lobes, or ruffled or crinkled, curled edges, some sharply pointed; ½"-8" (12-200 mm); colored light greens through black greens; striated and margined with color variations; textured paper-thin through leathery; some stemmed with aerial roots; foregoing all depending on species.

Flower: insignificant; greenish shade.

Fruit: orange, yellow, or blackish berries; seldom in indoor culture.

Size: up to 10' (3 m).

Location: WINTER—southeastern or southwestern exposure. SUMMER—*Inside* or *Outside:* eastern or western exposure. FALL: move indoors by mid-September; site in eastern or western exposure.

Dormancy: none, but light resting period; slowly diminish watering, keeping soil barely moist; cease fertilizing, November through February.

Water: keep moderately and evenly moist.

Mist: daily, twice a day when possible.

Humidity: above normal for happiness 40%-45%.

Air circulation: helpful condition.

Feed: mild liquid manure every 2 weeks.

Soil: 2 parts standard potting mix, 1 part peat moss, 1 part perlite.

Temperature: Day—68°-80°F (20°-26°C). Night—55°-68°F (12°-20°C).

Potbound: repot or pot-on as needed and indicated by root growth being at least 50% of pot content.

Mature plants: hard pruning to reestablish plant should be done in early spring, prior to evidence of new growth. Take cuttings, easily rooted, for fresh replacement. Super specimen for training as topiary.

Propagate: by division or stem cuttings, root latter in water or moist vermiculite.

Insect alert: mealybug, mites, scale.

Notable: good artificial light specimen, a total of 14 light hours combined with natural; prune plant often to prevent legginess; must have good soil porosity; never allow soil to dry out completely; rinse foliage frequently in room-temperature or tepid water to prevent dust-clogged pores.

H. canariensis (kan-ar-ee-en'-siss) Algerian ivy, Canary Island ivy; native to Azores, Canary Islands, Morocco; leaves to 8" (.25 m); leathery; deep green, shiny; nondivided leaf face; stems with aerial roots; evergreen.

> Variety—Variegata (vay-ree-ag-gay'-tuh) meaning variegated; leaf has a creamy color margin.
> Variety—Foliis variegatis (foh'-lee-iss vay-ree-eh-gay'-tiss) leaf swathed or spotted with creamish shade.

H. helix (hee'-lix) Common ivy, English ivy; native to North Africa, Europe, Asia; leaf size from very small through large, 3 or 5 lobed, plain or variegated in color; leaf edges variable in character; all determined by varieties and cultivars.

> Variety—Cordata (kor-day'-tuh) heart-shaped leaf; slow growing.
> Variety—Gold Dust: green leaves, yellow variations.

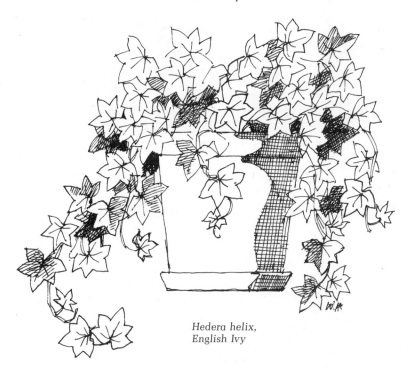

Hedera helix,
English Ivy

Variety—Hibernica (hye-ber'-nik-uh) Irish ivy; leaves up to 5" (127 mm); barely lobed.
Variety—Minor (mye'-nor) dainty leaf; grayish veining.
Variety—Pedata (ped-ay'-tuh) small leaf; silver veining; fast growing.

HELIOTROPIUM ARBORESCENS (hee-lee-oh-troh'-pee-um are-bore-ess'-enz) Common Heliotrope; nickname: Cherry Pie.

This evergreen shrub, softly and sweetly scented with summer through autumn flowering, will last for many years. *Helios,* the sun, and *trope,* to turn, *arborescens,* treelike. The arborescens species, merely 12"-18" (.30-.45 m) high, is a super embellishment for the small, plant-neglected site. Legend has it that although Apollo loved Clytie, he left her for greener pastures, and took up with her sister Levcothoe. Clytie couldn't handle this scene and slowly faded into death. Too late, Apollo rued his demeaning actions and, to make amends, changed Clytie into a flower which would always keep turning toward the sun.

Family Tree: Boraginaceae (bohr-uh-gin-ay'-see-ay) Borage family; from Peru.

Foliage: dark evergreen to purplish leaves; oblong, slightly hairy and veined.

Flower: delightful vanilla fragrance, although some varieties lack scent; 3"-6" (76-150 mm) flat umbels (a number of stalked flowers issuing from top center of stem); soft-textured, purple flowerlets year round; hybrids are lavender, purple, blue, white, or red.

Size: 6"-18" (.15-.45 m) tall; some species to 4' (1.20 m).

Location: WINTER—full sun; set in southern exposure. SUMMER—*Inside:* partial shade; set in eastern to southern exposure for direct rays of morning sun. *Outside:* partial shade; set in eastern exposure or under a protective structure where plant receives strong light but no direct rays. FALL: move indoors by mid-September.

Dormancy: starts along about September; slowly di-

Heliotropium arborescens,
Heliotrope

minish watering and allow to get on the dry side between waterings, until May; cease fertilizing.
Water: keep very moist; water check frequently.
Mist: daily, twice daily in hot weather.
Humidity: above normal, 45%-50%.
Air circulation: helpful condition.
Feed: weekly, with mild liquid manure, May through August.
Soil: 2 parts standard potting mix, 1 part peat moss, 1 part perlite.
Temperature: Day—68°-72°F (20°-22°C). Night—50°-55°F (10°-12°C).

Helleborus niger,
Christmas Rose

Potbound: happy; repot in spring before growth begins; pot-on only when root system becomes 60%-65% of soil content.
Mature plants: in spring, pinch tips when 4"-5" (100-127 mm) high, to make bushy plant. In fall, prune back after major blooming; tree or standard shape is achieved by pruning off side shoots.
Propagate: by spring or autumn stem cuttings, which root easily in moist sand or perlite; or seed.
Insect alert: aphids, red spider, mealybug, whitefly.
Notable: never allow soil to dry out completely; cannot take direct rays of sun; use pebble, water, and tray method to maintain "upped" humidity.

H. peruvianum (per-ooh-vee-ay'-num) same as species arborescens, but, as the name indicates, from Peru.

HELLEBORUS NIGER (hel-leb-boh'-rus nye'-jer) Christmas Rose, Hellebore.
The name comes from the Greek *helein*, to kill; *bora*, food; and the Latin *niger*, black, for some species are deadly poisonous. Handsome flowers to bloom cheerfully through winter months.
Family Tree: Ranunculaceae (ran-un-cue-lay'-see-ay) Buttercup family; from central and southern Europe, and Asia.
Foliage: dark green, leathery, deeply divided evergreen; leaves toothed at the apex.
Flower: 2" (50 mm) cup-shaped, white, on sturdy stems, November through March; varieties come in white and pink-flushed.
Size: 1'-2' (.30-.60 m).
Location: WINTER—southern exposure.
SUMMER—*Inside:* eastern exposure. *Outside:* northern exposure.
FALL: move indoors by mid-September; site in southeast exposure.
Dormancy: period starts in April; keep in shaded, cool area with lightly, evenly moist soil; when new growth begins move plant back to specified site for season; cease fertilizing.
Water: keep evenly moist.
Mist: daily; when flower buds open mist around plant, not directly on it.
Humidity: happy above normal, 40%-50%.
Air circulation: helpful condition.
Feed: mild liquid manure weekly, June through November.
Soil: 1 part standard potting mix, 1 part peat moss, 1 part perlite.
Temperature: Day—68°-72°F (20°-22°C). Night—60°-65°F (15°-18°C).
Potbound: repot each spring after dormancy, in soil specified for this genus; pot-on as indicated by crowding of pot.
Mature plants: better bloom if stems pinched back as they become straggly; pinch off to point where plant retains compact, uniform shape.
Propagate: by division when repotting, each section can be planted separately, disturb parent plant as little as possible; or by seed.
Insect alert: mealybugs, mites.

Disease alert: root rot from overwatering.
Notable: keep sited in coolish indoor habitat; soil must be porous and light; never allow to be water-logged or to completely dry out; repot very gently so as not to handle roots more than necessary.

H. corsicus (kor'-sic-cuss) meaning of Corsica in the Mediterranean; Corsican Hellebore; creamy green flowers 2″ (50 mm) across, on large trusses, winter through spring; waxy bluish, spiny leaves on 2″ (50 mm) stems.
H. orientalis (or-ee-en-tay'-lis) meaning from the East; common name, Lenten Rose, sturdier and more colorful than *H. Niger*; up to 2′ (.60 m) high; blooms to 15″ (.38 m) across; flowers in spring; variables of white, pink, maroon, cream, and purple fading to green; from Greece, Asia Minor.

HIBISCUS ROSA-SINENSIS (hye-bisk'-us roh-zuh-sin-nen'-sis) Rose of China, Tropical Hibiscus, Rose Mallow, Chinese Hibiscus.
Given adequate space, a truly fine plant of lovely bloom and easy maintenance. Previously available in a much varied selection of flower type and color, this genus now has new bi- and tri-colored cultivars in coffee brown, mauve, and tints, as well as ruffled and fringed shapes. This, the official flower of Hawaii, is the luscious posy gracing the dark hair of that state's beauties. Hibiscus is an ancient Greek name.
Family Tree: Malvaceae (mal-vay'-see-ay) Mallow family; native to China, Asia, and the tropics.
Foliage: dense group of coarsely toothed, dark, glossy, oval leaves.
Flower: 4″-8″ (100-200 mm) papery blossoms for most of the year; each usually open for just one day; colors range through white, yellow, orange, red, pink; shapes are single or double funnels with yellow pistils (the flower's female organ); some petals cut deeply and feathered.
Size: 3′-5′ (.90-1.50 m).

Hibiscus rosa-sinensis,
Rose of China

Location: WINTER—southern exposure.
SUMMER—*Inside* and *Outside*: eastern exposure.
FALL: move indoors by mid-September; site in eastern exposure.
Dormancy: period starts at end of flowering; or you may induce dormancy by withholding fertilizer and keeping water to minimum; will bloom in summer if dormant in winter, or vice versa.
Water: keep soil evenly moist.
Mist: daily, or when possible twice daily, with tepid water.
Humidity: moist, moist! 50%-60%.
Air circulation: helpful condition.
Feed: weekly dose of mild liquid manure.
Soil: 2 parts standard potting mix, 1 part peat moss.
Temperature: Day—70°-75°F (21°-23°C). Night—60°-65°F (15°-18°C).
Potbound: repot after dormant period; pot-on normally as indicated by plant's root system overbalancing soil content.
Mature plants: better bloom if stems pinched back as they become straggly; pinch off to point where plant retains compact, uniform shape throughout growing season. Best time for pruning is repotting or potting-on time.
Propagate: by air layering, seed, or from cuttings of new growth, using 3″ (76 mm) shoots in water, moist sand, or vermiculite.
Insect alert: red spider mite, whitefly, mites, aphids, mealybug, scale.
Disease alert: with too low humidity, leaves curl and buds may drop; also sharp changes in temperature may cause buds to drop.
Notable: do not keep in overly warm site; never allow soil to dry out completely; flourishes under normal care; keeping pot-bound restricts size of plant to keep from growing out-of-bounds, but allow pot size of 12″-14″ (.30-.36 m) or tub, prior to restraining root system to potbound status; plant will be happy in interior habitat 25 years and up.

H. schizopetalus (skye-zoh-pet'-al-us) meaning cut-petaled; Fringe Hibiscus: pendulous 2½″ (62 mm) orange red flowers with lacy-edged petals.
H. rosa-sinensis cooperi (roh-zuh-sin-nen'-sis koop'-per-ee) meaning Cooper's Rose of China; 2½″ (62 mm) scarlet flowers, narrow 2″ (50 mm) leaves marked with olive green, pink, crimson, and white.

HOWEA (how'-ee-uh) Flat Palm; Curly Palm.
Howea is a very graceful, arching genus of two species, previously named Kentia. It is erect and upright in habit, a good tub plant for eastern or western exposure. Handsome and tough, this rich dark green, evergreen palm does not grow too rapidly but needs a sizable site at maturity.
Family Tree: Palmae (pal-may') Palm family; native only to the Lord Howe Islands in the Pacific.
Foliage: long, feathery, arching fronds (leaves) composed of many leaflets, on a single trunk.
Size: up to 15′ (4.50 m), depending on species.
Location: WINTER—eastern or western exposure.
SUMMER—*Inside*: eastern or western exposure. *Outside*: eastern or western exposure, sheltered to protect fragile foliage from potentially damaging winds and heavy rains.

FALL: move indoors by mid-September; site in eastern or western exposure.

Dormancy: none, although light resting period in winter months; slowly diminish watering, keeping soil barely moist; cease fertilizing.

Water: thoroughly and evenly, allowing soil to dry between waterings.

Mist: daily, two or more times in warm weather.

Humidity: above normal, 45%-60%.

Air circulation: essential to have good moderate movement for top plant performance.

Feed: very, very mild liquid manure, ¼ strength of package recommendations, March through October.

Soil: 1 part standard potting mix, 2 parts peat.

Temperature: Day—68°-75°F (20°-23°C). Night—58°-65°F (14°-18°C).

Potbound: very happy; unless absolutely essential, do not disturb the root system of this genus, it can take years for plant to settle back into its previous contentment.

Mature plants: in repotting or potting-on, firm soil well but do not compact it.

Propagate: by seed.

Insect alert: mealybug, red spider mite, scale, thrips.

Notable: absolutely no drafts; do not allow soil to dry out completely, but *no soggy soil*; soil must be porous, for good drainage is essential to successful culture; use pebble, water, and tray method to maintain high humidity; good in artificial light, needing a total of 16 light hours, combining natural and artificial; leaves should be washed or wiped with moist cloth at least once a month to keep pores unclogged; no direct sun, or foliage will burn; remember that most palms are slow growing; frequently one finds several plants of a species potted together for a look of more fullness, giving a multitrunk effect.

H. belmoreana (bel-mor-ee-ay'-nuh) Sentry palm or Curly palm; previously known as Kentia belmoreana; slow growing, not too spreading in habit; curving green fronds in arched form.

H. forsteriana (for-ster-ee-ay'-nuh) Paradise palm or Flat palm, previously called Kentia forsteriana; fast growing, flat in growth habit; dark green feathery fronds to 10′ (3 m) long, open-type crown formed.

HOYA (hoy'-uh) Waxplant, Porcelain Flower.
A hanging or twining plant that blooms periodically, most profusely April through October. The lovely, sweetly aromatic flowers are a bonus produced only after this genus has totally settled into its interior habitat; this may take up to 5 years; the beauty of the foliage, however, will aid your patience.

Family Tree: Asclepiadaceae (as-klep-ee-uh-day'-see-ay) Milkweed family; from Java, East Asia, and Australia.

Foliage: pointed, oval, and fleshy, arranged in opposites on vines; 2″-4″ (50-100 mm); smooth texture, leathery; evergreen; very glossy; some have showy colors in swaths of pink, white, red, or variegated.

Flower: shiny, sweetly aromatic, pending in clusters of 12-15 blossoms; wheel-shaped, long-lasting, ½″-1″ (12-25 mm); brown, red, yellow, violet, or white, with pink centers.

Size: trailers up to 4′ (1.20 m).

Howea belmoreana,
Sentry Palm

Location: WINTER—full sun; set in southern exposure.
SUMMER—*Inside:* partial shade; set in eastern to southern exposure for direct rays of morning sun. *Outside:* partial shade; set in eastern exposure or under a protective structure where plant receives strong light but no direct rays.
FALL: move indoors by mid-September; site in eastern exposure.

Dormancy: period starts October; return to normal cultural program when new growth starts to appear in January; slowly diminish watering, keeping soil barely moist; cease fertilizing; keep on cooler side of recommended temperatures.

Water: thoroughly, but allow to dry out totally between waterings.

Mist: daily, twice a day throughout blooming and growing season; use only tepid water.

Humidity: normal, 30%-35%.

Air circulation: helpful condition.

Feed: with mild liquid manure every 3 weeks, late February through July.

Soil: 2 parts standard potting mix, 1 part peat moss, 1 part perlite.

Temperature: Day—70°-75° F (21°-23°C). Night—60°-65°F (15°-18°C).

Potbound: mature plants are happy, but repot young plants after dormancy in February.

Mature plants: do not remove stems of flowers that have bloomed, for on these leafless, seemingly dead stems, new flowering will occur; rest of the plant may be pruned any time for shaping. Keep plants in same sites, they dislike change of location; can be trained on a trellis.

Propagate: from stem cuttings in spring, root in moist vermiculite.

Insect alert: mites, mealybugs, nematodes, scale, aphids.

Disease alert: root rot from soggy soil.

Notable: when blooming, plant is most visually effective if seen from below in hanging container; if plant is over-

Hoya bella,
Waxplant

fed, excessive vigor of growth causes dropping of flower buds; water less during cool or cloudy weather; blossoms sometimes drop nectar; a slow-growing, long-lasting plant.

H. australis (os-tray'-liss) meaning from Australia; vigorous vine with red-centered bluish-white flowers in fall; leaves broadly oval, pointed, leathery, spotted silver; fuzzy beneath; some blooms waxy pink with red crowns.
H. bella (bell'-uh) meaning pretty; previously called *H.*

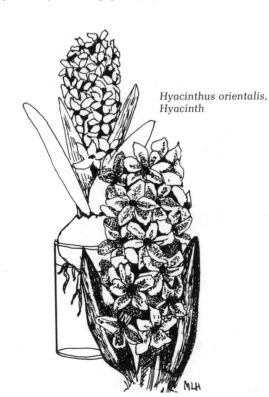

Hyacinthus orientalis,
Hyacinth

paxtonii; 20″ (.55 m), bushy plant with branches drooping in maturity; flowers, in summer, white with rosy violet centers; dark green, tiny, oval leaves.
H. carnosa (kar-noh'-suh) meaning fleshy; from India; vining plant up to 8′ (2.45 m) long; 2″-4″ (50-100 mm) oval, dark green, succulent leaves, sometimes edged with pink and cream; blossoms arranged in rounded clusters, creamy white with centers of tiny, pink, 5 pointed stars; old flower stems will bloom again.
H. cinnamomifolia (sin-nam-moh-me-foh'-lee-uh) bears yellowish green flowers with purple red centers.
H. coronaria (kor-oh-nay'-ree-uh) meaning crowned or wreathed; a rare species with lettuce green leaves and yellow flowers, bearing 5 red dots at their base.
H. purpurea-fusca (poor-poor'-ee-uh-fus'-kuh) meaning having a shade of purple; fall blooming, brownish red flowers have white hairs in a purple center; also called Silver Pink because of silvery pink blotches on its leaves.
H. keysii (kee-see-eye) grows to 30″ (.75 m), with white flowers and gray green leaves.
H. motoskei (mow-tosk'-ee-eye) to 4′ (1.20 m); pink blooms with maroon crown, broadly elliptic leaves with silver spots.

HYACINTHUS ORIENTALIS (hye-uh-sinth'-us or-ee-en-tay'-liss) Hyacinth. A Greek myth has Hyakinthos, much favored by Apollo, killed by this god while playing quoits; Apollo's jealousy was caused by Zephyrus, the West Wind. Where the blood of Hyakinthos spilled, Hyacinths sprang up.
This highly scented genus is very easy to force in the interior habitat. The wide spectrum of colors from which to choose is limited only by definite blooming seasons for each variety. *Orientalis* means from the East.
Family Tree: Liliaceae (lil-ee-ay'-see-ay) Lily family; native of eastern Mediterranean and Asia Minor.
Foliage: cluster of long, narrow, boat-shaped, light green leaves.
Flower: many small, bell-shaped, waxy blooms clustered on spikes; richly fragrant; available in many varieties; red, white, blue, pink, or yellow.
Size: 6″-1½′ (.15-.45 m).
Mist: daily, lightly, around plant, not on it.
Humidity: normal, 30%-35%.
Air circulation: helpful condition.
Feed: for pot culture, mild liquid manure every 2 weeks; nothing for water culture (see entry below).
Soil: 2 parts standard potting mix, 1 part perlite or sand.
Pot culture: fill flower pots with soil, add and cover specially precooled bulbs to a depth of ¾″ (19 mm). Water, set in cool, dark site, keeping evenly moist. Have temperature between 40°-50°F (4-10°C). Feed every 2 weeks with mild liquid manure. About 3 months later, when tops are 3″ (76 mm) high, remove to warm site, keeping soil evenly moist. Place in cooler position when bulbs are in full flower (which should be in about a week), to extend blooming period. After flowering when the foliage has yellowed, cease watering and store in cool, dark site, to hold until outside fall planting.
Water culture: use specially precooled bulbs ordered in September, early flowering varieties are available for Christmas bloom. Fill special hyacinth glasses with tap

water, to level just below bottom of bulb resting in top (bulb) section. Place glasses in cool dark site, periodically replenishing water to same level. When thick, white roots fill glasses, and sprouts are 4″ (100 mm) tall, take plants into warm room with bright light. When foliage has yellowed after blooming, remove bulb from glass. Dry and store in paper bag to plant outdoors in fall.

Propagate: by side bulbs—not a task for the amateur.

Notable: if blooming bulbs are kept in coolish site, the flower should hold for 1½-2 weeks; a forced bulb cannot be reforced but will recycle for years of growth if planted outside; for water culture, drop a few pieces of horticultural charcoal into glasses to keep the water clear and sweet.

H. amethystinus (am-meth-thist′-in-us) meaning of amethyst color; Spanish hyacinth, originates in the Pyrenees; delicate bright blue flowers borne on stems seldom exceeding 8″ (200 mm).

HYDRANGEA MACROPHYLLA (hye-drayn′-jee-uh mak′-roh-fill-uh).

Of the six or seven species of hydrangea, only H. macrophylla, a native of Japan, is used as an indoor plant. Commonly referred to as the house hydrangea or common big leaf hydrangea, it is handsome and one of the earliest spring flowering plants. An interesting feature is that the color of the huge, soft-textured flower clusters can be manipulated by soil chemistry, very simply (see *Notable*); *H. macrophylla* is sometimes listed by its previous name, *H. hortensis* (hor-ten′-siss).

Family Tree: Saxifragaceae (saks-i-fra-gay′-see-ay) Saxifrage family; native to China and Japan; hybridized by growers in Europe.

Hydrangea macrophylla

Foliage: shiny, oval, dark green leaves, 2″-6″ (50-150 mm) long; opposite and tooth-edged.

Flower: dense clusters, small, 1″-1½″ (25-37 mm), with some larger, showy flowers; outer florets usually pale; blooms often last 6 weeks or more; colors range blue through lavender to pink, also red and white.

Size: generally kept to 3′ (.90 m) high.

Location: WINTER—full sun; set in southern exposure. SUMMER—*Inside:* partial shade; set in eastern to southern exposure for direct rays of morning sun. *Outside:* partial shade; set in eastern exposure or under a protective structure where plant receives strong light but no direct rays. FALL: move indoors by mid-September.

Dormancy: indoors in fall, store in cool, dim site with temperature as close to a low of 45°F (7°C) as possible; slowly diminish watering, keeping soil evenly and moderately moist; cease fertilizing.

Water: needs frequent, thorough, even watering; check plant daily for moisture needs.

Mist: daily, twice daily if possible.

Humidity: above normal for happiness, 45%-50%.

Air circulation: helpful condition.

Feed: weekly, with very mild liquid form of acid fertilizer, a 21-7-7 balance; start feeding program 1½ months after repotting or potting-on plant, and continue through July.

Soil: 2 parts standard potting mix, 2 parts peat moss, and 1 part perlite.

Temperature: Day—70°F (21°C). Night—60°F (15°C).

Potbound: pot-on with spacious pots after flowering cycle; using soil as specified for this genus.

Mature plants: too tall a plant for standing upright; stake and tie main trunk (leave small amount of slack in ties to eliminate potential of injury from tie cutting into fleshy stem). After flowering, cut back shoots which have bloomed, newly developed shoots will bloom following year. Give rest period in 65°F (18°C), for 6 weeks prior to dormancy.

Propagate: by cuttings in March, after flowering; place in moist sand or vermiculite.

Forcing culture: midwinter, January, move to 60°F (15°C) site, with good, bright light; water thoroughly and evenly to encourage growth; when leaves start to form, feed biweekly with mild liquid manure, till spring flowering.

Insect alert: whitefly, thrips, scale, mite, aphid.

Notable: soil must have porosity; no soggy conditions; do not set in direct sun when flowering; to control color, add a tablespoon of aluminum sulfate (after new leaves appear) to each pot every 2 weeks for 6 to 8 feedings; this turns soil acidic, which results in blue flowers; flowers turn pink in basic soil; white flowering varieties will not change, regardless of soil conditions.

HYPOCYRTA NUMMULARIA (hye-poh-sert′-uh nummew-lay-ree-uh) Candy Corn Plant, Goldfish Plant.

An excellent genus for hanging container in shaded site with its masses of pouch-shaped flowers in spring and summer months. Enjoy the Hypocyrta as a graceful evergreen trailer, for a small area.

Family Tree: Gesneriaceae (jes-near-ee-ay′-see-ay) Gesneria family; native of Brazil, tropical America.

Foliage: ¾″-2½″ (19-62 mm) oval, opposite leaves; some velvety, some glossy or waxy; all evergreen.

Flower: 1″ (25 mm) blossoms hanging from stems look like puffy tropical fish, the purple-ringed openings of pouched lobes look like tiny mouths; blooms throughout the year; heavier at times, light resting in between.

Size: stems grow 9″-2′ (.23-.60 m).

Location: WINTER—southern exposure.

SUMMER—*Inside:* eastern exposure. *Outside:* northern exposure.

FALL: move indoors by mid-September; site in eastern exposure.

Dormancy: starts after major blooming ends but is actually more of a resting period; slowly diminish watering; cease fertilizing; prune back to compact shape; leave no straggly branches.

Water: keep evenly moist.

Mist: daily, twice a day when possible.

Humidity: high for happiness, 50%-60%.

Air circulation: helpful condition.

Feed: mild liquid manure every 2 weeks, March through September.

Soil: 1 part standard potting mix, 2 parts peat moss, 1 part sharp sand or perlite.

Temperature: Day—72°-78°F (22°-25°C). Night—65°-70°F (18°-21°C).

Potbound: very happy; if repotting, do so in February; pot-on only as necessary, when there is 80% root growth to 20% soil.

Mature plants: maintain warm, even temperature, especially in December and January when buds begin their development.

Propagate: old plants, by division in spring, seed, or 3″ (76 mm) stem cuttings, latter at any time. Root cuttings in small pots of moist sandy soil or vermiculite.

Offspring established: after transplanting rooted cuttings into small pots of soil specified for this genus, pinch tops several times for fuller plant; site same as mature plants.

Insect alert: whitefly, mealybug, mite, scale.

Disease alert: misting or watering with too cold a shower can cause circle spotting on leaves.

Notable: must have good drainage; soil must never be completely dry or soggy; set on tray with pebbles and water for consistent humidity; a good artificial light specimen, give a total of 14 hours of light combining natural and artificial light culture; pay attention to proper culture for success.

H. strigillosa (stry-jill-oh′-suh) Goldfish Plant; orange red flowers in winter and spring; leaves are lancelike, velvety dark green.

H. wettsteinii (wet-sty-nee′-eye) Clog Plant; flowers with red and yellow pouches; ¾″ (19 mm) leaves are glossy, oval, on thick stems.

H. radicans (rad′-i′kanz) meaning rooting, especially along stems; flowers are almost round; orange red with orange yellow rim; blooming time through spring and summer.

HYPOESTES SANGUINOLENTA (hye′-poh-ess-teez san-gwin′-oh-len-tuh) Freckle Face, Pink Polka Dot.

"Little ole′ Freckle Face" is a rather charming, small-scaled, evergreen foliage species. The special characteristic is coloration; the green leaves so prettily splashed with

Hypocyrta strigillosa,
Goldfish Plant

shades of pink. Moderate in growth pace, of simple care, the *H. sanguinolenta* is quite at home in the interior environment when sited in good bright light. A pinch and a nip to retain good shape will ensure a totally aesthetic display at blooming time. It may be listed or referred to by its previous names, *Eranthemum sanguinolentum* or *H. phyllostachya*.

Family Tree: Acanthaceae (uh-kanth-ay′-see-ay) Acanthus family; native to Madagascar.

Foliage: green spotted with pink through light red; oval to point, rather deeply center-veined; evergreen.

Flower: spike blossoms; lavender, white-throated.

Size: up to 2′ (.60 m).

Location: WINTER—southern exposure.

SUMMER—*Inside:* southeastern or southwestern exposure. *Outside:* eastern or western exposure.

FALL: move indoors by mid-September; site in eastern or western exposure.

Dormancy: none, but light resting period; after flowering; slowly diminish watering, keeping soil barely moist; cease fertilizing.

Hypoestes sanguinolenta,
Freckle Face

Water: keep moderately and evenly moist.

Mist: daily, twice a day when possible.

Humidity: above normal for happiness, 40%-45%.

Air circulation: helpful condition.

Feed: mild liquid acid fertilizer, every 2 weeks; using 21-7-7 balance.

Soil: 1 part standard potting soil, 2 parts peat moss, 1 part perlite.

Temperature: Day—68°-80°F (20°-26°C). Night—55°-68°F (10°-20°C).

Potbound: repot, or pot-on as needed and indicated by root growth being at least 50% of pot content.

Mature plants: hard pruning to reestablish plant should be done in early spring prior to evidence of new growth. Depending upon cultural and environmental circumstance, it is conceivable that after flowering, this plant just may wither and die down to soil level; keep soil barely moist; new growth will be evident within a short period of time.

Propagate: by seed or stem cuttings.

Insect alert: mealybug, whitefly, mites, scale, slugs.

Notable: good artificial light specimen, a total of 14 light hours combined with natural; prune plant often to prevent legginess; must have good soil porosity; never allow soil to dry out completely; rinse foliage frequently in room-temperature or tepid water to prevent dust-clogged pores; the brighter light site will produce the more interesting shadings and patterns of foliage.

IMPATIENS (im-pay′-shee-enz) Touch-Me-Not, Patient Lucy, Busy Lizzie, Snapweed, Lousy Lucy.

The Latin, *impatiens*, refers to the way the seed pods of some species burst and scatter their seed when touched. A bushy plant with delicate charm; the small-scaled flower with profusion of bloom. Dwarf varieties are best suited for interior growing because of visual appearance; an old-fashioned garden plant to remind one of the importance of indoor greenery throughout our heritage.

Family Tree: Balsaminaceae (ball-sam-min-ay′-see-ay) Balsam family; native of Africa and tropical Asia.

Foliage: 1″-2″ (25-50 mm) leaves may be green, maroon, or variegated green and white.

Flower: soft, single, flat flowers 1″-2″ (25-50 mm) across; pink, red, orange, purple, tangerine or red and white; fast growing; bloom all year with varying degrees of profusion.

Size: 6″-24″ (.15-.60 m).

Location: WINTER—southern exposure.

SUMMER—*Inside:* eastern to southern location. *Outside:* northeastern exposure.

FALL: move indoors by mid-September; site in southeastern exposure.

Water: keep evenly moist through frequent, thorough waterings.

Mist: daily, twice a day if possible, year-round.

Humidity: above normal, 50%-60%.

Air circulation: helpful condition.

Feed: weekly, with mild liquid manure.

Soil: standard potting mix.

Temperature: Day—70°F (21°C) or higher. Night—60°-65°F (15°-18°C).

Potbound: normal; pot-on when plant indicates it by root system overpowering soil content.

Mature plants: better bloom if stems pinched back as they become straggly, pinch off to point where plant retains compact, uniform shape; pinch center out of young shoots, especially after heavy blooming periods, for a wide plant.

Propagate: by seed or leaf cuttings obtained when pinching tops back; root in water or moist vermiculite; remove flowers and buds while rooting.

Offspring established: transplant each seedling into 2½″-3″ (62-76 mm) pot with standard potting mix; pinch out tips regularly for better branching and flowering; pinch premature flower buds until plant matures.

Insect alert: red spider mite, whitefly, aphids.

Notable: flower buds will drop off from lack of light and/or too low humidity; if not fed regularly, flowering will be very light; a good artificial light genus, 14 hours a day is the recommended combined total of natural and artificial light; keep on lower side of recommended temperatures.

I. walleriana (wal-ler-ee-ay′-nuh).

I. holstii (hole′-stee-eye).

I. sultanii (sul-tan′-ee-eye) meaning after sultan or Zanzibar; all 3 are the same species; bloom in winter with irregular red, pink, white, purple, or salmon flowers; some hybrids are colored salmon, rose, and purple; leaves are reddish; height to 1′-2′ (.30-.60 m).

I. petersiana (pea-ter′-sy-ay′-nuh) blooms in late spring and summer with 2″ (50 mm) scarlet flowers; elliptic, purple bronze evergreen leaves to 1½″ (37 mm) long; height up to 1½′ (.45 m).

I. oliveri (ol-li-vay′-ree) 2″ (50 mm) lavender flowers; pale leaves up to 4″ (100 mm) long; large plant becomes straggly easily.

I. platypetala aurantiaca (plat-ee-pet′-ta′-luh aw-ran-tie-

Impatiens walleriana,
Busy Lizzie

ay'-cuh) meaning flat-petalled; dark yellow or salmon orange flowers with red center; green foliage; to 26″ (.65 m).

I. repens (ray'-penz) meaning with stems which creep or root; delightful, red-branched trailer with golden yellow, brown striped, hooded flowers; up to 20″ (.55 m).

IPOMOEA RUBRO-CAERULEA (eye-poh-mee'-uh roob-roh-sear-ooh'-lee-uh) Morning Glory, Sweet Potato.
From the Greek *ips*, bind weed; and *homoios*, a twining growth habit. *Rubro-caerulea*, red sky (or true) blue. Flowers last but a day, yet each is large and magnificent, in profuse display, with more to follow the next day. A climbing, vining aesthetic accent for a sunny interior site. One may hear this plant referred to as the Pharbitis.
Family Tree: Convolvulaceae (con-vol-view-lay'-see-ay) Morning Glory family; native of central tropical America.
Foliage: slender, pointed, heart-shaped, 2″-3″ (50-76 mm) leaves.
Flower: purple upon opening, turns sky blue when mature; trumpet shaped; 2½″-8″ (62-203 mm) blooms with yellow throats; others are scarlet, pink, white, or multicolor.
Size: twining, 5′-10′ (1.50-3 m).
Location: WINTER—full sun, southern exposure.
SUMMER—*Inside and Outside:* southern exposure.
FALL: move indoors by mid-September, site in southern exposure.
Dormancy: none, actually, but resting period indicated by plant not forming new buds for flowering; slowly diminish watering to approximately ½ normal amount; when new growth shows, gradually increasing to normal cultural process; cease fertilizing.
Water: keep thoroughly, constantly moist.

Ipomoea rubro-caerulea,
Morning Glory

Mist: daily, twice daily whenever possible.
Humidity: above normal, 45%-50%.
Air circulation: helpful condition.
Feed: when 4′ (1.20 m) high, fertilize with mild liquid manure, April through September.
Soil: standard potting mix.
Temperature: Day—70°-75°F (21°-23°C). Night—60°-65°F (15°-18°C).
Potbound: very happy! keep in small pot; when crowded, divide and repot.
Mature plants: remove dead blossoms to encourage better blooming.
Propagate: by seed, in March for summer flowers, in mid-summer for winter flowers; or purchase tuber: to root, set tuber in glass container with narrow end of tuber down, water level should cover 1″ (25 mm) of tuber; site in dark area; when growth starts, move to eastern exposure; when root system is firmly established, leave in glass container or pot in 6″-7″ (150-177 mm) pot with standard potting mix; site in full sun.
Offspring established: when 8-9 leaves are out, pinch out tip; pinch buds out of axils (where leaf stem is joined to main stem) of remaining leaves; as new branches grow and develop 6-7 leaves, pinch back to 3 leaves; keep pinching branch tips and alternate (every other) flower buds for finest plant form and large blossoms.
Notable: avoid drafts.

I. batatas (bat-tay'-tass) trailing, blue-flowered "sweet potato."
I. nil (nill) brilliant purple blue or pink flowers up to 4″ (100 mm); single and semidouble; rapid growing, large-leaved vine to 8′ (2.45 m); sometimes listed as I. imperialis.

IRESINE (eye-res-sye'-nee) Blood Leaf, Gizzard Plant.
Iresine is of easy maintenance, needing attention in light pruning to maintain its aesthetic form. Site this perennial foliage genus in full sun to bring out the brilliant color of its translucent, heavily veined foliage. The common name, blood leaf, indicates the depth of color of the leaves, retained as the plant ages and tends to trail.
Family Tree: Amaranthaceae (am-ar-ranth-aye'-see-ay) Amaranth family; native to South America.
Foliage: oppositely arranged, usually oval, to 5″ (127 mm) long; prominent greenish yellow veins, on red or green leaves; red stems; bushy growth habit.
Flower: small, insignificant.
Size: up to 18″ (.45 m).
Location: WINTER—southern exposure.
SUMMER—*Inside:* southern exposure. *Outside:* southern exposure; protect fragile foliage from potentially damaging elements, preferably by overhang.
FALL: move indoors by mid-September; site in southern exposure.
Dormancy: none, but light resting period, October through February; slowly diminish watering, keeping soil barely moist; cut fertilizing program in half.
Water: keep moderately and evenly moist.
Mist: daily, twice a day when possible.
Humidity: above normal for happiness, 40%-45%.
Air circulation: helpful condition.

*Iresine herbstii,
Blood Leaf*

Feed: mild liquid manure every 2 weeks.
Soil: 2 parts standard potting soil, 1 part peat moss, 1 part perlite.
Temperature: Day—68°-80°F (20°-26°C). Night—55°-68°F (12°-20°C).
Potbound: repot; or pot-on as needed and indicated by root growth being at least 50% of pot content.
Mature plants: need constant pruning for retention of good form. Take cuttings, easily rooted, for fresh replacement. Pinch off flower buds as soon as evident to encourage nurturing of plant into foliage growth.
Propagate: by division or stem cuttings, root latter in water or moist vermiculite.
Insect alert: mealybug, whitefly, mites, scale, slugs.
Notable: good artificial light specimen, a total of 14 light hours combined with natural; prune often to prevent legginess; do not overwater as plant will rot easily; must have good soil porosity; never allow soil to dry out completely; rinse foliage frequently in room-temperature or tepid water to prevent dust-clogged pores.

I. herbstii (herbs'-tee-eye) previously named Achyranthes verschaffeltii; purplish red leaves, notched at tip; light red veins.
I. lindenii (lin-deen'-ee-eye) narrow leaves, sharp tips; upright; strong red.

IXORA (ik-soh'-ruh) Flame of the Woods, Star Flower, Jungle Geranium.
Be aware that, generally, summer flowering Ixora goes into shock with change of environment; therefore this tropical genus drops its flower heads when first sited in the new environment. When adjusted and not disturbed it will favor you with very special, lovely flowers. Although not related, it is similar in appearance—on a much smaller scale—to the hydrangea.
Family Tree: Rubiaceae (roo-be-ay'-see-ay) Madder family; from tropical Asia and the East Indies.
Foliage: elliptical and bronze toned at first, maturing into dark, shiny evergreen, leathery leaves with red veins; about 4" (100 mm) long.
Flower: fragrant, 1" (25 mm), 4-petalled blooms in 4"-6" (100-150 mm) clusters; blooms intermittently all year, most profusely in summer and fall; orange, salmon, pink, white, or yellow.
Size: 12"-4' (.30-1.20 m); varying with species.
Location: WINTER—full sun; set in southern exposure.
SUMMER—*Inside:* partial shade; set in eastern to southern exposure for direct rays of morning sun. *Outside:* partial shade; set in eastern exposure or under a protective structure where plant receives strong light but no direct rays.
FALL: move indoors by mid-September.
Dormancy: starts when heaviest blooming ends, about August, allow to rest through December, plant will indicate when hibernation time is over; slowly diminish watering to about half normal amount, keeping soil barely moist; cease fertilizing; resume feeding program when new growth shows.
Water: keep soil evenly moist.
Mist: daily, twice daily if possible; only tepid water.
Humidity: high for happiness, 60%-70%.
Air circulation: helpful condition.
Feed: mild liquid fertilizer of 21-7-7 balance, weekly March through August.
Soil: 1 part standard potting mix, 2 parts peat moss, 1 part perlite, 1 part sand.
Temperature: Day—70°-80°F (21°-26°C). Night—65°-68°F (18°-20°C).
Potbound: pot-on when indicated by root growth overbalancing soil content.
Mature plants: pinch at branch tips and clip leading shoots during growing season (March through August), or until flower buds appear, to encourage fuller plant and abundance of bloom; after resting period (late winter through early spring), cut plant back to equalized compact size; every second or third year repot at this time.
Propagate: by soft or young stem cuttings usually in spring, in moist vermiculite.

*Ixora coccinea,
Star Flower*

Offspring established: pinch tips for a fuller plant and better flowering.
Insect alert: mealybugs, scale, aphids.
Disease alert: too much sunlight will cause rolled-up leaves; too low a soil temperature, or watering with too cold water, will cause yellowing or falling.
Notable: needs acid soil; if leaves pale, add iron, such as Sequesfrene, in water once a month; do not allow soil to dry out completely; cannot stand lime so beware of house water; use room-temperature water; remove faded flower heads faithfully to make possible the setting of new buds; do not change site of plant during its flowering cycle or it will lose its flower heads; maintain humidity with pebbles, water, and tray or slider culture.

I. javanica (jav-van'-ik'uh) salmon red flowers; slender, pointed leaves 7″ (177 mm) long; willowy, red branches; once established, a long-lasting plant.
I. coccinea (kok-sin'-ee-uh) meaning bright, deep pink; large semispherical flower umbels (quantities of stalked flowers arise from central point at top of stem) of orange red or salmon red.

Jacobinia carnea,
King's Crown

JACOBINIA (jak-ob-bin'-ee-uh) King's Crown, Brazilian Plume, Plume Flower.
An unusually lovely flower spike is produced by this vigorously growing genus. The flowers generally last a few weeks.
Family Tree: Acanthaceae (uh-canth-ay'-see-ay) Acanthus family; native to Brazil.
Foliage: quiltlike, thin and velvety; arranged oppositely on square, branched stems; size, 1″-8″ (25-200 mm).
Flower: borne in pompomlike, long clusters at end of branches, all opening at the same time during the spring season; each bloom is two-lipped; orange, scarlet, yellow, rose, purple, pink, and crimson.
Size: 1′-3′ (.30-.90 m).
Location: WINTER—full sun; set in southern exposure.
SUMMER—*Inside:* partial shade; set in eastern to southern exposure for direct rays of morning sun. *Outside:* partial shade; set in eastern exposure or under a protective structure where plant receives strong light but no direct rays.
FALL: move indoors by mid-September; site in southeastern exposure.
Dormancy: no true dormancy, but plant is resting when not flowering; maintain normal culture during this time.
Water: keep soil evenly moist.
Mist: daily; twice a day when possible.
Humidity: happy when above normal, 40%-50%.
Air circulation: essential for healthy plant.
Feed: mild liquid manure every 3 weeks during growing season, March through August.
Soil: 2 parts standard potting mix, 1 part peat moss.
Temperature: Day—70°-75°F (21°-23°C). Night—65°-70°F (18°-21°C).
Potbound: repot in February after watering thoroughly; pot-on as needed for good root and soil balance.
Mature plants: when repotting, cut back old plants to encourage new, bushy growth. Remove dried up blooms as they fade.

Propagate: by stem cuttings, in spring for winter bloom, in fall for summer bloom.
Offspring established: pinch tips for bushy growth.
Insect alert: whitefly, red spider mite, scale.
Disease alert: too dry an air makes leaf edges roll up.
Notable: pruning is necessary to assure pleasing, wide shape; never allow soil to dry out completely; flower buds will blast from overwatering, also leaves turn brown.

J. carnea (karr'-nee-uh) meaning flesh-colored (the flowers); blooms are pink or rosy purple; fall blooming.
J. pauciflora (paw-sif-floh'-ruh) meaning few-flowered; once called J. Paucifolia, having few leaves; 1′ (.30 m) tall, it blooms late winter through April; solitary, 1″ (25 mm) long, tubular scarlet, yellow-tipped flowers; leaves are 3″ (76 mm) ovals; repot in May after flowering.
J. umbrosa (um-broh'-suh) meaning found in shady places; 2″ (50 mm) yellow flowers in dense, terminal clusters; large, egg-shaped leaves; to 12′ (3.65 m).
J. ghiesbeghtiana (geese-beg-tie-ay'-nuh) light green leaves; orange flowers.
J. obtusior (ob-too'-see-ohr) meaning with blunt apex; sub-shrub to 2′ (.60 m) tall; pink to crimson flowers in dense terminal clusters.
J. suberecta (soob-ber-rec'-tuh) 1″ (25 mm) orange scarlet flowers in clusters; 2½″ (62 mm) velvety leaves.

JASMINUM (jas'-min-um) Jasmine, Jessamine.
Jasminum is a latinized Persian name. The genus will display a profuse production of blooms when kept warm, permeating your interior site with delightful fragrance. It is twining in habit; a shrubby vine which performs regardless of size to which it is pruned; know it to be of vigorous growth. Some species included have slightly different cultural needs from those specified in the general culture for the genus; variants are noted.

Family Tree: Oleaceae (oh-lee-ay'-see-ay) Olive family; native to China, Canary Islands, Madeira, and Persia.

Foliage: 2″ (50 mm) waxy oval leaves; lobes, deciduous or evergreen, square-stemmed, opposite or alternate, simple or compound; depending on species.

Flower: fragrant clusters of star-shaped, white or yellow blossoms; most species blooming early spring through late fall.

Size: 8″ (.25 m), 15′-40′ (4.50-12 m) if vining.

Location: WINTER—full sun; set in southern exposure.

SUMMER—*Inside:* partial shade; set in eastern to southern exposure for direct rays of morning sun. *Outside:* partial shade; set in eastern exposure or under a protective structure where plant receives strong light but no direct rays.

FALL: move indoors by mid-September.

Dormancy: resting period only, October through February; slowly diminish watering, keeping soil barely moist; cease fertilizing.

Water: keep soil thoroughly and evenly moist.

Mist: twice a day when possible.

Humidity: above normal, 50%-60%.

Air circulation: helpful condition.

Feed: mild liquid manure, weekly March through September.

Soil: 2 parts standard potting mix, 1 part vermiculite.

Temperature: Day—68°-72°F (20°-22°C). Night—60°-65°F (15°-18°C).

Potbound: repot after blooming as needed; or pot-on when root growth is 50% of pot content.

Mature plants: prune as necessary, after blooming, to retain desired size.

Propagate: by seed, layering, or stem cuttings, latter in spring; root in moist sand or perlite.

Insect alert: mealybug, scale, whitefly.

Notable: high humidity and temperatures over 70°F (21°C) are required for good blooming; needs good drainage; most plants need support of small trellis or mesh wire; height can be controlled by basketweaving branches through support. Never allow soil to dry out completely; soil must have porosity.

J. grandiflorum (gran-di-flaw'-um) large, showy flowers; Spanish jasmine; resembles *J. officinale;* arching branches; white flowers with crimson outside.

J. humile (hew'-mil-ee) meaning of humble growth; common name, Italian jasmine; 1″ (25 mm) lemon yellow flowers, June through September; feathery, dark green leaflets, 2″ (50 mm); temperature requirements: night—50°-60°F (10°-15°C), day—68°F (20°C) or lower.

J. mesnyi (mess'-nee-eye) Primrose jasmine; native to China; 2″ (50 mm), sometimes double, yellow flowers with dark centers; no fragrance; thick, shiny green leaflets on beautiful evergreen vine; to 10′ (3 m).

J. nudiflorum (new-di-floh'-rum) Winter jasmine; bright yellow, 1″ (25 mm) flowers; deciduous vine to 15′ (4.50 m); late winter to early spring bloom; can be trained to fan shape or espalier.

J. odoratissimum (oh-door-uh-tis'-si-mum) native to Canary Islands and Madeira; small inflorescences (clusters) of delicately fragrant, yellow flowers, not abundant but throughout year; slender green shoots with dark green leaflets.

J. officinale (off-fiss-i-nay'-lee) meaning of the shop (the

Jasminum polyanthum, Jasmine

herbalist's), of value and service to man; common name, Poet's jasmine; from the Orient; clusters of star-shaped, ⅞″ (22 mm), white double flowers, blooms June through October; glossy green leaflets, 2″ (50 mm) long; deciduous shrub to 30′ (9 m).

J. parkeri (par-ker-eye) small, star-shaped yellow flowers in summer; to 12″ (.30 m) tall.

J. polyanthum (poll-ee-an-thum) native to China; clusters of star-shaped, fragrant, ¾″ (19 mm), white and rose flowers, in spring; can be forced to bloom until Christmas.

J. sambac (sam'-bak) Arabian jasmine; native to India and Indonesia, where these flowers are used as offerings to Buddha; clusters of rosette-shaped, semidouble, delicately fragrant blooms; colored white turning to purple as they fade.

KALANCHOE (kal-an'-koh'ee) Christmas Kalanchoe, Good Luck Plant, Panda Plant, Air Plant.

A genus of the succulent group whose varieties have attractive and long-lasting flowers. Kalanchoe is a latinized Chinese name for an ornamental of at least 20 different appearances among its various species. While waiting for blooms, one can enjoy the extremely interesting foliage. Catalogues sometimes list Kalanchoe as Bryophyllum or Kitchingia.

Family Tree: Crassulaceae (crass-yew-lay'-see-ay) Orpine family; native to South Africa, Asia, Madagascar.

Foliage: depending on species, linear, cylindrical, or orate; all are succulent and thick.

Flower: in clusters of little stars of greenish yellow, scarlet red, white, rust, or rose; generally bloom twice, winter and spring.

Size: 8″-10′ (.25-3 m), shrubby or trailing.

Location: WINTER—southern exposure.

SUMMER—*Inside and Outside: southern exposure.*

FALL: move indoors by mid-September; site in southern exposure.

Dormancy: period starts in fall; cease fertilizing; provide only natural light as normal for short fall and winter days; water lightly only when soil becomes completely dry; do not allow foliage to dry or wither; plant will indicate needs.

Water: thoroughly and evenly, allowing soil to dry out partially in between.

Mist: daily, lightly, around plant.

Humidity: low normal, 20%-25%.

Air circulation: helpful condition.

Feed: every 2 weeks, May through August with mild liquid manure.

Soil: 2 parts standard potting mix, 1 part perlite.

Temperature: Day—72°-78°F (22°-25°C). Night—60°-65°F (15°-18°C).

Potbound: normal, repot or pot-on into 3″-4″ (76-100 mm) pots every second year or when root system overbalances soil content.

Mature plants: better bloom if stems pinched back as they become straggly; pinch off to point where plant retains compact, uniform shape. Pinch center out of young shoots for wide plant; too tall a plant for standing upright, stake and tie main trunk (leave small amount of slack in ties to eliminate potential of injury from tie cutting into fleshy stem). Remove flower stalks when flowers fade.

Propagate: by stems, leaves, or petiole (leaf stalk); plant cuttings in moist sand or perlite any time of year; or from baby plants which form in the air on leaf edges of some varieties, root in moist sand or perlite.

Insect alert: mealybugs, aphids, mites, scale.

Disease alert: avoid mildew from too humid an atmosphere.

Notable: with proper culture, seed sown in March will flower the following winter; provide porous soil for good drainage; if treating insect pests, avoid Malathion which severely or fatally injures this plant; flowering season can

be humanly manipulated by setting this short-day plant in a dark area, or covering with tent of black plastic, for 14 out of every 24 hours, 4 weeks in a row, then setting it in full sun; overfeeding will foster fantastic foliage but little or no bloom; brightest flower color is obtained in full sun.

K. uniflora (yew-nif-floh'-ruh) meaning bearing one flower, each stem; one flower, delicate, pitcher-shaped, red on each stem; climbing, trailing species; up to 2′ (.60 m); bright green 1″ (25 mm) leaves; blossoms early spring; excellent for hanging basket; prune when becoming leggy.

K. verticillata (ver-tiss-ill-ay'-tuh) meaning in circles around stem; linear, cylindrical leaves, up to 6″ (150 mm); profusion of tubular orange red flowers in drooping clusters.

K. fedtschenkoi (fet-shenk'-oi) creeping habit, good subject for hanging basket; blue green leaves edged in purple, clusters of buff rose flowers.

K. beharensis (bee-har-en'-siss) 3′-10′ (.90-3 m) plant; broad-lobed arrow-shaped leaves, to 18″ (.45 m) long, silvery beneath, rust-colored felty upper surface; branched clusters of yellowish green to white flowers.

K. tomentosa (toh-men-toh'-suh) meaning with a covering of short hair; commonly known as Panda Plant; once called *K. Lanceolata*, meaning having small, lance-shaped leaves; hairy stemmed, branching habit; 1′-3′ (.30-.90 m) tall; spoon-shaped, bluish green leaves, 3″ (76 mm) long, arranged in loose rosettes at top of stems; leaf fuzz is silvery; flowers white with brownish stripes.

K. blossfeldiana (bloss-fel-dee-ay'-nuh) Christmas Kalanchoe; glossy green leaves edged in red; clusters of scarlet flowers, fall blooming; consider treating as an annual, less attractive in second year; blooms continuously through year; flowers stay open day and night.

Variety—Yellow Tom Thumb: bright yellow flowers, which close at night; 8″ (200 mm) tall.

Variety—Scarlet Gnome: large scarlet blossoms which close at night; 7″ (177 mm) tall.

KOHLERIA (koh-leer'-ee-uh).

Previously known as Tydaea or Isoloma, this tuber has lovely, sizable flowers for winter bloom, on a screen of large, soft, velvety leaves. Most species are trailers, though some are upright. A fine hanging specimen, not too large, for colorful display to brighten a snowy day.

Family Tree: Gesneriaceae (jes-ner-ee'-ay-see-ay) Gesneria family; native to Central and South America.

Foliage: very ornamental, velvety brown or purple coloring along the veins of leaves. Green oval leaves on fuzzy stems.

Flower: to 2″ (50 mm); 5-petalled, tubular or bell-shaped flower, thickly covered with down; blooms late winter through spring; yellow, orange, red, pink, or white, often spotted with contrasting hues.

Size: 8″-30″ (.25-.75 m).

Location: WINTER—full sun; set in southern exposure.

SUMMER—*Inside:* partial shade; set in eastern to southern exposure for direct rays of morning sun. *Outside:* partial shade; set in eastern exposure or under a protective structure where plant receives strong light but no direct rays.

FALL: move indoors by mid-September.

Dormancy: occurs to some extent in summer between

Kalanchoe

Kohleria lindeniana,
Longwood

Mature plants: prune lightly during resting periods, after blooming.
Propagate: from stem cuttings of new growth, covering pot with clear plastic bag to build humid atmosphere; or by division of tubers.
Insect alert: thrips.
Notable: do not allow soil to dry out completely; temperature must be warm; all water for this plant to be at room temperature; keep fed as specified for a happy plant that will produce well; excellent artificial light subject, give 14-16 hours of light combining natural and artificial.

K. bogotensis (boh-gah-ten'-siss) 1″ (25 mm), red-spotted, yellow flowers; to 24″ (.60 m) tall.
K. eriantha (ehr-ee-anth'-uh) 1″ (25 mm), red orange flowers, with red spots; 2″-4″ (50-100 mm) dark green leaves marked with red edges.
K. amabilis (am-mab'-il-iss) meaning lovely, usually referring to the flower; leaves are silver green, hairy, veined with brown; flowers are bright pink with red spots; borne on airy, fuzzy stem tops; blooms for several months.
K. lindeniana (lin-den-ee-ay'-nuh) ½″ (12 mm), blue-throated white flowers, lightly fragrant; leaves shaded olive green, silver-veined; plant to 10″ (254 mm) high; blooms continuously with proper culture.

blooming periods; slowly diminish watering, keeping soil barely moist; cease fertilizing.
Water: keep evenly moist.
Mist: daily, twice daily during growing period.
Humidity: above normal for happy, 50%-60%.
Feed: every 3 weeks, April through August, with diluted liquid manure.
Soil: 1 part standard potting mix, 2 parts peat moss, 1 part sharp sand or perlite.
Temperature: Day—72°-78°F (22°-25°C). Night—65°-70°F (18°-21°C).
Potbound: normal; pot-on into flat pots if root growth overbalances soil content; pot-on, repot, or side-dress in March.

LAMPRANTHUS (lamp-ran'-thus) Ice Plant, Afternoon Flower, Livingstone Daisy.
A perennial evergreen, frequently listed in catalogues as Mesembryanthemum, available with many varieties and different colored flowers; visually dazzling. An interestingly different hanging plant when mature.
Family Tree: Aizoaceae (ay-zoh-ay'-see-ay) Carpetweed family; native to South Africa.
Foliage: muted medium green color; soft, narrow, fleshy leaf; graceful form in branching habit.
Flower: in summer, full sun produces a profusion of blooms, large and showy; many varieties colored pink, white, salmon, carmine, or yellow, shaped like daisies.
Size: 1″-3′ (25 mm-.90 m).
Location: WINTER—southern exposure.
SUMMER—*Inside and Outside:* southern exposure.
FALL: move indoors by mid-September, site in southern exposure.
Dormancy: period starts November through February; slowly diminish watering, keeping barely moist; allow plant to indicate needs; cease fertilizing; site in 45°-65° F (7°-18°C), in full sun.
Water: keep soil evenly moist; check daily in summer months.
Mist: daily, twice daily when possible.
Humidity: very high, 50%-60%.
Air circulation: helpful condition.
Soil: cactus potting soil; available packaged at garden supply centers.
Temperature: Day—68°-80°F (20°-26°C). Night—60°-70°F (15°-21°C).
Potbound: repot in spring with soil as specified for this genus; pot-on when root growth overbalances soil content in pot.

Lampranthus blandus,
Afternoon Flower

Mature plants: better bloom if stems pinched back as they become straggly; pinch off to point where plant retains compact, uniform shape; pinch center out of young shoots for wide plant.

Propagate: from 3″ (76 mm) cuttings, spring through fall; root in moist sandy soil or vermiculite.

Offspring established: when 7-9 weeks old, plant each established seedling in 2″ (50 mm) pot with soil specified for this genus.

Insect alert: mealybug, scale, thrips.

Notable: imperative to have full sun for blossoms to open; fertilization not really necessary, but do repot each spring, and do move outside for summer months; soil must be porous for good drainage.

L. aureus (aw′-ree-us) meaning golden; 1½′ (.45 m) tall; 2″ (50 mm) long, narrow, fleshy leaves; golden flowers to 2″ (50 mm) across.

L. coccinus (kok-sin′-ee-us) meaning bright, deep pink; to 3′ (.90 m) tall; angled leaves; scarlet flowers.

L. roseus (roh′-zee-us) meaning rose colored, pink; 1½′ (.45 m) tall; rose flowers.

L. blanders (blann′-dus) meaning pleasant; large pink flowers.

Lantana camara,
Red Sage

LANTANA CAMARA (lan-tay′-nuh kam-mar′-uh) Red Sage, Yellow Sage.

Total sunshine, as much as possible. Interestingly, the darkest flowers, which are the oldest, are always on the outside of the clusters. Not too challenging a plant at which to try your hand. Prune to a standard form, or basket-up as a fine hanging genus. Whatever, an easily maintained, prime subject for inside culture.

Family Tree: Verbenaceae (ver-ben-nay′-see-ay) Verbena family; native to tropical America.

Foliage: 2″-6″ (50-150 mm) long; rough, gray green oval leaves; pungent; oppositely arranged.

Flower: in flat-topped cluster, 1″-2″ (25-50 mm) across; colors change as they mature; white, yellow, pink, red, orange, and bicolored; blooms are tiny, fragrant, densely grouped; occurring mostly in spring and summer, intermittently in fall and winter.

Fruit: black and berrylike, miniature and round.

Size: 4″ to 4′ (100 mm-1.20 m); depending on species.

Location: WINTER—southern exposure.

SUMMER—*Inside and Outside:* southern exposure.

FALL: move indoors by mid-September; site in southern exposure.

Dormancy: resting period, starting about October, fear not if some leaves shed; slowly diminish watering, keeping soil barely moist and allowing soil to become slightly dry between waterings; increase watering gradually as new growth begins, around late February; cease fertilizing.

Water: thoroughly and evenly, when soil has somewhat dried.

Mist: daily.

Humidity: low normal, 25%-30%.

Air circulation: helpful condition.

Feed: weekly, mild liquid manure, April through September.

Soil: standard potting mix.

Temperature: Day—68°-75°F (20°-23°C). Night—55°-60°F (12°-15°C).

Potbound: repot or pot-on in February; pot-on only when root growth has developed to more than 50% of soil content.

Mature plants: better bloom if stems pinched back as they become straggly; pinch off to point where plant retains compact, uniform shape; pinch center out of young shoots for wide plant; may be trained into standard form (tree form) by proper pruning or pinching; old flowers wither and fall, bursting buds follow; when repotting in February, cut plant back at least 1/3 of size or to point of removing all straggly, unsightly stems, this will encourage bushier growth and better flowering; if not repotting or potting-on at this time, be sure to side-dress for nourishment.

Propagate: by seed, branch cuttings, or stem cuttings, place latter in small pot with moist sandy soil or vermiculite in September and/or February.

Offspring established: when transplanted and seedlings are 6″ (150 mm) high, pinch out tips for branching of plant; continue practice on newly branched stems until plant is of pleasing multistemmed growth.

Insect alert: whitefly, red spider, mealybug, scale.

Notable: at least one if not two hard prunings are needed yearly for a good bushy, trailing and blooming plant; loved by whitefly; pest is discouraged by regular misting; don't overhumidify, especially during winter months; do not allow soil to dry out completely, this is obvious when foliage becomes tired and drooping in appearance; soil must be porous for good drainage.

L. montevidensis (mon-tev-id-den′-sis) once called *L. sellowiana* (sell-oh-ee-ay′-nuh); known as trailing or weeping Lantana; 1″ (25 mm) leaves; trailers up to 4′ (1.20 m); fragrant flower clusters, 1½″ (37 mm) across, white, yellow, rosy lilac, pink red, and blue purple; heaviest blooming time in summer months.

LAURUS NOBILIS (law'-rus noh'-bil-iss) Sweet Bay, Bay Tree, Laurel.

The Laurus nobilis has served several interesting uses. The leaves were fashioned into wreaths to crown heroes of ancient Greece and Rome; then and now are utilized as food seasoning. Sweet bay is a very slow growing herb in need of sun and coolish temperatures along with attention to pruning for growth control.

Family Tree: Lauraceae (law-ray'-see-ay) Laurel family; native to Mediterranean, probably originally from Asia Minor or southeast Asia.

Foliage: leathery, dark green leaves, to 4″ (100 mm) long, 1″ (25 mm) wide; develops multiple stems with maturity; fragrant leaves usable for flavoring.

Flower: green-toned to yellowish white, small blossoms.

Fruit: black berries.

Size: up to 20′ (6 m).

Location: WINTER—southern exposure.

SUMMER—*Inside and Outside:* southern exposure.

FALL: move in by mid-September; site in southern exposure.

Dormancy: none, a resting time during winter months, after flowering has ceased; slowly diminish watering; plant will indicate needs by appearance, becoming limp and droopy; develop sensitivity to feel of soil moisture level; cease fertilizing.

Water: evenly and thoroughly, allowing soil to dry between waterings.

Mist: daily, twice a day when possible.

Humidity: normal, 30%-35%.

Air circulation: essential for good cultural response.

Feed: weekly with mild liquid manure throughout growing season, April through August.

Soil: 3 parts standard potting mix, 1 part sharp sand or perlite.

Temperature: Day—65°-75°F (18°-23°C). Night—40°-64°F (4°-17°C).

Potbound: very happy; repot or pot-on only when soil is totally overpowered by root system, roots completely filling plant housing.

Mature plants: prune species as needed to maintain size desired.

Propagate: by seed or cutting, root latter in moist vermiculite or sharp sand.

Insect alert: aphid, mealybug, mite, scale.

Notable: soil must have porosity; no soggy conditions; keep on lower side of recommended temperatures; important to wipe or wash foliage every 2 weeks; *Note:* good air circulation needed for top performance.

LIGUSTRUM JAPONICUM (li-gust'-rum ja-pon'-ik-um) Privet, Wax-leafed Ligustrum.

Members of this genus are found in many parts of the world; the *L. japonicum* is native to Japan. This particular species is a rapid grower, with both flower and fruit, making it a rather special ornamental, evergreen tub plant. Site the *L. japonicum* in drafts without harmful effect, which is unusual. Happiness is a bright light site. The entire plant is poisonous, so be careful with children, pets, and curious adults.

Family Tree: Oleaceae (oh-lee-ay'-see-ay) Olive family; native to many, many countries.

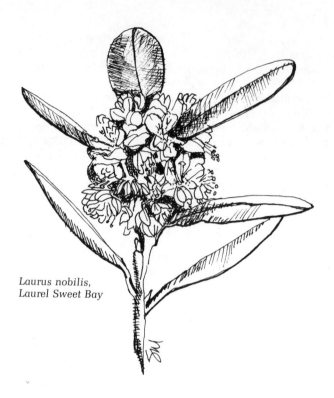

Laurus nobilis,
Laurel Sweet Bay

Foliage: glossy or waxy, leathery, deep evergreen, to 6″ (150 mm) long.

Flower: creamy white flowers, in clusters, to 6″ (150 mm) long; in summer.

Fruit: bluish or black berries.

Size: up to 6′ (1.80 m).

Location: WINTER—southeastern or southwestern exposure.

SUMMER—*Inside and Outside:* eastern or western exposure.

FALL: move indoors by mid-September; site in eastern or western exposure.

Dormancy: none, a resting time during winter months, generally September through March; slowly diminish

Ligustrum japonicum,
Japanese Privet

watering; plant will indicate needs by appearance, becoming limp and droopy; develop sensitivity to feel of soil moisture; cease fertilizing.

Water: evenly and moderately, allowing soil to dry between waterings.

Mist: daily, twice a day when possible.

Humidity: normal, 30%-35%.

Air circulation: essential for good cultural response.

Feed: every 2 weeks with mild liquid manure throughout growing season, April through August.

Soil: 3 parts standard potting mix, 1 part sharp sand or perlite, 1 part peat moss.

Temperature: Day—68°-75°F (20°-23°C). Night—40°-64°F (4°-17°C).

Mature plants: prune as hard as desired to retain height or shape of plant; if plant becomes ragged in growth pattern, it can be pruned back to 4″ (100 mm) from soil level without permanent damage; this is best done around March.

Propagate: by stem cuttings in moist sharp sand or vermiculite.

Insect alert: aphid, mealybug, mite, scale, leaf miner.

Notable: soil must have porosity; no soggy conditions; keep on lower side of recommended temperatures; important to wipe or wash foliage every 2 weeks; good air circulation needed for top performance; do not overpot, use pot only 2″ (50 mm) larger than previous housing; good artificial light genus, combine artificial and natural for a total of 14 light hours.

LILIUM LONGIFLORUM (lil'-ee-um lon-jif-floh'-rum) Bermuda Lily, Easter Lily.

Of historic longevity, the lily has meaning from both the Persian, *laleh* and the Greek, *leiron*. In cultivation 3000 years ago in parts of the Old World, The Madonna lily can be seen in ancient Cretan wall paintings. Modern hybrids are easy to maintain with modest attention to cultural needs.

Family Tree: Liliaceae (lil-ee-ay'-see-ay) Lily family; native to Bermuda, the Orient, southern Europe, and North America.

Foliage: almost grasslike; 6″ (150 mm) long; of narrow, erect nature.

Flower: pure white, funnel shaped, with strong, sweet aroma; 6″-8″ (150-200 mm) long and 4″-5″ (100-127 mm) across. Blooms last a week or more and occur in July; borne one at a time at the tip of a stalk; some are upright, some drooping; have 3 petals and a 3-leafed calyx (the chalice-shaped growth which protects buds before opening).

Size: varies from 1'-6' (.30-1.80 m).

Location: WINTER—southeastern exposure.

SUMMER—*Inside:* eastern exposure. *Outside:* northeastern exposure.

FALL: move indoors by mid-September; site in southeastern exposure.

Dormancy: period starts in fall when blooming has ended and leaves and stem have died down; remove bulb from pot; clean and dry bulb before storing during winter season, place in moist peat litter or sand, in a cool cellar.

Water: keep soil evenly moist.

Mist: lightly, daily, twice daily during forcing time.

Humidity: normal, 30%-35%.

Air circulation: essential to successful culture.

Soil: 2 parts standard potting mix, 1 part sand.

Temperature: Day—62°-68°F (16°-20°C). Night—40°-55°F (4°-12°C).

Forcing Culture: about August, plant a bulb in deep, 16″ (.40 m) pot, in soil specified for this genus; cover bottom of pot with a 1″ (25 mm) thick gravel bed; set bulb on gravel bed with soil covering bulb to its own height; site pot in cool, 40°-45°F (4°-7°C), shaded or dark area; when growth is obvious, move pot to northern exposure of 60°-70°F (15°-21°C); approximately 115 days after this, blooming should occur, at which time resite in eastern to southern exposure. Cut off withered flowers after last of these dies, just below lowest blossom but just above tallest leaf; keep watering as bulb is now manufacturing and storing food for next season's growth; when leaves die, cut off stalk completely. Remove bulb from pot and clean off; store it in damp peat litter in a cool, dark area. Either plant outdoors in spring when chance of frost is past, or leave untouched until following August for reforcing inside.

Propagate: by seed or bulb scales (the outer, curved coverings of the bulb).

Insect alert: aphid, borer, bulb fly, mealybug, scale, thrips.

Disease alert: botrytis rot—leaves, stems, and flower buds develop orange brown spots, this fungus spreads in cool, wet weather; bulb rot develops from soggy soil.

Notable: keep on cooler side of recommended temperatures; good soil drainage of top priority; usually, bulb can be forced the second year in the interior site.

Most popular, because of their low stature, are varieties:

L. longiflorum Croft: 2' (.60 m).

L. longiflorum Ace: 1'-2' (.30-.60 m).

L. longiflorum Estate: 3' (.90 m).

Lilium longiflorum,
Bermuda or Easter Lily

LITHOPS BELLA (lith'-ops bell'-uh) Living Stones.
Lithops is a fun, interesting, oddly charming, and extremely small succulent. Its pebblelike form has a narrow slit across the top, from which the flower appears. In its native habitat, it actually grows among pebbles and frequently becomes lost to sight among them. It seldom flowers inside, even with maximum full sun year round.

Family Tree: Aizoaceae (ay-zoh-ay'-see-ay) Carpetweed family; native to South Africa.

Foliage: thick, brownish yellow leaves in joined pairs, notch or fissure on top, resemble pebbles.

Flower: single white or yellow, to 1¼" (32 mm) wide, in late summer or fall.

Size: 1" (25 mm) high.

Location: WINTER—southern exposure.

SUMMER—*Inside and Outside:* southern exposure.

FALL: move indoors by mid-September; site in southern exposure.

Dormancy: none, just a resting period from October through February; slowly diminish watering to just enough to keep leaves from shriveling.

Water: allow soil to become quite dry between thorough, even waterings, March through September.

Mist: daily, very lightly, around plant but not directly on it.

Humidity: low normal, 20%-25%.

Air circulation: helpful condition.

Feed: do not feed.

Soil: 1 part standard potting mix, 2 parts sharp sand.

Temperature: Day—68°-80°F (20°-26°C). Night—50°-70°F (10°-21°C).

Potbound: please do not disturb; *never* repot or pot-on.

Mature plants: growth of plant is determined by the water culture; do not moisten the foliage.

Propagate: by seed or division.

Insect alert: scale, mealybug.

Disease alert: root rot from overwatering.

Notable: soil must have excellent porosity; do not try to create a humid condition; normal interior air, even a dry site, is most suitable. *Most notable:* plants rot very easily; a good artificial light plant, up to 16 hours combined natural and artificial light hours; do not allow soil to dry out completely.

L. leslei (less'-lee-eye) olive brown and rust foliage, yellow blooms.

L. pseudotruncatella (sood-oh-trunk-uh-tell'-uh) grayish green or grayish brown, ball-shaped foliage, narrow slit through center of top; 2" (50 mm), yellow flowers, grow out of the slit; keep on warm side of recommended temperatures.

LIVISTONA CHINENSIS (liv-is-toh'-nuh chin-en'-siss) Fountain Palm, Chinese Fan Palm.
A densely crowned palm with fronds (leaves) springing forth in a gracefully arching manner, and so referred to as Fountain Palm. The *L. chinensis* is a slow grower, as is the habit of most of its palm cousins. A handsome species for tub growth in a sunless but bright light site; of simple cultural needs. Chinensis means belonging to China.

Family Tree: Palmae (pal-may') Palm family; native to tropical eastern Asia, Australia, Malaya, Philippines, and New Guinea.

Foliage: fronds (leaves) to 6' (1.80 m) long, form huge semicircles resembling open fans, 12"-18" (.30-.45 m) across, on young plants, larger as they mature; barely visible threadlike fibers hang between fingerlike segments of fronds; thick, 1" (25 mm) spines cover lower half of each leaf stalk; solitary trunk, arching stems.

Fruit: black, smooth; to ½" (12 mm) long.

Size: up to 10' (3 m).

Lithops bella,
Living Stones

Livistona chinensis,
Chinese Fan Palm

Location: WINTER—eastern or western exposure.

SUMMER—*Inside:* eastern or western exposure. *Outside:* eastern or western exposure, sheltered to protect fragile foliage from potentially damaging winds and heavy rains.

FALL: move indoors by mid-September; site in eastern or western exposure.

Dormancy: none, although light resting period in winter months; slowly diminish watering, keeping soil barely moist; cease fertilizing.

Water: thoroughly and evenly, allowing soil to dry between waterings.

Mist: daily, two or more times in warm weather.

Humidity: above normal, 45%-60%.

Air circulation: essential to have good moderate movement for top plant performance.

Feed: very, very mild liquid manure, ¼ strength of package or manufacturer's recommendations, March through October.

Soil: 2 parts standard potting mix, 1 part peat moss, 1 part vermiculite.

Temperature: Day—68°-75°F (20°-23°C). Night—58°-65°F (14°-18°C).

Potbound: pot-on young plants each year to 2″ (50 mm) larger pot; older plants happy when somewhat potbound; side-dress each year, pot-on every 2 or 3 years, when indicated by plant's root growth being 80% to 20% soil in pot; this cultural attention to be implemented late winter or early spring, February or March; deep pots are best shape for submerged aerial roots.

Mature plants: in repotting or potting-on, firm soil well, but do not compact it.

Propagate: by seed.

Insect alert: mealybug, red spider mite, scale, thrips.

Notable: absolutely no drafts; do not allow soil to dry out completely, but *no soggy soil*; soil must be porous, for good drainage is essential to successful culture; use pebble, water, and tray method to maintain high humidity; good in artificial light, needing a total of 16 light hours, combining natural and artificial; leaves should be washed or wiped with moist cloth at least once a month to keep pores unclogged; no direct sun, or foliage will burn; remember that most palms are of slow growing habit.

L. australis (os-tray′-liss) meaning southern; known as Australian Fan Palm; dense crown of stiff, dark green fronds, to 5′ (1.50 m) across, on spiny stems to 5′ (1.50 m) long; fronds divide to midrib into narrow segments; small greenish flowers; round fruit to ¾″ (19 mm).

LOBULARIA MARITIMA (lob-yew-lay′-ree-uh mar-rittee′-muh) Sweet Alyssum, Sweet Alison, Alyssum Maritima.

The name of this genus is derived from Latin *lobulus*, little lobe, and *maritimus*, from the sea coast areas. This very small plant related to the true Alyssum has four species but only one is in cultivation. The *Lobularia maritima flore pleno* referred to here for inside cultivation has double flowers. It trails handsomely without becoming too straggly, therefore proves to be a superior selection for a sunny site of limited size inside.

Family Tree: Cruciferae (kru′-see-fer′-aye) Mustard family; native to the Mediterranean.

Foliage: very small, gray, hairy, alternately arranged leaves grow compactly on trailing stems.

Flower: tiny, double, honey-scented clusters of white blossoms throughout the year, at times with more profusion.

Size: 3″-12″ (76-304 mm).

Location: WINTER—full sun; set in southern exposure.

SUMMER—*Inside:* partial shade; set in eastern to southern exposure for direct rays of morning sun. *Outside:* partial shade; set in eastern exposure or under a protective structure where plant receives strong light but no direct rays.

FALL: move indoors by mid-September.

Water: keep soil evenly moist.

Mist: daily.

Humidity: above normal, 40%-50%.

Air circulation: helpful condition.

Feed: once a month with mild liquid manure.

Soil: 2 parts potting soil, 1 part perlite.

Temperature: Day—68°-72°F (20°-22°C). Night—50°-55°F (10°-12°C).

Potbound: pot-on when root growth exceeds soil by 50%.

Mature plants: clip nonbudded, nonblooming stems to keep plant bushy and compact, and to induce constant flowering.

Propagate: by stem cuttings, any time; or by seed.

Notable: ensure porosity of soil for good drainage; the cultivars listed for this genus can be grown with total success as indoor plants, but do cultivate as annuals; discard the plants when they have completed their blooming cycle; propagate cultivars below from seed.

L. cultivars

New Carpet of Snow: white; dwarf, to 2½″ (62 mm), spreading.

Rosie O'Day: dark rose pink; to 3″ (76 mm).

Royal Carpet: violet purple; to 3″-4″ (76-100 mm).

Pastel Carpet: dark violet rose, pink white, and cream yellow, all with white centers; dwarf.

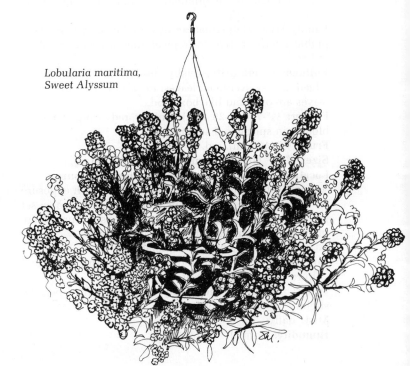

Lobularia maritima,
Sweet Alyssum

Malpighia coccigera,
Singapore Holly

MALPIGHIA COCCIGERA (mal-pig′-ee-uh kok-sig′-er-uh)
Holly Malpighia, Singapore Holly, Miniature Holly.
An exquisite small plant with proper culture. This woody, shrub-type plant, frequently used as a bonsai, is literally covered with delicate blossoms throughout spring and early summer; light blooming spasmodically through the year. The plant is natured to rapid growth. Named after Dr. Marcello Malpighi, 1628-94, an Italian anatomist whose botanical contribution was to discover and prove that a tree's age can be determined by counting rings in its trunk's cross section.
Family Tree: Malpighiaceae (mal-pig′-ee-ay-see-ay) Malpighia family; native to tropical America and the West Indies.
Foliage: in maturity, bushy, hollylike, sharp, spiny-edged, glossy evergreen leaves; to ¾″ (19 mm); immature leaves are oval and like boxwood.
Flower: ½″-1″ (12-25 mm) pink or red, fringed petals; blooms in spring and summer.
Fruit: ½″ (12 mm), red.
Size: 4″-12″ (100-300 mm), and up to 3′ (.90 m).
Location: WINTER—full sun; set in southern exposure.
SUMMER—*Inside:* partial shade; set in east to south exposure for direct rays of morning sun. *Outside:* partial shade; set in eastern exposure or under a protective structure where plant receives strong light but no direct rays.
FALL: move indoors by mid-September.
Dormancy: none, mild resting periods; maintain normal culture throughout the year.
Water: thoroughly and evenly, allowing soil to become slightly dry between waterings.
Mist: daily.
Humidity: normal, 30%-35%.

Air circulation: essential for good culture.
Feed: once in late winter with fertilizer high in potassium and phosphate to encourage bloom; the last of three numbers on the container indicates potassium content; choose one indicating #10; 5-10-10 is suggested.
Soil: 1 part standard potting mix, 1 part vermiculite, 1 part peat moss.
Temperature: Day—68°-72°F (20°-22°C). Night—60°-65°F (15°-18°C).
Potbound: normal; pot-on when root system overbalances soil content; repot or pot-on in late winter, March.
Mature plants: better bloom if stems pinched back as they become straggly; pinch off to point where plant retains compact, uniform shape; want wide plant, so pinch center out of young shoots; excellent for developing as bonsai.
Propagate: by seed or young, firm, woody stem cuttings; latter root easily in moist vermiculite in spring or summer.
Insect alert: mealybug, scale.
Notable: to keep size to below 10″ (254 mm), repot into pots no larger than 4″ (100 mm); to avoid root rot, ensure a porous soil, and never allow soggy soil conditions.

MANETTIA (man-net′-ee-uh) Firecracker Vine.
This colorful evergreen trailing vine is a dwarf shrub, delicate in nature, never overpowering. Site in bright light, either natural or artificial. A pretty firecrackerlike blossom appears, sometimes profusely, sometimes sparsely, all year.
Family Tree: Rubiaceae (roo-bee-ay′-see-ay) Madder family; native to tropical America.
Foliage: evergreen; slender, 2″ (50 mm) long, delicate, oval leaves, colored a lively green; densely grouped around fine, twining woody stems.
Flower: ¾″ (19 mm) long white, yellow, and red miniature urn shapes with hairy petals; bloom primarily in summer but frequently throughout year.
Size: 4′-5′ (1.20-1.50 m).
Location: WINTER—full sun; set in southern exposure.
SUMMER—*Inside:* partial shade; set in eastern to southern exposure for direct rays of morning sun. *Outside:* partial shade; set in eastern exposure or under a protective structure where plant receives strong light but no direct rays.
FALL: move indoors by mid-September.
Dormancy: none really; merely a resting period, November through January; slowly diminish watering, keeping soil barely moist, allow plant to indicate needs; cease fertilizing.
Water: keep soil evenly moist.
Mist: daily, twice daily if possible.
Humidity: very happy, 50%-60%.
Air circulation: essential to successful culture.
Feed: mild liquid manure weekly, February through October.
Soil: 2 parts standard potting mix, 1 part sand, 1 part peat moss.
Temperature: Day—68°-80°F (20°-26°C). Night—68°-70°F (20°-21°C).
Potbound: unhappy; pot-on (late winter, in February or March) only when root system becomes 80% of pot content, handle with sensitivity.
Mature plants: older plants do not like to be disturbed, so

side-dress instead of repotting, carefully so as not to injure roots. Can be pruned very hard and retained as a bushy vine 6″-12″ (150-300 mm) high. If left as twining vine, prune lightly after flowering to encourage new growth.
Propagate: by rooting cuttings, any time.
Offspring established: should be supported on wire screen or bamboo trellis.
Insect alert: aphids, whitefly.
Disease alert: yellowing of leaves caused by too cold and damp soil or too cold water.
Notable: keep on warmer side of recommended temperatures, especially while in bloom; needs good soil drainage; water with rain water or pure, chemically uncontaminated water; good genus for artificial light growth, giving total of 12-14 hours combined natural and artificial light.

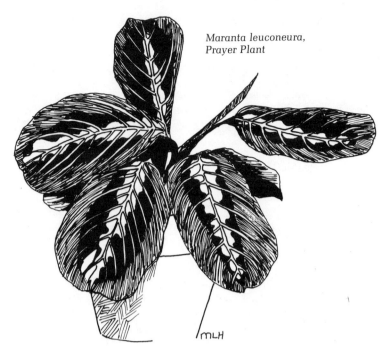

Maranta leuconeura,
Prayer Plant

Manettia
Firecracker Vine

M. bicolor (bye′-kol-or) meaning of two colors; smooth vine, summer blooming; single red, yellow-tipped, ¾″ (19 mm) flowers; leaves lance shaped, 4″-6″ (100-150 mm).
M. glabra (glay′-bruh) meaning smooth or hairless; known as Firecracker Vine; 1½″ (37 mm) crimson flowers; similar to M. bicolor but taller, with larger flowers.
M. inflata (in-flay′-tuh) meaning blown up; native to Paraguay and Uruguay; similar to bicolor; lance shaped leaves, hairy on underside.

MARANTA (mar-ant′-uh) Prayer Plant, Arrowroot; nickname: Ten Commandment Plant, Banded Plant.
Leaves fold at night into a position of praying hands; therefore the common name, prayer plant. Strong design in leaf patterns, or variegated foliage, and/or extremely colorful veining characterize this genus and make it commonly recognizable and also a most desirable possession. Basic, undemanding culture, good bright light; an ornamental foliage plant that asks so little and gives so much.
Family Tree: Marantaceae (mar-an-tay′-see-ay) Maranta family; native to South America.
Foliage: oval, grayish green leaves, highlighted shadings of brighter and deeper greens, some with purple undersides, red vein coloring throughout; 3″-6″ (76-150 mm) long.
Flower: if culturally happy, in maturity produces small white or pink flowers, on long stem.
Size: to 3′ (.90 m) tall, depending on species.
Location: WINTER—southeastern or southwestern exposure.
SUMMER—*Inside:* northeastern or northwestern exposure.
Outside: northeastern or northwestern exposure; site in shelter to protect foliage.
FALL: move indoors by mid-September: site in eastern or western exposure.
Dormancy: none, but a resting period of slower growth during winter months of less intensity, generally October through February; slowly diminish watering, plant will indicate needs as determined by environmental conditions; develop sensitivity to feel of soil moisture; cease fertilizing.
Water: thoroughly and evenly, allowing soil to dry out between waterings.
Mist: daily, twice a day when possible.
Humidity: above normal for happiness, 45%-55%.
Air circulation: helpful condition.
Feed: mild liquid manure every 2 weeks.
Soil: 1 part standard potting mix, 1 part perlite, 2 parts peat moss.

Temperature: Day—70°-80°F (21°-26°C). Night—62°-68°F (16°-20°C).

Potbound: very happy; pot-on only when root growth of plant is 80%, soil 20% of pot content; top- or side-dress yearly, preferably spring.

Mature plants: if plant becomes too tall, cut growing ends; start in rooting media; remove dried or withered leaves as they appear.

Propagate: by stem cuttings or air layering.

Insect alert: mealybug, red spider, scale, thrip, aphids.

Notable: good artificial light plant; total of 14-16 hours, combining natural and artificial light; do not allow soil to dry out completely; soil must have porosity, eliminating possibility of soggy conditions; use pebble, water, and tray method to maintain humidity level; rinse foliage at least every 3 weeks, always use room-temperature water; leaf shiners and/or oils are an *absolute no-no*.

M. arundinacea (ar-un-di-nay'-see-uh) meaning bamboolike grasses, southern care; white flowers; zig-zag rows of gray green, arrow-shaped leaves; to 3' (.90 m) tall; grown commercially for its starchy root.

Variety—Variegata; large, cream-edged leaves.

M. bicolor (bye-kol'-or) meaning two-colored; oval, dark gray green leaves, spotted with brown, wavy margins, 12" (.30 m) long; white flowers spotted with purple.

M. leuconera (lew-koh-new'-ruh)

Variety—Kerchoveana (ker-koh-vee-ay'-nuh) pale gray green leaves; reddish brown spots, becoming dark green with age, run parallel to central ribs of leaves.

Variety—Massangeana (mas-san-jee-ay'-nuh) gray green leaves, fish-bone pattern of veins, purple undersides.

MIMOSA PUDICA (mi-moh'-suh pew'-dik-uh) Sensitive plant.

Mimosa pudica is characterized by springy branches of a graceful, slightly arching nature and soft, delicate foliage. Named Sensitive plant because the leaves fold up, merely temporarily, when touched. This species, native to Brazil, is good for a small site in full sun.

Family Tree: Leguminosae (le-gum-in-oh-say) Pea family; native to tropical America.

Foliage: alternate, compound leaves with many leaflets; gray green; feathery appearance; branching nature.

Flower: pinkish red; pompon-type, exotic.

Size: up to 1' (.30 m).

Location: WINTER—southern exposure,

SUMMER—*Inside and Outside:* southern exposure.

FALL: bring inside by mid-September; site in southern exposure.

Dormancy: none, but a resting period of slower growth during winter months of less intensity, generally October through February; slowly diminish watering, plant will indicate needs as determined by environmental conditions; develop sensitivity to feel of soil moisture-level; cease fertilizing.

Water: moderately and evenly.

Mist: daily, twice a day when possible.

Humidity: above normal for happiness, 45%-55%.

Air circulation: helpful condition.

Mimosa pudica,
Sensitive Plant

Feed: mild liquid manure every 2 weeks, April through August.

Soil: 3 parts standard potting mix, 1 part perlite.

Temperature: Day—70°-80°F (21°-26°C). Night—62°-68°F (16°-20°C).

Mature plants: start pinching back when 6th leaf develops, for good branching; will grow in bright light, sunless site, but is better in full sun.

Propagate: from seeds in late winter, early spring; sow several seeds to single pot, using soil as specified for this genus.

Insect alert: scale, mealybug.

Notable: good artificial light plant; total of 14-16 hours, combining natural and artificial light; do not allow soil to dry out completely; soil must have porosity, eliminating possibility of soggy conditions; use pebble, water, and tray method to maintain humidity level.

MONSTERA (mon-ster'-uh) Cut- or Split-Leaved Philodendron, Hurricane Plant; nickname: Swiss Cheese Plant.

One of the most durable plants for interior habitat, it provides a delightful surprise: an edible fruit, aromatic and tasting rather like a combination of banana and pineapple. Monstera actually is a vine, so generally a bark slab is provided for self-support. Rapidly growing, a monstera attaches itself via aerial roots to the support. Young leaves so resemble the philodendron that this plant often is confused with a species of philodendron.

Family Tree: Araceae (uh-ray'-see-ay) Arum family; native to jungles of Mexico and Guatemala.

Foliage: broad, dark green leaves; lobes, incisions, holes.

Flower: creamy white spathe (large leaflike sheath surrounding actual flower); around 5"-10" (127-254 mm) spadix (spike) rising from center.

Fruit: spadix becomes edible, cone-shaped fruit, maturing in 1 year.

Size: up to 8′ (2.45 m).
Location: WINTER—southeastern or southwestern exposure.
SUMMER—*Inside:* northeastern or northwestern exposure.
Outside: northeastern or northwestern exposure; site in shelter to protect foliage.
FALL: move indoors by mid-September; site in eastern or western exposure.
Dormancy: none; but a resting period of slower growth during winter months of less intensity; generally October through February; slowly diminish watering, plant will indicate needs as determined by environmental conditions, develop sensitivity to feel of soil moisture; cease fertilizing.
Water: thoroughly and evenly, allowing soil to dry out between waterings.
Mist: daily, twice a day when possible.
Humidity: above normal for happiness, 45%-55%.
Air circulation: helpful condition.
Feed: mild liquid manure every 2 weeks.
Soil: standard potting soil.
Temperature: Day—70°-80°F (21°-26°C). Night—62°-68°F (16°-20°C).
Potbound: very happy; pot-on only when root growth of plant is 80%, soil 20% of pot content; top- or side-dress yearly; preferably spring.
Mature plants: if plant becomes too tall, cut growing ends (can start in rooting media). Remove dried or withered leaves as they appear. Aerial roots develop which eventually root into soil at base of plant, aiding in nourishment.
Propagate: by stem cuttings or air layering.
Insect alert: mealybug, red spider, scale, thrip, aphids.
Notable: good artificial light plant; total of 14-16 hours, combining natural and artificial light; do not allow soil to dry out completely; soil must have porosity, eliminating possibility of soggy conditions; use pebble, water, and tray

Monstera deliciosa,
Swiss Cheese Plant

method to maintain humidity level; sponge foliage at least every three weeks, always use room-temperature water; leaf shiners and/or oils are an *absolute no-no.*

M. acuminata (a-kew-mi-nay′-tuh) meaning tapering to a point; 14″ (.35 m) leaves, plant habit as other species.
M. deliciosa (de-lis-i-o′-sa) meaning delicious; common name, Ceriman or Mexican breadfruit; incorrectly called Philodendron pertusum; roughly circular, lobed and perforated leaves, 8″-24″ (.25-.60 m); new leaves light green, darkening as they unfold.
M. dubia (dew′-bee-uh) leaves to 2½′ (.75 m); rather pinnate (leaf division like that of a feather) segments, 1½″ (37 mm) wide; spadix about 1′ (.30 m) long and 2″ (50 mm) thick.
M. pertusa (per-too′-suh) incorrectly referred to as a variety of *M. deliciosa*; small leaves, many aerial roots; vigorous, rapid grower.

MUSCARI (muss-kar′-eye) Grape Hyacinth.
Muscari is derived from the Greek *moschos,* musk, a description of the scent of some species. One thinks of the miniature erect stature of these bulbous plants as a mass of deep, colorful exterior spring performance; yet I know the Grape Hyacinth as a wonderful spot of color to warm the winter months. Successive plantings in late summer and early fall present delightful additions to the plant family come log-burning season.
Family Tree: Liliaceae (li-lee-ay′-see-ay) Lily family; native to central and southern Europe, southern Russia, and the Mediterranean.
Foliage: slender, grasslike, blue green; 6″-8″ (.15-.25 m) long.
Flower: fragrant 6″-8″ (.15-.25 m) spikes of tiny bell-shaped blossoms, forced in mid-winter or early spring; colors range through shades of blue, violets, and purples, and striated purples, yellows, golds, and white, and, by the 1970s, a species colored to pink.
Size: 6″-12″ (.15-.30 m).
Interior site: eastern to southern, or southern to western exposure.
Dormancy: cease watering after flowers and foliage wither; store in cool dark site until next forcing or until planted outdoors the following fall.
Water: keep thoroughly moist until foliage withers.
Mist: daily, light around foliage; never directly on flowers when blooming.
Humidity: normal, 30%-35%.
Air circulation: helpful condition.
Feed: do not fertilize.
Soil: 2 parts standard potting mix, 1 part perlite.
Temperature: Day—60°-68°F (15°-20°C). Night—50°-55°F (10°-12°C).
Forcing culture: place bulbs (corms) in shallow, 4″ (100 mm) pots or bowls; put bulbs close together but not touching; site in cool, around 50°F (10°C), dark area; keep soil moist but not saturated; when shoots are about 2″ (50 mm) long, move to slightly warmer, 55°-60°F (12°-15°C), sunny spot, and increase water supply; or place corms in trays filled with pebbles, set so bottom of corm is barely below level of pebbles, do not twist bulb to get it into place; fill tray with water so level is just below top of pebble surface

line, and keep water level thus; site trays as for soil planting, follow same culture; after bloom, remove corms from pots, bowls, or trays, and plant in the garden or discard.
Propagate: by seeds or by the small offsets or bulbs that develop on parent bulb.
Notable: keep on lower side of recommended temperatures, bulbs must have a cool environment; will take full sun, but blooms will not last quite as long; the variety Early Giant, of the species *M. armeniacum* and *M. botryoides* are two of the better types available for forcing; in seed propagation, know that flowering time is 2-3 years from seed sowing; if soil dries out completely, flower bud may not open.

M. armeniacum (arr-men-eye'-ak-kum) meaning of Armenia; flower stalk to 6″ (.15 m); velvety dark blue to pale blue or cream flowers topping stalk.

> Variety—Early Giant: many pale blue flowers, very fragrant.

M. botryoides (bot-rye-oy'-deez) meaning like a bunch of grapes (the shape of the flower cluster); pink, white, and pale blue; lance-shaped leaves, 8″-10″ (200-254 mm) long, ½″ (12 mm) across.
M. comosum (kom-moh'-sum) meaning with tufts of hair, Feather Hyacinth; leaves to 18″ (.45 m), 1″ (25 mm) wide; two kinds of flowers appear on the same stalk; lower florets are nodding olive drab, upper, a cluster of greenish white or purple.
M. moschatum (mos-kay'-tum) meaning having a musky perfume; known as Musk Grape Hyacinth; to 8″ (200 mm); musk-scented; purple flowers that fade to yellow and brown.
M. neglectum (neg-lek'-tum) meaning neglected or overlooked; up to 9″ (230 mm) high; very narrow leaves; dark blue flowers in dense clusters.
M. paradoxum (par-ad-doks'-um) known as Caucasus Grape Hyacinth; but a few leaves, ¾″ (19 mm) wide; blue black flowers in dense clusters.
M. tubergenianum (too-ber-jen-ee-ay'-num) a fine species; flower spike two-toned or particolored, dark blue florets above, lighter blue lower on spike.

MYRTUS COMMUNIS (mert'-us kom-mew'-niss) Greek Myrtle.

Greek myrtle, of glossy foliage and petite blossoms, is simply maintained. The leaves are pleasantly aromatic when crushed. This genus is used in northern European countries in bridal trousseaus; it was a ritual plant in ancient Greece. Myrtus resembles Buxus, boxwood; it can be pruned to boxwood or special bonsai shape.
Family Tree: Myrtaceae (mert-ay'-see-ay) Myrtle family; native of southern Europe to western Asia, to New South Wales.
Foliage: shiny, dark green leaves, ½″ (12 mm) long, on slender, twiggy branches; evergreen foliage, sparsely placed.
Flower: tiny, fragrant, fuzzy white.
Fruit: bluish black berries.
Size: up to 4′ (1.20 m).
Location: WINTER—southern exposure.
SUMMER—*Inside:* southeastern or southwestern exposure.
Outside: eastern or western exposure.
FALL: move inside by mid-September; site in southeastern or southwestern exposure.
Dormancy: none, a resting time during winter months, generally September through March; slowly diminish watering, plant will indicate needs by appearance, becoming limp and droopy, develop sensitivity to feel of soil moisture level; cease fertilizing.
Water: evenly and thoroughly, allowing soil to dry between waterings.

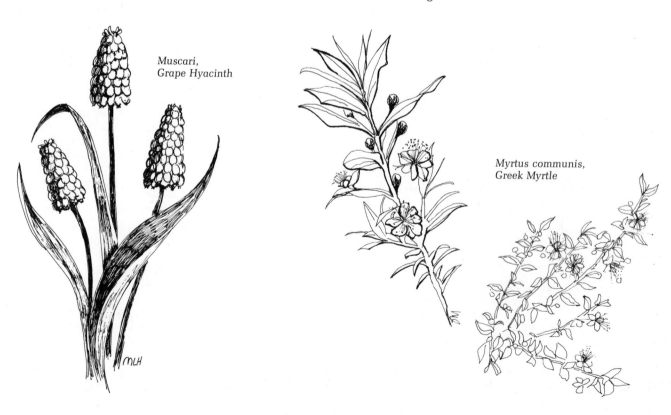

Muscari,
Grape Hyacinth

Myrtus communis,
Greek Myrtle

Mist: daily, twice a day when possible.
Humidity: normal, 30%-35%.
Air circulation: essential for good cultural response.
Feed: every 2 weeks with mild liquid manure throughout growing season, April through August.
Soil: 3 parts standard potting mix, 1 part sharp sand or perlite.
Temperature: Day—68°-78°F (20°-25°C). Night—40°-64°F (4°-17°C).
Potbound: slightly for happiness, when root growth is approximately 65% of pot contents; best repotted or potted-on before new growth develops, in March.
Mature plants: prune to maintain shape of plant.
Propagate: by cuttings; in moist sand and/or vermiculite.
Insect alert: aphid, mealybug, mite, scale, leaf miner.
Notable: soil must have porosity; no soggy conditions; keep on lower side of recommended temperatures; important to wipe or wash foliage every 2 weeks. *Note:* good air circulation needed for top performance; do not overpot, use pot only 2″ (50 mm) larger than previous housing.

M. communis
 Variety—Compacta (kom-pak′-tuh) dwarf, dense foliage.
 Variety—Nana (na′-nuh) very tiny leaves.
 Variety—Variegata (var-ee-eh-gay′-tuh) green and white leaves.
 Variety—Microphylla (mye-kroh-fil′-luh) smaller leaves than M. communis; plant more compact.

NARCISSUS (nar′siss′-us) Daffodil, Jonquil.
The common name, daffodil, assures familiarity with this naturally nodding genus, shaded from minty golds through whites. Simple it is to force the bulbs indoors and provide a breath of spring throughout the winter's starkness. Some species have narcotic properties, as the name Narcissus indicates; in Greek, *narke* is stupor, *narkeo*, to be stupefied. In Greek mythology, the Furies used the Narcissus to stupefy those whom they wished to destroy, thus the flowers were consecrated to them. Legend has it that Narcissus was a beautiful youth loved by the nymph Echo, but he gave her the "buzz off, Echo" business. Aphrodite intervened by causing the lad to fall in love with his own image, mirrored in a fountain, as punishment. He died in despair and was transformed into a flower growing beside the fountain.
Family Tree: Amaryllidaceae (am-ar-rill-i-day′-see-ay) Amaryllis family; native to Japan, western Asia, western Europe, and North Africa.
Foliage: lancelike, gray green, 2″-12″ (50-300 mm) long.
Flower: single or clustered blooms topping a stem; a ring of segments at right angles to a trumpet-shaped center; basically yellow or white, with many variations, including scarlet, apricot, and shell pink trumpets, and now pinkish hybrids.
Size: 3″ (76 mm) to 2′ (.60 m).
Water: for soil culture, keep evenly moist, never allowing to dry out; keep well watered till foliage yellows.
Mist: daily during forcing, lightly while flowering.
Humidity: normal, 30%-40%.

Air circulation: helpful condition.
Soil: 2 parts standard potting mix, 1 part sand.
Temperature: Day—68°-75°F (20°-23°C). Night—60°-68°F (15°-20°C).
Soil culture: select large bulbs, preferably pretreated. Handling them gently, bury 7 to 9 of them, with sides touching, in soil specified for this genus, to only half their height. Use proper potting procedure, a shallow pot or bulb pan. Moisten soil by setting this into pan of water, allowing to absorb "bottoms up" until patches of moisture appear on top of soil. Place in cool, about 50°F (10°C), dark site, keeping soil barely moist until shoots are approximately 4″ (100 mm) high. This root-producing period takes 8-12 weeks. Move pot to north light site of 50°-55°F (10°-12°C) for 3-4 days, then move pot on to sunny southern location. Newly potted-up bulbs can also be set outside in cold frame or plunged into ground and covered with 4″ (100 mm) of soil. Temperatures should be around 40°F (4°C). With shoots 4″ (100 mm) high, move inside and proceed with culture as above. After flowering and foliage has yellowed and withered, set pot in dry cool area until fall planting season; the bulbs can be removed from the pot, old soil removed, and planted outside for next spring's blooming.
Water culture: place pretreated bulbs in a container 2/3 filled with gravel, water to top level of gravel. Gently set bulbs atop the gravel, then half cover bulbs with more gravel, carefully keeping them upright. Maintain water level at base of bulbs. Site the pot in a cool, 50°-60°F (10°-15°C), dark, airy location until shoots sprout to 3″ (76 mm). Then move to north window for 3-4 days and, finally, to full sun.
Propagate: by division of offshoots (side bulbs).
Insect alert: aphids, mealybugs, thrips, mites, slugs.
Notable: extremely high temperatures cause bulbs to blast—produce excessive foliage—thus obscuring the flowers; fertilization not necessary, as all nutrients are stored in bulbs; have temperature cool for longer lasting flowers.

Narcissus, Daffodil

N. asturiensis (as-tur-ee-en'-siss) meaning from Asturia, now northern Spain; common name, Pygmy daffodil; miniature, 4"-5" (100-127 mm) tall; narrow leaves 2"-4" (50-100 mm) long; yellow flowers, ½" (12 mm) long; blooming in winter.

N. bulbocodium (bulb-oh-koh'-dee-um) meaning with a fleecy covering on bulb; common name, Petticoat daffodil; 15" (.38 m) tall; light yellow flowers, many varieties; from southern Europe.

N. jonquilla (jon-kwil'-luh) Jonquil; 2 to 5 fragrant yellow flowers, wavy-edged crown.

N. poeticus (poh-et'-ik-us) Poet's narcissus or Pheasant eye; very delicate and fragrant, white, single, cup-shaped flowers, crowns edged with red.

N. tazetta (taz-zet'-tuh) Polyanthus narcissus; 6 to 8 flowers appear together; delicate, fragrant, star-shaped flowers; pale yellow, paper white; leaves to 1½' (.45 m).

> Variety—Orientalis (or-ee-en-tay'-liss) meaning from the East; common name, Chinese sacred lily; sulfur yellow blooms; native to Canary Islands, Japan.

> Variety—Polyanthos (pol-ee-anth'-os) sprays of 10-20 blossoms.

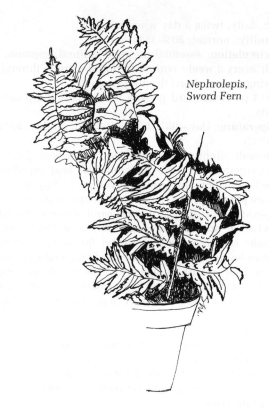

Nephrolepis, Sword Fern

NEPHROLEPIS (nef-frol'-ep-iss) Sword Fern.

Evergreen, rapid growers of easy cultural maintenance, members of this genus are happiest when least disturbed. The Boston Fern, the species *N. exaltata*, is considered by many to be the best all-around inside fern; it was very popular in great, great, grandparents' day!

Family Tree: Polypodiaceae (pol-ee-poh-dee-ay'-see-ay) Common Fern family; originally from Africa and tropical America.

Foliage: fronds (leaves) are up to 5' (1.20 m) in length, medium green, long and slender, pendulous; growth is dense; many species appear feathery.

Size: 1'-5' (.30-1.50 m).

Location: WINTER—eastern exposure.

SUMMER—*Inside:* eastern exposure. *Outside:* northern exposure.

FALL: move indoors by mid-September; site in eastern exposure.

Dormancy: none, really, but rests lightly through fall and winter.

Water: an extremely important part of the culture of these plants; be guided by the following: ordinarily, water thoroughly, allowing moderate drying between waterings, never allow to dry out completely; be aware of cool weather, when slower evaporation should mean less frequent watering; use room-temperature water only.

Mist: daily, twice a day if possible; use room-temperature water.

Humidity: very high, 60%-70%; especially March through September.

Air circulation: essential for super success, but avoid drafts.

Feed: very, very weak solution of mild liquid manure (cut recommendation of manufacturer to 2/3) every 3 weeks.

Soil: 2 parts standard potting mix, 1 part vermiculite, 2 parts peat moss.

Temperature: Day—68°-75°F (20°-23°C). Night—50°-60°F (10°-15°C).

Potbound: very happy; do not pot-on until root system is 80% of pot content (best done in February or March). Roots adhere to interior pot walls, therefore, work gently to avoid excessive injury, easing them loose. Rapping pot against end of a table is an aid, as well as running a spatula around inside of pot, pressing against pot wall with tool to avoid slipping into root ball. Wrap fronds of a large fern in newspaper for protection while handling. Set plant on 1½" (37 mm) layer of gravel, then add soil.

Mature plants: if fern looks sad, cut back to 2" (50 mm) above soil line; repot and proceed in proper culture. If aerial roots develop, cut them off. Wash foliage at least every 3 weeks. Remove yellowed or withered fronds as they appear.

Propagate: by division of mature plant, best done around March; or by spores (little brown dots) attached to underside of leaflets.

Insect alert: mealybugs, aphids, thrips, red spider; control with soap and water remedy, repeat every 3 days until eradicated.

Notable: ferns need coolness at their roots, so use pebble, water, and tray method for cooler temperature and high humidity; best to grow in clay pots, as their porosity allows evaporation and aids in keeping roots cool; if fronds droop from too dry soil, they cannot be revived; fronds of young plants cannot stand water directly on them; fronds bruise easily so plant should be located where it will not touch or be touched; ferns cannot stand pesticides, which will kill insects and your plant, too.

N. exaltata bostoniensis (ex-al-tay'-tuh bos-ton-ee-en'-siss) meaning extremely tall; Boston fern; arching fronds to 3' (.90 m) long; 3"-4" (76-100 mm) closely set leaflets. N. exaltata bostoniensis compacta, dwarf Boston fern, has 15"-18" (.38-.45 m) fronds.

> Variety—Childsii: dwarf, slow growing, waxy, green leaves.

Variety—Fluffy Ruffles: heavily ruffled fronds; lush growth.

Variety—Norwoodii: lacelike fronds, up to 18″ (.45 m); fresh, green, dense growth.

Variety—Verona: popular Boston fern; lacy, pendulous fronds.

N. acuminata (ak-kew-mi-nay'-tuh) meaning tapering to a point; known as Java sword fern; from Malaya; coarsely toothed, drooping fronds, 1′ (.30 m) wide, 2′-3′ (.60-.90 m) long.

N. biserrata (bye-ser-ray'-tuh) from Malaya; drooping or arching fronds, 1′ (.30 m) wide, 4′-5′ (1.20-1.50 m) long.

N. cordifolia (kor-di-foh'-lee-uh) tuberous rooted species; bright green, divided fronds, 2″ (50 mm) wide, to 2′ (.60 m) long.

N. pectinata (pek-ti-nay'-tuh) meaning like a comb; Basket fern; compact, grayish green fronds, to 1′ (.30 m).

N. philippinensis (fil-ip-pin-en'-siss) compact, upright plant; narrow, dark green fronds; brown stalk.

NERIUM (neer'-ee-um) Oleander, Rose Bay.

A sizable, spring and summer blooming evergreen genus. Tub size, of graceful, erect nature, it features simple or double flanged clusters of delicate flowers of delicate fragrance, depending on variety.

Family Tree: Apocynaceae (ap-oh-sin-ay'-see-ay) Dogbane family; native to Mediterranean countries, southern Europe, and North Africa.

Foliage: long, narrow, lance shaped, similar to willow; dark gray green, leathery; some varieties variegated in color.

Flower: 2″ (50 mm) diameter, fragrant, single or double blooms; perched at tip of 1 year-old canes; white through buff, creamy yellow to pinks and reds; primary blooming time, spring and summer; colors and shapes vary with species.

*Nerium oleander,
Rose Bay*

Size: long-caned, upright, slender shrub to 5′ (1.50 m).

Location: WINTER—southern exposure.

SUMMER—*Inside and Outside:* southern exposure.

FALL: move indoors by mid-September; site in southern exposure.

Dormancy: starts in September, prune back severely; slowly diminish watering, keeping soil barely moist; allow to dry out completely between waterings; cease fertilizing.

Water: keep very moist, with room-temperature water.

Mist: daily, lightly.

Humidity: low normal, 20%-25%.

Air circulation: helpful condition.

Feed: every 3 weeks, April through August, with mild liquid manure.

Soil: 2 parts standard potting mix, 1 part peat moss, 1 part vermiculite.

Temperature: Day—68°-75°F (20°-23°C). Night—60°-68°F (15°-20°C).

Potbound: very unhappy; in February, if needed, pot-on —whenever root system overbalances soil content; mature plant needs 12″ (.30 m) pot.

Mature plants: prune canes when blooming has ceased. May be trained into standard form (tree form) by proper pruning.

Propagate: from 6″ (.15 m) stem tip cuttings, in late May; root in water.

Insect alert: mealybug, scale, whitefly.

Notable: do not burn any trimmings of this plant because all parts and their fumes are fatally poisonous; good for growth under artificial light; full sun exposure essential to flowering; plants do not become truly showy until 3 years old; do protect from overabundance of rain when summering outdoors.

N. oleander (oh-lee-and'er) known as Oleander or Rose Bay; native to Mediterranean region; single flowers in terminal clusters, colored yellow, pink, red, purple, or white; flower to 2″ (50 mm); bloom spring and summer; leaves to 8″ (200 mm) long.

Variety—Variegatum (var-ee-eh-gay'-tum) meaning with another color, generally on leaves; in this case, white edges on leaves.

NICODEMIA DIVERSIFOLIA (nik-oh-dee'-mee-uh dye-ver-si-foh'-lee-uh) Indoor Oak.

The indoor oak is medium-sized, bushy, and evergreen. Diversifolia refers to the variable leaf shape, which generally resembles the foliage of the English oak tree. A branching growth habit and foliage hued to a misty, shimmering blue combine to offer a very attractive species to grace a dimmish interior site.

Family Tree: Loganiaceae (loh-gan-ee-aye'-see-ay) Logania family; native to Madagascar.

Foliage: succulent green leaves with metallic blue sheen; shape is lobed to point; up to 2″ (50 m) long; on branching reddish brown stems.

Size: up to 2′ (.60 m) high.

Location: WINTER—northeastern to eastern exposure.

SUMMER—*Inside:* northern exposure. *Outside:* northern exposure; site in sheltered area to protect foliage.

FALL: move indoors by mid-September; site in northern exposure.

Nicodemia diversifolia,
Indoor Oak

Dormancy: none, a resting time during winter months, generally September through March; slowly diminish watering, plant will indicate needs by appearance, becoming limp and droopy; develop sensitivity to feel of soil moisture level; cease fertilizing.

Water: evenly and thoroughly, allowing soil to dry between waterings.

Mist: daily, twice a day when possible.

Humidity: normal, 30%-35%.

Air circulation: essential for good cultural response.

Feed: every 2 weeks with mild liquid manure throughout growing season, April through August.

Soil: 3 parts standard potting mix, 1 part sharp sand or perlite, 1 part peat moss.

Temperature: Day—68°-78°F (20°-25°C). Night—40°-64°F (4°-17°C).

Potbound: slightly, for happiness, when root growth is approximately 65% of pot content; best repotted or potted-on before new growth develops, in March.

Mature plants: prune to maintain plant to size and form, preferably in late winter, prior to evidence of new growth. Remove withered foliage as it occurs.

Propagate: by cuttings, in spring, April or May.

Insect alert: red spider, mites, scale.

Notable: soil must have porosity; no soggy conditions; keep on lower side of recommended temperatures; important to cleanse foliage regularly. *Note:* good air circulation needed for top performance; do not overpot, use pot only 2″ (50 mm) larger than previous housing.

NICOTIANA (nik-oh-shee-ay′-nuh) Flowering Tobacco, Tobacco Plant. This plant is named for scholar-diplomat Jean Nicot, French Ambassador to Portugal, 1559-61. He sent seeds of the plant to the Queen Mother Catherine de Medici of France. On his return, he raised tobacco and promoted the fashion of smoking in the French court.

The tobacco plant flowers in winter. Many of the older varieties have habit of closed blooms during the day, they open in late afternoon to release the heady fragrance into the evening hours. Newer varieties whose blooms open all day are now available. All are generous in their flowering habits. This, along with easy maintenance, makes the flowering tobacco a pleasure to possess.

Family Tree: Solanaceae (soh-luh-nay′-see-ay) Nightshade family; native to Brazil and Australia.

Foliage: soft, hairy, oval leaves, 4″-6″ (100-150 mm) long, on erect plant.

Flower: tubular, trumpet-shaped, 2″ (50 mm) flowers, fragrant in the evening; white, pink, scarlet, shades of lime green, yellow, chartreuse, wine red, chocolate, crimson, and purple.

Size: 8″ (.25 m) to 2½′ (.75 m), depending on species.

Location: WINTER—direct sun; set in southern exposure.

SUMMER—*Inside:* partial shade; set in eastern to southern exposure for direct rays of morning sun. *Outside:* partial shade; set in eastern exposure or under a protective structure where plant receives strong light but no direct rays.

FALL: move indoors by mid-September.

Water: keep soil evenly moist.

Mist: daily.

Humidity: normal, 30%-35%.

Air circulation: necessary for successful culture.

Feed: every 2 weeks with mild liquid manure.

Soil: standard potting mix.

Temperature: 68°-72°F (20°-22°C). Night—50°-60°F (10°-15°C).

Propagate: by seed, in midsummer for midwinter flowering; or take plants from garden in late summer, cut back to 6″ or 8″ (150-200 mm) before potting; plant in small pot to restrict growth in height; will branch and flower in midwinter.

Offspring established: seedlings should be well rooted within 6-8 weeks; plant each in 4″ (100 mm) pot, use soil

Nicotiana alata,
Tobacco Plant

specified for this genus; set pots in bright light—but not direct sun—for 7-10 days; then follow light culture for nicotiana.

Insect alert: aphids, whitefly.

Notable: keep on cool side of recommended temperatures; plan to enjoy as an annual and therefore discard plant when flowering has ceased; will be happy in full sun or light shade.

N. alata (al-lay'-tuh) meaning with wings or flanges, usually the edges; common name, Flowering tobacco or Jasmine tobacco; former name, N. affinis; fragrant white, pink, rose, crimson, tubular flowers; 3'-5' (.90-1.50 m).

    Variety—Grandiflora (gran-di-flo'-ra) meaning large flowered; most common; larger white flowers; blooms in afternoon.

N. glauca (glaw'-kuh) meaning grayish or bluish green; common name, Tree tobacco; bluish green leaves, yellow flowers, 15'-20' (4.50-6 m) tall; needs long growing season to bloom.

N. sanderae (san'-der-ee) fragrant rose blossoms, 3" (76 mm) long, in clusters; large leaves, bushy plant, to 2½' (.75 m).

N. suaveolens (swav-ee'-ol-enz) meaning sweet smelling; purple-tinged, green flowers, sweetly fragrant, night blooming; 1'-1½' (.30-.45 m).

N. sylvestris (sil-vess'-triss) fragrant, drooping white flowers, tube shaped on stout central stem; night bloomer but will open in dim daylight; easily grown.

OLEA EUROPAEA (oh'-lee-uh yew-roh-pee'-uh) Olive.
Olea, the olive tree, grown commercially for its fruit, especially in the areas surrounding the Mediterranean. In cultivation for centuries, it is known to have longevity and to be a genus tolerant of adverse conditions. O. europaea is attractive trained to standard form.

Family Tree: Oleaceae (oh'-lee-ay'-see-ay) Olive family; native to Mediterranean area.

Foliage: leathery textured, green leaves, silvery undersides, 1½"-3" (37-76 mm) long.

Flower: fragrant, tiny white blooms.

Fruit: rarely in interior environment.

Size: up to 20' (6 m).

Location: WINTER—southern exposure.

SUMMER—*Inside and Outside:* southeastern or southwestern exposure.

FALL: move indoors by mid-September; site in southeastern or southwestern exposure.

Dormancy: none, a resting time during winter months, generally September through March; slowly diminish watering, plant will indicate needs by appearance, becoming limp and droopy; develop sensitivity to feel of soil moisture level; cease fertilizing.

Water: evenly and thoroughly, allowing soil to dry between waterings.

Mist: daily, twice a day when possible.

Humidity: normal, 30%-35%.

Air circulation: essential for good cultural response.

Feed: every 2 weeks with mild liquid manure throughout growing season, April through August.

Olea europaea,
European Olive Tree

Soil: 3 parts standard potting mix, 1 part sharp sand or perlite.

Temperature: Day—68°-78°F (20°-25°C). Night—40°-64°F (4°-17°C).

Potbound: happy; repot when root growth is 80% of pot content.

Mature plants: prune drastically in spring to establish desired shape and height.

Propagate: by seed or cuttings.

Insect alert: aphid, mealybug, mite, scale, leaf miner.

Notable: soil must have porosity; no soggy conditions; keep on lower side of recommended temperatures; important to wipe or wash foliage every 2 weeks. *Note:* good air circulation needed for top performance; do not overpot, use pot only 2" (50 mm) larger than previous housing.

ORCHID FAMILY (or'-kid).
Botany breaks the Orchid family into groups or tribes for classification. The genera included within the specific categories relate in certain characteristics of structure and native habitat; therefore, it follows that a generalization in cultural needs can be attributed within these specific breakdowns. Orchids growing in trees or upon rocks are referred to as *epiphytes,* or air plants. The genera under this category are nourished from humus, or a breakdown of natural materials, which accumulates in the area of the host, the tree or rock to which it has rooted. Also, these air plants receive nourishment from the moisture in the air. Frequently one finds the epiphytes have obese or thick leaves and stems in which they store water. *Terrestrials* are plants rooted into the ground. Orchids in this classification select moist areas rich in humus, but with excellent drainage, in their native environment. The cultural needs of the various genera vary to such a degree, that each

genus will have a detailed breakdown for attention in the interior environment.

In generalization, concerning this family vast in potential of exciting plant species, it can only be stated that truly fantastic blooms in such variety suffice to fill all needs. Proud-statured species vary: gracefully cascading to erect. All display blooms of fragility, most of delicate design form, all handsome regardless of size, color, or structure. With almost all varieties, many with a blooming period spanning 3 months or more, one can safely bring a plant in bloom from its cultural site to an interior site, placing it in a location for full enjoyment throughout the blooming cycle.

Family Tree: Orchidaceae (or-kid-day'-see-ee) Orchid family; native to tropical areas of the world.

Orchid

The following specifics on the general culture of the Orchid family are important. If there is a deviation, the needed cultural treatment will be noted under that genus.

Dormancy: a resting time after flowering; slowly diminish watering, keeping potting mix barely moist; cease fertilizing, until new growth is evident.

Mist: daily, twice a day when possible; when plant is blooming do not mist directly on flowers.

Humidity: high for happiness, 50%-60%.

Air circulation: essential for good cultural response.

Mature plants: thoroughly happy with outside summer vacation. Remove spent blooms as they occur. No harm in moving plant from its accustomed cultural site during its blooming period. Washing plants on a regular schedule will prevent an infestation of insects.

Insect alert: slugs, snails, scale, aphids, mealybugs, thrips.

Disease alert: yellow leaves mean too much light; dark green foliage with poor or no bloom, too little light; soft or wrinkled foliage, too much or too little watering. Orange powder on under leaf caused by a rust or fungi, treat with proper fungicide; leaf spots or discolored leaves caused by bacteria and fungi controlled by spraying two or three times, approximately 10 days between sprays, with proper fungicide; gray mold on flower petals caused by drops of water.

Notable: use pebble, water, and tray method to maintain high humidity; potting mixture must have excellent porosity; no compacted or soggy potting medium, please; use only pure water, rain water or other nonchemical for watering; use only tepid or room-temperature water; good artificial light specimen, giving total of 14 hours combined natural and artificial light. When purchasing new plant select fresh, white tipped, healthy green growth.

Cattleya labiata Genus of Orchid tribe. (kat'-lee-a lay-bee-a'-ta) *labiata*, having flowers with a lip. Cattleya tribe; native to Brazil.

Foliage: thickened stems, pseudobulbs, club shaped; produce up to 1 leathery leaf, up to 7″ (177 mm) long; green.

Flower: on stalks up to 18″ (.45 m) tall; 2-5 flowers, each up to 6″ (150 mm) wide; flower has purple lip, yellow throat is orange spotted; blooms generally October and June; recognized as the corsage flower.

Location: WINTER—southern exposure.

SUMMER—*Inside:* southeastern exposure. *Outside:* southeastern or southwestern exposure; preferably protect under tree boughs.

FALL: move indoors by mid-September; site in southeastern or southwestern exposure.

Water: thoroughly and evenly, do not allow potting medium to dry.

Feed: every 2 weeks with mild liquid manure.

Soil: use shredded fir bark or osmunda fiber, both available packaged at garden supply outlets.

Temperature: Day—68°-80°F (20°-26°C). Night—62°-70°F (16°-21°C).

Potbound: repot or pot-on only when potting medium has rotted or decomposed; or roots overflow confines of pot; best done when new growth is evident by new shoots. Do not water for 1 week after repotting.

Propagate: by division; taking pseudobulb with roots from parent plant; leave at least 4 stems on parent plant.

Paphiopedilum Genus of Orchid tribe. (pap-ee-oh-ped'-il-um) Lady's slipper. *Cypripedium* (sip-pri-pee'-di-um) tribe; native to tropical Asia.

Foliage: grows from fibrous or fleshy root system; short stemmed; generally small leaves with deep center vein giving leaf characteristic fan shape; generally pale green, splotched or spotted; leaf length to 18″ (.45 m) long, and 1½″ (37 mm) wide, all depending on species.

Flower: of erect nature; petals generally narrow and spreading; lip blossom pouchlike; 1 to several flowers per stem; stems up to 18″ (.45 m); flowers combinations of pink through purple, greens, white; striped, spotted; blooming time usually between October and March, all depending on species.

Location: WINTER—southeastern exposure.

SUMMER—*Inside:* eastern exposure. *Outside:* eastern exposure; preferably protect under tree boughs.

FALL: move indoors by mid-September; site in eastern exposure.

Water: thoroughly and evenly, keeping planting medium lightly damp, no harm in using tap water.

Feed: every 2 weeks with mild liquid manure.

Soil: shredded fir bark, osmunda fiber, both available packaged at garden supply outlets.

Temperature: Day—for mottled-leaved species, 68°-80°F (20°-26°C); others 62°-70°F (16°-21°). Night—for mottled-leaved species, 62°-70°F (20°-26°C) others 50°-62°F (10°-16°C).

Potbound: repot or pot-on only when potting medium has rotted or decomposed, or roots overflow confines of pot; best done when new growth is evident by new shoots; do not water for 1 week after repotting.

Propagate: by division or seed.

P. barbatom (bar-bay′-tum) meaning barbed or bearded; native to Malaya; mottled leaves in checked pattern, up to 6″ (150 mm) long, and 3″ (76 mm) wide; flowers white to purplish with pale green base, up to 4″ (100 mm) wide, narrow petals tipped purple, margin black-dotted, lip purplish-brown; single stem, up to 10″ (254 mm) tall; blooms generally February to June.

P. callosum (kal-loh′-sum) meaning callused; native to China; leaves to 9″ (230 mm) long, 2″ (50 mm) wide, marbled, blackish green; flowers colored white, with stripes of green and purple, lip of purplish brown; one flower, on up to 1′ (.30 m) stems; bloom long-lasting; keep in temperature about 65°F (18°C).

P. insigne (in-sig′-nee) meaning distinguished or remarkable; native to India; up to 12″ (.30 m), unmarked, pale green leaves, ¾″ (19 mm) wide; waxy flower, up to 4″ (100 mm) wide, white to yellowish green, brown spotted, purple veining, petal has hairy margins; lip greenish yellow muted with brown hue; stemless blooms; short, hairy flower stalk; blooms generally November to January.

Cymbidium insigne Genus of Orchid tribe. (sim-bid′-ee-um in-sig′-nee) The Greek, *cymbidium*, boat, refers to the lip shape; *insigne*, distinguished or remarkable. Cymbidium tribe; native to Asia.

Foliage: up to 12 leaves, 3′ (.90 m) long and ½″ (12 mm) wide, sword shaped; from pseudobulbs, the stemlike base of the leaf; blue green.

Flower: up to 4′ (1.20 m) long, erect stems; bloom generally February or March; each flower up to 4″ (100 mm) wide, lightish rose, white lip, crimson-spotted or lined.

Location: WINTER—southern exposure.

SUMMER—*Inside:* southeastern exposure. *Outside:* south-eastern or southwestern exposure; preferably protect under tree bough.

FALL: move indoors by mid-September; site in southeastern or southwestern exposure.

Water: thoroughly and evenly, do not allow potting medium to dry.

Feed: every 2 weeks, with mild liquid manure.

Soil: shredded fir bark or osmunda fiber, both available packaged at garden supply outlets.

Temperature: Day—62°-70°F (16°-21°C). Night—55°-65°F (12°-18°C).

Potbound: repot or pot-on only when potting medium has rotted or decomposed, or roots overflow confines of pot; best done when new growth is evident by new shoots; do not water for 1 week after repotting.

Propagate: by division; taking pseudobulb with roots from parent plant; leave at least 4 stems on parent plant.

C. lowianum (low-ee-ay′-num) native to Burma; narrow, curved leaves 2′-3′ (.60-.90 m) long, from pseudobulb; flowers, each to 4″ (100 mm) wide, in arching clusters of up to 20 blooms per cluster (raceme), streaked reddish brown on greenish yellow petals; lip front purplish red with yellow margin, side lobe of lip yellowish tan.

Odontoglossum pulchellum Genus of Orchid tribe. (o-don-to-gloss′-um pull-kell′-um) The Greek, *odontoglossum*, tooth and tongue, *pulchellum*, beautiful or merely pretty; *Odontoglossum* tribe native to Mexico and Central America.

Foliage: 2-3 leaves growing from pseudobulb; narrow leaf, up to 12″ (.30 m) long; colored dark green.

Flower: fragrant; clustered blooms of 8-10 flowers, clusters to 15″ (.38 m) long; flower to 1″ (25 mm) wide; white, yellow lip with purple dots; blooms winter months.

Location: WINTER—southern exposure.

SUMMER—*Inside:* southeastern exposure. *Outside:* south-eastern or southwestern exposure; preferably protect under tree boughs.

FALL: move indoors by mid-September; site in southeastern or southwestern exposure.

Water: thoroughly and evenly, do not allow potting medium to dry.

Feed: every 2 weeks, with mild liquid manure.

Soil: shredded fir bark, or osmunda fiber, both available packaged at garden suppy outlets.

Temperature: Day—55°-68°F (12°-20°C). Night—45°-58°F (7°-14°C).

Potbound: repot or pot-on only when potting medium has rotted or decomposed, or roots overflow confines of pot; best done when new growth is evident by new shoots; do not water for 1 week after repotting.

Propagate: by division, taking pseudobulb with roots from parent plant; leave at least 4 stems on parent plant.

O. grande (gran′-dee) *grande*, larger, showy; common name, Tiger Orchid; native to Guatemala; up to 14″ (350 mm) leaves, up to 2″ (50 mm) wide, generally 2 rising from each pseudobulb, 3-6 clustered flowers, up to 9″ (230 mm) across; yellow, striped or spotted brown, with wavy creamish lip; fall blooming.

O. pendulum (pen'-dew-lum) meaning hanging; previously classified as *O. citrosmum*; native to Mexico; generally 2 leaves up to 3″ (76 mm) wide, 1′ (.30 m) long, rising from pseudobulb; 3″ (76 mm) wide flower clusters; drooping clusters to 16″ (.40 m) long; white or shaded rose, lip deeper rose; fall blooming; this species will take a temperature up to 5°F (2.8°C) warmer.

ORNITHOGALUM (or-nith-thog'-al-um) Star of Bethlehem; False Sea Onion.

The genus name is from the Greek, *ornis* or *ornithos*, a bird, and *gala*, milk. "Bird's milk," a colloquialism of ancient Greek, means something wonderful. Small, lilylike blossoms cluster to form a gracefully tapering, long flower which lasts several weeks. A sweet-scented bulb plant for late winter-early spring enjoyment.

Family Tree: Liliaceae (lil-ee-ay'-see-ay) Lily family; native to Asia Minor and South Africa.

Foliage: extremely narrow, grasslike green leaves, 18″ (.45 m) long, 1″-2″ (25-50 mm) wide.

Flower: loose clusters; fragrant, white or yellow, small, waxy stars, on central stalk taller than leaves.

Size: 1′-2′ (.30-.60 m).

Location: WINTER—full sun; set in southern exposure.

SUMMER—*Inside:* partial shade; set in eastern to southern exposure for direct rays of morning sun. *Outside:* partial shade; set in eastern exposure or under a protective structure where plant receives strong light but no direct rays.

FALL: move indoors by mid-September.

Dormancy: after flowering, let foliage mature, yellow and die; store bulbs in dry soil of original pots until the next September or October; in cool, dark site; when foliage has yellowed, cease watering; cease fertilizing.

Water: allow soil to become slightly dry between thorough and even waterings.

Mist: daily during growing season, around plant but not on flowers.

Ornithogalum umbellatum,
Star of Bethlehem

Humidity: 40%-50%.

Air circulation: helpful condition.

Feed: every 2 weeks, with mild liquid manure.

Soil: 2 parts standard potting mix, 1 part sharp sand or perlite.

Temperature: Day—68°-72°F (20°-22°C). Night—50°-60°F (10°-15°C).

Potbound: repot after each dormancy period in fresh potting mix specified for this genus; remove offsets to avoid crowding.

Bulb culture: pot-up offsets in soil specified for this genus; set bulbs (offsets) very close together; keep cool and moderately watered until top growth is evident; move to full sun site, keeping on cooler side of recommended temperatures.

Propagate: by offsets.

Notable: offsets usually flower by the second year; all parts of *Ornithogalum umbellatum* are poisonous. Soil must have porosity, no soggy conditions; never allow soil to dry out completely during growth season.

O. arabicum (ar-ab'-ik-um) meaning of Arabia; 6-12 white flowers, 2″ (50 mm) long, bear black, pollen-receiving pistils (female reproductive organ); slender green leaves; 2′ (.60 m) stems bear flowers.

O. biflorum (bye-floh'-rum) meaning having 2 flowers or pairs of flowers arranged along stem; 4″ (100 mm) long flower cluster; native to Chile and Peru.

O. caudatum (cau-day'-tum) meaning bearing a tail, usually a shape relating to the flower itself; common name, False sea onion; mass of 50-100 small white flowers bearing green center line on each petal; 18″-36″ (.45-.90 m) stalk, grows from 3″-4″ (76-100 mm) bulb that is almost entirely out of the soil.

O. nutans (new'-tanz) meaning nodding or drooping flowers; clustered white flowers with green bands on outside; foliage 1′ (.30 m) tall; flower stalks up to 2′ (.60 m) high.

O. thyrsoides (thy-roh-soy'-dez) meaning flower head like a thyrse; common name, Chincherinchee; long lasting white or yellow flowers on 6″-18″ (.15-.45 mm) stalk; leaves 2″ (50 mm) wide, 1′ (.30 m) long.

O. umbellatum (um-bel-lay'-tum) meaning bearing the flowers in umbels; common name, Star of Bethlehem; white, green-edged, starlike flowers, on up to 1′ (.30 m) stalks; open flat in late morning, close late afternoon; leaves 1′ (.30 m) long, grooved along midrib. *Note:* all parts of this species are poisonous.

OSMANTHUS (os-manth'-us) Holly Osmanthus, False Holly.

Osmanthus, a durable, slow growing shrub, adjusts readily to interior environments. False holly's ornamental foliage appears very much like English holly, and displays most attractively, particularly when flowering, with fragrant white blossoms.

Family Tree: Oleaceae (oh'-lee-ay'-see-ay) Olive family; native to Asia.

Foliage: glossy, dark green leaves, 1½″-4″ (37-100 mm) long; spiny edged, resembling holly leaves; all depending on species.

Flower: clusters of tiny white, fragrant flowers, bloom year round.

Size: up to 5' (1.50 m) tall.
Location: WINTER—southern exposure.
SUMMER—*Inside and Outside:* southeastern or southwestern exposure.
FALL: move indoors by mid-September; site in southeastern or southwestern exposure.
Dormancy: none, a resting time during winter months, after major flowering; slowly diminish watering, plant will indicate needs by appearance, becoming limp and droopy; develop sensitivity to feel of soil moisture level; cease fertilizing.
Water: evenly and thoroughly, allowing soil to dry between waterings.
Mist: daily, twice a day when possible.
Humidity: normal, 30%-35%.
Air circulation: helpful condition.
Feed: every 2 weeks with mild liquid manure throughout growing season, April through August.
Soil: 3 parts standard potting mix, 2 parts sharp sand.
Temperature: Day—68°-78°F (20°-25°C). Night—40°-64°F (4°-17°C).
Potbound: slightly for happiness, when root growth is approximately 65% of pot contents; best repotted or potted-on before new growth develops, in March.
Mature plants: remove flowers as they fade.
Propagate: by seed or cuttings, latter best in summer.
Insect alert: aphid, mealybug, mite, scale.

O. fragrans (fray'-granz) meaning fragrant; common name Sweet olive; 4" (100 mm), oval leaves; small, white fragrant flowers; to 24" (.60 m) tall.
O. heterophyllus (het-er-oh-fil'-lus) Holly osmanthus or False holly; 1½"-2" (37-50 mm), extremely dark green, spiny-edged leaves; previously called *O. aquifolium* and *O. ilicifolius* (ill-li-see-fo'-li-a).

Variety—Variegatus (var-ee-eh-gay'-tus) green leaves, cream-colored edges, sometimes tinged pink.

Osmanthus fragrans,
Sweet Olive

Oxalis braziliensis,
Shamrock

OXALIS (ox'-al-iss).
A bit of a charmer in size and loveliness, undemanding yet high in performance. I refer to it as a "primer plant," for it is amost an "I can do no wrong," no-care genus. Some species are pleasing for hanging baskets.
Family Tree: Oxalidaceae (ox-al-lid-ay'-see-ay) Oxalis family; native to the Americas and South Africa.
Foliage: leaves are cloverlike, some 3, some 4 bladed; green tops and burgundy undersides, 2"-4" (50-100 mm) in size; all fold up at night.
Flower: fold up with descending evetime, as well as on cloudy days; profuse, almost ever blooming, but peak in summer and fall; dainty 1"-2" (25-50 mm) with 5 broad petals, in clusters of satiny yellow, pink, white, or red.
Size: 4"-18" (100 mm-.45 m).
Location: WINTER—full sun; set in southern exposure.
SUMMER—*Inside:* partial shade; set in eastern to southern exposure for direct rays of morning sun. *Outside:* partial shade; set in eastern exposure or under a protective structure where plant receives strong light but no direct rays.
FALL: move indoors by mid-September.
Dormancy: period starts when foliage withers in winter; rest pots in 50°F (10°C) coolness, keeping barely moist; do not allow soil to dry out completely; cease fertilizing in September, until end of February.
Water: keep soil evenly moist.
Mist: daily, lightly.
Humidity: normal, 30%-35%.
Air circulation: helpful condition.
Feed: every 2 weeks with diluted liquid manure March through August.

Soil: 2 parts standard potting mix, 1 part vermiculite, and a sprinkling of lime.

Temperature: Day—68°-72°F (20°-22°C). Night—50°-60°F (10°-15°C).

Potbound: repot each year at end of dormancy, about February, in fresh soil as specified for this genus; pot-on if not removing offset bulbs to establish individual young offspring.

Mature plants: remove faded blossoms and foliage.

Propagate: by seed, root division or from small bulbs that develop beside the parent bulb; in fall or February, plant 4″-6″ (100-150 mm) tubers ½″ (12 mm) deep in 6″ (150 mm) pot of soil specified for this genus.

Insect alert: aphids, mites.

Notable: prefer cool night air; keep on cool side of recommended temperatures; good for artificial light culture; never allow soil to dry out completely; must have good soil drainage, never soggy soil; totally a sun-loving plant.

O. adenophylla (ad-en-oh-fill′-uh) tuberous-rooted native of Chile; densely clustered leaflets on short stalks; flowers are pink, with dark pink veins; winter blooming.

O. lasiandra (las-ee-and′-ruh) crimson purple flowers in summer and fall.

O. melanostica (mel-an-os′-tik-uh) silvery leaves with 5-10 blades; yellow blooms in fall; needs 2 months rest in spring and summer; native of Mexico.

O. ortegiesii (or-teg-eez′-ee-eye) leaves olive green and red; yellow flowers intermittently all year; no rest period; 1½′ (.45 m) tall with 5-10 blades; called "Tree Oxalis."

O. rubra (roob′-ruh) meaning red; also called *O. rosea*; clusters of pink, lilac, or white flowers in summer; rest in winter; from Brazil.

O. hedysaroides rubra (hed-ee-sahr-oy′-deez roob′-ruh) firefern; satiny reddish, fernlike foliage; profusion of butter yellow flowers; grows to 6″ (150 mm); from South America; can be propagated from tip cuttings.

O. variabilis (var-ee-ay′-bil-liss) white, pink, or lavender blossoms.

O. bowiei (bow′-ee′-eye) also known as *O. purpurata* bowiei and *O. bowieana*; rose red flowers 2″ (50 mm) across on 1″ (25 mm) stems; summer and fall blooming.

O. braziliensis (braz-il-ee-en′-siss) meaning from Brazil; bulbous plant with firm, bright green leaves of 3 blades on long stems; 1″ (25 mm) rosy colored blooms in winter and spring; plant size to about 6″ (150 mm) sold as shamrock by florists.

O. carnosa (kar-noh′-suh) a succulent species grown from horizontal rhizome (stem which sends up sprouts); gray green, long-stemmed shiny leaflets; ¾″ (19 mm) yellow flowers in spring.

O. deppei (dep′-ee-eye) Good Luck Plant, Lucky Clover; beet-like, edible root; large leaves with 4 blades and brownish tracing; rosy flowers with yellow base, bloom in winter; propagate from bulblets.

O. herrerae (her-rar′-ay-ee) also known as *O. henrei*; succulent; fibrous-rooted; densely branched with light green leaflets and small yellow flowers in clusters on long stalks; good for hanging baskets.

O. hirta (hert′-uh) meaning with small hairs; fernlike; having tuberous roots, trailing stems, short-stalked leaves; large cup-shaped bright rose or lavender flowers; good for hanging baskets; from South Africa.

PACHYPHYTUM (pak-ee-fit′-um) Moonstones, Sugared Almonds, Silver Bract.

This genus of small succulents, as with most succulents, needs little attention, has most attractive foliage and charming flowers; a good choice for a site with full sun.

Family Tree: Crassulaceae (krass-yew-lay′-see-ay) Orpine family; native to Mexico.

Foliage: fleshy, thick leaves in rosette forms; up to 12″ (.30 mm) long; depending on species.

Flower: generally red or white; delicate, bell-shaped flowers on stems.

Size: up to 12″ (.30 m).

Location: WINTER—southern exposure.

SUMMER—*Inside and Outside:* southern exposure.

FALL: move indoors by mid-September; site in southern exposure.

Dormancy: none, although a rest period from October through February; slowly diminish watering, giving just enough moisture to keep leaves from shrivelling; cease fertilizing.

Water: allow soil to become quite dry between even, thorough waterings; March through September.

Mist: daily, very lightly, around plant but not directly on it.

Humidity: low normal, 20%-25%.

Air circulation: helpful condition.

Feed: once a month, April through July, with mild liquid manure.

Soil: 1 part standard potting mix, 2 parts sharp sand.

Temperature: Day—68°-80°F (20°-26°C). Night—50°-70°F (10°-21°C).

Potbound: normal; repot or pot-on when foliage appears overcrowded or root growth is 50% of pot content; best done in early spring prior to new growth evidence.

Mature plants: older plants frequently lose bottom leaves; bright light and sun improve richness of colors of foliage.

Pachyphytum oviferum,
Moonstones

Propagate: by leaf or tip cuttings (any time); or by offsets; pot-up in soil as specified for this genus; do not have damp soil and do not water for 5 days after potting.
Insect alert: scale, mealybug.
Disease alert: root rot from overwatering.
Notable: soil must have excellent porosity; do not try to create humid conditions; normal interior air, even a dry site, is most suitable. *Most notable:* plants rot very easily; a good artificial-light plant, up to 16 hours combined natural and artificial light hours; do not allow soil to dry out completely.

P. bracteosum (brak-tee-oh'-sum) Silver bract; thick, tongue-shaped leaves, grayish white, upward curving; to 1' (.30 m) high.
P. compactum (kom-pak'-tum) partially flattened, very thick, cylindrical leaves, to 1" (25 mm) long, in dense rosettes; red flowers; 8"-12" (.25-.30 m) tall.
P. oviferum (oh-vif'-er-um) Moonstones or Sugared almonds; thick, egg-shaped leaves, ½"-¾" (12-19 mm); densely growing; pearllike cast, becoming pinkish in sun; red or white flowers, tubular shape, ¾" (19 mm) long.

PANDANUS (pan-day'-nus) Screw-Pine.
Pandanus, a latinized Malayan name, is seldom used when referring to this decorative tropical genus with spiny-edged foliage. The screw pine resembles a palm tree without a trunk. It is sturdy, undemanding, and long-lived. Its dried fruit, when frayed, is used as a brush by Polynesians to paint on tapa cloth.
Family Tree: Pandanaceae (pan-dan-ay'-see-ay) Screw-pine family; native to Polynesia.
Foliage: evergreen; swordlike leaves in spiral rosettes; spiny margin and midrib; to 3' (.90 m) long.
Flower: rare in cultivation; in heads or spikes.
Fruit: conelike mass of nuts.
Size: up to 10' (3 m).
Location: WINTER—southeastern or southwestern exposure. SUMMER—*Inside:* northeastern or northwestern exposure. *Outside:* northeastern or northwestern exposure; site in shelter to protect foliage.
FALL: move indoors by mid-September; site in eastern or western exposure.
Dormancy: none, but a resting period of slower growth during winter months of less intensity, generally October through February; slowly diminish watering, plant will indicate needs as determined by environmental conditions; develop sensitivity to feel of soil moisture; cease fertilizing.
Water: thoroughly and evenly, allowing soil to dry out between waterings.
Mist: daily, twice a day when possible.
Humidity: above normal for happiness, 45%-55%.
Air circulation: helpful condition.
Feed: mild liquid manure every 2 weeks.
Soil: standard potting soil.
Temperature: Day—70'-80°F (21°-26°C). Night—62°-68°F (16°-20°C).
Potbound: very happy; pot-on only when root growth of plant is 80%, soil 20% of pot content; top- or side-dress yearly, preferably in the spring.
Mature plants: if plant becomes too tall, cut growing

Pandanus veitchii,
Screw-Pine

ends, start in rooting media. Remove dried or withered leaves as they appear.
Propagate: any time, from suckers that spring up at base of plant; when 6" (150 mm), remove, pot-up each individually, using soil specified for this genus.
Insect alert: mealybug, red spider, scale, thrip, aphids.
Notable: good artificial light plant; total of 14-16 hours, combining natural and artificial light; do not allow soil to dry out completely; soil must have porosity, eliminating possibility of soggy conditions; use pebble, water, and tray method to maintain humidity level; sponge foliage at least every 3 weeks, always use room temperature water; shiners and/or oils are an *absolute no-no.*

P. baptistii (bap-tiss'-tee-eye) stiff, blue green and yellow leaves.
P. sanderi (sand'-er-eye) yellow- and green-striped foliage.
P. utilis (yew'-til-iss) meaning useful; long, curving, bluish green leaves; reddish thorns at edges.
P. veitchii (veech'-ee-eye) the basic species; narrowed, pointed green leaves, bordered with creamy margin; up to 3' (.90 m) long, 3" (76 mm) wide.
   Variety—Compacta (kom-pak'-tuh) dark green leaves with white margins; 12"-18" (.30-.45 m) long, 1"-2" (25-50 mm) wide.

PASSIFLORA (pass-i-floh'-ruh) Passion Flower, Granadilla.
A rapidly growing vine which needs support for climbing. The flowers are fantastic; large, delicate loveliness to possess. They open in daylight with a delightful perfume but close tightly at night. Although each single flower lasts but one day, the supply is renewed daily in abundance. Remove a few flowers and float them in a floral arrangement to enhance your interior habitat. Named by missionaries who saw in the flower a representation of the Passion of Christ. Legend has it that various parts represent the crown of thorns, Christ's wounds, the chalice, and the nails in the cross.
Family Tree: Passifloraceae (pass-i-floh-ray'-see-ay) Pas-

Passiflora caerulea,
Passion Flower

sion flower family; native to tropical America, Asia, and Australia.

Foliage: simple or lobed; slender, alternate leaves; mostly evergreen, on 4-angled stems.

Flower: 10 outer petals surround intricate inner crown, to 4″ (100 mm) wide; red, purple, pink, yellow, scarlet, or white; blooms most profusely July through September but lightly off and on throughout the year.

Fruit: many seeded, pretty berry; purple, yellow, or orange; edible in some species; 2″-9″ (50-230 mm).

Size: climbing vines 6′-35′ (1.80-10.50 m).

Location: WINTER—southern exposure.

SUMMER—*Inside or Outside:* eastern or western exposure.

FALL: move inside by mid-September; site in southeastern or southwestern exposure.

Dormancy: October through December or January, after profuse blooming period, allow to rest these months in full sun; slowly diminish watering, keeping soil lightly dry; cease fertilizing, until signs of new growth are evident in early spring.

Water: keep soil evenly moist, never allowing to dry out completely.

Mist: daily, twice a day during growing season.

Humidity: high for happiness, 40%-50%.

Air circulation: helpful condition.

Feed: weekly with mild liquid manure, April through September.

Soil: standard potting mix.

Temperature: Day—68°F (20°C) or higher. Night—55°-65°F (12°-18°C).

Potbound: repot in early spring before new shoots develop; pot-on as needed when root growth overbalances soil content.

Mature plants: in January, cut flowering shoots of previous year back to 6″-8″ (150-200 mm) to force branching and encourage better blooms. Vines need support, even with heavy pruning.

Propagate: by layering, stem cuttings, or seed, any time; spring cuttings, when young shoots are 3″ (76 mm) long, will root easily in water.

Offspring established: when well rooted, plant each seedling in 4″ (100 mm) pot, using standard potting mix.

Insect alert: red spider mites, scale, mealybug.

Notable: keep on cooler side of recommended temperatures; if propagated from seed, plant will not bloom first year; usually young plants will have to be potted-on to 6″ (150 mm), then 8″ (200 mm) pot within a year; never allow soil to dry out completely.

P. x. alata-caerulea (al-ay′-tuh-see-rew′-lee-uh) meaning winged-dark blue; hybrid climber; 3 lobed leaves; fragrant flowers, 4″ (100 mm) across; white and pink with purple, blue, and white crown; 2″ (50 mm) ornamental fruit.

P. caerulea (see-rew′-lee-uh) meaning dark blue; 5 lobed, 4″-5″ (100-127 mm) gray green leaves; 3″-4″ (76-100 mm) pink and purple flowers; egg-shaped, yellow, ornamental fruit, to 2″ (50 mm).

P. coccinea (koh-sin′-ee-uh) meaning scarlet; 3″-6″ (76-150 mm), oval, coarsely toothed leaves; 4″-5″ (100-127 mm), scarlet flowers; small edible fruit.

P. edulis (ed′-yew-liss) meaning edible; common name, Apple bell or Purple Granadilla; 4″-6″ (100-150 mm) shiny leaves; 2½″ (62 mm) purple and white flowers; edible purple fruit.

P. manicata (man-i-kay′-tuh) meaning long-sleeved; leathery lobed leaves, whitish undersides; flowers scarlet with blue crown, 4″ (100 mm) across; yellowish green, non-edible fruit, to 2″ (50 mm).

P. quadrangularis (kwad-ran-gew-lay′-riss) Apple bell; unlobed leaves, bright red flowers, 3″-5″ (76-127 mm) across; 9″ (230 mm) long, edible passion fruit, called Granadilla.

P. racemosa (ras-em-oh′-suh) meaning flowers along a stream; a rampant climber; 5″ (127 mm) long, 3 lobed leaves; dark red flowers with white and purple crown; 3″ (76 mm) greenish yellow, non-edible fruit.

P. trifasciata (trye-fass-kee-ay′-tuh) 4″-6″ (100-150 mm) leaves, olive to bronze, silver pink markings, purple undersides; 1″-1½″ (25-37 mm) yellow white flowers.

PEDILANTHUS TITHYMALOIDES (ped-il-anth′-us tith-im-al-loy′-deez) Devil's Backbone, Redbird Cactus, Slipper Flower, Jewbush.

Common names for this species are interestingly derived: Devil's backbone has stems like a spinal column; Redbird cactus has spring blooming petite, red blossoms. P. tithamaloides is a succulent, happy only with cactus culture, sandy-type soil, and full sun.

Family Tree: Euphorbiaceae (yew-forb′-ee-ay-see-ay) Spurge family; native to tropical America.

Foliage: succulent stems; alternate leaf pattern; foliage rigid, lance shaped to a point, edges crinkled, up to 2″ (50 mm); variegations of swathed pink to red on creamish base with green highlighting.

Flower: nondescript; small, red, spring blooming; seldom in interior habitat.

Size: up to 2′ (.60 m).

Location: WINTER—southern exposure.

SUMMER—*Inside and Outside:* southern exposure.

Pedilanthus tithymaloides,
Devil's Backbone

Pelargonium hortorum,
Fish Geranium

FALL: move indoors by mid-September; site in southern exposure.

Dormancy: none, but a light resting period October through February; slowly diminish watering, keeping soil barely moist; cease fertilizing.

Water: keep moderately and evenly moist.

Mist: daily, twice a day when possible.

Humidity: normal, 30%-35%.

Air circulation: helpful condition.

Feed: mild liquid manure every 2 weeks.

Soil: 1 part standard potting mix, 1 part sharp sand.

Temperature: Day—68°-80°F (20°-26°C). Night—55°-68°F (12°-20°C).

Potbound: repot or pot-on as needed and indicated by root growth being at least 50% of pot content.

Mature plants: leaf drop will occur if soil dries out.

Propagate: by division or stem cuttings, root latter in water or moist vermiculite.

Insect alert: mealybug, mites.

Notable: good artificial light specimen, a total of 14 light hours combined with natural; prune plant often to prevent legginess; must have good porosity; never allow soil to dry out completely.

PELARGONIUM (pel-ahr-goh´-nee-um) Geranium.

The geranium family is extensive in its genera, but the cultural attention possible within an interior environment limits the selection. The Pelargonium is an herb, many heavily scented, flowers and leaves are used in potpourri; many types were used as medical herbs in generations past. Regardless of bloom or leaf size—these features vary with species and varieties—all are most colorful and attractive, the majority prefer a sunny site. Actually evergreen genera, these plants usually are handled as tender

specimens, and many times disposed of and replaced with fresh young plants. With care, there is no reason why the geranium cannot be carried on through several seasons. In fact, if one wishes to prune to a standard form, it will take a minimum of 3-4 years to produce a mature plant, properly shaped.

Family Tree: Geraniaceae (ger-ray-nee-aye´-see-ay) Geranium family; native to South Africa.

Foliage: depending on species, the leaf forms vary extensively through deeply lobed, serrated, ivy shaped, oval, smooth-margined; textures smooth through somewhat hairy, of soft nature; striations, heavily margined, vein accented; colors on green, highlights of white, cream, shadings of red; many heavily scented.

Flower: clusters tipping leafless stems; colored from pure whites, shadings of pinks to deep reds.

Size: to 3′ (.90 m).

Location: WINTER—southern exposure.

SUMMER—*Inside and Outside: southern exposure.*

FALL: move indoors by mid-September; site in southern exposure.

Dormancy: none, light resting period after each heavy blooming session.

Water: moderately but evenly, allowing soil to dry out between waterings.

Mist: daily, twice a day when possible.

Humidity: slightly above normal, 40%-45%.

Air circulation: helpful condition.

Feed: mild liquid manure, once a month.

Soil: standard potting mix.

Temperature: Day—68°-80°F (20°-26°C). Night—60°-68°F (15°-20°C).

Potbound: happy; top-dress in late winter or early spring; pot-on only when root growth is 75%, soil 25% balance of pot.

Mature plants: better bloom if stems pinched back as they become straggly, pinch off to point where plant retains compact, uniform shape; pinch center out of young shoots for wide plant; too tall a plant for standing upright, stake and tie main trunk (leave small amount of slack in ties, eliminating potential of injury from tie cutting into fleshy stem) may be trained into standard form (tree form) by proper pruning or pinching. Remove faded blooms as they occur; remove yellowed foliage.

Propagate: by seed or top cuttings, root latter in moist vermiculite.

Insect alert: mealybug, mites, sow bugs, whitefly, aphids.

Disease alert: root and stem rot from overwatering.

Notable: use pebble, water, and tray method to maintain an "up" humidity level; do not overwater for fear of stem rot and yellow leaves; overfertilization will produce abundance of foliage, very poor blooming; good artificial-light plant, give a total of 14 hours combined natural and artificial.

P. hortorum (hor-to'-rum) meaning of the garden; native to South Africa; common name, Fish geranium; named for faint fishlike odor of plant; stems of upright nature, thick, branching habit, fleshy; leaves up to 5″ (127 mm) wide, horseshoe shaped, scalloped margin; green with brownish green zone in horseshoe pattern on surface; flower heads consisting of many small blossoms, tightly clustered, single or double florets; white, shades of salmon, pink, and lavender through red; up to 3′ (.90 m).

P. peltatum (pell-tay'-tum) meaning leaf blade attached to stem not at leaf edge; common name, Ivy geranium; trailing stems; ivy-shaped leaves, 5-pointed, bright green, shiny; flowers white through shades of lavender and reds; stems to 4′ (1.20 m); pinching essential for good branching.

P. domesticum (do-mes'-ti-kum) meaning domesticated; common name, Lady Washington geranium; bush form, low, branching nature, up to 2′ (.60 m) high; soft, roundish, barely lobed, up to 4″ (100 m) wide leaves; stems hairy, fleshy; florets clustered to form rounded head of flower, white, shaded pinks through reds.

P. tomentosum (toe-men-toe'-sum) meaning dense coverage of flat hairs; common name, Peppermint geranium; up to 3′ (.90 m) high; shrubby nature; highly peppermint scented; 3-5 lobed leaves, velvet texture, white hairs, serrated margins, up to 4″ (100 mm) wide; florets cluster to form flower head; generally white; needs less sun than other species.

PELLAEA (pel-lee'-uh) Cliff Brake Fern.
The Greek, *pellos*, dusky, fathered the name of this genus, the reference is to the dark frond (leaf) stalks. The Pellaea is a lovely, delicate fern, with special need for sun and dry soil conditions. Virginia protects all native species. Unusual foliage for the fern genera makes it a "special" for interesting interior embellishment.

Family Tree: Polypodiaceae (pol-i-po'-di-ay'-see-ay) Common Fern family; native to New Zealand, some species native to United States.

Foliage: bluish green fronds, rounded like a coin; on dark, wiry stems; spreading growth habit.

Size: 4″ (100 mm) up to 2′ (.60 m), depending on species.

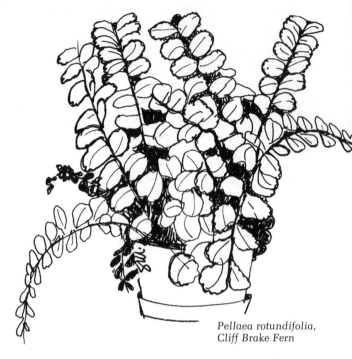

Pellaea rotundifolia,
Cliff Brake Fern

Location: WINTER—southern exposure.

SUMMER—*Inside and Outside:* southeastern exposure.

FALL: move indoors by mid-September; site in southeastern exposure.

Dormancy: none really, but rests lightly through fall and winter.

Water: an extremely important part of the culture of these plants; be guided by the following—water evenly and moderately, allowing water to drip through drainage hole; ensure soil has lost moisture but not dried out completely before rewatering.

Mist: daily, twice a day if possible; use room-temperature water.

Humidity: normal, 30%-35%.

Air circulation: helpful condition.

Feed: very, very weak solution of mild liquid fertilizer, balance 15-30-15 (cut recommendation of manufacturer by 2/3) every 3 weeks.

Soil: 2 parts standard potting mix, 1 part limestone, 1 part vermiculite.

Temperature: Day—68°-75°F (20°-23°C). Night—50°-60°F (10°-15°C).

Potbound: very happy; do not pot-on until root system is 80% of pot content (best done in February or March). Roots adhere to interior pot walls, therefore, to avoid excessive injury, work gently easing them loose. Rapping pot against end of a table is an aid, as well as running a spatula around inside of pot, pressing against pot wall with tool to avoid slipping into root ball. Wrap fronds of a large fern in newspaper for protection while handling. Set plant on 1½″ (37 mm) layer of gravel, then add soil.

Mature plants: if fern looks sad, cut back to 2″ (50 mm) above soil line; repot and proceed in proper culture. Wash foliage at least every 3 weeks. Remove yellowed or withered fronds as they appear.

Propagate: by division of mature plant, best done around March; or by spores (little brown dots) attached to underside of leaflets.

Insect alert: mealybugs, aphids, thrips, red spider; con-

trol with soap and water remedy, repeat every 3 days until eradicated.
Notable: ferns cannot stand pesticides, which will kill insects and your plant, too; soil must have good drainage; keep on the cooler side of recommended temperatures.

P. viridis (vihr'-id-iss) meaning green; known as False Holly Fern; native to West Indies; narrowly divided fronds to 2' (.60 m) long; on brown stalks; leaflets are holly shaped at maturity; high humidity, 40%-50%.
P. hastata (has-tay'-tuh) meaning like arrowhead; small, refined version of P. viridis.
P. rotundifolia (roh-tun-di-foh'-lee-uh) meaning round leafed; native to New Zealand; yellow green, dime-sized leaflets on young plant become brilliant green, holly shaped at maturity; 1' (.30 m) long fronds, on wiry, dark stems; low and spreading growing habit.

PELLIONIA (pell-ee-oh'-nee-uh) Trailing Watermelon Begonia.
The Pellionia, an herb genus, has a small-scale growth habit. The interesting leaf patterns of the delicate, evergreen foliage create an attractive display from a hanging container as the pendulous stems with good leaf coverage descend in moderate growth.
Family Tree: Urticaceae (ur-tye-kay'-see-ay) Nettle family; native to Asia and Pacific islands.
Foliage: strongly patterned veining on leaf surface, serrated edges, up to 2½" (62 mm); greens or deep purples; creeping stems, succulent, pink or purple; all depending on species.
Flower: insignificant; small, greenish.
Size: to 2' (.60 m).
Location: WINTER—southeastern or southwestern exposure.
SUMMER—*Inside:* northeastern or northwestern exposure. *Outside:* northeastern or northwestern exposure; protect fragile foliage from potentially damaging elements; preferable by overhang.
FALL: move indoors by mid-September; site in eastern or western exposure.
Dormancy: none, but light resting period, October through February; slowly diminish watering, keeping soil barely moist; cease fertilizing.
Water: keep moderately and evenly moist.
Mist: daily, twice a day when possible.
Humidity: above normal for happiness, 40%-45%.
Air circulation: helpful condition.
Feed: mild liquid manure every 2 weeks.
Soil: standard potting mix.
Temperature: Day—68°-80°F (20°-26°C). Night—55°-68°F (12°-20°C).
Potbound: repot; or pot-on as needed and indicated by root growth being at least 50% of pot content.
Mature plants: pruning to reestablish plant should be done in early spring, prior to evidence of new growth. Take cuttings, easily rooted, for fresh replacement.
Propagate: by stem cuttings, root in water or moist vermiculite.
Insect alert: mealybug, whitefly, mites, scale, slugs.
Notable: good artificial light specimen, a total of 14 light hours combined with natural; prune plant often to prevent legginess; do not overwater as plant will rot easily; must

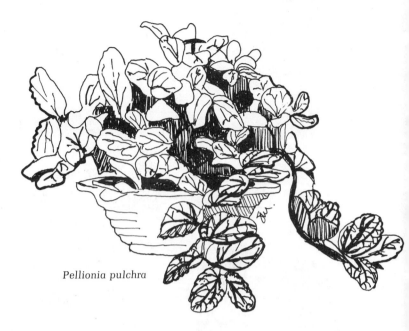

Pellionia pulchra

have good soil porosity; never allow soil to dry out completely; rinse foliage frequently in room-temperature or tepid water to prevent dust-clogged pores.

P. daveauana (day-vee-oh-ay'-nuh) Trailing watermelon-begonia; foliage grayish green; light red stems are succulent.
P. pulchra (pull'-kruh) leaf topside black, reverse side reddish black; stems reddish black are succulent.

PENTAS LANCEOLATA (pen'-tass lan-see-oh-lay'-tuh) Egyptian Star Cluster.
Pentas lanceolata means shaped like small lances (the leaves). It may be listed or referred to by the previous name, *P. carnea*, meaning flesh colored (the flowers). Delicate, lovely, miniature star-shaped flowers are arranged in clusters on small evergreen plant. Pentas are simple in culture but need periodic pruning attention to maintain attractive plant.
Family Tree: Rubiaceae (roo-bee-ay'-see-ay) Madder family; native to tropical Africa.
Foliage: hairy oval leaves, deeply veined, alternate placement; compact bushy genus; woody, flexible branches, covered with soft hairs.
Flower: 4" (100 mm) flat clusters of ½" (12 mm), star-shaped flowers, red, pink, lavender, or white; hairy at throat; bloom mainly fall through late winter.
Fruit: oval-shaped fruit.
Size: 12"-24" (.30-.60 m).
Location: WINTER—southern exposure.
SUMMER—*Inside and Outside:* southern exposure.
FALL: move inside by mid-September; site in southern exposure.
Dormancy: none, when pinching and feeding program is maintained.
Water: keep soil thoroughly and evenly moist.
Mist: daily, twice a day when possible.
Humidity: high, minimum 50%-60%.
Air circulation: helpful condition.
Feed: weekly with mild liquid manure.

Pentas lanceolata,
Egyptian Star Cluster

Soil: standard potting mix.
Temperature: Day—68°-80°F (20°-26°C). Night—60°-65°F (15°-18°C).
Potbound: normal; pot-on as plant indicates by root growth being more than 50% of pot content.
Mature plants: keep sited in full sun to ensure sturdy stems, helping to remain erect and support heavy flower heads. Pinch for retention of bushiness. Repot each spring, cutting plant back to 8″ (203 mm) all around to encourage compactnesss and better bloom.
Propagate: from soft wood cuttings any time, in water or moist vermiculite; or by seed (approximately 20 days for germination).
Offspring established: pot-up in soil recommended for this genus; each seedling to a 4″ (100 mm) container; place in north to east exposure for 3-4 days, then move to full sun; start normal cultural program.
Insect alert: scale.
Notable: genus can be handled as annual, and cuttings propagated in water, replacing parent plant with a succession of timed seedlings; blooming occurs within 9 or 10 weeks of seed sowing; a good artificial-light plant, a total of 14 hours combined natural and artificial.

PEPEROMIA (pep-er-roh′-mee-uh).
Small scaled plants, most no more than 1′ (.30 m) tall, make up a genus thought to have over 1,000 varieties. Characterized by many variations of leaf form, texture, shape, coloration, Peperomia is an evergreen of succulent nature, either creeping or erect in habit. Regardless of ap-

pearance, all species are interesting and attractive and require the same culture. North to east or west site, no sun, and care in moisture level concerns are the only demands for happiness. The name is from the Greek and means similar to pepper.
Family Tree: Piperaceae (Pye-per-aye′-see-ay) Pepper family; native to South America.
Foliage: small leaves; succulent; shades of green with striations, variegations, blotches, spots; colored stems, generally pink through red; texture crinkled, quilted, ridged; growth habit erect or creeping trailers; all depending on species.
Flower: tipping stems, usually of erect habit, protruding above foliage with clustered petite florets, resulting in mouse tail appearance.
Size: up to 1′ (.30 m) tall.
Location: WINTER—southeastern or southwestern exposure. SUMMER—*Inside:* northeastern or northwestern exposure. *Outside:* northeastern or northwestern exposure; protect fragile foliage from potentially damaging elements; preferably by overhang.
FALL: move indoors by mid-September; site in eastern or western exposure.
Dormancy: none, but light resting period, October through February; slowly diminish from full watering to keeping soil barely moist; cut fertilizing in half.
Water: keep moderately and evenly moist; allow soil surface to become dry to touch before rewatering.
Mist: daily, twice a day when possible.
Humidity: above normal for happiness, 40%-45%.
Air circulation: helpful condition.
Feed: mild liquid manure every 2 weeks.
Soil: 1 part standard potting mix, 1 part peat moss, 1 part perlite.
Temperature: Day—68°-80°F (20°-26°C). Night—55°-68°F (12°-20°C).
Potbound: repot; or pot-on as needed and indicated by root growth being at least 75% of pot content.
Propagate: by stem cuttings, of vining species; or by leaf cuttings.
Insect alert: mealybug, whitefly, mites, slugs.
Notable: good artificial-light specimen, a total of 14 light hours combined with natural; prune plant often to prevent legginess; do not overwater as plant will rot easily; must have good soil porosity; never allow soil to dry out completely; rinse foliage frequently in room-temperature or tepid water to prevent dust-clogged pores; exposure to strong sun discolors foliage; a genus which prefers being potted in shallow containers.

P. acuminata (ak-kew-min-nay′-tuh) meaning prickly; native to Mexico; fleshy leaf; marked with red rings; narrow, almost grasslike.
P. bicolor (bye′-kol-or) Silver velvet; native to Ecuador; velvety, round leaves; grayish green, silver edges and veins, red undersides.
P. caperata (kap-per-ay′-tuh) Wrinkle-leaved peperomia; ridged, heart-shaped leaves, red stemmed; to 5″ (127 mm) high.
　Variety—Emerald Ripple: emerald green leaves, brownish valleys, ¾″-1½″ (19-37 mm) across; 3″-4″ (76-100 mm) tall.
　Variety—Little Fantasy: emerald green leaf surfaces, brownish valleys; smaller than Emerald Ripple.

Peperomia caperata,
Wrinkle-Leaved Peperomia

Variety—Tricolor: red-veined, creamy leaves, central area of pale green; red stemmed; 3″-4″ (76-100 mm) high.

P. clusiaefolia (kloo-zay-ee-foh′-lee-uh) metallic green leaves edged with red, narrow, 4″ (100 mm); prominent spikes of flowers.

P. crassifolia (krass-if-foh′-lee-uh) meaning thick leaved; common name, Leather peperomia; pale green, round leaves; erect habit.

P. glabella (glay′-bell-uh)
Variety—Variegata (var-ee-eh-gay′-tuh) light green and yellow leaves; creeping habit; 12″ (.30 m).

P. griseo-argentea (griss′-ee-oh-ar-jen′-tee-uh) Ivy peperomia, nicknamed Blackie; previously known as *P. hederaefolia*; wrinkled leaf, silvery, with wide black green swath of color; long pink stems; 6″-8″ (150-200 mm).

P. incana (in-kay′-nuh) thick, heart-shaped, grayish leaves; will take sun.

P. maculosa (mak-yew-loh′-suh) meaning spotted; native to Santo Domingo; grayish green leaves, veined green and white, spotted bluish black; narrow, waxy leaves; spotted stem; erect to 12″ (.30 m).

P. marmorata (mar-moh-ray′-tuh) meaning mottled; common name, Silver heart; dark green, heart-shaped leaves, ridged with grayish silver; stems pink.

P. metallica (meh-tal′-ih-kuh) meaning with metallic cast; brown colored, waxy leaves, striped light green; erect up to 12″ (.30 m)

P. obtusifolia (ob-tew-sif-foh′-lee-uh) meaning with blunt apex; common name, Blunt-leaved peperomia; native to tropical America; waxy, smooth, deep green leaves, splashed with yellow and white spots; short, curving stems; 8″-10″ (200-250 mm); trailing.
Variety—Alba (al′-buh) all-white leaves.
Variety—Variegata (var-ee-eg-gay′-tuh) pale green leaves, cream-white edges.

P. ornata (or-nay′-tuh) deep green leaves, veined maroon; erect to 12″ (.30 m).

P. rotundifolia (roh-tun-dif-foh′-lee-uh) meaning round-leaved; succulent, round leaves; creeping habit; previously known as P. nummularifolia.

P. argyreia (are-jy-rei-a) Watermelon peperomia, Watermelon begonia, Football plant; native to South America, particularly Brazil; light green, heart-shaped, fleshy leaves, 2″-4″ (50-100 mm); grayish white stripes between veins running lengthwise on red stems; flowers on tall stems, resemble mouse tail; previously named *P. arifolia argyreia*.

P. velutina (vel-yew-tye′-nuh) Velvet peperomia; native to Ecuador; thick, hairy leaves, deep bronze green with whitish green center rib topside; underneath colored reddish; red stems; keep shaded or in dim site.

PETUNIA HYBRIDS (pe-tew′-nee-uh).

Summer, fall, winter, and sometimes into spring accents of color to enliven interiors. Seemingly endless availability for a selection of choice in color, aside from black or true blue, upright or trailing in habit, Petunia is a generous bloomer, both in length of flowering time and quantity of blossoms, when given full sun. Consider Petunias as an annual, for new plants yearly are more handsome in display, and propagation an easy, enjoyable involvement. The Brazilian, *petun*, means tobacco. This plant is closely related to Nicotiana, a group of 40 or so annuals and perennials of South American habitat.

Family Tree: Solanaceae (soh-lan-ay′-see-ay) Nightshade family; native to South America.

Foliage: small, fuzzy, sticky leaves.

Flower: up to 4″ (100 mm) funnel-shaped flowers usually single, often fringed or double-flowered; colors from white and yellow through pink and red to violet blue and deep purple; varieties are bicolored, multicolored, and striped in addition to shaded solids.

Petunia hybrids

Size: 6″-18″ (.15-.45 m), depending on species.

Location: WINTER—full sun; set in southern exposure.

SUMMER—*Inside:* partial shade; set in eastern to southern exposure for direct rays of morning sun. *Outside:* partial shade; set in eastern exposure or under a protective structure where plant receives strong light but no direct rays.

FALL: move indoors by mid-September.

Dormancy: treat as an annual.

Water: allow soil to become slightly dry between thorough waterings.

Mist: daily.

Humidity: normal, 30%-35%.

Air circulation: helpful condition.

Feed: weekly, with mild liquid manure.

Soil: 2 parts standard potting mix, 1 part peat moss, 1 part perlite.

Temperature: Day—68°-75°F (20°-23°C). Night—55°-60°F (12°-15°C).

Mature plants: better bloom if stems pinched back as they become straggly, pinch off to point where plant retains compact, uniform shape.

Propagate: by seeds; or cut back outdoor plants to 4″ (100 mm), pot in September for winter blooming indoors.

Insect alert: aphids, mealybug, mites.

Notable: must have full sun with as much daylight as possible; soil must have good drainage; aerate soil every 2 weeks; keep on lower side of recommended temperatures; if night temperature too high, flower buds will not set; when transplanting, use large earth ball, for petunias do not like roots disturbed.

P. x. hybrida (hib′-rid-uh) meaning hybrid; technically a perennial though used as an annual; entire color spectrum; all forms, shapes, including dwarf, bedding, and large flowering varieties, upright and trailing.

P. violacea (vye-oh-lay′-see-uh) meaning of the violet family; a prostrate form; rose violet flowers; stems to 10″ (250 mm).

P. axillaris (ax-il-lay′-riss) meaning of the axil; 2½″ (62 mm) white flowers; 2′ (.60 m) high.

PHILODENDRON (fil-oh-den′-dron).

The name of this tropical genus derives from Greek, *phileo* meaning love and *dendron* meaning tree; a tree-loving plant. Over 200 known species, most very adaptable to interior environments, ask little for their return in steadfastness. Vining, pending, shrubby, or erect uprights provide lush evergreen foliage, much varied, depending on species and variety.

Family Tree: Araceae (uh-ray′-see-ay) Arum family; native to Central and South American and Caribbean islands.

Foliage: high glossed, rich green leaves; arrow, lance, heart shaped and other forms; size, shape vary widely among the many species.

Flower: inconspicuous, creamy or greenish color; held close to stem; generally concealed by leaves; resemble calla lily.

Size: up to 7′ (2.10 m) depending on species.

Location: WINTER—southeastern or southwestern exposure.

SUMMER—*Inside:* northeastern or northwestern exposure. *Outside:* northeastern or northwestern exposure; site in shelter to protect foliage.

Philodendron selloum,
Saddle-leaved Philodendron

FALL: move indoors by mid-September; site in eastern or western exposure.

Dormancy: none, but a resting period of slower growth during winter months of less intensity, generally October through February; slowly diminish watering, plant will indicate needs as determined by environmental conditions; develop sensitivity to feel of soil moisture; cease fertilizing.

Water: thoroughly and evenly, allowing soil to dry out between waterings.

Mist: daily, twice a day when possible.

Humidity: above normal for happiness, 45%-55%.

Air circulation: helpful condition.

Feed: mild liquid manure every 2 weeks.

Soil: standard potting soil.

Temperature: Day—70°-80°F (21°-26°C). Night—62°-68°F (16°-20°C).

Potbound: very happy; pot-on only when root growth of plant is 80%, soil 20% of pot content; top- or side-dress yearly, preferably spring.

Mature plants: if plant becomes too tall, cut growing ends (can start in rooting media); on vine types, prune or pinch back if they become spindly or leggy; treatment depends on growth habit of species. Remove dried or withered leaves as they appear. Cut off aerial roots *only* if they become unsightly.

Propagate: by stem cuttings, air layering, seed, aerial rooting, or water.

Insect alert: mealybug, red spider, scale, thrip, aphids.

Disease alert: brown spots on leaves or yellowing, dropping leaves from overwatering; spindly look, too little light.

Notable: good artificial light plant; total of 14-16 hours, combining natural and artificial light; do not allow soil to dry out completely; soil must have porosity, eliminating possibility of soggy conditions; use pebble, water, and tray method to maintain humidity level; sponge foliage at least every 3 weeks; always use room-temperature water; leaf shiners and/or oils are an *absolute no-no;* good light intensity encourages larger leaves, brighter and deeper color; many species drop leaves with abrupt environmental changes; no drafts, please.

P. burgundy (ber-gun'-dee) Burgundy philodendron; very shiny reddish leaves, 8"-12" (200-300 mm) long.

P. florida (flor'-i-duh) Florida philodendron; 4"-8" (100-200 mm) leaves divided into 5 widely spaced lobes, brownish red undersides; leaf stalks have reddish fuzz.

P. hastatum (has-tay'-tum) meaning like arrowhead; common name, Spearhead philodendron; 8"-12" (200-300 mm) dark green leaves; shaped like spearheads.

P. micans (mye'-kanz) meaning glittering, sparkling; common name, Velvet-leaved philodendron; 2"-3" (50-76 mm) heart-shaped leaves, iridescent bronze green tops, reddish brown underside; a climber.

P. oxycardium (oks-si-kar'-dee-um) previously known as *P. cordatum;* Heart-leaved philodendron, the most common philodendron; 2"-10" (50-254 mm) heart-shaped leaves.

P. panduraeforme (pan-dew'-ray-form) meaning fiddle-shaped; common name, Fiddle-leaved philodendron; previously known as *P. bibennifolium;* large, dense, overlapping leaves, violin-shaped, 5"-8" (127-200 mm) long; a climber.

P. radiatum (ray-dee-ay'-tum) meaning rayed; previously named *P. dubium;* climber; 4"-10" (100-254 mm) heart-shaped leaves, deeply lobed in maturity; native to Guatemala.

P. selloum (see-low'-um) Saddle-leaved philodendron; leaves deeply lobed, 2'-3' (.60-.90 m) wide; stemless plant; 4'-5' (1.20-1.50 m) tall, 4'-6' (1.20-1.80 m) spread; short trunk; a tub plant.

P. wendlandii (wend-land'-ee-eye) Wendland's philodendron or Bird's Nest philodendron; native to Costa Rica; paddle-shaped leaves; occasionally blooms in cultivation, white spathes (petal at base of flower, frequently mistaken for flower); 6"-8" (150-200 mm) long.

PHOENIX (fee'-nix) Miniature or Pygmy Date Palm. Although not thought to be as graceful as many species of other palm genera, this is nevertheless a handsome plant with fruit that is very obvious and quite visually exciting. A slow growing and sturdy plant, it will take abuse and withstand neglect. Bright light exposure a necessity.

Family Tree: Palmaceae (pal-may'-see-ay) Palm family; native to Africa and Asia.

Foliage: varies with species, some with fronds up to 15' (4.50 m) long; shades of green to blue green; most species have arching habit.

Flower: petite yellow blooms appear, supported on long drooping stalks; two types, male and female, each on separate plants; broad, clustered, drooping habit up to 1' (.30 m) long; size and color vary with species.

Fruit: date.

Size: 3'-15' (.90-4.50 m), depending on species and cultural conditions.

Location: WINTER—eastern or western exposure.

SUMMER—*Inside:* eastern or western exposure. *Outside:* eastern or western exposure, sheltered to protect fragile foliage from potentially damaging winds and heavy rains.

FALL: move indoors by mid-September; site in eastern or western exposure.

Dormancy: none, although light resting period in winter months; slowly diminish watering, keeping soil barely moist; cease fertilizing.

Water: thoroughly and evenly, allowing soil to dry between waterings.

Mist: daily, two or more times in warm weather.

Humidity: above normal, 45%-60%.

Air circulation: essential to have good moderate movement for top plant performance.

Feed: very, very mild liquid manure, ¼ strength of package or manufacturer's recommendations, March through October.

Soil: 2 parts standard potting mix, 1 part peat moss, 1 part vermiculite.

Temperature: Day—68°-75°F (20°-23°C). Night—58°-65°F (14°-18°C).

Potbound: pot-on young plants each year to 2" (50 mm) larger pot; older plants happy when somewhat potbound; side-dress each year, pot-on every 2 or 3 years, when indicated by plant's root growth being 80% to 20% soil in pot; this cultural attention to be implemented late winter or early spring, February or March; deep pots are best shape for submerged aerial roots.

Mature plants: in repotting or potting-on, firm soil well, but do not compact it.

Propagate: by seed or by suckers.

Insect alert: mealybug, red spider mite, scale, thrips.

Notable: absolutely no drafts; do not allow soil to dry out completely, but *no soggy soil;* soil must be porous, for good drainage is essential to successful culture; use pebble, water, and tray method to maintain high humidity; good in artificial light, needing a total of 16 light hours, combining natural and artificial; leaves should be washed or wiped with moist cloth at least once a month to keep pores unclogged; no direct sun or foliage will burn; remember that most palms are of slow-growing habit.

Phoenix roebelenii,
Pygmy Date Palm

P. canariensis (kan-ar-ee-en'-siss) native to Canary Islands; glossy, light green leaflets on feathery fronds to 15' (4.50 m) long; ¾" (19 mm) long yellowish red fruit in clusters to 8' (2.45 m) long; a moderate grower, erect and stately in appearance.

P. dactylifera (dak-til-if'-er-uh) meaning fingerlike, known as Date palm, native to the tropics; blue green foliage; rigid, long, scratchy, needlelike leaves; oblong fruit to 3" (76 mm), clustered habit; suckers at base of plant; fast growing species.

P. roebelenii (roh-be-leen'-ee-eye) known as Pygmy date palm, native to East Indies and Burma; multistemmed, arched, pending, plumelike foliage on slender stems; brown, hairy trunk; black, berry-type fruit to ½" (12 mm) wide; clusters to 1' (.30 m) long; delicate, feathery visual display; to 12' (3.65 m) high, highly recommended for indoor culture; survives neglect; at times referred to as *P. loureirii*.

PILEA (pye'-lee-uh) Aluminum Plant, Panamiga, Artillery Plant.

Pileas, evergreen, have a small growth form with richly patterned and textured foliage being the attractive feature. This rather slow-growing genus varies in form from natural to erect or creeping habits. All species prefer a good light site, and most need minor pruning attention to be retained as good-looking, full specimens. The name is derived from *pileus*, which means a Roman cap and refers to the seed covering. Certain varieties cause stinging sensations when touched.

Family Tree: Urticaceae (ur-tye'-kuh-see-ay) Nettle family; native to Indochina and tropical America.

Foliage: oval fleshy leaves, textured to ridged, deeply veined, crinkled, quilted or puckered, some hairy; up to 3"-4" (76-100 mm) long; blunt, rounded tips, serrated margins; erect or creeping in habit, many creepers rooting from nodes, or joints on stems when in contact with soil; good branching nature; greens with variations of red, blue green, blue silver, purple, copper brown; hairy stems; all depending on species.

Flower: petite; greenish or white; rather inconspicuous; summer blooming; all depending on species.

Size: up to 2' (.60 m).

Location: WINTER—southeastern or southwestern exposure. SUMMER—*Inside*: eastern or western exposure. *Outside*: eastern or western exposure; protect fragile foliage from potentially damaging elements, preferably by overhang.

FALL: move indoors by mid-September; site in eastern or western exposure.

Dormancy: none, but light resting period after heavy flowering, generally late fall through February; slowly diminish watering, to keeping soil barely moist; cease fertilizing.

Water: keep moderately and evenly moist.

Mist: daily, twice a day when possible.

Humidity: above normal for happiness, 40%-45%.

Air circulation: helpful condition.

Feed: mild liquid manure weekly.

Soil: 2 parts standard potting soil, 1 part peat moss, 1 part perlite.

Temperature: Day—68°-80°F (20°-26°C). Night—55°-68°F (12°-20°C).

Potbound: repot; or pot-on as needed and indicated by root growth being at least 50% of pot content.

Mature plants: hard pruning to reestablish plant should be done in early spring prior to evidence of new growth. Take cuttings, easily rooted, for fresh replacement.

Propagate: by stem cuttings, root in water or moist vermiculite.

Insect alert: mealybug, scale, slugs.

Notable: good artificial light specimen, a total of 14 light hours combined with natural; prune plant often to prevent legginess; must have good soil porosity; never allow soil to dry out completely; rinse foliage frequently in room-temperature or tepid water to prevent dust-clogged pores; keep on lower side of recommended temperatures.

P. cadierii (cad-ee-air'-ee-eye) Aluminum plant, Watermelon pilea; native to Vietnam; succulent, 2½"-3½" (62-88 mm) puckered leaves, 3 conspicuous depressed veins; green tops, highlighted with metallic silver gray; erect growth habit, to 1½' (.45 m) high; flowers tiny, inconspicuous.

  Variety—Minima (min'-ih-muh) meaning small; common name, Artillery plant; dwarf, good for terrariums; small, oval, green leaves; fernlike; fleshy stemmed; erect habit; 2" (50 mm) to 1' (.30 m).

P. crassifolia (kras-si-foh'-lee-uh) meaning thick-leaved; shiny, bright green, quilted leaves, to 2" (50 mm); height to 10" (254 mm).

P. depressa (de-pres'-sa) native to Puerto Rico; creeping habit, roots at nodes; light green leaves, ¼" (6 mm) wide; good in hanging containers.

P. grandis (gran'-diss) corrugated leaf, indented veins; small white flowers in clusters.

P. involucrata (in-vol-yew-kray'-tuh) meaning rolled inward; common name, Panamiga or Pan-American friendship plant; native to Panama and Peru; leaves arranged oppositely; heavily quilted texture, deeply indented veins, oval, 2"-3" (50-76 mm) long; hairy, coppery tops, reddish

Pilea crassifolia

Pilea cadierii,
Aluminum Plant

undersides; erect stems; tiny, greenish pink flowers in flat-topped clusters; good for terrariums.

P. microphylla (mye-kroh-fill′-uh) meaning with small leaves; common name, Artillery plant; native to West Indies; an annual; shrubby, erect form; fleshy, fine, twiggy branches; densely set, tiny, medium light green leaves; petite greenish flowers; fernlike effect; to 1′ (.30 m) tall; keep warmer than others; discharges ripe pollen explo-

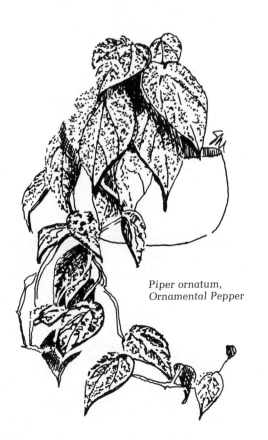

Piper ornatum,
Ornamental Pepper

sively when touched, hence its common name; very slow grower.

P. moon valley small, compact growth; medium green leaves, brown-veined, quilted texture; slow growing.

P. nummularifolia (num-mew-lair-i-fo′-lee-a) Creeping Charlie; native to Peru and West Indies; light yellowish green; round leaves, somewhat hairy, quilted; greenish rose flowers; creeping habit; plants root at stem sections when in contact with soil, good for hanging containers.

P. pubescens (pew-bes′-enz) meaning with soft, downy hair; common name, Silver panamiga; oval, scalloped leaves, 2″-3″ (50-76 mm); 3 dark gray, indented veins; glossy bluish silver surface, grayish green underneath; succulent; 8″-10″ (200-254 mm) tall.

P. repens (ree′-penz) meaning creeping, rooting stems; common name, Black-leaved panamiga; round, hairy leaves, 1½″ (37 mm), with copper brown tops, purple undersides; low creeping habit, 4″-8″ (100-200 mm) high.

P. silver tree cultivar of the Caribbean; 2″-3″ (50-76 mm), oval, quilted leaves, serrated margins; bronze green with wide silver center stripe, silver dots; deeply indented veins; undersides hairy; very branching; 8″-12″ (200-300 mm) tall.

PIPER NIGRUM (pye′-per nye′-grum) Pepper.

The fruit of *P. nigrum* is used commercially for supplying black and white pepper. Its fruit, clustered berries, when dried, is peppercorn. A genus consisting of tropical herbs of shrub and vine growth habits, it prefers a soft-light area and a good humidity level to display attractively veined foliage. This species of Pepper, slow growing and climbing, vining, has lovely, shiny, heavily veined, heart shaped leaves, *P. nigrum* previously was classified as *P. aromaticum.*

Family Tree: Piperaceae (pye′-per-aye-see-ay) Pepper family; native to Malabar Coast.

Foliage: leaves oval to heart shaped, pointed tips; glossy, generally smooth margins, deeply veined in pinks, yellows, silvers; leaf surfaces, shadings of green with undersides purple through greens; frequently red-stemmed, some with white hairs; erect or vining growth; all depending on species.

Flower: rare in indoor culture.

Fruit: green turning to red, then black berry; clustered.

Size: up to 6′ (1.80 m).

Location: WINTER—southeastern or southwestern exposure. SUMMER—*Inside:* eastern or western exposure. *Outside:* eastern or western exposure; protect fragile foliage from potentially damaging elements, preferably by overhang.

FALL: move indoors by mid-September; site in eastern or western exposure.

Dormancy: none, but light resting period after fruit bearing; cease fertilizing.

Water: keep moderately and evenly moist.

Mist: daily, twice a day when possible.

Humidity: normal, 30%-35%.

Air circulation: helpful condition.

Feed: mild liquid manure every 2 weeks.

Soil: standard potting mix.

Temperature: Day—68°-80°F (20°-26°C). Night—55°-68°F (12°-20°C).

Potbound: repot; or pot-on as needed and indicated by root growth being at least 50% of pot content.

Propagate: by shoot cuttings, in early spring; need warm area to root.

Insect alert: red spider mites.

Notable: must have good soil porosity; never allow soil to dry out completely; rinse foliage frequently in room-temperature or tepid water to prevent dust-clogged pores.

P. crocatum (kroh-kay'-tum) Saffron pepper; green leaves, 4″-6″ (100-150 mm); pink veins, purple underneath.

P. ornatum (or-nay'-tum) Celebes pepper or Ornamental pepper; heart-shaped, waxy, dark green leaves, up to 5″ (127 mm) long; lacy veining of silvery pink, pale green undersides; slender red stems; more attractive than P. nigrum; give young plant support.

P. porphyrophyllum (por-fear'-oh-fill-um) Porphyry-leaved pepper; heart-shaped leaves; bronze green, yellow veins, pink spots, purplish undersides; stiff white hairs, covering red stems.

Pittosporum tobira,
Japanese Pittosporum

PITTOSPORUM TOBIRA (pit-tosp'-or-um toh-bye'-ruh) Japanese Pittosporum.

Pittosporum tobira, evergreen, sturdy, decorative, is easy to satisfy and an excellent species for a bonsai specimen. *P. tobira*, although considered a foliage plant, produces small greenish white blossoms under proper cultural environment. Provide a very good, bright light site; even though there is no danger in full sun, this genus will be happier when partially protected.

Family Tree: Pittosporaceae (pit-tosp'-or-ay-see-ay) Pittosporum family; native to Australia, New Zealand, Japan.

Foliage: broad, thick, leathery leaves, shiny dark green, 3″-4″ (76-100 mm) long, in clustered whorls at tips of branches; when bruised it has foul odor; resembles rhododendron foliage.

Flower: fragrant creamy white blooms; petite; in clusters.

Fruit: sticky seeds within long, oval, capsule-type shapes; fragrance like unto an orange blossom.

Size: to 3′ (.90 m), height and width.

Location: WINTER—southeastern or southwestern exposure. SUMMER—*Inside:* northeastern or northwestern exposure. *Outside:* northeastern or northwestern exposure; site in sheltered area to protect foliage. FALL: move indoors by mid-September; site in eastern or western exposure.

Dormancy: none, but a resting time after flowering; slowly diminish watering, plant will indicate needs by appearance, becoming limp and droopy; develop sensitivity to feel of soil moisture level; cease fertilizing.

Water: evenly and thoroughly, allowing soil to dry between waterings.

Mist: daily, twice a day when possible.

Humidity: normal, 30%-35%.

Air circulation: essential for good cultural response.

Feed: every 2 weeks with mild liquid manure throughout growing season, April through August.

Soil: 3 parts standard potting mix, 1 part sharp sand or perlite.

Temperature: Day—68°-78°F (20°-25°C). Night—40°-64°F (4°-17°C).

Potbound: happy; pot-on when pot content is 80% root growth, 20% soil.

Mature plants: remove dead foliage which periodically occurs, it is of no harm to plant; prune as necessary to maintain size, preferably late winter, prior to new growth evidence.

Propagate: by seed or cuttings of half-ripened wood, latter in moist vermiculite.

Insect alert: aphid, mealybug, mite, scale, leaf miner.

Notable: soil must have porosity; no soggy conditions; keep on lower side of recommended temperatures; important to wipe or wash foliage every two weeks; good air circulation needed for top performance; do not overpot, use pot only 2″ (50 mm) larger than previous housing.

P. tobira
Variety—Variegata (var-ee-eh-gay'-tuh) meaning variegated; pale grayish green leaves, 4″ (100 mm) long, irregular, creamy outlines; greenish white flowers.

P. undulatum (un-dew-lay'-tum) meaning wavy surface or margin; common name, Victorian Laurel; leaves deep green, glossy, waved margin, to 6″ (150 mm) long; white flowers, very fragrant.

PLATYCERIUM (pla-ti-seer'-ee-um) Staghorn Fern.
Watering is problematic, yet the pleasure derived from ownership of the rapidly growing Staghorn fern far outweighs a slight cultural inconvenience. Generally grown on a slab of cork bark and hung on a wall, the fertile, broad fronds (leaves) so resembling a stag's horns prove to be quite a conversation piece. In maturity, they branch densely in a gracefully pending nature. Platycerium is from *platys*, broad, and *kevas*, horn. In natural habitat, this fern grows on tree branches and trunks.

Family Tree: Polypodiaceae (poh-lee-poh-dee-ay'-see-ay) Common Fern family; native to Australia, some Pacific islands, eastern Africa, and islands of the Indian Ocean.

Foliage: there are two types of fronds: sterile and fertile.

The former are flat, disc shaped, and cover the roots and rooting medium; young sterile fronds are bright green, cycling into a tan demise. Fertile fronds—erect, lobed, antler shaped, pending in an overlapping nature—are shades of green, from grayish to medium true green with deeper green veins. The sterile fronds age into a papery brown, these dying leaves become a humus to feed the fern; this is a continuing cycle of new sterile fronds, a lovely, delicate green, growing in replacement; small plants called pups grow out from between sterile leaves.

Size: 1'-7' (.30-2.10 m), spread and height depending on species.

Location: WINTER—eastern exposure.

SUMMER—*Inside*: eastern exposure. *Outside*: northern exposure.

FALL: move indoors by mid-September; site in eastern exposure.

Dormancy: none, really, but rests lightly through fall and winter.

Water: an extremely important part of the culture of these plants; be guided by the following: ordinarily, water thoroughly, allowing moderate drying between waterings, never allow to dry out completely; be aware of cool weather, when slower evaporation should mean less frequent watering; use room-temperature water only; dip bark or basket into tepid water; do not soak the fertile fronds.

Mist: daily, twice a day if possible; use room-temperature water.

Humidity: very high, 60%-70%, especially March through September.

Air circulation: essential for super success, but avoid drafts.

Feed: do not fertilize.

Soil: use osmunda fiber or sphagnum moss, the whole fiber not the shredded product, as the planting medium; it is commercially packaged and available at garden supply outlets.

Propagate: by suckers, spores, or division of mature plants. Young or divided plants should be rooted either in an orchid basket (for hanging) or a slab of cork bark or tree fern bark. For bark culture, tie the rooting medium onto the surface of the bark; place base of plant on rooting medium and tie or wire securely in place. Also can be planted in clay pot in rooting medium specified for this genus.

Insect alert: mealybugs, aphids, thrips, red spider; control with soap and water remedy; repeat every 3 days until eradicated.

Notable: do not use a potting soil as it smothers roots; no direct sun; no drafts; do not use pesticide sprays for they are fatal to the plant.

P. grande (gran-dee') meaning large or impressive, from Australia; broad, soft pale green sterile fronds; fertile fronds, to 6' (1.80 m) glossy green, spreading, cascading; generally grow in pairs.

P. stemmaria (ste-mer'-ee-uh) thick, gray green fronds to 3' (.90 m).

P. veitchii (vetch'-ee-eye) rounded basal fronds to 2' (.60 m).

P. wilhelminae reginae (will-hel-min'-ay rej'-in-ay) meaning queenly; glossy, silvery green fronds to 3' (.90 m).

Platycerium bifurcatum,
Staghorn Fern

P. pumilum (pew'-mi-lum) meaning dwarf; light green sterile fronds with dark veining; grows in rounded habit; up to 1' (.30 m) circular.

P. hillii (eye-til'-ee-eye) same features as *P. pumilum*.

P. bifurcatum (bye-fur-kay'-tum) meaning twice forked; known as Common Staghorn; from *Australia, Java, East Indies, Madagascar*; also known as *P. alcicorne* (al'-si-korn), this is the hardiest of the species; sterile fronds, downy when young, colored gray green, wavy-edged; fertile fronds to 3' (.90 m) long, narrow, forked segments.

Variety—Majus: meaning greater or larger; the greenest and most vigorous of this most popular species.

PLECTRANTHUS (plek-tranth'-us) Swedish Ivy.

Plectranthus was named Swedish ivy because it was first grown as a house plant in Sweden. Super as a hanging basket or pot plant, it grows in either soil or water culture with equal success. Its thick textured, fleshy, scalloped leaves give a soft visual effect. Place this evergreen plant in a bright light site, and it will grow rampantly. So lush a grower, it's great to root stem cuttings in water, pot-up and take as a hostess gift—thus doing your own thing . . . and inexpensively. This is not an ivy but is referred to because of its trailing habit, so like the ivies.

Family Tree: Labiatae (lay-bee-ay'-tee) Mint family; native to Africa, Australia and China.

Foliage: 1"-3" (25-76 mm) leaves on trailing stems, to 2' (.60 m) long; coloring varies with species, bronze green, purplish, or dark green; hairy or velvety; contrasting veins and undersides.

Flower: delicate white or lavender flowers, depending on species.

Size: 1½'-2' (.37-.60 m), depending on species.

Location: WINTER—full sun; set in southern exposure.

SUMMER—*Inside*: partial shade; set in eastern to southern exposure for direct rays of morning sun. *Outside*: partial

Plectranthus oertendahlii,
Swedish Ivy

tiny, whitish pink flowers; 1½'-2' (.45-.60 m) trailing stems.

P. coleoides (coh-lee-oy'-deez)
> Variety—Marginatus (mar-ji-nay'-tus) white-edged Swedish ivy; 2"-3" (50-76 mm) hairy green leaves, creamy white edges; bushy plant, 8"-12" (.20-.30 m) tall.

P. oertendahlii (err-ten-dal'-ee-eye) Swedish Ivy; 1" (25 mm), bronze green leaves with network of silvery veins; old leaf undersides and stalks are purplish; trailing stems to 2' (.60 m)
> Variety—Variegatus (var-i-e-ga'-tus) dark green leaves with broad, irregular white blotches; lavender flowers.

P. purpuratus (per-per-ay'-tus) meaning of purple; common name, Purple-leaved Swedish ivy; ¾" (19 mm) purplish green leaves, velvety hairs dull purple undersides; trailing stems to 2' (.60 m) long.

PLEOMELE REFLEXA (plee-oh'-may-lee ree-flex'-uh)
Song of India.

The Pleomele and Dracaena families are very similar in appearance; however, Pleomele is more irregularly shaped and a denser, bushier plant. Consider the sturdy P. reflexa a tub plant because of eventual size, and site this species in a bright area.

Family Tree: Liliaceae (lil-ee-ay'-see-ay) Lily family; native to India and southeastern Asia.

Foliage: narrow, leathery leaves, spikelike; in reflexed clusters, edged with pale yellow stripes; 6"-10" (.15-.26 m) long.

Size: up to 12' (3.65 m).

Location: WINTER—southeastern or southwestern exposure. SUMMER—*Inside:* northeastern or northwestern exposure. *Outside:* northeastern or northwestern exposure; site in shelter to protect foliage.

FALL: move indoors by mid-September; site in eastern or western exposure.

Dormancy: none, but a resting period of slower growth during winter months of less intensity, generally October through February; slowly diminish watering, plant will indicate needs as determined by environmental conditions, develop sensitivity to feel of soil moisture level; cease fertilizing.

Water: thoroughly and evenly, allowing soil to dry out between waterings.

Mist: daily, twice a day when possible.

Humidity: above normal for happiness, 45%-55%.

Air circulation: helpful condition.

Feed: mild liquid manure every 2 weeks.

Soil: standard potting soil.

Temperature: Day—70°-80°F (21°-26°C). Night—62°-68°F (16°-20°C).

Potbound: very happy; pot-on only when root growth of plant is 80%, soil 20% of pot content; top- or side-dress yearly; preferably spring.

Mature plants: if plant becomes too tall, cut growing ends, start in rooting media. Remove dried or withered leaves as they appear.

Propagate: by cuttings.

Insect alert: mealybug, red spider, scale, thrip, aphids.

Notable: good artificial light plant; total of 14-16 hours, combining natural and artificial light; do not allow soil to

---

shade; set in eastern exposure or under a protective structure where plant receives strong light but no direct rays.

FALL: move indoors by mid-September.

Dormancy: none, but a resting period, September through February; slowly diminish watering, keeping soil barely moist, to prevent drying out completely; plant will indicate needs; if foliage loses its perkiness, water in more quantity but not more frequently; cease fertilizing, until signs of new growth are evident.

Water: thoroughly and evenly, allow to dry between waterings.

Mist: daily, twice a day when possible.

Humidity: normal, 30%-35%.

Air circulation: helpful condition.

Feed: mild liquid manure every 2 weeks, April through August.

Soil: 2 parts standard potting mix, 1 part peat moss, 1 part perlite.

Temperature: Day—65°-75°F (18°-23°C). Night—55°-65°F (12°-18°C).

Potbound: normal; repot or pot-on when root growth is 50% of pot contents, after flowering has ceased.

Mature plants: better bloom if stems pinched back (as they become straggly), pinch off to point where plant retains compact, uniform shape, pinch center out of young shoots for a wide plant.

Propagate: seeds in spring or from stem cuttings after flowering.

Insect alert: mealybugs, whitefly.

Notable: a good specimen for artificial light culture, combining with natural light for total 12-14 hours daily; do not allow soil to dry out completely; do not allow soggy condition; soil must be porous; pinch back regularly to prevent straggly appearance.

P. *australis* (os-tray'-liss) meaning southern; waxy, dark green leaf, shallow, scalloped edges, 1" (25 mm) wide;

Pleomele reflexa,
Song of India

Podocarpus macrophyllus maki,
Chinese Podocarpus

dry out completely; soil must have porosity, eliminating possibility of soggy conditions; use pebble, water, and tray method to maintain humidity level; sponge foliage at least every 3 weeks, always use room-temperature water; leaf shiners and/or oils are an *absolute no-no.*

P. angustifolia honoriae (an-gus-ti-foh′-lee-uh hon-ohr-eye′-ah-ee) meaning with narrow leaves; Narrow-leaved pleomele; leathery green leaves, cream yellow edges.

PODOCARPUS MACROPHYLLUS MAKI (poh-doh-karp′-us mak-roh-fil′-lus mak′ee) Chinese or Shrubby Podocarpus.

Podocarpus means evergreen tree or shrub, macrophyllus refers to its large leaves. This genus gives a soft pine needle effect. It is easily pruned to desirable size, and is suitable for low light areas. The interesting pattern of this species frequently has an espaliered effect in natural growth.

Family Tree: Podocarpaceae (poh-doh-karp′-ay-see-ay) Podocarpus family; native to China and Japan.

Foliage: dense, soft-textured needles, 1½″-4″ (37-100 mm) long, ¼″-½″ (6-12 mm) wide; bright green when young, changing to dark green.

Size: 6′ (1.80 m) or more, but may be pruned to keep smaller size.

Location: WINTER—southeastern or southwestern exposure. SUMMER—*Inside:* northeastern or northwestern exposure. *Outside:* northeastern or northwestern exposure; site in sheltered area to protect foliage.

FALL: move indoors by mid-September; site in eastern or western exposure.

Dormancy: none, a resting time during winter months, generally September through March; slowly diminish

watering, plant will indicate needs by appearance, becoming limp and droopy; develop sensitivity to feel of soil moisture level, cease fertilizing.

Water: evenly and thoroughly, allowing soil to dry between waterings.

Mist: daily, twice a day when possible.

Humidity: normal, 30%-35%.

Air circulation: helpful condition.

Feed: every 2 weeks with mild liquid manure throughout growing season, April through August.

Soil: 3 parts standard potting mix, 1 part sharp sand or perlite.

Temperature: Day—68°-75°F (20°-23°C). Night—40°-64°F (4°-17°C).

Potbound: happy; repot when root growth approximately 80%, soil 20% of pot content.

Propagate: by seed or cuttings.

Insect alert: aphid, mealybug, mite, scale, leaf miner.

Notable: soil must have porosity, no soggy conditions; keep on lower side of recommended temperatures; important to wipe or wash foliage every 2 weeks; *Note:* good air circulation needed for top performance; do not overpot, use pot only 2″ (50 mm) larger than previous housing.

P. nagi (nay′-gee) broader leaves, keep drier than other species.

POLYPODIUM (pol-i-poh′-dee-um) Hare's Foot Fern, Golden Polypody Fern.

This is a fern with fronds (leaves) of deepest green that arch most gracefully. An "untouchy" genus that needs minimum attention, it frequently is passed by for more delicate appearing genera, which generally are more demanding in cultural needs.

Polypodium crispum glaucum,
Blue Fern

against end of a table is an aid, as well as running a spatula around inside of pot, pressing against pot wall with tool to avoid slipping into root ball. Wrap fronds of a large fern in newspaper for protection while handling. Set plant on 1½″ (37 mm) layer of gravel, then add soil.

Mature plants: if fern looks sad, cut back to 2″ (50 mm) above soil line; repot and proceed in proper culture. If aerial roots develop, cut them off. Wash foliage at least every 3 weeks. Remove yellowed or withered fronds as they appear.

Propagate: by division of mature plant (best done around March), or by spores (resemble little brown dots) attached to underside of leaflets.

Insect alert: mealybugs, aphids, thrips, red spider. Control with soap and water remedy, repeat every 3 days until eradicated.

Notable: ferns need coolness at their roots, so use pebble, water, and tray method for cooler temperature and high humidity; best to grow in clay pots, as their porosity allows evaporation and aids in keeping roots cool; fronds of young plants cannot stand water directly on them; fronds bruise easily so plant should be located where it will not touch or be touched; ferns cannot stand pesticides, which will kill insects and your plant, too.

P. polypodioides (pol-ip-pod-ee-oy′-deez) known as Resurrection Fern; when dry, they have habit of curling up into tight ball but unfold when placed in water; this species is a total deviation from most ferns, for which drought means fatality: it is drought-resistant; gray green fronds 6″ (150 mm) long, 2″ (50 mm) wide; native to North America.

P. vulgare (vul-gay′-ree) meaning common or ordinary; known as common polypody or Adder's Fern; native to rocky woodlands of North America, Europe, Asia; thick, erect, evergreen fronds 1′-2′ (.30-.60 m) long, 2″-5″ (50-127 mm) across; more leathery texture than other species.

P. polycarpon (pol-i-kar′-pon) small, upright habit; broadly triangular yellow green fronds; tonguelike leaves, tipped with fanlike crowns, grow at close intervals.

P. subauriculatum (sub-aw-ri-kew-lay′-tum) known as Jointed polypody; very slow grower; handsome; graceful fronds, on heavy rhizomes.

P. aureum (aw′-ree-um) meaning golden; known as Hare's Foot or Golden polypody fern; scaled, glossy brown rhizomes give it its name; blue green fronds; wavy-edged leaflets; fronds 2′-5′ (.30-1.50 m) long, 1′ (.30 m) wide; vigorous grower.

P. crispum glaucum (krisp′-um glaw′-kum) known as Blue Fern; fronds have a blue cast; broad leaved, wavy-edged, to a 4′ (1.20 m) spread, 6′ (1.80 m) high.

Family Tree: Polypodiaceae (pol-i-po′-di-ay-see-ay) Common Fern family; native to tropics, North America, Europe and Asia.

Foliage: blue green, gray green, or true deep green fronds grow out of creeping rhizomes (rootstock); fronds are deeply cut, almost to midrib; arching to pending in habit.

Size: 1′-6′ (.30-1.80 m) in spread and height, depending on species.

Location: WINTER—eastern exposure.

SUMMER—*Inside:* eastern exposure. *Outside:* northern exposure.

FALL: move indoors by mid-September; site in eastern exposure.

Dormancy: none, really, but rests lightly through fall and winter.

Water: an extremely important part of the culture of these plants; be guided by the following: ordinarily, water thoroughly, allowing moderate drying between waterings, never allow to dry out completely; be aware of cool weather, when slower evaporation should mean less frequent waterings; use room-temperature water only.

Mist: daily, twice a day if possible; use room-temperature water.

Humidity: very high, 60%-70%, especially March through September.

Air circulation: essential for super success, but avoid drafts.

Feed: very, very weak solution of mild liquid manure (cut recommendation of manufacturer to 2/3) every 3 weeks.

Soil: 2 parts standard potting mix, 1 part vermiculite, 2 parts peat moss.

Temperature: Day—68°-75°F (20°-23°C). Night—50°-60°F (10°-15°C).

Potbound: very happy; do not pot-on until root system is 80% of pot content; best done in February or March. Roots adhere to interior pot walls, therefore, to avoid excessive injury, work gently, easing them loose. Rapping pot

POLYSCIAS (pol-iss′-ee-us).
Sometimes still referred to by its previous name Aralia or Panax, Polyscias, a foliage genus, thrives in bright light; handsome evergreen plant, treelike in form, should be approached as tub culture to realize mature growth site area needed.

Family Tree: Araliaceae (uh-ray-lee-ay′-see-ay) Aralia family; native to the Pacific islands, Africa, and Asia.

Foliage: compound leaves of many shapes and colors; colors shaded greens, solid, blotched or swathed in creamy tones; foliage smooth or toothed; all depending on species.

Size: to 20' (6 m) tall.

Location: WINTER—southeastern or southwestern exposure. SUMMER—*Inside:* northeastern or northwestern exposure. *Outside:* northeastern or northwestern exposure; site in shelter to protect foliage.

FALL: move indoors by mid-September; site in eastern or western exposure.

Dormancy: none, but a resting period of slower growth during winter months of less intensity; generally October through February; slowly diminish watering, plant will indicate needs as determined by environmental conditions; develop sensitivity to feel of soil moisture level; cease fertilizing.

Water: thoroughly and evenly, not allowing soil to dry out between waterings.

Mist: daily, twice a day when possible.

Humidity: 50%-60%.

Air circulation: helpful condition.

Feed: mild liquid manure every 2 weeks.

Soil: standard potting soil.

Temperature: Day—70°-80°F (21°-26°C). Night—62°-68°F (16°-20°C).

Potbound: very happy; pot-on only when root growth of plant is 80%, soil 20% of pot content; top or side-dress yearly; preferably spring.

Mature plants: if plant becomes too tall, cut growing ends; start in rooting media. Remove dried or withered leaves as they appear.

Propagate: by stem cuttings, air layering, or root division.

Insect alert: mealybug, red spider, scale, thrip, aphids.

Notable: good artificial light plant; total of 14-16 hours, combining natural and artificial light; do not allow soil to become dry at any time; use pebble, water, and tray

Polyscias

method to maintain humidity level; sponge foliage at least every 3 weeks, always use room-temperature water; leaf shiners and/or oils are an *absolute no-no.*

P. balfouriana (bal-foor-ee-ay'-nuh) previously known as *Aralia balfouriana* and *Panax balfourii* (Balfour aralia). Native to New Caledonia; in maturity, to 20' (6 m) high; dense foliage, fernlike, lightly pendulous.

Variety—Balfour (bal-for') shiny, dark green leaves; with 3 roundish leaflets, 2"-4" (50-100 mm) across.

Variety—Marginata (mar-gin-ay'-tuh) native to New Caledonia; dark green, white-edged, round, leathery textured leaves.

Variety—Victoria (vik-tor'-ee-a) white-edged, dark leaves; milky green, edged in dark green.

P. fruticosa (frew-tik-koh'-suh) meaning shrubby; native tive to South Sea Islands; tall shrub with fernlike leaves; bright green.

P. fruticosa (frew-tih-koh'-suh) meaning shrubby; native to Polynesia; twisted willowlike branches, finely cut, parsleylike foliage; fernlike appearance; to 5' (1.50 m).

P. guilfoylei (gil-foy'-lee-eye) Victoria aralia

Variety—Victoria (vik-tor'-ee-a) white-edged, dark green leaves, 12"-16" (.30-.40 m) or more long, with 3-7 sawtoothed leaflets, end leaflet 6" (150 mm), side leaflets 2"-3" (50-76 mm) long; in maturity, to 20' (6 m) high.

POLYSTICHUM (pol-list'-ik-um) English Hedge Fern, Soft Shield Fern, Leather Leaf Fern, Holly Fern, Dagger Fern, Christmas Fern.

Mostly an evergreen species, this genus has narrow, shiny green leaves that arch gracefully. One may find it referred to or listed under its former genus name, Aspidium. The fronds (leaves) sprout from rhizomes (rootstock) which have an attractive creeping habit, edging over the rims of pots.

Family Tree: Polypodiaceae (pol-i-po'-di-ay-see-ay) Common Fern family; native to tropical Asia and Africa.

Foliage: fronds with habit of growing in clustered circles, have dense appearance, are narrowly segmented; plume shaped to a pointed tip.

Size: 1'-3' (.30-.90 m) long.

Location: WINTER—eastern exposure.

SUMMER—*Inside:* eastern exposure. *Outside:* northern exposure.

FALL: move indoors by mid-September; site in eastern exposure.

Dormancy: none really, but rests lightly through fall and winter.

Water: an extremely important part of the culture of these plants; be guided by the following: ordinarily, water thoroughly, allowing moderate drying between waterings, never allow to dry out completely; be aware of cool weather, when slower evaporation should mean less frequent watering; use room-temperature water only.

Mist: daily, twice a day if possible; use room-temperature water.

Humidity: very high, 60%-70%, especially March through September.

Air circulation: essential for super success, but avoid drafts.

Feed: very, very weak solution of mild liquid manure (cut recommendation of manufacturer to 2/3) every 3 weeks.

Soil: 2 parts standard potting mix, 1 part vermiculite, 2 parts peat moss.

Temperature: Day—68°-75°F (20°-23°C). Night—50°-60°F (10°-15°C).

Potbound: very happy; do not pot-on until root system is 80% of pot content, best done in February or March. Roots adhere to interior pot walls, therefore, to avoid excessive injury, work gently, easing them loose. Rapping pot against end of a table is an aid, as well as running a spatula around inside of pot, pressing against pot wall with tool to avoid slipping into root ball. Wrap fronds of a large fern in newspaper for protection while handling. Set plant on 1½" (37 mm) layer of gravel, then add soil.

Mature plants: if fern looks sad, cut back to 2" (50 mm) above soil line; repot and proceed in proper culture. If aerial roots develop, cut them off. Wash foliage at least every 3 weeks. Remove yellowed or withered fronds as they appear.

Propagate: by division of mature plant (best done around March), or by spores (resemble little brown dots) attached to underside of leaflets.

Insect alert: mealybugs, aphids, thrips, red spider; control with soap and water remedy, repeat every 3 days until eradicated.

Notable: ferns need coolness at their roots, so use pebble, water, and tray method for cooler temperature and high humidity; best to grow in clay pots, as their porosity allows evaporation and aids in keeping roots cool; if fronds droop from too dry soil, they cannot be revived; fronds of young plants cannot stand water directly on them; fronds bruise easily so plant should be located where it will not touch or be touched; ferns cannot stand pesticides, which will kill insects and your plant, too.

P. aculeatum (ak-yew-lee-ay'-tum) meaning prickly; vigorous grower; stems scaly and nonfragile; deep, dark green fronds, segmented, narrow and hollylike, up to 2' (.60 m) long.

P. tsus-simense (suss-sim-men'-see) native of Japan; small species, 1'-2' (.30-.60 m); species for baskets and terrariums; fronds of double division, metallic sheen.

P. munitum (mew'-ni-tum) known as Holly Fern; a large species with arched, evergreen fronds up to 3' (.90 m) long; leaves are deeply segmented to heavy midrib, plume shaped.

P. acrostichoides (ak-ros-ti-koy'-deez) Dagger or Christmas Fern, native to United States; fronds up to 3' (.90 m) long, 4" (100 mm) wide, taper to a point; leathery, rough-edged leaflets.

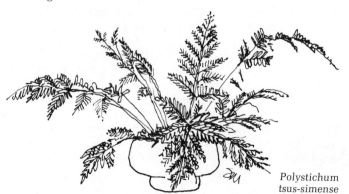

Polystichum tsus-simense

Primula malacoides, Primrose

PRIMULA (prim'-yew-luh) Primrose.

This ornamental plant, generally evergreen, provides winter through spring color, flowering for 3-4 months. It should be selected only if one is happy in cool inside temperatures, for coolness is an essential factor in good culture of the Primrose. A plant difficult to surpass in beauty, it must have cool roots; one way to "skin the cat" is to plant it in a clay pot, then spray the pot itself several times daily (evaporation cools the roots). Primrose does well in artificial light.

Family Tree: Primulaceae (prim-yew-lay'-see-ay) Primrose family; native of Asia, Europe, Africa.

Foliage: long-stemmed rosettes of broad, oval leaves; some species with hairs or down on underside.

Flower: winter and spring blooming flowers appear on tall stems; many colors, shades of red, white, pink, blue, and lilac; some species have fringed blossoms.

Size: to 2' (.60 m).

Location: WINTER—eastern exposure.

SUMMER—*Inside:* northeastern exposure. *Outside:* northern exposure.

FALL: move indoors by mid-September; site in eastern exposure.

Dormancy: none, but after flowering there is a rest period; change fertilizing program to feeding every 2 weeks with mild solution of a balance 21-7-7, an acid fertilizer.

Water: keep soil moist constantly; watering several times daily if needed, with tepid water.

Mist: daily, when blooming mist around, not directly on flowers.

Humidity: most happy when high, 50%-60%.

Air circulation: helpful condition.

Feed: every 2 weeks, mild liquid manure.

Soil: 1 part standard potting mix, 2 parts peat, and 1 part sand.

Temperature: Day—65°-68°F (18°-20°C). Night—40°-50°F (4°-10°C).

Potbound: unhappy; whenever flowering ceases, repot, keeping pots small.

Mature plants: remove stems that have ceased flowering, to encourage new flower stems to extend the flowering season.

Propagate: pot-up young plants that grow at side of parent; or plant seeds—in autumn for spring flowers, in spring for fall flowers.

Insect alert: aphids, mites, slugs, whitefly, mealybug.

Notable: soil must have good drainage but never allow to dry out completely or leaves will develop yellow edges; certain species have hairy or downy leaves which can cause skin irritation; too bright light fades blossoms; if using artificial light, give total of 12-14 light hours daily, combining artificial and natural; overfeeding will burn roots.

P. malacoides (mal-a-koy′-dez) meaning soft; from China; called Fairy Primrose or Baby Primrose; a popular species; clouds of pink, red, or white blossoms arranged in whorling tiers, on slender 8″-10″ (200-254 mm) stalks; blooms winter and spring; leaves are oval, hairy, bright green; tallest of the species to 26″ (.65 m); difficult plant to force the second time, best considered an annual.

P. obconica (ob-kon′-i′-ka) meaning inversely conical; can stand more heat than other species; large flower heads on long stems; white, pink, red, and violet; leaves and stems are hairy; soil should be 1 part standard potting mix, 2 parts sand; a perennial.

P. sinensis (sin-en′-siss) meaning of China; Chinese Primrose; large flowers 1″-1½″ (25-37 mm) across; single, double, frilled, or star-shaped; winter blooming; colors range in many shades from white through dark red; leaves are lobed, dark green, large, and hairy; plant to 1′ (.30 m) tall.

PTERIS (tehr′-iss) Table, Brake, or Ribbon Fern.

An easily cultured fern. Many species are tropical, with foliage lasting well, even in dimmest of sites. With so many species so varied in their nature, it is difficult to project a general description for this genus, yet all are feathery and softly graceful, from the charming small species through the few large plants. The Greek *pteris* refers to feather; the fronds are so shaped.

Family Tree: Polypodiaceae (pol-i-po′-di-ay-see-ay) common fern family; native to the Himalayas but mainly from the tropics.

Foliage: fronds are various shades of solid green, some with silvery highlights; certain species narrow, others broad; spear shaped or fan shaped; texture ranges from papery to leathery; there are fronds with deeply serrated edges, other with long, narrow segments; most species' habit is erect nature; wiry stalks; uneven divisions.

Size: 1′-3′ (.30-.90 m).

Location: WINTER—eastern exposure.

SUMMER—*Inside:* eastern exposure. *Outside:* northern exposure.

FALL: move indoors by mid-September; site in eastern exposure.

Dormancy: none really, but rests lightly through fall and winter.

Water: an extremely important part of the culture of these plants; be guided by the following: ordinarily, water thoroughly, allowing moderate drying between waterings, never allow to dry out completely; be aware of cool weather, when slower evaporation should mean less frequent watering; use room-temperature water only.

Mist: daily, twice a day if possible; use room-temperature water.

Humidity: very high, 60%-70%, especially March through September.

Air circulation: essential for super success, but avoid drafts.

Feed: very, very weak solution of mild liquid manure (cut recommendation of manufacturer to 2/3) every 3 weeks.

Soil: 1 part standard potting mix, 2 parts sharp sand or perlite, 1 part peat moss.

Temperature: Day—68°-75°F (20°-23°C). Night—50°-60°F (10°-15°C).

Potbound: very happy; do not pot-on until root system is 80% of pot content; best done in February or March. Roots adhere to interior pot walls, therefore, to avoid excessive injury, work gently, easing them loose. Rapping pot against end of a table is an aid, as well as running a spatula around inside of pot, pressing against pot wall with tool to avoid slipping into root ball. Wrap fronds of a large fern in newspaper for protection while handling. Set plant on 1½″ (37 mm) layer of gravel, then add soil.

Pteris tremula,
Trembling Brake Fern

Mature plants: if fern looks sad, cut back to 2″ (50 mm) above soil line; repot and proceed in proper culture. If aerial roots develop, cut them off. Wash foliage at least every 3 weeks. Remove yellowed or withered fronds as they appear.

Propagate: by division of mature plant (best done around March) or by spores (resemble little brown dots) attached to underside of leaflets.

Insect alert: mealybugs, aphids, thrips, red spider; control with soap and water remedy, repeat every 3 days until eradicated.

Notable: ferns need coolness at their roots, so use pebble, water, and tray method for cooler temperature and high humidity; best to grow in clay pots, as their porosity allows evaporation and aids in keeping roots cool; if fronds droop from too dry soil, they cannot be revived; fronds of young plants cannot stand water directly on them; fronds bruise easily so plant should be located where it will not touch or be touched; ferns cannot stand pesticides, which will kill insects and your plant, too.

P. cretica (kreet'-ik-uh) meaning of Crete, The Mediterranean; known as Brake or Ribbon fern; native to the Himalayas; leathery textured fronds are long and narrow, to 1' (.30 m) length; on erect, wiry stems.

    Variety—Albolineata (al-boh-lin-ee-ay'-tuh) slightly taller than most species; each leaflet with silver band.

    Variety—Victoriae (vik-toh'-ree-ee) white bands on segments; serrated edges.

P. quadriaurita (kwa'-dree-uh-ew-ree'-tuh) known as dense growth; lively green fronds, to 2' (.60 m) long; finely serrated leaves.

P. ensiformis (en-sif-form'-iss) meaning sword shaped; known as sword brake; narrow segments on narrow fronds, to 20″ (.55 m) long.

    Variety—Victoriae (vik-toh'-ree-ee) white bands on segments; serrated edges;

P. quadriaurita (kwa'-dree-uh-ew-ree'-tuh) known as silver brake; leathery fronds, to 3' (.90 m) long.

    Variety—Argyraea (ar-gee-ray'-uh) vivid green leaflets, white-banded, taillike tips, to 3' (.90 m).

P. multifida (mull-tif'-id-uh) meaning many times parted or cleft; may still be referred to by previous name, *P. serrulata*; known as spider brake fern, graceful; deeply segmented fronds, up to 1½' (.45 m) long, 10″ (.27 m) wide.

P. tremula (trem'-yew-luh) meaning quivering, trembling; known as Trembling brake or Australian brake fern; native to New Zealand; muted green fronds, up to 3' (.90 m) long, up to 2' (.60 m) wide; feathery, broad.

RHAPIS HUMILUS (ray'-piss hew'-mil-iss) Slender Lady Palm.

Rhapis means low, reedlike, tufted fan palms, *humilus* means low-growing or dwarf. This is one of the most graceful palms adaptable to interior habitats, a small shrub type taking a bushy form because of suckers that grow from the base and rise around the stem. Like most of the Palm family, it is very slow growing.

Family Tree: Palmae (pal-may') Palm family; native to eastern Asia.

Rhapis excelsa,
Lady Palm

Foliage: dark green, fan-shaped fronds (leaves) 7'-10' (2.10-3 m) long; form semicircular fans; on bamboolike stems, covered with hairy brown fibers.

Flower: male and female, on separate plants.

Size: up to 5' (1.50 m).

Location: WINTER—eastern or western exposure.

SUMMER—*Inside:* eastern or western exposure. *Outside:* eastern or western exposure, sheltered to protect fragile foliage from potentially damaging winds and heavy rains.

FALL: move indoors by mid-September; site in eastern or western exposure.

Dormancy: none, although light resting period in winter months; slowly diminish watering, keeping soil barely moist; cease fertilizing.

Water: thoroughly and evenly, allowing soil to dry between waterings.

Mist: daily, two or more times in warm weather.

Humidity: above normal, 45%-60%.

Air circulation: essential to have good moderate movement for top plant performance.

Feed: very, very mild liquid manure, ¼ strength of package or manufacturer's recommendations, March through October.

Soil: 2 parts standard potting mix, 1 part peat moss, 1 part vermiculite.

Temperature: Day—68°-75°F (20°-23°C). Night—58°-65°F (14°-18°C).

Potbound: pot-on young plants each year to pot 2″ (50 mm) larger; older plants happy when somewhat potbound; side-dress each year, pot-on every 2 or 3 years, when indicated by plant's root growth being 80% to 20% soil in pot; implement this cultural attention late winter or early spring, February of March; deep pots are best shape for submerged aerial roots.

Mature plants: in repotting or potting-on, firm soil well

but do not compact it. As plant ages, it develops a more shrubby form.
Propagate: by seed or by suckers.
Insect alert: mealybug, red spider mite, scale, thrips.
Notable: absolutely no drafts; do not allow soil to dry out completely, but *no soggy soil;* soil must be porous, for good drainage is essential to successful culture; use pebble, water, and tray method to maintain high humidity; good in artificial light, needing a total of 16 light hours, combining natural and artificial; leaves should be washed or wiped with moist cloth at least once a month to keep pores unclogged; no direct sun, or foliage will burn; remember that most palms are of slow-growing habit.

R. excelsa (ex-sel'-suh) meaning tall; may also be referred to or listed as *R. aspera* and *R. flabelliformis*, its previous names; known as Lady Palm or Broad-leaved Lady Palm; a bushy plant to 10' (3 m) tall; fan-shaped fronds, with 5-10 curving leaflets; 1" (25 mm) thick, stiff, erect stems.

Rhododendron indicum,
Indica Azalea

RHODODENDRON INDICUM (roh-doh-den'-dron indik'-um) Indica Azalea.

Azaleas are species of the Rhododendron genus, so know, no error has been made in this research. Azaleas can be maintained and carried over, given correct cultural attention. Timing of placing in proper location, light, and watering are the important considerations for causing held over plant to bud and blossom. Delicate, evergreen foliage is ornamentally pleasing to span the time between flowering periods of this species.
Family Tree: Ericaceae (er-i-kay'-see-ay) Heath family; native to eastern Asia.
Foliage: evergreen leaves; slightly hairy; lighter colored on undersides.
Flower: 1"-4" (25-100 mm) blossoms in clusters; appear for 2-4 weeks in late summer or early spring; various bell and funnel shapes; single, double, semidouble flowers may be red, pink, white, yellow, purplish, or multicolored.
Size: 6"-2' (.15-.60 m).
Location: WINTER—southeastern or southwestern exposure. SUMMER—*Inside and Outside*: eastern exposure.
FALL: move indoors by mid-September; site in eastern exposure.
Dormancy: rest period begins in September; keep cool, 50°F (10°C) or as close to as possible for flower buds to form between September and January; slowly diminish watering, keeping soil evenly but barely moist; cease fertilizing.
Water: keep soil thoroughly and evenly moist.
Mist: daily, twice daily if possible.
Humidity: above normal, 50%-60%.
Air circulation: helpful condition.
Feed: formula 21-7-7, an acid fertilizer, every 2 weeks from time flowers fade in spring until new buds form in fall.
Soil: 1 part standard potting mix, 2 parts peat moss, 1 part sharp sand or perlite; or purchase packaged acid potting mix at garden supply outlet.
Temperature: Day—65°-74°F (18°-22.50C). Night—40°-60°F (4°-15°C).
Potbound: repot immediately after blooming, press soil firmly around roots.
Mature plants: may be trained into standard form (tree

form) plant by proper pruning. Absolutely do not feed after flower buds have formed. Remove faded blooms as they occur.
Propagate: from stem cuttings of new growth in July; root in moist mixture of 2 parts sand, 1 part peat moss.
Insect alert: whitefly, aphid, borer, mealybug, scale, thrips.
Disease alert: leaf drop caused by lack of water, or light; yellowness in leaf tips or new shoots caused by calcium in soil.
Notable: should be protected from scorching of leaves and flowers; cannot stand lime; soil must be porous; never allow soggy soil; never allow soil to dry out; do not pot-on, keep in as small a pot as possible.

RHOEO SPATHACEA (ree'-oh spath-ay'-see-uh) Moses-in-the-Cradle, Moses-in-the-Bulrushes, Man-in-a-Boat, Boat Lily, Oyster Plant.

R. spathacea was so named because of the flower almost concealed deep within boat-shaped, petallike leaves or bracts; this growth habit is referred to as a spathe—a leaf, of which several make up the bract, this characteristic is generally mistakenly thought to be the flower. The evergreen foliage is very handsome, the flowers charming, although shortlived, and the genus needs few attentions. There is but one species; it was previously classified as R. discolor. Site in medium light and keep humidity level high.
Family Tree: Commelinaceae (kom-el-lye-nay'-see-ay) Spiderwort family; native to West Indies, Mexico, Central America.
Foliage: growth habit of rosette form; sword-shaped

leaves have olive green surfaces, metallic purple reverse sides.

Flower: small, white; near base of plant.

Size: up to 15″ (.38 m).

Location: WINTER—southeastern or southwestern exposure. SUMMER—*Inside:* eastern or western exposure. *Outside:* eastern or western exposure; protect fragile foliage from potentially damaging elements; preferably by overhang.
FALL: move indoors by mid-September; site in eastern or western exposure.

Dormancy: none, but light resting period after flowering; slowly diminish watering, keeping soil barely moist; cease fertilizing.

Water: keep moderately and evenly moist.

Mist: daily, twice a day when possible.

Humidity: above normal for happiness, 40%-45%.

Air circulation: helpful condition.

Feed: mild liquid manure every 2 weeks.

Rhoeo spathacea,
Moses-in-the-Cradle

Soil: 1 part each standard potting mix, peat, perlite or sharp sand.

Temperature: Day—68°-80°F (20°-26°C). Night—60°-70°F (15°-21°C).

Potbound: repot or pot-on as needed and indicated by root growth being at least 50% of pot content.

Mature plants: remove seedlings that tend to grow around plant, species most attractive when grown as single plant.

Propagate: by offsets, growing from plant, or by seedlings growing from soil at base of plant.

Insect alert: mealybug, mites.

Notable: good artificial light specimen, a total of 14 light hours combined with natural; must have good soil porosity; never allow soil to dry out completely; rinse foliage frequently in room-temperature or tepid water to prevent dust-clogged pores; take care in watering in winter months so soil surface shoots do not rot; use pebble, water, and tray method to maintain humidity level; leaves roll up if not enough air moisture.

R. spathacea
   Variety—Vittata (vit-tay′-tuh) meaning striped; sword-shaped, narrow leaves, purple, with yellow and white striations on surface; slow growing.

Rosmarinus officinalis,
Rosemary

ROSMARINUS OFFICINALIS (ross-muh-rye′-nus off-iss-in-nay′-liss) Rosemary. "Reverend sirs, for you there's Rosemary and Rue/these keep seeming and savour all the winter long."

In Shakespeare's *Winter's Tale*, we have the romanticism of a delightfully fragrant herb, with a spicy and gingery odor, which seems to flourish in sea spray, therefore its nickname, dew of the sea. The name derived from the Latin, *ros*, dew or spray, and *marinus*, sea, refers to the seaside habitat in southern Europe of this genus. In the Middle Ages it was thought to be medicine to cure "all manner of evils of the body." Too, it became a symbol of remembrance, as in Ophelia's reference in *Hamlet*. *Officinalis* means of the shop, the herbalist's, of value and service to man. An edible herb either fresh or dried, it adds savor in culinary usage.

Family Tree: Labiatae (lay-bi-ay′-te) Mint family; of the Mediterranean.

Foliage: evergreen, oppositely arranged, narrow, shiny leaves, dark green above, fuzzy white beneath; aromatic, ¾″-2″ (19-50 mm) long.

Flower: two-lipped, violet blue, fragrant short spikes of flower clusters; bloom in midwinter or early spring.

Size: 8″ (.25 m) and up to 6′ (1.80 m) trailing stems.

Location: WINTER—southern exposure.
SUMMER—*Inside and Outside:* eastern or western exposure.
FALL: move indoors by mid-September.

Water: let soil dry out between thorough waterings.

Mist: daily.

Humidity: normal, 30%-35%.

Air circulation: helpful condition.
Feed: monthly, mild liquid manure.
Soil: standard potting mix, add small amount of lime.
Temperature: Day—68°-72°F (20°-22°C). Night—50°-55°F (10°-12°C).
Mature plants: better bloom if stems pinched back as they become straggly, pinch off to point where plant retains compact, uniform shape; want wide plant, pinch center out of young shoots.
Propagate: from stem cuttings when their tip ends are firm; or from seeds, any time. Cuttings can be rooted in moist sand, vermiculite, or in water culture.
Offspring established: when seedlings are sturdy, pot individually in 2″ (50 mm) pots in soil specified for genus; water thoroughly and set in northern exposure for 4 or 5 days, then move to eastern site as plant matures.
Notable: consider Rosmarinus a visual pleasure as a feathery foliage plant in its nonflowering periods; keep plant neat and compact by pinching tips off branches and using them for seasoning; soil must have good drainage— avoid soggy potential; regard this genus as an annual, discarding when unsightly. For your pleasure, I include the following:

ROSEMARY POTPOURRI

Mix together:
 4 cups Rosemary clippings
 2 cups fresh lemon verbena leaves
 4 ground cinnamon sticks
 ¼ cup ground cloves
For color add:
 dried bachelor's buttons
 dried pinks
 dried peony petals
If mixture is placed in open bowl, it will
emit a sweet fragrance for several months.

 Variety—Prostratus (pros-tra′-tus) meaning lying flat; a charming, small hanging basket subject, sprawling and creeping; can be kept below 15″ (.38 m) by pinching off stem tips; blue flower.
 Variety—Lockwood deForest: brighter foliage, more intensely blue flower.
 Variety—Albiflorus (al-bi-flo′-rus) meaning white flowered.

RUELLIA (rew-ell′-ee-uh) Trailing Velvet Plant.
Several species of the Ruellia are excellent for terrarium use. Both foliage and flowers are equally decorative. Many of the species are of a bushy habit.
Family Tree: Acanthaceae (uh-kanth-ay′-see-ay) Acanthus family; native to Brazil.
Foliage: 4″-6″ (100-150 mm) oval leaves, variegated, velvety texture.
Flower: bell shaped, 5-lobed blooms; colored white through pink, rosy shades to purple and crimson; sizes and blooming times vary with species.
Size: 1′-3½′ (.30-1 m).
Location: WINTER—southeastern exposure.
SUMMER—*Inside and Outside:* eastern exposure.
FALL: move indoors by mid-September; site in eastern exposure.

Dormancy: period starts after blooming, generally in September; slowly diminish watering, keeping soil barely moist; cease fertilizing until plant's new growth has been established, along about March or April.
Water: keep soil constantly and evenly moist, use room-temperature water.
Mist: daily, with room-temperature water; when possible, twice a day.
Humidity: very high for very happy, 60%-70%.
Air circulation: helpful condition.
Feed: every 2 weeks during growing season, March through August, with mild liquid manure.
Soil: 2 parts peat moss, 1 part standard potting mix, 1 part sharp sand or perlite.
Temperature: Day—68°-75°F (20°-23°C). Night—55°-65°F (12°-18°C).
Potbound: repot in flat pots (like bulb pots) after flowering has ceased.
Mature plants: better bloom if stems pinched back as they become straggly, pinch off to point where plant retains compact, uniform shape, in late winter or early spring; want wide plant, pinch center out of young shoots.
Propagate: by seed or stem cuttings; root young shoots 3″ (76 mm) long in moist sandy soil in spring or summer.
Insect alert: red spider mite, thrips.
Disease alert: rolled-up leaves mean too dry air or too much sun.
Notable: pebble, tray, and water culture should be used to maintain much needed high humidity; ensure porosity of soil for good drainage; do not allow soggy soil conditions.

R. amoena (a-mee′-nuh) meaning charming, pleasing; 18″-24″ (.45-.60 m) tall; 2″ (50 mm) crimson flowers; blooms year round.
R. makoyana (ma-ko-yeh′-nuh) trailing, muted olive green foliage with silvery violet veins and purple undersides; 1″ (25 mm) rosy red flowers; bloom in fall and winter; plant to 18″ (.45 m) tall.
R. devosiana (dee-voh-see-ay′-nuh) Christmas Pride; na-

*Ruellia devosiana,
Christmas Pride*

tive to Brazil; fine hanging basket plant; oval, olive green leaves to 2″ (50 mm), with network of veins and reddish brown undersides; single, tubular white flowers streaked with rose or lilac.

R. macrantha (ma-cran′-thuh) meaning large flowered; winter blooming; pink flowers; 2″ (50 mm) across.

SAINTPAULIA (saint-paul′-ee-uh) African Violet. This plant was named for Baron Walter von Saint Paul, a German colonial official who, in 1892, collected specimens of African violets from the Usambara Highlands of Tanganyika.

A banner year, 1936, introduced this velvety, miniature jungle genus. The delicate beauty of the African violet, whetting the interest of many professional and amateur botanists, eventuated into a proliferation of thousands of varieties, delighting millions of owners. The original flower color presented, purple, still the most common and of the richest hue, is now available shaded through a spectrum of mostly muted colors, pinks, blue, and whites. Site the Saintpaulia properly, care about watering program, have proper soil porosity, keep foliage dust-free and protected from clay pot rim, all so simple; and there is absolutely no reason not to possess a specimen plant.

Family Tree: Gesneriaceae (jes-ner-ee-ay′-see-ay) Gesneria family; native to Africa.

Foliage: rosette arrangement of thick, oval- to heart-shaped leaves, usually downy, on stems close to the soil; margins of leaves are of many natures, smooth, fringed, or wavy; tips rounded or pointed; solid green or swathed with cream, all depending on varieties.

Flower: clusters of up to 2″ (50 mm) blossoms may be single, double, semidouble, with fringed or ruffled as well as smooth-edged petals; reds and pinks through purples and blues, including green, white, multi and bicolored varieties; colors and blooming time all varying with varieties.

Saintpaulia,
African Violet

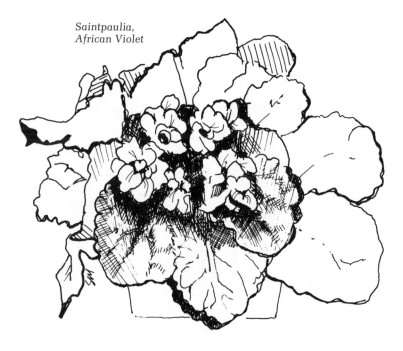

Size: 3″-6″ (76-150 mm) tall.

Location: WINTER—southeastern or southwestern exposure. SUMMER—*Inside:* eastern or western exposure. *Outside:* eastern or western exposure; site under protective shelter to protect fragility of plant from potentially damaging weather elements.

FALL: move in by mid-September; site in eastern or western exposure.

Dormancy: none, only a rest period after each blooming, be it light or heavy.

Water: keep evenly moist with tepid water.

Humidity: very high for happiness, 60%-70%.

Air circulation: helpful condition.

Feed: every 2 weeks, fertilizer formulated for African violets or 21-7-7 fertilizer in mild solution.

Soil: African violet soil, or mix 1 part each standard potting mix, peat moss, and perlite.

Temperature: Day—75°F (23°C) or higher. Night—65°-70°F (18°-21°C).

Potbound: repot or top-dress annually, prior to peak blooming period; pot-on younger plants only, when root system is 50% of soil content of pot; in planting, keep crown of plant high with soil gently sloping away from it, an aid in preventing crown rot.

Mature plants: plant shape, strength, and flower size improved by removing additional growing crowns—a crown is formed by several stems protruding from same area of soil surface into obvious formation of new plant. Remove by division at time of repotting or potting-on, or with sharp, sterile knife, slicing off at soil level; can be rooted for new plants. Keep foliage dust-free with soft bristled artist's paintbrush, or by rinsing in container of water.

Propagate: by rooting leaf cuttings in water or moist vermiculite; for best results use a mature leaf—but not an aged, spent one—leaving 1″ (25 mm) of stem for insertion for rooting; or by division of crowns when repotting; or by seed.

Insect alert: aphids, mealybug, red spider, mites.

Disease alert: botrytis blight, crown rot from soggy soil, ring spot from cold water on foliage; leaf and stem damage from touching accumulated salts on pot rim; leaves crisp with brittle edges from too low humidity; also buds will not open without good moist air.

Notable: soil must have porosity; no soggy soil; use pebble, water, and tray method to maintain essential high humidity; good artificial light specimen, giving total of 14 light hours combined with natural light; flush soil to remove accumulated salts; generally poor or no bloom caused by too low light intensity, too many crowns on plant where all plant's energy is directed to foliage nurturing rather than flower product, or, too high room temperature, too low area humidity, or too cold water.

S. confusa (con-few′-suh) dark violet flowers; blooms freely in less light than most.

S. grotei (groh′-tee-eye) trailing, hanging basket specimen.

S. pusilla (pew-sil′-luh) grows only 5″ (127 mm) in diameter; with blue and white flowers.

S. ionantha (eye-oh-nanth′-uh) parent of many varieties.

　　Variety—Butterfly white: huge, double white blooms; neat-shaped leaves.

　　Variety—Tiny Blue and Snow: miniatures; dark leaves; double blooms.

Variety—Cochise: semidouble star-shaped red.
Variety—Honeyette: miniature, bicolored.
Variety—Oriental Red: double bloom, bright red; leaves compound, smooth, dark green.
Variety—Seafoam: quilted wavy foliage on small plant; medium blue flowers, single, fringed, with broad white edges.
Variety—Hi Friend: semiminiature with notched foliage, blooms are double, deep blue with white, uncurved edges.

SANSEVIERIA TRIFASCIATA (san-seh-veer′-ee-uh try-fas-see-ay′-tuh) Snake plant; nickname: Mother-in-law Plant; Bowstring Hemp.

Snake plant will thrive in good or adverse conditions of culture and environment; it "could care less" about light requirements, is most tolerant of temperature extremes, or dryness, and the whatever of total neglect. It provides a strong visual accent, with vertical leaves often boldly striped. *Sansevieria trifasciata* may be listed or referred to by its previous name *S. zebrina*.

Family Tree: Liliaceae (lil-ee-ay′-see-ay) Lily family; native to Africa and India.

Foliage: thick, upright, sword-shaped leaves 18″-30″ (.45-.75m) tall and 2″-3″ (50-76 mm) wide, rise in rosettes from thick underground rhizomes; horizontally striped with white or pale green zigzags, on dark green foliage.

Flower: usually do not appear in interior habitats; but fragrant pink white or greenish white sprays of flowers on erect stems may occur in some species.

Size: up to 5′ (1.50 m), depending on species.

Location: WINTER—southeastern or southwestern exposure.
SUMMER—*Inside and Outside*: northeastern or northwestern exposure.
FALL: move indoors by mid-September; site in eastern or western exposure.

Dormancy: none, but a resting period of slower growth during winter months, generally October through February; slowly diminish watering, plant will indicate needs as determined by environmental conditions, develop sensitivity to feel of soil moisture; cease fertilizing.

Water: thoroughly and evenly, allowing soil to dry out between waterings.

Mist: daily, twice a day when possible.

Humidity: low normal, 25%-30%.

Air circulation: helpful condition.

Feed: mild liquid manure, weekly.

Soil: standard potting soil.

Temperature: Day—70°-80°F (21°-26°C). Night—62°-68°F (16°-20°C).

Potbound: very happy; pot-on only when root growth of plant is 80%, soil 20% of pot content; top or side-dress yearly; preferably spring.

Mature plants: if plant becomes too tall, cut growing ends, start in rooting media. Remove dried or withered leaves as they appear.

Propagate: by dividing rhizomes (root stock), or by leaf cuttings rooted in moist sand; or by offsets.

Notable: good artificial light plant; total of 14-16 hours, combining natural and artificial light; do not allow soil to dry out completely; soil must have porosity, eliminating possibility of soggy conditions; sponge foliage at least

every 3 weeks, always use room-temperature water; leaf shiners and/or oils are an *absolute no-no*; plant can withstand full sun, having best leaf coloring in this exposure.

S. trifasciata (trye-fas-see-ay′-tuh)
Variety—Golden Hahnii; gray green leaves, lengthwise yellow stripes, crosswise gray bands; leaf growth forms rosette pattern from soil level.
Variety—Laurentii; broad yellow edges; do not propagate by leaf cuttings for distinctive coloring will be lost.
Variety—Silver Hahnii; silver green leaves with scattered, horizontal, dark green bands; leaf growth forms rosette pattern from soil level.

S. cylindrica (sye-lin′-dri-kuh) meaning cylindrical; spearlike leaves with deep grooves; dark green, gray bands; to 5′ (1.50 m).

S. ehrenbergii (eh-ren-berj′-ee-eye) flat-sided, round-bottomed, angled leaves spread to fan from basal center stem, blue green with white edges; to 5′ (1.50 m).

S. grandicuspis (grand-i-kusp′-iss) narrow, slightly furrowed leaves ending in anvil-shaped tip, dark green with light gray crossbands, brown edges; to 20″ (.55 m).

S. grandis (gran′-diss) meaning large, showy; erect, flat, broad, fleshy leaves, dark green.

S. nelsonii (nel′-son-ee-eye) graceful, dark green leaves.

S. parva (par′-vuh) narrow, concave leaves, dark green crossbands, long circular tip; rosette formation, to 1½′ (.45 m).

S. thyrsiflora (thir-si-floh′-ruh) long, narrow, pointed leaves, 1′-2′ (.30-.60 m) long, 3″ (76 mm) wide, yellow margins.

S. zeylanica (zee-lay′-nee-kuh) meaning of Ceylon; concave or nearly cylindrical leaves in rosettes, 2½′ (.75 m) long, 1″ (25 mm) wide; banded light green or grayish white.

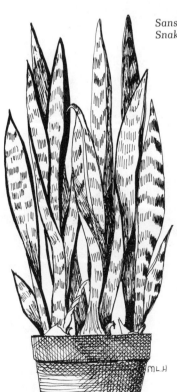

Sansevieria trifasciata, Snake Plant

SAXIFRAGA STOLONIFERA (sax-iff'-ruh-guh stoh-lon-nif'-er-uh) Strawberry Geranium, Strawberry Begonia, Aaron's Beard, Mother of Thousands; nickname: Roving Sailor.

S. stolonifera may be listed or referred to by its previous name, *Saxifraga parmentosa* (par-men-toh'-suh). It is a dwarf perennial of small growth habit, easy to maintain and propagate. Allow runners to pend from the hanging container. The good-looking foliage and the profusion of flowers, when in bloom, display an interesting and rather pretty, lacy effect. The name is from *saxum*, meaning stone, and *frango*, to break. A variety of *S. stolonifera* is Tricolor (try'-co-lor), its common name, Magic carpet; a smaller shade-loving plant sporting green and white leaves with softly pinked edges and purplish rose undersides.

Family Tree: Saxifragaceae (sax-i-fra-gay'-see-ay) Saxifrage family; native of China and Japan.

Foliage: 4″-6″ (100-150 mm) rosettes of 1″-1½″ (25-37 mm), hairy, round leaves, slightly scalloped edges; reddish green with light veins and purplish red undersides; resembles geranium in leaf coloration.

Flower: clouds of tiny white to light red flowers; on 9″-12″ (.23-.30 m) wiry stalks; blooms in summer, May to August.

Size: to 20″ (.55 m).

Location: WINTER—full sun; set in southern exposure.
SUMMER—*Inside:* partial shade; set in eastern to southern exposure for direct rays of morning sun. *Outside:* partial shade; set in eastern exposure or under a protective structure where plant receives strong light but no direct rays.
FALL: move indoors by mid-September.

Dormancy: September, after flowering; slowly diminish watering, keeping soil barely but evenly moist until May or when flower buds begin to form; cease fertilizing, September through February.

Water: let dry slightly between thorough and even waterings.

Mist: daily, with tepid water; around plant, not directly on it.

Humidity: low normal, 20%-30%.

Air circulation: helpful condition.

Feed: mild liquid manure every 2 weeks, March through September.

Soil: 2 parts standard potting mix, 1 part peat moss, 1 part perlite.

Temperature: Day—68°-75°F (20°-23°C). Night—55°-68°F (12°-20°C).

Mature plants: remove faded blossoms. If more soil surface foliage is desired, simply place plantlets attached to runners onto soil surface for rooting. Use soft, clean artist's brush to dust leaves for unclogging of pores and best cultural conditions.

Propagate: from plantlets at tips of runners, place lightly but securely in new pot, with soil proper for this genus.

Insect alert: mealybugs, whitefly, scale.

Notable: soil must have porosity; no soggy soil conditions; do not allow soil to dry out completely.

Saxifraga stolonifera, Strawberry Geranium

SCHIZOCENTRON ELEGANS (skye-zoh-sent'-ron ell'-e-ganz) Spanish Shawl.

Previously referred to or listed as Heterocentron or Haeria elegans, this succulent forms a dense mat of leaves on reddish stems and a covering in summer of purple blooms pending gracefully from a hanging container. Provide a bright light site and good humidity.

Family Tree: Melastomaceae (mel-uh-stom-ay'-see-ay) Melastoma family; native to Mexico.

Foliage: hairy, dark green leaves, ½″ (12 mm) long, diamond shaped; stem develops nodes, a joint or knob, which root where touching soil surface.

Flower: 1″ (25 mm), satiny, rosy purple flowers; appear in late spring or early summer.

Size: up to 2′ (.60 m).

Location: WINTER—full sun; set in southern exposure.
SUMMER—*Inside:* partial shade; set in eastern to southern exposure for direct rays of morning sun. *Outside:* partial shade; set in eastern exposure or under a protective structure where plant receives strong light but no direct rays.
FALL: move indoors by mid-September.

Dormancy: none, but resting period after heavy summer blooming time; slowly diminish watering, keeping soil moderately and evenly moist; cease fertilizing, until signs of new growth are evident in late winter.

Water: keep thoroughly and evenly moist, allowing soil to dry between waterings.

Mist: daily, twice a day if possible.

Humidity: quite high for happiness, 50%-60%.

Air circulation: helpful condition.

Feed: mild liquid manure every 2 weeks.

Soil: standard potting mix.

Temperature: Day—68°-78°F (20°-25°C). Night—58°-65°F (14°-18°C).

Potbound: repot or top-dress in late winter before new growth is evident; or pot-on as indicated by plant's root system being 50% or more of soil content of pot.

Schizocentron elegans,
Spanish Shawl

Mature plants: better bloom if stems pinched back, as they become straggly; pinch off to point where plant retains compact, uniform shape; want wide plant, pinch center out of young shoots.

Propagate: by stem cuttings in moist vermiculite; or by seeds any time, or from stems where they root naturally at the nodes; plant rooted pieces in soil as specified for this genus.

Insect alert: mealybug, mites, whitefly, scale.

Notable: use pebble, water, and tray method to maintain good humidity level; soil must have porosity; no soggy soil; do not allow soil to dry out completely; good artificial light specimen; give a total of 14 hours combining natural and artificial light.

SCHLUMBERGERA BRIDGESII (shlum-berj'-ee'-ruh brij'-zee-eye) Christmas Cactus.

This species of our past displays a lovely array of blooms for the holiday season. Follow cultural directions, not difficult but essential for assurance of bloom at proper season. Natured to arching, pending branching of the succulent foliage, S. bridgesii and its sister species, the Easter cactus, S. gaertneri, display well from hanging containers.

Family Tree: Cactaceae (kak-tay'-see-ay) Cactus family; native to Brazil.

Foliage: dark green, glossy, linklike segments, fleshy stem joints, 1"-1½" (25-37 mm) long, with scalloped margins, form arching pendulous branches.

Flower: scarlet to purple whorls of nesting petals.

Size: 1'-2' (.30-.60 m) long.

Location: WINTER—full sun; set in southern exposure.
SUMMER—*Inside:* partial shade; set in eastern to southern

exposure for direct rays of morning sun. *Outside:* partial shade; set in eastern exposure or under a protective structure where plant receives strong light but no direct rays. FALL: move indoors by mid-September.

Dormancy: begins after flowering; slowly diminish watering, keeping just barely moist but not so dry as to allow foliage to shrivel; cease fertilizing.

Water: keep moderately but evenly moist, allowing soil to dry between waterings.

Mist: daily, twice a day when possible; around plant, not directly on it.

Humidity: high, about 60%.

Air circulation: helpful condition.

Feed: every 2 weeks with mild liquid manure.

Soil: 2 parts standard potting mix, 1 part sharp sand or perlite, 1 part peat moss.

Temperature: Day—65°-75°F (18°-23°C). Night—55°-65°F (12°-18°C).

Potbound: enjoys being totally potbound; if in time it looks sad and all other cultural procedures have been followed, you may wish to pot-on or top-dress; I advise against this treatment.

Culture: to ensure blooming, at end of dormancy, follow this procedure for 4-6 weeks: temperatures at 55°-65°F (12°-18°C), 10 light hours daily, with 14 hours of *absolute* darkness—not even a bit of stray artificial light. Good buds should form during this period and bloom about 10-12 weeks after inception of this routine.

Propagate: by cuttings of 2 or 3 segments long, rooted in damp vermiculite; or by seed.

Insect alert: not prone to pests.

Disease alert: incorrect temperature, moisture, turning of plant may cause buds to shed.

Notable: plant dislikes being disturbed and will react by skipping flowering cycle or dropping buds, if they have formed; although confused with the Thanksgiving cactus, *Zygocactus truncatus*, it differs in that the Thanksgiving cactus has elongated blooms and claw-shaped joints.

S. gaertneri (gert'-ner-eye) Easter cactus; less sensitive to site change, brilliant red flowers bloom easily in March or April. *Note:* this species now reclassified as *Rhipsalidopsis gaertneri.*

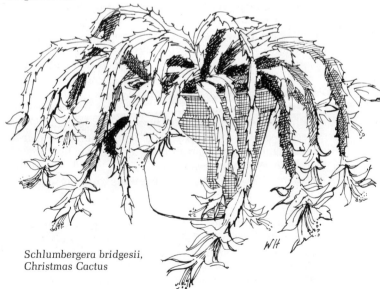

Schlumbergera bridgesii,
Christmas Cactus

SCINDAPSUS (sin-dap'-sus) Devil's Ivy, Golden Pothos. Interesting and attractive variations in leaf color and pattern of the *Scindapus* species, vigorous trailers, make this a genus of perennial trailing vines for handsome display from hanging containers. Devil's Ivy and other species of this genus are just as frequently seen growing erectly, supported on bark, to which they attach themselves by their aerial roots. Sited in a bright light, no sun area, and attended to with basic, simple cultural needs, these plants are well-behaved year round.

Family Tree: Araceae (uh-ray'-see-ay) Arum family; native to East Indies, Malaya, Solomon Islands.

Foliage: waxy, green and white to yellow leaves 2″-6″ (50-150 mm) long; heart shaped.

Flower: if occurring in interior environment, very tiny blossom in spikes surrounded by a spathe (petallike leaf at base of flower, usually mistaken for part of flower).

Size: to 15′ (4.50 m) long, depending on species.

Location: WINTER—southeastern or southwestern exposure.

SUMMER—*Inside:* northeastern or northwestern exposure. *Outside:* northeastern or northwestern exposure; site in shelter to protect foliage.

FALL: move indoors by mid-September; site in eastern or western exposure.

Dormancy: none, but a resting period of slower growth during winter months of less intensity, generally October through February; slowly diminish watering, plant will indicate needs as determined by environmental conditions, develop sensitivity to feel of soil moisture level; cease fertilizing.

Water: thoroughly and evenly, allowing soil to dry out between waterings.

Mist: daily, twice a day when possible.

Humidity: above normal for happiness, 45%-55%.

Air circulation: helpful condition.

Feed: mild liquid manure every 2 weeks.

Soil: 3 parts standard potting mix, 1 part peat moss, 1 part perlite.

Temperature: Day—70°-80°F (21°-26°-C). Night—62°-68°F (16°-20°C).

Potbound: normal, pot-on as needed, when plant's root growth is over 50% of soil content of pot.

Mature plants: remove dried or withered leaves as they appear. Older leaves have tendency to drop. Prune hard to reestablish plant.

Propagate: by stem cuttings; or by division; cuttings root in water.

Notable: good artificial light plant; total of 14-16 hours, combining natural and artificial light; do not allow soil to dry out completely; soil must have porosity, eliminating possibility of soggy conditions; use pebble, water, and tray method to maintain humidity level; sponge foliage at least every 3 weeks, always use room-temperature water; leaf shiners and/or oils are an *absolute no-no*; good light intensity increases pattern and color detail of foliage; when pruning older plant, take stem cutting with 2 or 3 leaves and root in water.

S. aureus (aw'-ree-us), Devil's Ivy meaning golden pothos; previously known as *Epipremnum aureum, Pothos aureus, Raphidophora aurea*; waxy green and yellow leaves, when young 2″-4″ (50-100 mm) long, mature 6″-10″ (150-254 mm); on vine stems; growth up to 40′ (12 m).

Scindapsus aureus,
Devil's Ivy

Variety—Marble Queen: young leaves extensively marked with white, turn greener with age; takes closer attention than S. aureus; absolutely no soggy soil.

Variety—Tricolor: medium green leaves blotched with cream, yellow, pale green.

S. pictus (pik'-tus) meaning painted or variegated; 6″ (150 mm) long, 3″ (76 mm) wide heart-shaped leaves; colored dark green with small, spotlike greenish silver pattern; slower growing than other species.

Variety—Argyreus (ar-ji-re'-us) Silver pothos; known previously as *Pothos argyreus;* 2″-3″ (50-76 mm) heart-shaped leaves blackish green leaves blotched irregularly with silver, edged with silver line; grows to any length in good cultural climate.

SEDUM MORGANIANUM (seed'-um mor-gan-ee-ay'-num) Burro's or Donkey's Tail, Stonecrop.

The name, *Sedum,* comes from the Latin, *sedere,* meaning to sit; most species are of a low, spreading habit. The genus is succulent, perennial, and most species evergreen. Flowers generally appear in clusters of white, pink through red shades, and various yellows. Provide a full sun site. Burro's tail is really super in a hanging container. It displays chains of waxy blue green leaves. All species native to the U.S. are on preservation lists.

Family Tree: Crassulaceae (krass-yew-lay'-see-ay) Orpine family; native to Northern Hemisphere, central Asia, Peru, and Mexico.

Foliage: green leaves, 1″ (25 mm) long, tear shaped; covered with blue dust called bloom; overlapping on pendant stems to form 1″-1½″ (25-37 mm) thick braids; leaves flimsily attached; fall easily if disturbed.

Flower: pale pink or red, in spring and summer.

Size: to 36″ (.90 m) long.

Location: WINTER—southern exposure.

SUMMER—*Inside and Outside:* southern exposure.

FALL: move indoors by mid-September; site in southern exposure.

Dormancy: none, although a resting time from October through February; slowly diminish watering, having

Sedum morganianum,
Burro's Tail

early spring; tender, bushy plant native to Mexico; to 6″ (150 mm) tall.

S. allantoides (al-lan-toy′-deez) slightly curved, alternate, club-shaped leaves, silvery green; on stems branching from base; ½″ (12 mm) greenish white flowers in early summer; erect growth; native to Mexico.

S. dasyphyllum (das-if-fill′-um) tiny, swollen blue gray leaves, pinkish white, hairy flowers in summer; plant to 2″ (50 mm) tall; creeping habit.

S. lineare (lin′-ee-ay-ree) meaning long, narrow; small, almost needlelike leaves; plant to 6″ (150 mm) high; trailer; yellow flowers in summer.

S. multiceps (mul′-ti-seps) shrubby miniature, treelike plant to 4″ (100 mm); leaves dark green; yellow flowers in summer; native to Algeria.

S. prealtum (pree-alt′-um) tender evergreen shrub; oval, fleshy, shiny green leaves, 2½″ (62 mm) long; ¾″ (19 mm) yellow flowers in May-June; plant to 2′ (.60 m) tall; native to Mexico.

S. rubrotinctum (roo-broh-tink′-tum) tender, branching form; thick, dark green leaves, become somewhat coppery in sun; yellow flowers; native to Mexico.

S. sieboldii (see-bol′-dee-eye) round, blue green flowers with notched narrow red edges; slender stems spread 6″-8″ (150-200 mm) from central root; pink flowers in fall; native to Japan.

Variety—Medio-variegatum (mee-dee-oh-vay-ree-eg-gay′-tum) cream yellow variegation.

S. stahlii (stah′-lee-eye) Coral beads; miniature, slow growing to 8″ (200 mm) high; green leaves, downy, oval, fat; to ½″ (12 mm) long; small yellow flowers in summer; do not use rich soil, no humus; better color in poor soil; creeping habit; native to Mexico.

SELAGINELLA (sell-uh-jin-ell′-uh) Moss Fern, Sweat Plant.

Natural habitat of this genus is the forest floor, a moist, cool, shady environment. Some species are super for terrariums, where a low, creeping habit lends itself to use as ground cover, adding a delicate, airy, mosslike effect. Other species charm from a petite hanging container, and the larger species tend to be interesting, as up to foot high accents in bright light.

Family Tree: Selaginellaceae (sel-uh-jin-el-lay′-see-ay) Selaginella or Spike Moss family; native to South America and tropical Africa.

Foliage: densely tufted branches, fernlike foliage, with many tiny opposite leaves.

Size: 2″-12″ (50-300 mm) high.

Location: WINTER—southeastern or southwestern exposure. SUMMER—*Inside:* northeastern or northwestern exposure. *Outside:* northeastern or northwestern exposure; site in shelter to protect foliage.

FALL: move indoors by mid-September; site in eastern or western exposure.

Dormancy: none; but a resting period of slower growth during winter months of less intensity, generally October through February; slowly diminish watering, plant will indicate needs as determined by environmental conditions, develop sensitivity to feel of soil moisture; cease fertilizing.

Water: keep thoroughly moist.

sufficiently moist soil to keep leaves from shriveling; cease fertilizing.

Water: allow soil to become quite dry between thorough, even waterings.

Mist: daily, very lightly, around plant but not directly on it.

Humidity: low normal, 20%-25%.

Air circulation: helpful condition.

Feed: mild liquid manure, once a month, April through July.

Soil: 1 part standard potting mix, 2 parts sharp sand.

Temperature: Day—68°-80°F (20°-26°C). Night—50°-70°F (10°-21°C).

Potbound: normal; repot or pot-on when foliage appears crowded, and/or root growth is 50% of pot content; best done in early spring prior to new growth evidence.

Mature plants: trim off dried foliage.

Propagate: by seed, in spring; or by 3″ (76 mm) leaf cuttings, or by inserting bottom of entire leaf into sharp dry sand; do not water for 5 days after insertion.

Insect alert: scale, mealybug.

Disease alert: root rot from overwatering.

Notable: soil must have excellent porosity; do not try to create a humid condition; normal interior air, even a dry site, is most suitable. *Most notable:* plants rot very easily; a good artificial-light plant, up to 16 hours combined natural and artificial light hours; do not allow soil to dry out completely.

S. adolphii (a-dolf′-ee-eye) Golden sedum; lance-shaped, alternate, fleshy leaves, greenish yellow, red edges, 1″ (25 mm) long; dense, branched clusters of white flowers, in

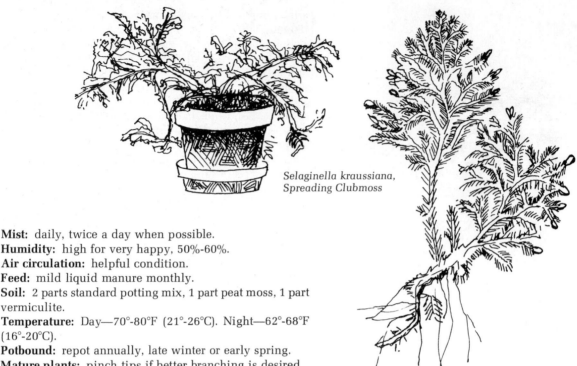

Selaginella kraussiana,
Spreading Clubmoss

Mist: daily, twice a day when possible.
Humidity: high for very happy, 50%-60%.
Air circulation: helpful condition.
Feed: mild liquid manure monthly.
Soil: 2 parts standard potting mix, 1 part peat moss, 1 part vermiculite.
Temperature: Day—70°-80°F (21°-26°C). Night—62°-68°F (16°-20°C).
Potbound: repot annually, late winter or early spring.
Mature plants: pinch tips if better branching is desired.
Propagate: by cuttings, layering, or spores.
Notable: good artificial light plant; total of 14-16 hours, combining natural and artificial light; do not allow soil to dry, ever; use pebble, water, and tray method to maintain high humidity level; this genus prefers shallow pots; always use room-temperature water.

S. caulescens (caw-less'-enz)
　　Variety—Argentea (ar-jen-tee'-uh) meaning silvery; native to China, Japan, Mexico; to 12″ (.30 m).
S. emmeliana (em-mel-ee-ay'-nuh) Sweat plant; lacy, fernlike green tufts.
S. kraussiana (kraw-see-ay'-nuh) Spreading Clubmoss; mosslike, stems root as they creep.
　　Variety—Brownie: more compact; green.
　　Variety—Aurea: yellow.
S. lepidophylla (le-pid-oh-fil'-luh) Resurrection plant, or Desert perennial; native to Texas and South America; common names describe the way in which plant curls up in a ball when dry, expands, coming back to life, when put into water; this species will take full sun and normal humidity levels.
S. martensii (mar-ten'-see-eye) many branched; upright when young; semicreeping when older.
　　Variety—Variegata; marked with white.

SENECIO MIKANIOIDES (seh-nee'-see-oh mick-an-ee-oy'-deez) Parlor Ivy, German Ivy.
Delicate, very thin leaves, formed ivy shaped, are ample in an overlapping fashion on the vining species, happiest in a bright light indoor site. Light green leaves on graceful stems are a display of gentle softness.
Family Tree: Compositae (kom-poh'-sit-ay) Composite family; native to South Africa.
Foliage: compact, thickly foliaged plant with 2″-4″ (50-100 mm), multilobed leaves, resembles English ivy.
Flower: small clusters of yellow flowers.

Size: to 4′ (1.20 m).
Location: WINTER—full sun; set in southern exposure.
SUMMER—*Inside:* partial shade; set in eastern to southern exposure for direct rays of morning sun. *Outside:* partial shade; set in eastern exposure or under a protective structure where plant receives strong light but no direct rays.
FALL: move indoors by mid-September.
Dormancy: none really, a resting period during winter months, November through February; slowly diminish watering, keeping soil constantly but lightly moist; if foliage begins to droop, water more thoroughly, not more frequently; cease fertilizing, until new growth is evident, generally March.
Water: thoroughly and evenly, allowing soil to dry between waterings.
Mist: daily, lightly.
Humidity: normal, 30%-35%.
Air circulation: helpful condition.
Feed: mild liquid manure every 2 weeks.
Soil: 3 parts standard potting mix, 1 part perlite.
Temperature: Day—65°-75°F (18°-23°C). Night—55°-62°F (12°-16°C).
Potbound: repot annually, around February; pot-on when root growth is 50% of pot content.
Mature plants: better bloom if stems pinched back, as they become straggly, pinch off to point where plant retains compact, uniform shape; want wide plant, pinch center out of young shoots.
Propagate: by pinched-off tips; or by cuttings of plants; root in water or moist sand.
Notable: frequently loses lower leaves if twining around a vertical support; essential for soil to have good porosity; cannot have soggy conditions. Never allow soil to dry out completely, it could be the demise of the plant; keep on lower side of recommended temperatures.

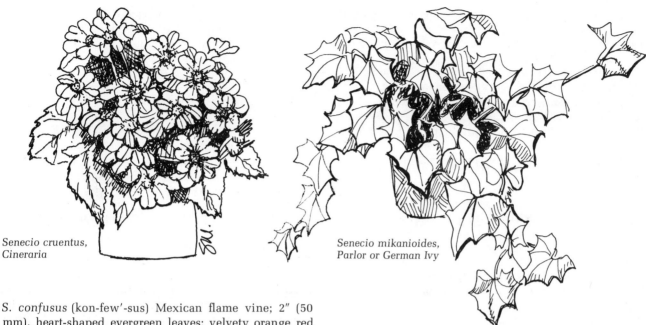

Senecio cruentus,
Cineraria

Senecio mikanioides,
Parlor or German Ivy

S. confusus (kon-few'-sus) Mexican flame vine; 2" (50 mm), heart-shaped evergreen leaves; velvety orange red flowers, 1½" (37 mm) across, daisylike; bloom on and off throughout the year.

S. cruentus (krew-en'-tus) meaning bloody; previously called *Cineraria grandiflora* and *C. hybrida*; densely grouped, 3"-4" (76-100 mm) leaves; velvety, daisylike flowers 1"-4" (25-100 mm) across; range entire spectrum of white through red and blue, with centers or concentric circles of contrasting colors.

SETCREASEA PURPUREA (set-crease'-ee-uh per-pew'-ree-uh) Purple Heart, Purple Queen.

The vivid depth of purple coloring of the foliage names this species in the common reference. Good, bright light produces charming though small, pinkish lilac blossoms on stem tips. An evergreen, or "everpurple," pendulous for the proverbial hanging container or soft cascades from a shelf or fern stand, it will produce a full foliage plant in a brief time. Pinching will aid in retaining fullness. It grows well in soil or water culture.

Family Tree: Commelinaceae (kom-el-lye-nay'-see-ay) Spiderwort family; native to Mexico.

Foliage: purple, lance-shaped leaves, slightly hairy, some slightly waxy, 5"-7" (127-177 mm) long; fleshy stems, quite brittle or tender.

Flower: small, on stem tips; each blossom lasts but a day, but flowers over long period of time; generally, summer blooming; colored pink to lilac.

Size: up to 2' (.60 m).

Location: WINTER—southeastern or southwestern exposure.

SUMMER—*Inside*: northeastern or northwestern exposure. *Outside*: northeastern or northwestern exposure; protect fragile foliage from potentially damaging elements; preferably by overhang.

FALL: move indoors by mid-September; site in eastern or western exposure.

Dormancy: none, but light resting period, October through February; slowly diminish watering, keeping soil barely moist; cut fertilizing program in half.

Water: keep moderately and evenly moist.

Mist: daily, twice a day when possible.

Humidity: above normal for happiness, 40%-45%.

Air circulation: helpful condition.

Feed: mild liquid manure every 2 weeks.

Soil: 2 parts standard potting soil, 1 part peat moss, 1 part perlite.

Temperature: Day—68°-80°F (20°-26°C). Night—55°-68°F (12°-20°C).

Potbound: repot; or pot-on as needed and indicated by root growth being at least 50% of pot content.

Mature plants: hard pruning to reestablish plant should

Setcreasea purpurea,
Purple Heart

be done in early spring, prior to evidence to new growth. Take cuttings, easily rooted, for new, fresh replacement.
Propagate: by stem cuttings; root in water or moist vermiculite; or by division.
Insect alert: mealybug, whitefly, mites, scale, slugs.
Notable: good artificial light specimen, a total of 14 light hours combined with natural; prune plant often to prevent legginess; do not overwater as plant will rot easily; must have good soil porosity; never allow soil to dry out completely; rinse foliage frequently in room-temperature or tepid water, to prevent dust-clogged pores; overfeeding will cause a paleness of leaf color.

SINNINGIA SPECIOSA (sin-ninj′-ee-uh spe-shee-oh′-suh) Gloxinia.

Confined to its native Brazil until 1847, when it was introduced in England, the Gloxinia has become known and loved for its lush beauty as well as longevity, up to 50 years if its simple needs are met. A tuberous plant, its brilliant flowers, against velvety leaves, provide great decorative accent in a small space.
Family Tree: Gesneriaceae (jes-ner-ee-ay′-see-ay) Gesneria family; native to Brazil.
Foliage: large, rounded, dark green, velvety leaves on short stems are brittle and juicy; leaves form 12″-15″ (.30-.38 m) circle around blossoms.
Flower: bell-shaped, velvety flowers, 3″-6″ (76-150 mm) across, colored blue, white, red or red with white edges; appear May through October.
Size: 6″-18″ (.15-.45 m), depending on species.
Location: WINTER—southern exposure.
SUMMER—*Inside and Outside:* eastern exposure.
FALL: move indoors by mid-September; site in southeastern exposure.
Dormancy: period starts around October, move to cooler, dark site; allow leaves to wither and die down; remove foliage at finalization or demise; slowly diminish watering, keeping soil barely moist; cease fertilizing.
Water: keep evenly moist with tepid water.

Mist: twice daily, around but not directly on plant; use tepid water.
Humidity: very high for happiness, 60%-70%.
Air circulation: helpful condition.
Feed: mild acid fertilizer, using a 21-7-7 formula, every 2 weeks.
Soil: African violet soil; or 1 part each standard potting mix, peat moss, perlite.
Temperature: Day—75°F (23°C) or higher. Night—65°-70°F (18°-21°C).
Repotting: when new growth develops after dormancy, place each tuber in a 5″-6″ (127-150 mm) pot filled with soil as specified herein, covering tuber to depth of ¾″ (19 mm).
Propagate: by tubers, seed, offsets, or leaf and stem cuttings, in damp vermiculite.
Insect alert: mites, aphids.
Disease alert: crown or leaf rot from improper drainage; leaf edges brown and rolled from too dry air.
Notable: use pebble, water, and tray culture to maintain essential humidity level; can't take drafts; if using seed for propagation, one should have blooming plants within the year.

S. pusilla (pew-sil′-luh) miniature plant; bears ¼″-½″ (6-12 mm) violet flowers continuously.
S. macrophylla (mak-roh-fil′-luh) leaves olive green, magenta undersides, patterned above with silvery white veins; small, tubular, slipperlike flower is dark purple.
S. barbata (bar-bay′-tuh) 4″-6″ (100-150 mm) blue green leaves; white flowers streaked with red.
S. concinna (con-sin′-nuh) 2″ (50 mm) tubular flowers are lavender with white throats.
S. regina (ray-jeen′-uh) dark green leaves with white veins, silver undersides, to 10″ (254 mm); 2″ (50 mm) tubular, slipper-shaped, dark purple flowers.
S. speciosa (spee-shee-oh′-suh) ovate green leaves to 12″ (.30 m), nodding pink, blue and purple slipper-shaped flowers have ruffled edges.

SMITHIANTHA (smith-ee-anth′-uh) Temple Bells.

Shaped like a bell flower, colored in a warm orange spectrum, this genus is a relative of the Gloxinia and African violet. Smithiantha displays its aesthetics in both an ornamental foliage and very unusual pendular blooms, flowering in summer months, in good light site.
Family Tree: Gesneriaceae (jes-ner-ee-ay′-see-ay) Gesneria family; from tropical America and Mexico.
Foliage: heart-shaped, deep green leaves, covered with red hairs; often marbled with red and purple; rising from scaly rhizome; leaves opposite in pattern.
Flower: bell-shaped 1½″ (37 mm) long, double-lipped flowers in terminal clusters; white, pink, red, orange, and yellow, often streaked or spotted inside; blooms from summer into late fall or early winter.
Size: about 1′-2′ (.30-.60 m) tall.
Location: WINTER—eastern exposure.
SUMMER—*Inside and Outside:* eastern exposure.
FALL: move indoors by mid-September; site in eastern exposure.
Dormancy: around October when flowering ceases; move to cool dark site, allow leaves to wither, then remove; slowly diminish watering, keeping soil barely moist until

Sinningia speciosa,
Gloxinia

Smithiantha cinnabarina,
Temple Bells

SOLANUM PSEUDO-CAPSICUM (so-lay'-num sood-oh-kap'-sik-um) Jerusalem Cherry, Cleveland Cherry.

A cheerful red and green Christmas plant, Jerusalem Cherry often is discarded as an annual; yet, with proper culture it can be nursed to a beautiful medium size shrub. Happy indoors, that is where it prefers to stay. The name cherry could be misleading. This inedible, poisonous fruit is decorative only. Do keep away from children and pets, or curious adults.

Family Tree: Solanaceae (soh-luh-nay'-see-ay) Nightshade family; native to Madeira and South America.

Foliage: narrow pointed, dark green leaves, 4″ (100 mm) long, 2″-2½″ (50-62 mm) wide; alternately arranged.

Flower: ½″ (12 mm) white, starlike flowers; bloom July through September.

Fruit: shiny, orange scarlet or yellow berries, cherry-sized, appear in November and December; poisonous to eat.

Size: 10″-3′ (.25-.90 m).

Location: WINTER—full sun; set in southern exposure.

SUMMER—*Inside:* partial shade; set in eastern to southern exposure for direct rays of morning sun. *Outside:* partial shade; set in eastern exposure or under a protective structure where plant receives strong light but no direct rays.

FALL: move indoors by mid-September.

Dormancy: rest after fruiting, in January or February; trim vigorously and move to cool, about 60°F (15°C) site; slowly diminish watering; cease fertilizing.

Water: keep thoroughly and evenly moist.

Mist: daily, twice daily if possible.

Humidity: above normal, 40%-50%.

Air circulation: helpful condition.

Feed: every 6 weeks with mild liquid manure.

Soil: standard potting mix.

Temperature: Day—68°-72°F (20°-22°C). Night—50°-55°F (10°-12°C).

Mature plants: better bloom if stems pinched back as they become straggly; pinch off to point where plant retains

foliage has withered, then cease watering; cease fertilizing.

Water: keep thoroughly and evenly moist, with tepid water.

Mist: daily, lightly; around but never directly on plant; use tepid water.

Humidity: very high for happiness, 60%-70%.

Air circulation: helpful condition.

Feed: mild acid fertilizer, 21-7-7 formula, every 2 weeks.

Soil: African violet soil, or 1 part each of standard potting mix, perlite, and peat moss.

Temperature: Day—70°-80°F (21°-26°C). Night—65°-70°F (18°-21°C).

Repotting: in March; place each rhizome (tuber-root) in 5″-6″ (127-150 mm) pot filled with soil as specified herein; cover to depth of ¾″ (19 mm).

Mature plants: care with handling plant for stems and leaves are very brittle. Remove faded blossoms as they occur.

Propagate: by seed, rhizomes, offsets, or leaf and stem cuttings; in damp vermiculite.

Insect alert: red spider, mites, aphids, thrips.

Disease alert: crown or leaf rot from improper drainage, leaf edges brown and rolled from too dry air; brown spots on leaves from too cold water.

Notable: do not site in drafty area; soil must be porous; do not allow soggy conditions; do not allow soil to dry out completely; good artificial light specimen, providing 14-16 light hours combining with natural and artificial; do not allow water on foliage or flowers.

S. cinnabarina (sin-nab-ar-rye'-nuh) red, rose, or orange red flowers; plant to 2′ (.60 m) high; native to Mexico.

S. zebrina (zeb-rye'-nuh) bushy plants with yellow, pink and red-spotted blossoms; very, very hairy leaves, with red or dark colored veins; fall flowering; native to Brazil.

Solanum capsicastrum,
Winter Cherry

compact, uniform shape. Cut back severely after fruiting. Too tall a plant for standing upright, stake and tie main trunk (leave small amount of slack in ties, eliminating potential of injury by tie cutting into fleshy stem). May be trained into standard form (tree form) or espaliered plant by proper pruning or pinching.

Propagate: from stem cuttings or seed.

Insect alert: whitefly, aphid, scale.

Disease alert: leaves and cherries drop from excessive heat or excessive shade.

Notable: keep on cooler side of recommended temperatures; have porosity to soil; no soggy conditions; do not allow soil to dry out completely.

S. capsicastrum (kap-si-kas'-trum) known as Winter Cherry; orangelike fruit lasts longer in cooler room; green leaves have unpleasant smell.

S. jasminoides (jaz-min-oy'-deez) meaning like jasmine; known as Potato Vine; shrubby climber to 6' (1.80 m); star-shaped, lilac flowers in clusters; nonedible fruit; tends to self-seed.

SPATHIPHYLLUM WALLISI (spath-if-fill'-um wal-lees-ee) Flame Plant, White Sail.

This warmth, shade, and moisture-loving evergreen is an excellent perennial house plant. A large flame-shaped, white spathe (petallike white leaf) backdropping a regal yellow spike is obviously an exotic tropical. There is a basic resemblance to the Calla Lily. This genus is unique in beauty with longevity of bloom.

Family Tree: Araceae (ar-ay'-see-ay) Arum family. Native to Central and South American jungles, particularly Colombia.

Foliage: leaves are shiny, dark evergreen, long, narrow lance shapes, on wiry stems; have pronounced veins.

Flower: rises simply from stem at leaf base; a straight spike of close set tiny yellow blooms (spadix) set off by white spathe directly behind it, about 3" (76 mm) long.

Size: to 9" (230 mm) tall.

Location: WINTER—partial shade; set in eastern to southern exposure so plant will get some direct rays; when plant is in flower, however, keep out of direct rays.

SUMMER—*Inside:* northeastern exposure. *Outside:* northern exposure.

FALL: move indoors by mid-September; site in eastern exposure.

Dormancy: none; maintain proper culture throughout year.

Water: keep soil evenly moist.

Mist: daily, twice a day if possible.

Humidity: very high for happy; around 80%.

Air circulation: helpful condition.

Feed: every 2 weeks, February through July, mild liquid manure.

Soil: 1 part standard potting soil, 1 part fir bark.

Temperature: Day—72°-85°F (22°-29°C). Night—65°-70°F (18°-21°C).

Potbound: very happy; do not pot-on until root system is at least 80% of pot content.

Mature plants: new roots may appear on the surface of soil, if such occurs, place a layer of sphagnum moss over the roots, moistening moss daily. The Spathiphyllum is a

Spathiphyllum wallisi, Flame Plant

sizable plant needing a large pot, yet needs to be kept potbound. Ensure good drainage for the needed moist conditions by having the bottom 1/3 of the pot full of broken crocks (pieces of broken clay pots). Insecticide sprays injure flowers.

Propagate: by seed, or division of young shoots formed at base of plant. The latter may be removed complete with roots and grown in separate pots; pot in osmunda fiber or fir bark; place in cooler spot for this period.

Offspring established: once established, repot (not pot-on) in fresh soil and return to warmer, proper environment.

Insect alert: red spider mites, mealybug, whitefly, scale.

Notable: retain high humidity; never allow soil to dry out completely; soil must be well aerated and have good drainage; roots sensitive, therefore can be easily burned if fertilizer is too strong; eliminate all harsh light; do not grow under artificial light.

S. floribundum (floh-rib-bund'-um) white spathes to 2½" (62 mm), enclosing a greenish yellow or white spadix (flower spike); dwarf size plant with matte green oval leaves 7" (177 mm) long and 3" (76 mm) wide, borne on 6" (150 mm) stems.

S. x. Mauna Loa (maw-nuh low'-uh) large bold form, hybridized in California; has glossy leaves and spathes 5"-8" (127-200 mm) long.

STENOTAPHRUM SECUNDATUM (sten-oh-taff'-rum sek-un-day'-tum) St. Augustine Grass, Buffalo Grass, Variegated Grass.

Ornamental and perennial foliage plant, a fairly indestructible genus, which thrives in the interior environment. Of easy culture and maintenance, it will grow in sun or in light shade. A nifty species for a hanging container; unusual in an angular creeping habit; exceptionally handsome in variegated form.

Family Tree: Gramineae (gram-min-ee'-ay) Grass family; native to South America, naturalized in southern Europe and Canary Islands.

Foliage: green, grasslike, coarse leaves; very narrow, with straight to rounded tips.

Size: 3"-12" (76-300 mm) high.

Location: WINTER—southeastern or southwestern exposure. SUMMER—*Inside:* northeastern or northwestern exposure. *Outside:* northeastern or northwestern exposure; protect fragile foliage from potentially damaging elements, preferably by overhang. FALL: move indoors by mid-September; site in eastern or western exposure.

Dormancy: none, but light resting period, October through February; slowly diminish watering, keeping soil barely moist; cut fertilizing program in half.

Water: keep moderately and evenly moist.

Mist: daily, twice a day when possible.

Humidity: above normal for happiness, 40%-45%.

Air circulation: good movement essential for totally successful culture.

Feed: mild liquid manure every 2 weeks.

Soil: 2 parts standard potting soil, 1 part peat moss, 1 part perlite.

Temperature: Day—68°-80°F (20°-26°C). Night—55°-68°F (12°-20°C).

Potbound: repot; or pot-on as needed and indicated by root growth being at least 50% of pot content.

Propagate: from shoots, selecting already rooted sprigs; or by clump division.

Insect alert: mealybug, whitefly, mites, scale, slugs.

Notable: good artificial light specimen, a total of 14 light hours combined with natural; do not overwater as plant will rot easily; must have good soil porosity; never allow soil to dry out completely; rinse foliage frequently in room-temperature or tepid water to prevent dust-clogged pores; plant several sprigs of genus in one pot for attractive, full plant.

S. secundatum
 Variety—Variegatum (var-ee-eh-gay'-tum) meaning variegated; same form but green and white striped foliage.

STRELITZIA REGINAE (stre-litt'-see-uh re-jye'-nay) Bird of Paradise.

A long-lived, slow-growing perennial that, because of its eventual size, must be considered a tub plant in maturity. An unusual, exotic plant, truly grandiose in appearance, undemanding and uncomplicated in culture. Obviously a tropical genus in its staging of radiant colors when flowering; leaves similar to its cousin, the banana tree. Commemorates the maiden name of a queen of England, Charlotte Sophia of Mecklenburg-Strelitz, who spent a great deal of time in the Royal Gardens at Kew. Sir Joseph Banks, a naturalist travelling with Captain Cook, discovered the Bird of Paradise near the Cape of Good Hope in 1771 and named it after his queen.

Family Tree: Musaceae (muss'-ay'-see-ay) Banana family; native to South Africa and Canary Islands.

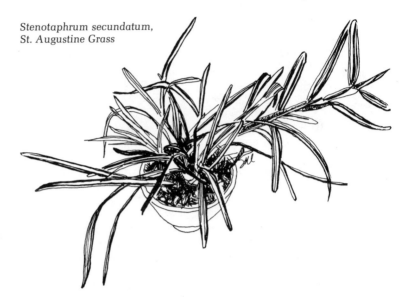

Stenotaphrum secundatum,
St. Augustine Grass

Foliage: gray blue spear-shaped leaves, up to 3" (76 mm) wide, 12"-18" (.30-.45 m) long; rise palmlike, from a central clump.

Flower: Spectacular, 6" (150 mm) flowers, shaped like heads of tropical birds on 12"-18" (.30-.45 m) stalks, in spring and early summer; multicolored, combining orange, blue, and white with purplish green bracts; only mature 7 to 8-year-old plants bearing 7-10 leaves bloom.

Size: 3'-5' (.90-1.50 m).

Location: WINTER—full sun; set in southern exposure. SUMMER—*Inside:* partial shade; set in eastern to southern exposure for direct rays of morning sun. *Outside:* partial shade; set in eastern exposure or under a protective structure where plant receives strong light but no direct rays. FALL: move indoors by mid-September.

Strelitzia reginae,
Bird of Paradise

Dormancy: none, a resting period in November and December; slowly diminish watering to approximately half the amount of full growth period water needs, plant will indicate by visual appearance; cease fertilizing; keep on lower side of recommended temperatures.

Water: keep thoroughly and evenly moist, allowing soil to dry between waterings.

Mist: daily, twice a day when possible.

Humidity: normal, 30%-35%.

Feed: weekly, mild liquid manure.

Soil: 1 part standard potting mix, 2 parts peat moss, 1 part perlite.

Temperature: Day—68°-75°F (20°-23°C). Night—58°-65°F (14°-18°C).

Potbound: essential for blooming; pot-on only after root system outbalances soil, 80% to 20% balance and threatens to break pot. Roots are easily damaged, so handle carefully.

Mature plants: prompt removal of dead leaves and flowers contributes both to health and appearance.

Propagate: by division.

Insect alert: mealybug, scale.

Notable: ensure soil porosity, no soggy soil conditions; never allow plant to dry out completely; propagation by seed can take up to 10 years for maturity into flowering.

S. nicolai (nik-oh-lay′-eye) evergreen leaves large and handsome, overpower flowers; white and purple blooms; grows to 20′ (6 m).

Streptocarpus,
Cape Primrose

STREPTOCARPUS (strep-toh-carp′-us) Cape Primrose.
Not truly a primrose, though leaves are similar, this biennial has behavior like and needs the same care as its relative the African violet. Several lovely species, varieties, and hybrids, range the blue-pink-reddish-purple color spectrum, as well as white. An excellent indoor plant, though rather uncommon in the U.S. Its flowering period is long, and better the second year.

Family Tree: Gesneriaceae (jes-ner-ee-ay′-see-ay) Gesneria family; native to Cape of Good Hope, South Africa.

Foliage: ground-hugging rosettes of stemless leaves, quilted and furry; leaf width varies with species; rosettes 10″-20″ (.27-.55 m).

Flower: bell or funnel-shaped, 2″-5″ (50-127 mm), can be grown to bloom at any time of year; colors of white, pink, rose, red, blue, or purple; frilled edges, often marked with veins or spots of contrasting color; several blooms clustered on a stem to 9″ (230 mm) high.

Size: 6″-1′ (.15-.30 m).

Location: WINTER—full sun; set in southern exposure.

SUMMER—*Inside:* partial shade; set in eastern to southern exposure for direct rays of morning sun. *Outside:* partial shade; set in eastern exposure or under a protective structure where plant receives strong light but no direct rays.

FALL: move indoors by mid-September.

Dormancy: rest period for 2 or 3 months after blooming; slowly diminish watering, plant will indicate needs; cease fertilizing.

Water: keep evenly moist.

Mist: daily, twice a day when possible.

Humidity: high for happiness, 60%-70%.

Air circulation: helpful condition.

Feed: monthly with mild liquid manure.

Soil: African violet mix; or 1 part standard potting mix, 2 parts peat moss, 1 part sharp sand or perlite.

Temperature: Day—75°F (23°C) or higher. Night—55°-70°F (12°-21°C).

Mature plants: cut back after flowering; will blossom again at end of rest period.

Propagate: by division, gently separating crowns, when dormant; or by seed, for blooms in 6-8 months; or by leaf cuttings any time. Cut leaf into small pieces and place in small pot filled with damp soil specified for this genus.

Insect alert: red spider mites, thrips, whitefly.

Disease alert: root rot from improper drainage.

Notable: needs gentle handling; soil must be porous; no soggy conditions; do not allow soil to dry out completely.

S. dunnii (dun′-nee-eye) a single leaf 1′-3′ (.30-.90 m) long; after 16 months produces generally one large leaf, a 6′-8′ (1.80-2.45 m) scape of rose to brick red flowers.

S. saxorum (sak-soh′-rum) grows and blooms fairly evenly with no rest period; trailer to 16″ (.40 m) with succulent leaves, 1½″ (37 mm) succulent lavender flowers on thin, wiry stems.

S. caulescens (caw-less′-senz) meaning with long stems; small, white-throated purple flowers on 10″-12″ (.27-.30 m) shiny-leaved plant.

S. kewensis (cue-en′-siss) meaning referring to Kew Gardens; summer and fall blooming plant; flowers blue, purple, pink with darker markings.

Streptosolen jamesonii,
Orange Browallia

STREPTOSOLEN JAMESONII (strep-toh-soh′-len jaym-
soh′-nee-eye) Orange Browallia.
Although at times referred to as Orange browallia because
of flora similarity to the Browallia, this genus is in no way
a relative. *Streptosolen*, a climber, is lovely in hanging
baskets, displaying a profusion of bloom. Or, with patience, apply creativeness and train as an upright, little
tree shape; a standard, as we say in "greenland."
Family Tree: Solanaceae (soh-lan-ay′-see-ay) Nightshade
family; from Colombia and Ecuador.
Foliage: shrubby growth; evergreen, 1″-2″ (25-50 mm)
oval leaves.
Flower: clusters of tubular, bell-shaped, bright orange
flowers; about 1″ (25 mm) across; appear in winter and
intermittently throughout the year.
Size: up to 8′ (2.45 m).
Location: WINTER—full sun; set in southern exposure.
SUMMER—*Inside:* partial shade; set in eastern to southern
exposure for direct rays of morning sun. *Outside:* partial
shade; set in eastern exposure or under a protective struc-
ture where plant receives strong light but no direct rays.
FALL: move indoors by mid-September.
Dormancy: rest period only, beginning after major flower-
ing; cut plant back to compact form, removing all
stragglers; slowly diminish watering; cease fertilizing.
Water: keep soil thoroughly and evenly moist, allowing
to dry between waterings.
Mist: daily, twice a day when possible.
Humidity: normal, 30%-35%.
Air circulation: helpful condition.
Feed: mild liquid manure every 2 weeks.
Soil: standard potting mix.

Temperature: Day—68°-72°F (20°-22°C). Night—50°-55°F
(10°-12°C).
Potbound: normal; pot-on when root system overbalances
soil content.
Mature plants: better bloom if stems pinched back, as
they become straggly; pinch off to point where plant retains compact, uniform shape; want wide plant, pinch center out of young shoots. Too tall a plant for standing upright; stake and tie main trunk (leave small amount of
slack in ties, eliminating potential of injury by tie cutting
into fleshy stem). May be trained into standard form, tree
form, or espaliered plant by proper pruning or pinching.
Propagate: by year-old stem cuttings anytime; root under
polyethylene in moist mixture of equal parts sand and peat
moss.
Offspring established: keep young plants out of direct
sun until growing strongly; blooming begins when 12″-18″
(.30-.45 m) high.
Insect alert: whitefly, leaf miner, aphid.
Notable: if training on a stake, prune in treelike form to
approximately 3′ (.90 m); new growth will trail in umbrella shape; soil must have good drainage; do not allow to
dry out completely.

SYNGONIUM (sin-goh′-nee-um) Arrowhead Leaf.
Syngonium is easily cultured, of few demands, growing
with equal success in water or soil. Various species, all
attractive, differing in growth forms, offer either crowned
trailers or erect, upright types. Therefore, fill hanging container or support on stake or trellis. Frequently, particu-

Syngonium albolineatum,
Arrowhead Leaf

larly when this genus is quite young, it is mistakenly identified as a philodendron.

Family Tree: Araceae (uh-ray'-see-ay) Arum family; native to tropical America.

Foliage: arrowhead-shaped leaves, to 3″ (76 mm) long when young; with age, up to 11 leaflets, fan shaped to 11″ (274 mm) breadth; increased variegation with age.

Flower: greenish, callalike; generally concealed by foliage.

Size: 2′-3′ in length or height.

Location: WINTER—southeastern or southwestern exposure. SUMMER—*Inside:* northeastern or northwestern exposure. *Outside:* northeastern or northwestern exposure; site in shelter to protect foliage. FALL: move indoors by mid-September; site in eastern or western exposure.

Dormancy: none, but a resting period of slower growth during winter months of less intensity, generally October through February; slowly diminish watering, plant will indicate needs as determined by environmental conditions, develop sensitivity to feel of soil moisture; cease fertilizing.

Water: thoroughly and evenly, allowing soil to dry out between waterings.

Mist: daily, twice a day when possible.

Humidity: above normal for happiness, 45%-55%.

Air circulation: helpful condition.

Feed: mild liquid manure every 2 weeks.

Soil: 2 parts standard potting mix, 1 part each peat moss and perlite or sharp sand.

Temperature: Day—70°-80°F (21°-26°C). Night—62°-68°F (16°-20°C).

Potbound: very happy; pot-on only when root growth of plant is 80%, soil 20% of pot content; top or side-dress yearly, preferably spring.

Mature plants: if plant becomes too tall, cut growing ends; start in rooting media. Remove dried or withered leaves as they appear. If plant is pruned to be kept small, it will retain arrowhead-shaped foliage. Aerial roots may develop.

Propagate: by stem cuttings, in water or moist vermiculite; or by air layering; or by aerial roots potted-up.

Insect alert: mealybug, red spider, scale, thrip, aphids.

Notable: good artificial light plant; total of 14-16 hours, combining natural and artificial light; do not allow soil to dry out completely; soil must have porosity, eliminating possibility of soggy conditions; use pebble, water, and tray method to maintain humidity level; sponge foliage at least every 3 weeks, always use room-temperature water; leaf shiners and/or oils are an *absolute no-no*; generally insect resistant; will grow well in water culture.

S. albolineatum (al-boh-lin-ee-ay'-tum) previously named *S. podophyllum albolineatum*; arrowhead leaf, white-veined.

    Variety—Green Gold: green foliage, washed with yellow.

    Variety—Imperial white: greenish white leaves, edged in dark green.

S. wendlandii (wend-land'-ee-eye) small plant; dark green leaves, veined white when young, change to solid green when mature.

TETRAPANAX PAPYRIFERUS (tet-rap'-ay-nax pap-ih-rif'-er-us) Rice Paper Plant.

The Chinese Rice Paper Plant is so named because the pith (white tissue) of the stem is used to make rice paper; handsome genus displaying large, lobed, rather umbrellalike leaves and angular stems. *T. papyriferus* may be referred to or listed by previous names, *Aralia papyrifera* or *Fatsia papyrifera*.

Family Tree: Araliaceae (uh-ray-lee-ay'-see-ay) Aralia family; native to Formosa.

Foliage: green, fan-shaped leaves, 12″ (.30 m) across; sometimes multistemmed clumps; undersides of leaves and young stems covered with white feltlike substance.

Flower: yellowish white flowers, in woolly cluster, to 1½′ (.45 m) across.

Fruit: small, round berries.

Size: 3′-5′ (.90-1.50 m).

Location: WINTER—southeastern or southwestern exposure. SUMMER—*Inside:* northeastern or northwestern exposure. *Outside:* northeastern or northwestern exposure; site in shelter to protect foliage. FALL: move indoors by mid-September; site in eastern or western exposure.

Dormancy: none; but a resting period of slower growth during winter months of less intensity; generally October through February; slowly diminish watering, plant will indicate needs as determined by environmental conditions, develop sensitivity to feel of soil moisture level; cease fertilizing.

Water: thoroughly and evenly, allowing soil to dry out between waterings.

Mist: daily, twice a day when possible.

Humidity: above normal for happiness, 45%-55%.

Air circulation: helpful condition.

Feed: mild liquid manure every 2 weeks.

Tetrapanax papyriferus,
Rice Paper Plant

Soil: standard potting soil.

Temperature: Day—70°-80°F (21°-26°C). Night—62°-68°F (16°-20°C).

Potbound: very happy; pot-on only when root growth of plant is 80%; soil 20% of pot content; top or side-dress yearly, preferably spring.

Mature plants: if plant becomes too tall, cut growing ends; start in rooting media. Remove dried or withered leaves as they appear. Prune in late winter, about February, for better, fuller branching.

Propagate: by stem cuttings; or by air layering; or by suckers; root in damp mixture of equal parts perlite and standard potting mix.

Insect alert: mealybug, red spider, scale, thrip, aphids.

Notable: good artificial-light plant; total of 14-16 hours, combining natural and artificial light; do not allow soil to dry out completely; soil must have porosity, eliminating possibility of soggy conditions; use pebble, water, and tray method to maintain humidity level; sponge foliage at least every 3 weeks, always use room-temperature water; leaf shiners and/or oils are an *absolute no-no*; keep on cooler side of recommended temperatures, particularly during rest period.

THUNBERGIA ALATA (thun-berj'-ee-uh al-ay'-tuh)
 Black-eyed Susan Vine, Clock Vine.

A cheerful, fast growing vine that must be supported by stake or trellis. Although a perennial, it is most frequently treated as an annual for interior growth. Started from seed, one can have either a summer or winter blooming plant. Also, this genus is a handsome hanging basket specimen. Great looking, variously colored flowers. Named for

Thunbergia grandiflora,
Clock Vine

Swedish botanist, Carl Peter Thunberg, pupil of the famed Carl Linneaus and his successor at Uppsala in 1781. In 1775, Thunberg was the only European botanist to enter Japan, during a 150-year span, to study plant life there.

Family Tree: Acanthaceae (uh-canth-ay'-see-ay) Acanthus family; native to southeastern Africa.

Foliage: medium green, tooth-edged leaves, 1"-2" (25-50 mm) long; heart shaped.

Flower: trumpet-shaped flowers, 1"-2" (25-50 mm) across, with black or dark purple centers; paper-thin white, buff, yellow, or orange petals.

Size: 2'-4' (.60-1.20 m) long.

Location: WINTER—southern exposure.

SUMMER—*Inside and Outside*: southern exposure.

FALL: move in by mid-September; site in southern exposure.

Dormancy: when flowering has ceased; approach as annual for best looking plants.

Water: keep evenly, thoroughly moist.

Mist: daily, twice daily if possible.

Humidity: normal, 30%-35%.

Air circulation: helpful condition.

Feed: mild liquid manure every 2 weeks.

Soil: standard potting mix.

Temperature: Day—70°-80°F (21°-26°C). Night—60°-65°F (15°-18°C).

Propagate: by seeds, in mixture of moist sand and peat; in midsummer to have plants for winter blooms, or in early spring for summer bloom; or by layering; or small cuttings in same mixture for seeds.

Offspring established: when new plants are 4" (100 mm) tall, transplant to permanent pots in potting mix specified for this genus.

Insect alert: scale, mealybug, red spider mites.

Notable: never let soil of Thunbergia plant dry out completely; keep on cooler side of recommended temperatures; soil must have porosity for good drainage.

T. erecta (ee-rek'-tuh) meaning upright; known as King's mantle; grows to 6' (1.80 m); dark green foliage; gloxinialike flowers, colored purple with yellow throat.
T. grandiflora (gran-di-floh'-ruh) meaning with larger flowers than other species; known as Sky vine; to 5' (1.50 m); large, pale blue flowers, in fall.
T. gregorii (gre-goh'-ree-eye) 3'-15' (.90-4.50 m); twining vine; triangular leaves 2"-3" (50-76 mm) long; waxy orange flowers.

TOLMIEA MENZIESII (tol-mee-ee'-uh men-zee'-zee-eye)
 Piggy-back Plant, Pick-a-back Plant, Mother-of-Thousands.

This species is called Piggyback because *T. menziesii* has a reproduction habit of plantlets, young leaves, growing out of mature leaves. As the young buds develop into formal leaves, they are of a very erect nature, giving a special, interesting character to the visual effect of this species. The foliage is muted in color and of somewhat delicate appearance, in a slightly pending growth habit. Tolmiea prefers shade and has a rather avid thirst which needs quenching. It may be listed by previous classification of Tiarella menziesii.

Tolmiea menziesii,
Piggy-back Plant

Family Tree: Saxifragaceae (sax-iff′-ra-gay′-aye′-see-ay) Saxifrage family; native to western coast of North America.
Foliage: heart-shaped leaf, to 3″ (76 mm) long, soft-textured, hairy; colored muted green; on stems up to 1′ (.30 m); growth habit of stem rising in rosette form; perennial; plantlets formed in axils, at base of leaf; generally plantlets develop on lower circle of mature leaves.
Flower: ½″ (12 mm); pale green or pale purple; elongated; in clusters up to 15″ (.38 m) long.
Size: up to 2′ (.60 m), height and/or breadth.
Location: WINTER—southeastern or southwestern exposure.
SUMMER—*Inside:* northeastern or northwestern exposure. *Outside:* northeastern or northwestern exposure; protect fragile foliage from potentially damaging elements, preferably by overhang.
FALL: move indoors by mid-September; site in eastern or western exposure.
Dormancy: none, but light resting period October through February; slowly diminish watering, keeping soil barely moist; cut fertilizing program in half.
Water: keep moderately and evenly moist.
Mist: daily, twice a day when possible.
Humidity: above normal for happiness, 40%-45%.
Air circulation: helpful condition.
Feed: mild liquid manure every week.
Soil: 2 parts standard potting soil, 1 part peat moss, 1 part perlite.
Temperature: Day—68°-80°F (20°-26°C). Night—55°-68°F (12°-20°C).
Potbound: repot; or pot-on as needed and indicated by root growth being at least 50% of pot content.
Propagate: by division; or by plantlets; place leaf with plantlet in water for rooting, or set lightly in moist sharp sand or vermiculite; or place runner of parent plant on moist soil as specified for this genus, pin to surface of soil; when rooted, sever runner from parent plant.
Insect alert: mealybug, whitefly, mites.
Notable: good artificial light specimen, a total of 14 light hours combined with natural; must have good soil porosity; never allow soil to dry out completely; rinse foliage regularly in room-temperature or tepid water, to prevent dust-clogged pores; plant must have damp soil at all times.

Tradescantia fluminensis,
Wandering Jew

TRADESCANTIA FLUMINENSIS (trad-es-kant′-ee-uh flew-mi-nen′-sis) Wandering Jew.
This well-known common name of Wandering Jew actually belongs to *T. fluminensis,* yet it is used as an incorrect colloquialism for other vining foliage genera. A genus, all perennial, which offers extensive selection of various natures, forms and habits. Vining and pendulous, excellent for hanging containers or setting on a shelf, display the cascading habit in a manner to be fully appreciated; be certain to site in a good bright-light area. Blooming season is summer to fall. Named for John Tradescant, 17th-century plant collector, who brought the only popular garden species of this genus from Virginia to England. He was responsible for introducing many new plant specimens to his native country. Mr. Tradescant was a gardener to Charles I and founder of a botanical garden at Lambeth in London.
Family Tree: Commelinaceae (kom-el-lye-nay′-see-ay) Spiderwort family; native to Central and South America.

Foliage: green leaves, violet undersides, oval, pointed, 2″ (50 mm) long; red stems; vining, branching growth habit.
Flower: white, very small; at tips of stem.
Size: up to 3′ (.90 m).
Location: WINTER—southeastern or southwestern exposure.
SUMMER—*Inside:* northeastern or northwestern exposure. *Outside:* northeastern or northwestern exposure; protect fragile foliage from potentially damaging elements, preferably by overhang.
FALL: move indoors by mid-September; site in eastern or western exposure.
Dormancy: none, but light resting period, October through February; slowly diminish watering, keeping soil barely moist; cut fertilizing program in half.
Water: keep moderately and evenly moist.
Mist: daily, twice a day when possible.
Humidity: above normal for happiness, 40%-45%.
Air circulation: helpful condition.
Feed: mild liquid manure every 2 weeks.
Soil: 2 parts standard potting soil, 1 part peat moss, 1 part perlite.
Temperature: Day—68°-80°F (20°-26°C). Night—55°-68°F (12°-20°C).
Potbound: repot; or pot-on as needed and indicated by root growth being at least 50% of pot content.
Mature plants: hard pruning to reestablish plant should be done in early spring prior to evidence of new growth. Take cuttings, easily rooted, for new, fresh replacement.
Propagate: by stem cuttings, root in water or moist vermiculite; or by division.
Insect alert: mealybug, whitefly, mites, scale, slugs.
Notable: good artificial light specimen, a total of 14 light hours combined with natural; prune plant often to prevent legginess; do not overwater as plant will rot easily; must

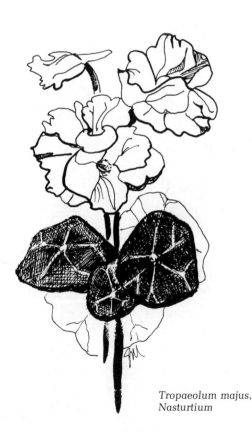

Tropaeolum majus,
Nasturtium

have good soil porosity; never allow soil to dry out completely; rinse foliage frequently in room-temperature or tepid water, to prevent dust-clogged pores; overfeeding will cause a paleness of leaf color.

T. albiflora (al-bi-floh′-ruh) meaning white; native to Central America; green leaves and stems; white flower, blooming summer through autumn.
  Variety—Albo-vittata: Giant white inch plant; narrow, dark bluish green leaves, to 4″ (100 mm) long; white stripes, white edges; 3-petaled white flowers.
  Variety—Laekenensis (leek-eh-nen′-siss) Rainbow inch plant; pale green, oval leaves, striped white, pink tinged; white flowers.
T. blossfeldiana (bloss-fel-dee-ay′-nuh) native to Brazil; leaves pale green on top, very thick white hair coverage, reddish underneath, oval, to 4″ (100 mm), leathery texture; flowers whitish pink; fast grower.
  Variety—Variegata (var-ee-eh-gay′-tuh) Blossfeld's variegated inch plant; leaves 1½″ (37 mm) long, striped white and yellow, purple undersides and center ribs; purple-tipped white flowers.
T. fluminensis
  Variety—Variegata (var-ee-eh-gay′-tuh) Variegated Wandering Jew; green leaves, white stripes of varying width, 1″ (25 mm) long; expose to sun to retain striping; very small, white flowers.
T. multiflora (mul-tih-floh′-ruh) meaning many flowers; native to Jamaica; smaller species, dark green leaves; white flowers.
T. navicularis (nay′-vik-yew-lahr′-iss) thick leaves, succulent; native to Peru; slower growing than other species; keep cool.
T. sillamontana (sye-lay-mon-tay′-nuh) White velvet Wandering Jew; deep green leaves, to 3″ (76 mm) long, tops covered with thick white fuzz, purplish green undersides and stems.

TROPAEOLUM MAJUS (troh-pee-ol′-um may′-jus) Nasturtium.
Not only an attractive winter through spring bloomer, the Nasturtium is quite edible. Green leaves, usable in salads, have a watercress flavor and are of the same family. The unripe seeds can be pickled and used as a substitute for capers. Even the flowers are used, in hors d′ oeuvres. Vivid colors sparkle from the vine of this genus when sited in full sun. A small species is a fine basket grower.
Family Tree: Tropaeolaceae (troh-pee-oh-lay′-see-ay) Tropaeolum family from Peru and American tropics.
Foliage: succulent; shield shaped, 1½″-2½″ (37-62 mm).
Flower: fragrant; crepe-textured flowers, up to 2″ (50 mm) across; a bit fringy at center; with few or many petals; colored white, yellow, orange, pink, red, or deep brown.
Size: 6″ (.15 m) up to 2′ (.60 m).
Location: WINTER—southern exposure.
SUMMER—*Inside and Outside:* southern exposure.
FALL: move indoors by mid-September; site in southern exposure.
Dormancy: none; generally approached as an annual.
Water: keep thoroughly and evenly moist.
Mist: daily, lightly.
Humidity: normal, 30%-35%.

Air circulation: helpful condition.
Feed: a 5-10-10 mild, liquid fertilizer, every 2 weeks, November through April.
Soil: 3 parts standard potting mix, 2 parts perlite, 1 part peat moss.
Temperature: Day—66°-74°F (19°-23°C). Night—55°-65°F (12°-18°C).
Mature plants: better bloom and compactness achieved through some amount of pinching back. Entwine vine on trellis or other support.
Propagate: by seed, sown in August for winter blooming; or by cuttings in some double forms; pea-sized seeds should be planted in final pot, in soil specified for this genus, seedlings hate transplanting.
Insect alert: aphids, mites.
Notable: Avoid fertilizers high in nitrogen, they produce too much leaf, too little flower; Nasturtium actually thrives in poor soil; soil must have porosity for good drainage; do not allow soil to dry out completely; keep on cooler side of recommended temperatures.

T. peregrinum (per-e-grin′-um) meaning exotic or foreign; also found listed or referred to as previous name, T. *canariense* (kan-air-ee-en′-see); known as the Canary Bird Vine; feathery, yellow flowers, deeply lobed leaves; climbs to 10′ (3 m).

TULIPA (tew-lip′-uh) Tulip.
A universally admired and known bulbous plant, named for the Turkish headdress, the turban, *tulipan*, it was brought to Vienna by an ambassador to Constantinople in 1554. Proliferation into hundreds of varieties, from regally handsome to demurely petite, in a full spectrum of colors and many differently designed flower heads was caused by its beauty, and in turn caused the further research and development into so large a genus. The species T. gesneriana is named for Konrad Gesner, a 16th-century Swiss naturalist who first observed Tulipa in bloom in Hupburg, Germany, and described and illustrated this plant.
Family Tree: Liliaceae (lil-ee-ay′-see-ay′) Lily family; native to the near East and southern Europe, especially Holland.
Foliage: rather large, narrow green leaves, size varying with species.
Flower: from 1″-7″ (25-177 mm) when open; usually a single bloom, on all height stems; some with several tiny flowers on one stem; colors range widely, including white, cream, yellow, orange, pink, red, blue, purple, brown, nearly black, green, and shades of these; many striated or striped.
Size: 3″ (76 mm) to 3′ (.90 m).
Water: for soil culture, keep soil evenly moist, never allowing to dry out; keep well watered till foliage yellows.
Mist: daily during forcing, but lightly while flowering.
Humidity: normal, 30%-40%.
Air circulation: helpful condition.
Feed: do not fertilize.
Soil: 2 parts standard potting mix, 1 part sand.
Temperature: Day—68°-75°F (20°-23°C). Night—60°-68°F (15°-20°C).
Culture: select bulbs which are preferably pretreated and large. Handling them gently, bury 7-9 of them, with sides touching, in soil specified for this genus, to only half their height. Use proper potting procedure and a shallow pot or bulb pan. Moisten soil by setting this into pan of water, allowing to absorb "bottoms up" until patches of moisture appear on top of soil. Place in cool, about 50°F (10°C), dark site, keeping soil barely moist until shoots are approximately 4″ (100 mm) high. This root-producing period takes 8-12 weeks. Move pot to north light site of 50°-55°F (10°-12°C), for 3-4 days; then move pot on to sunny southern location. Newly potted-up bulbs can also be set outside in cold frame or plunged into ground and covered with 4″ (100 mm) of soil. Temperatures should be around 40°F (4.4°C). With shoots 4″ (100 mm) high move inside, and proceed with culture as above. After flowering, and foliage has yellowed and withered, set pot in dry cool area until fall planting season. The bulbs can be removed from the pot, the old soil brushed off, and planted outside for next spring's blooming.
Propagate: division by offshoots and side bulbs.
Insect alert: aphids, mealybugs, thrips, mites, slugs.
Notable: extremely high temperatures cause bulb to blast (ripen too soon with immature or no flower) and/or excessive foliage; fertilization is not necessary, as all nutrients are stored in bulbs. Have temperatures cool for longer lasting flowers.

So much crossbreeding has occurred that Tulipa species are impossible to trace, so Dutch bulb growers classify instead into divisions. Some follow:

Darwin: stately; up to 30″ (.75 m) tall, complete range of outstandingly clear colors.
Early: on 10″-16″ (.27-.40 m) stem; single or double blooms, some scented, some variegated, colored orange, scarlet, yellow, or white.

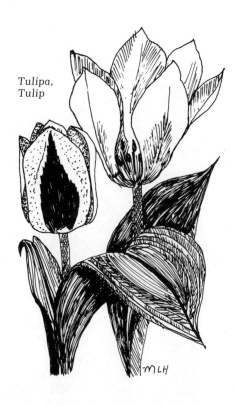

Tulipa,
Tulip

Cottage: stately, as Darwin, but flower forms are egg, urn or vase shaped, with pointed petals; wide color range including green and white with white inner parts.

Parrot: primarily irregular forms, such as feathering and deep fringing of petals, or striped colors.

Breeder: up to 40″ (1 m) tall; large globular flowers on sturdy stems; unusual colors, as bronze and apricot.

Mendel: stems up to 20″ (.55 m); single blossoms only; various colors include one red edged in orange, called Orange Wonder.

Bizarre: yellow background striped or marked with bronze, brown, maroon, or purple.

Rembrandt: streaked, flamed, or variegated in large range of colors.

Bybloems: white background with rose, lilac, or purple markings.

Woodwardia radicans,
Chain Fern

WOODWARDIA (wood-wahr'-dee-uh) Chain Fern.
When passing through the fern sites of Virginia, ignore the temptation to dig up and carry home one of these handsome species, for all are on that state's protected list. Fronds (leaves), large and coarser than most fern genera, with strong midrib, exhibit a very strong visual accent for an interior site. The common name was derived from the spore line, seeds, on the underleaf, the spore cases featured chainlike along the midrib of the frond. Rich green accents for a medium light, good humidity site, but sizable space is needed. Named for Thomas J. Woodward, an English botanist, 1745-1820.

Family Tree: Polypodiaceae (pol-ee-poh-dee-ay'-see-ay) Common fern family; native to North America.

Foliage: large, erect-natured fronds grow from creeping rootstocks; leaves shaped plumelike, with blade narrow, lance shaped, cut to midrib.

Size: up to 15′ (4.50 m).

Location: WINTER—eastern exposure.

SUMMER—*Inside:* eastern exposure. *Outside:* northern exposure.

FALL: move indoors by mid-September; site in eastern exposure.

Dormancy: none really, but rests lightly through fall and winter.

Water: an extremely important part of the culture of these plants; be guided by the following: ordinarily, water thoroughly, allowing moderate drying between waterings; never allow to dry out completely. Be aware of cool weather, when slower evaporation should mean less frequent watering. Use room-temperature water only.

Mist: daily, twice a day if possible; use room-temperature water.

Humidity: very high, 60%-70%, especially March through September.

Air circulation: essential for super success, but avoid drafts.

Feed: very, very weak solution of mild liquid manure (cut recommendation of manufacturer to 2/3) every 3 weeks.

Soil: 2 parts standard potting mix, 1 part vermiculite, 2 parts peat moss.

Temperature: Day—68°-75°F (20°-23°C). Night—50°-60°F (10°-15°C).

Potbound: very happy; do not pot-on until root system is 80% of pot content; best done in February or March. Roots adhere to interior pot walls, therefore, to avoid excessive injury, work gently, easing them loose. Rapping pot against end of a table is an aid, as well as running a spatula around inside of pot, pressing against pot wall with tool to avoid slipping into root ball. Wrap fronds of a large fern in newspaper for protection while handling. Set plant on 1½″ (37 mm) layer of gravel, then add soil.

Mature plants: if fern looks sad, cut back to 2″ (50 mm) above soil line; repot and proceed in proper culture. If aerial roots develop, cut them off. Wash foliage at least every 3 weeks. Remove yellowed or withered fronds as they appear.

Propagate: by division of mature plant, best done around March; or by spores (resemble little brown dots) attached to underside of leaflets.

Insect alert: mealybugs, aphids, thrips, red spider; control with soap and water remedy, repeat every 3 days until eradicated.

Notable: ferns need coolness at their roots, so use pebble, water, and tray method for cooler temperature and high humidity; best to grow in clay pots, as their porosity allows evaporation and aids in keeping roots cool; if fronds droop from too dry soil, they cannot be revived; fronds of young plants cannot stand water directly on them; fronds bruise easily so plant should be located where it will not touch or be touched; ferns cannot stand pesticides, which will kill insects and your plant, too.

W. areolata (aw-ree-oh-lay'-tuh) shiny fronds, colored dark green, some with slender green stripes; lightly serrated leaflets; creeping rootstock or rhizomes.

W. radicans (rad'-ik-anz) meaning rooting, especially along stem; native to Europe and Asia; erect growth of plumelike fronds to 15″ (.38 m) long, colored rich green; buds develop on main stem, root to form new plants.

W. orientalis (ohr-ee-en-tah'-liss) meaning Oriental, eastern; erect growth habit; arching, plumelike fronds, to 12″ (.30 m) long; lance-shaped leaflets; all rich green; good for hanging basket.

W. virginica (ver-jin'-ik-uh) erect nature; tall; fronds to 3′ (.90 m) long, 9″ (230 mm) wide; shiny purplish brown stalks; will take full sun; protected in state of Connecticut.

Zantedeschia aethiopica,
Calla Lily

ZANTEDESCHIA AETHIOPICA (zan-te-desh'-ee-uh eeth-ee-oh'-pik-uh) Calla Lily, Lily-of-the-Nile.

An elegant, long-flowering tuberous perennial, the Calla Lily is of strong decorative accent value, somewhat formal in style. Originally a bog plant native to marshlands. This sun and water loving plant is not difficult for success at home, if one heeds undemanding cultural needs. *Aethiopica*, which means of Ethiopia, was named in honor of an Italian physician and botanist of the 18th and 19th centuries, Francesco Zantedeschi.

Family Tree: Araceae (uh-ray'-see-ay) Arum family; native to South Africa.

Foliage: thick leaves shaped like arrowheads, to 8″ (200 mm) long and 5″ (127 mm) wide; frequently white markings appear.

Flower: rolled and flaring, waxy white petals, spathes (the sheath which protects the flower); rising from base of each is a pencil-shaped spike (spadix) bearing the plant's true flowers; spathes 4″-10″ (100-254 mm); blooming seasons vary with species and culture.

Size: 1′-3′ (.30-.90 m).

Location: WINTER—full sun; set in southern exposure.

SUMMER—*Inside:* partial shade; set in eastern to southern exposure for direct rays of morning sun. *Outside:* partial shade; set in eastern exposure or under a protective structure where plant receives strong light but no direct rays.

FALL: move indoors by mid-September.

Dormancy: a resting period at end of bloom when leaves yellow; remove plant from pot, cut off dead leaves, shake old and dry soil from roots; repot or put into garden until ready to begin new growth cycle; slowly diminish watering, keeping soil barely moist on repotted plant; cease fertilizing; when new growth shows and is established about one month, proceed with normal program.

Water: evenly and thoroughly moist.

Mist: daily.

Humidity: high for happiness, 50%-60%.

Air circulation: helpful condition.

Feed: weekly with mild liquid manure.

Soil: standard potting mix.

Temperature: Day—68°-75°F (20°-23°C). Night—50°-68°F (10°-20°C).

Propagate: at end of dormancy, divide tubers and plant each in 6″ (150 mm) pot with fresh soil specified for this genus; start in April for summer blooming, in September or October for winter bloom; proceed with normal cultural program.

Insect alert: aphid, mealybug, scale, thrips, mites.

Notable: soil must be porous for good drainage; also, never soggy; flower will last longer if not in too much direct sun while blooming.

Z. albo-maculata (al-boh-mak-yew-lay'-tuh) meaning with white spots, usually the leaves; Common Spotted Calla; white-spotted leaves to 1½″ (.45 m) long; cream-colored spathes with purple throats.

Z. elliottiana (el-lee-oh-tee-ay'-nuh) Golden Calla; dark sulfur yellow spathes; leaves 6″-10″ (150-254 mm) long, 4″-6″ (100-150 mm) across; propagate by seed.

Z. rehmannii (ray-man'-ee-eye) meaning showy, sticky perennials; Pink Calla; pink, rose or rose-edged white spathes; white-spotted leaves only 1″-1½″ (25-37 mm) wide, 10″-12″ (.27-.30 m) long.

ZEBRINA PENDULA (zeb-rye'-nuh pen'-dew-luh) Wandering Jew.

Definitely a hanging container genus, the Wandering Jew displays gracefully and with subtle beauty; cultural needs are minor. *Z. pendula* is happy in either water or soil culture; site in good bright light, and keep pinching to retain a full compact plant. The species and varieties are all rapid growers; they produce small flowers when contented. Listings of reference to *Z. pendula* could be under previous classification of *Cyanotis vittata*, *Tradescantia tricolor*, or *T. zebrina*.

Family Tree: Commelinaceae (kom-el-lye-nay'-see-ay) Spiderwort family; native to Mexico and Cental America.

Foliage: silvery leaves, center striped and edged with green, maroon undersides, to 3″ (76 mm) long; fleshy, trailing stems, segmented, will root when in contact with damp soil.

Flower: clustered; pinkish purple flowers; very small; generally bloom in spring.

Size: to 3′ (.90 m).

Location: WINTER—southern exposure.

SUMMER—*Inside*: southern to southwestern exposure. *Outside*: southern to southwestern exposure; protect fragile foliage from potentially damaging elements, preferably by overhang.

FALL: move indoors by mid-September; site in southern to southwestern exposure.

Dormancy: none, but light resting period, October through February; slowly diminish watering, keeping soil barely moist; cut fertilizing program in half.

Water: keep moderately and evenly moist.

Mist: daily, twice a day when possible.

Humidity: above normal for happiness, 40%-45%.

Air circulation: helpful condition.

Feed: mild liquid manure every 2 weeks.

Soil: 2 parts standard potting soil, 1 part peat moss, 1 part perlite.

Temperature: Day—68°-80°F (20°-26°C). Night—55°-68°F (12°-20°C).

Potbound: repot; or pot-on as needed and indicated by root growth being at least 50% of pot content.

Mature plants: hard pruning to reestablish plant should be done in early spring prior to evidence of new growth. Take cuttings, easily rooted, for new, fresh replacement.

Propagate: by stem cuttings; root in water or moist vermiculite; or by division.

Insect alert: mealybug, whitefly, mites, scale, slugs.

Notable: good artificial light specimen, a total of 14 light hours combined with natural; prune plant often to prevent legginess; do not overwater as plant will rot easily; must have good soil porosity; never allow soil to dry out completely; rinse foliage frequently in room-temperature or tepid water, to prevent dust-clogged pores; overfeeding will cause a paleness of leaf color; if air is too dry, leaves will roll up.

Z. minima (min′-ih-muh) purplish red leaves, striped silver; to 12″ (.30 m).

Z. pendula

    Variety—Discolor (dis′-kol-or) purple-tinged leaves, center stripe of bronze green.

    Variety—Quadricolor (kwad′-rih-kol-or) leaves striped green, white, pink, red, purple, with purple leaf margins; purplish undersides.

ZYGOCACTUS TRUNCATUS (zye-goh-kak′-tus trunkay′-tus) Thanksgiving Cactus, Crab-claw Cactus.

Catalogs may refer incorrectly to this species as *Epiphyllum truncatum* or Christmas cactus; as its common name implies, it blooms at Thanksgiving when handled properly. *Z. truncatus*, a lavish bloomer, performs beautifully if simple cultural directions are followed. Some hybrids produce flowers several times a year, in orange and crimson shades. The soft, draping nature of the Thanksgiving cactus display is a quite special visual pleasure as it cascades from a hanging container, *Z. truncatus* is the only species of this genus.

Family Tree: Cactaceae (kak-tay′-see-ay) Cactus family; from Brazilian jungle.

Zebrina pendula,
Wandering Jew

Zygocactus truncatus,
Thanksgiving Cactus

Foliage: dark green, glossy, linklike segments; fleshy stem joints, 1″-1½″ (25-37 mm) long, with scalloped margins; form arching pendulous branches.

Flower: 3″ (76 mm) long, hooded, multipetalled blossoms; satiny red; blooming once a year, with flowers blooming at least one month.

Size: 1′-2′ (.30-.60 m) in length.

Location: WINTER—full sun; set in southern exposure.

SUMMER—*Inside:* partial shade; set in eastern to southern exposure for direct rays of morning sun. *Outside:* partial shade; set in eastern exposure or under a protective structure where plant receives strong light but no direct rays.

FALL: move indoors by mid-September.

Dormancy: begins after flowering; slowly diminish watering, keeping just barely moist but not so dry as to allow foliage to shrivel; cease fertilizing.

Water: keep moderately but evenly moist, allowing soil to dry between waterings.

Mist: daily, twice a day when possible; around plant, not directly on it.

Humidity: high, about 60%.

Air circulation: helpful condition.

Feed: every 2 weeks with mild liquid manure.

Soil: 2 parts standard potting mix, 1 part sharp sand or perlite, 1 part peat moss.

Temperature: Day—65°-75°F (18°-23°C). Night—55°-65°F (12°-18°C).

Potbound: enjoys being totally potbound; if in time it looks sad and all other cultural procedures have been followed, you may wish to pot-on or top-dress. I advise against this treatment.

Culture: to assure blooming at end of dormancy, follow this procedure for 4 to 6 weeks: temperatures at 55°-65°F (12°-18°C), 10 light hours daily, with 14 hours of *absolute* darkness—not even a bit of stray artificial light; good buds should form during this period and bloom about 10-12 weeks after inception of this routine.

Propagate: by cuttings 2 or 3 segments long, rooted in damp vermiculite; or by seed.

Insect alert: not prone to pests.

Disease alert: incorrect temperature, moisture, turning of plant may cause buds to shed.

Notable: plant dislikes being disturbed and will react by skipping flowering cycle or dropping buds, if they have formed; although confused with the Christmas cactus, *Schlumbergera* (schlum-berj-ee′-ruh) *bridgesii* (brij-zee′-eye), it differs in having elongated blooms where the Christmas cactus's blooms form whorls; the Christmas cactus has flat, short joints, the Thanksgiving cactus has claw-shaped joints.

Section II
PLANT CARE AND CULTURE

General Do, Private Don't, Major Why of Plant Care

The "Major Why" of this section is to impress upon you the basics in plant culture. Many of these details are repeated later—with embellishments—within their respective arenas. Done with intent; repetition for permanent imprint.

Do try to know your source of supply. There should be a hardening-off period—a span of time of graduated temperature adjustment from hothouse to salesroom to your noncontrolled home environment, thus avoiding shock and potential demise.

Do check that the pot has drainage holes, especially if the plant was a gift whose pot was wrapped in foil. If not, beware of root rot; better to repot.

Do protect your new, or any, green plant from unaccustomed elements in any move: too hot, too cold, too windy, too rainy—too shocking.

Do be selective when acquiring new plants. Avoid yellowing, wilting leaves; check thoroughly for insects (in axils and under leaves).

Do keep a new member away from present plant family for several weeks . . . just in case you brought in an unhealthy plant.

Do protect. Give your new plant an immediate bath as a preventive measure; then treat it with a tea tonic (see tonic tea time, in *Washing: the Preventive Wisdom*).

Do ensure your new plant has its thirst thoroughly quenched; then add a pinch *only* of ant powder to top of soil. Now rewater, again thoroughly, till water drains from bottom of pot. You have just "debugged" the soil.

Do say "thank you" to a green plant today . . . in daily attention.

The timely interest in plant ownership has induced an explosion of exposure to plant culture in all media. One hears many technical words which I am, with purpose, avoiding; yet, photosynthesis is such a fun word to say—everyone but everyone is rolling it off verbose lips. A plant manufactures food for itself by using carbon dioxide taken from water and air combined with energy of the sun. This process is *photosynthesis*.

The *energy* source for plants is *light*. It is *essential* if all other growth factors are to be activated. Be alert to each plant's particular light needs by taking into consideration both the *intensity* and *length of time* light is available in a specific location. Note your plant stretching toward the light. Realistically, it is almost impossible to have a location where proper light can be received all hours of the day to all sides of your plant. Compensate by quarter-turning the pot each time you water.

A healthier habitat is created by extending the light hours through artificial means. Refer to Section I for the need of each genus. When the sun sets, use the proper night light (see *Artificial Light*). Not only does your plant look more attractive but, more importantly, you are stimulating a longer metabolism period. This produces robust physical condition. Winter months mean shorter days and weaker sunlight. Give your plant as much daylight as possible. The northern North American, for instance, should give full sun to almost all genera. However, always check Section I for the winter location of each genus.

Semidormancy or *dormancy* results as less daylight is available in winter months. (Remember, light is needed for metabolism.) With less time in which to grow, plants pace themselves accordingly. At this stage of minimal activity, stop feeding. Decrease amount of water to each plant's needs, testing moisture level using normal methods. With good humidity, you will discover plant's water consumption is at least one-third less during dormancy. As spring approaches, activity increases. The plant's tender new growth means it's time to increase the watering and reestablish the feeding program.

Do remove brown leaves and faded blossoms, thus directing the plant's energy to the production of healthy limbs only.

Do remember that *nitrogen* is the most important nutrient.

Do give your plant *pure rainwater* (see *Watering*) if possible. It's loaded with nitrogen.

Do use a good quality potting soil mix. A penny difference can mean good or bad.

Do use *only* plant foods that are water soluble.

Do consider the plant's health before your aesthetic happiness in selecting its site.

Do select a site with maximum humidity.

Do adjust care pattern when changing plant's location in house.

Plant and *people* relationship is a segment of the balance of nature. Now, take the "give and take" of breathing. People: in with oxygen—out with carbon dioxide. Plants: in with carbon dioxide—out with oxygen. Talk about planning! Talk to your plant . . . it's beneficial and it reacts. The closer we get, the more we give of what we each need. Note: you inhale 35 pounds of oxygen a day; it is all produced by plant life either on land or in the sea.

Reproduction *with control* is a "fun" challenge. I do not recommend or advise against an attempt at propagation. If you wish to feed more mouths,

Transporting plants
  a Wrap several layers of substantial paper around pot and above top rim securing wrapping with cord as an aid in stabilizing plant within its container.

  b Cautiously place pot on several layers of substantial paper and roll so as to have plant and pot completely encased.

  c Tie to secure; no plant material should extend beyond top edge of wrapping.

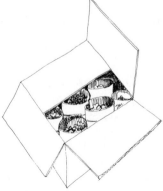

  d Brace plant or plants in carton of sufficient depth so lids can be closed flush without touching plant material.

that's your decision; *but* . . . so that you will enjoy the "birthing" experience, ease into the project. Review *Parenthood through Propagation*—and buy small quantities of materials.

Point: Young seedlings or cuttings are extremely touchy. Good light and air are very important. Overwatering is your main concern, for these dependent young ones are susceptible to "damping off" fungus (rotting where stem meets soil).

Point: If you insist on "going all the way" with many multiple births, you'd better buy a book *just* on propagation, and good luck! More important, enjoy!

Moving people and plant family to a new location? **Do** water potted plants to be moved the day *before* moving; the shock of the environmental change is sufficient without adding overly wet feet.

Do make appropriate arrangements for your plants when commercial moving companies are responsible for their care. Ask questions as to how your potted ones are handled and protected.

Do remember that your popularity rating zooms when presenting a plant as a present.

Do consider seriously giving your plant a summer vacation by placing it in proper outside location along about Mother's Day—around about mid-May (see *Summer Camp for Your Flora*).

If you have plants in window boxes, drainage outlets for excess water are vital.

Do move plants inside before nights chill to sweater weather along about the first of September, a must by mid-September. Provide proper care as detailed in *Settling in for the Winter*.

Do keep this handbook handy in area of plant care.

Do consider your plant's happiness in its type of pot before potting in Great Grandma's teakettle . . . if you must, then there is a way (see sections on *Pots* and *Repotting*).

Plant Tree—illustrated with Bromeliads. Select driftwood or well-preserved, aesthetically shaped tree branch. Be sure that it's pest-free. Method of establishing erect rigidity will vary with size of driftwood or branch. Plaster of Paris and pebbles are frequently used. The root system in its potting mix is completely wrapped with moist sphagnum moss, the moss being secured by nylon fish line. Tie plants to wood with fish line, keep sphagnum moss moist and mist frequently. Also, small African Violet trees are delicately charming.

Do realize that eventually your property will need feeding. Care enough to cater correctly (see the section on *Soil*).

Do water soil thoroughly before feeding time; otherwise, "hotfoot" results when fertilizer burns roots.

Do enjoy and glory in a plant's beauty without pampering—thus spoiling the pleasure of possession. As soon as plant is adjusted to and established in its new surroundings, *routine care* is the rule.

Do keep foliage from touching window glass in all seasons; freezing or burning can result.

Refrain from using insecticides indoors unless pests persist after all other methods have been tried. Follow all directions on labels precisely. *Please*, keep out of reach of children and pets. The latest information on insecticides and fungicides can be obtained by consulting your state agricultural extension service, the conservation and environmental protection agency, or a botanical garden.

The most "Private Don't" of total importance: please *don't* say "I *don't* have any luck with plants." Luck you don't need. Get yourself a little learning and give your plant a little loving and send Lady Luck along to your betting buddies.

Don't use artificial watering mechanisms except in emergencies (see *Watering*).

Don't use leaf shiners (see *Washing*).

Don't repot or pot-on unless necessary. Repotting is shocking and temporarily slows a plant's growth while it adjusts to new housing.

Don't use just artificial light if you can possibly have the plant in natural light for some part of each day. True, it's successful for the professional for certain plants.

Don't think that because a little fertilizing is good, more will give you a healthier plant. You don't want a "fat" plant, obesity is hard on any physical system.

Don't try to force your plant into activity during its dormancy period. Forced action in a tired period only strains greenery . . . time to rejuvenate is essential.

Don't try to be a parent just any old time. There is nothing more frustrating to the hopeful green parent than repeated attempts and no conception (see *Parenthood through Propagation*). Section I details the correct season for each genus to be propagated.

Bulb Forcing
Shoots of daffodils approximately 4" (100 mm) high, ready to be resited in bright light for 3-4 days prior to moving to full sun location.

Narcissus or paper-whites, lightly set into pebbles filling holeless container to minimum depth of 2" (50 mm). Add water to pebbles, keeping liquid level to base of bulbs at all times. Bulbs must not sit in water. Cool site and dim light.

Using bulb pan set bulbs, sides touching, into potting mix covering half-height of bulb. Keep soil slightly moist while sited in dim, cool location.

Watering: The Number One Cause for Funeral Dirges

In my extensive research for this handbook, not one single authority disagreed with the conclusion indicated by the title of this section. Water, the most essential life perpetuating element of plant care is, also, potentially the most fatal. Therefore, this section has top priority in this handbook. Study it well— learn your lesson!

More houseplants are lost from too wet soil rather than from insufficient moisture.

Your plant needs air for its root system just as much as air for its leaves.

A constantly wet soil does not allow porosity; therefore, there cannot be freedom or circulation of air in this potting soil. Result: the plant roots suffocate.

The following basic factors determine *the water needs of your plant:*
—size of plant
—plant's rate growth
—temperature of the area in which plant is located
—humidity in that area
—size and type of container
—plant's potting mix
—time of year
—plant's state of growth or dormancy

You want to feed your plant? Remember that nutrients cannot be absorbed unless they are dissolved in water.

In attempting to reproduce the factors of a plant's natural environment in home or office conditions, the most difficult is that of trying to maintain the correct moisture level of the soil. The many variables in our changing atmospheric conditions, based on the needs of the family, mean that one must be constantly sensitive to the needs of your plant.

You question why a plant may dry out with such rapidity. The loss of water is caused by *transpiration* (moisture emission) from the leaves, as well as by evaporation from the pot and the soil surface. One should therefore *water more frequently* if or when:
—pot is completely filled with roots
—oversized plant is in a very small pot
—humidity is low in your home
—plant is positioned in a sunny or windy location
—plant is in an unglazed clay (porous clay) container
—plant is in active growth with good light
—plant is located near a radiator or air convector
—plant is sitting in direct sunlight
—the season is winter and the heating system is in use.

Remember: Several continuous days of sunny weather will cause faster evaporation than intermittent or several successive days of cloudy or rainy weather.

Wather less frequently if and when:
—the dormant stage occurs (this is recognized when a healthy plant in a
   good location is getting enough light and warmth and yet has no sign of
   new growth
—humidity is high
—it is raining
—it is cloudy and the air is still
—it is below 65°F (18°C)
—your plant is just getting established

Gradually, as you become acquainted with your plants, you can see how and when a plant reacts to its environment. But there are ways of testing for assurance; learn *when to water:*

If in pressing dry finger tips to the top of the soil, particles adhere to your finger tips and the surface gives a little bit, add no additional moisture.

If you're not sure, take a toothpick and thrust it into the soil, just like testing a cake. If it comes out with particles of soil adhering to it, you have a moist condition. Or, with your knuckles or a small stick, rap the side of the pot. If the response is a dull sound, that means heavy, moist soil. A hollow sound means light, dry soil—that means watering time.

Please: if in testing your soil for moisture content, you find it solid with no resiliency, *do* take the time to loosen the top inch of soil with a fork or similar tool, thus enabling your plant to absorb the water with ease. (Do not get overzealous. Probing too deeply will injure the roots. It is the top layer of soil that so readily compacts from direct exposure to air.) At the same time, you will be doing the plant an additional favor: aeration, the freer passage of air.

Careful—as just noted—the top soil will dry out faster than the soil concealed below the level of the rim. Check thoroughly before watering to determine whether your plant is truly thirsty and not just "crying wolf." We must learn to avoid that overly moist root system! We belabor this point on purpose; for herein lies the major factor for success or failure with your new plant.

In review, a few watering do's:

Do water in the morning hours if possible.

Do water thoroughly.

Do soak the soil evenly; that is water every particle of soil (root development will be haphazard and occur most in a damper part of the pot with spotty watering).

Do use water at room temperatures (draw the water the night before as you sip your glass of warm milk; allow the water to sit till the following morning). Cold water causes foliage damage. The shock of cold water may cause your plant to wilt; also, it acts as a temporary growth retardent by cutting down the tempo of the plant activity.

If you really care, remember: Distilled water is good. Unchloradated bottled drinking water is excellent. Rainwater? The purity of this water depends upon the atmospheric pollutants, that is, the quality of the air through which it is drawn. Living in a "bad news" area? Then collected rainwater is a no-no . . . *unless* you allow it to rain for ten or so minutes to wash the pollutants from the air before collecting the water for your plants.

Never use: chemically softened water (the high sodium content is bad news); water kept in a galvanized metal or brass container; plain tap water; Important: If the above waters must be used—if one of these is the only convenient water supply—then *please* place a layer of agricultural charcoal over the top of the soil in your plant's pot. This filters out the chemicals, thus slowing down the chemical additive build-up in the potting mixture. Not only does the charcoal filter out many impurities, some of us feel it adds to the aesthetics. The charcoal also helps us remove smoke and food odors from the air.

Yes! There is a "how to" water: If a plant is potted properly, it is very simple to know when you have watered sufficiently. Water thoroughly—until water runs out of the drainage hole at the bottom of the pot. But to assure yourself that you have done the job properly, allow the water to drain through at least a second time. Some of our horticulturist friends advocate a third watering. One can set a pot of porous clay (if it has a drainage hole) in a container of water—the container's water level should be approximately half the height of the plant's pot—thereby watering your plant from the bottom up! When the top soil is thoroughly moist, you know the watering job has been adequate and thorough. For nonporous, plastic and glazed pots (drainage holes are essential), submerge in a container with water 1″ (25 mm) over the rim of the pot. *Do not remove* until air bubbles stop rising from the pot. Only then remove from the watering container and set aside to drain.

Note 1: Be extremely cautious when watering plants in containers without drainage holes. Good habit: take pot and turn it on its side—excess water then may drain off.

Note 2: Your plant's pot should be sitting on top of a layer of stones in a slider. Thus at no time will the pot be sitting directly in drainage water.

A number of commercial self-watering mechanisms are available. We have spoken to a few people who swear by them, but we have spoken to more who swear at them. Our suggestion: use only in dire need. Actually, watering time is check-up time; therefore, we definitely advocate you give your plants some personal attention. In addition to the pleasure received from the response to your tender touch of care, you have this opportunity to be aware of any symptom which is indicative of potential unhappiness.

So! When circumstances demand you provide substitute guardianship for your plant, we prevail upon you to make your selection from a species (human) with thinking capacity. As you pass your plant into their care, stage the "dewy eye." Then present that person with a gift copy of this handbook with your note of appreciation used as a bookmark at this section: "I found these particular pages so informative, sure you will enjoy it, too. Suggest you read it prior to general perusal. In fact, *demand* you read it before you touch my plant!"

Terrarium—humidity loving genera within antique leaded glass container. Moisture level is controlled by removable glass lid. Plants illustrated are Streptocarpus, Spathiphyllum, Chamaedorea elegans, and Aechmea.

Happiness is Humidity

If you are an early riser, you awaken to a dew-laden world each morning. This sparkling, moist freshness is condensation; the result when temperatures change as night passes into dawn. It is a consistent pattern to which plants become accustomed. Therefore, it follows that you should create this condition for plants in their interior habitat. Humidity is a happy word. Humidity creates that moist condition most similar to the environment in which plants grow in nature. No matter whether it be the aridness of a vast desert or the tropical rain forests, there is a certain percentage of moisture in the atmosphere.

A proper humidity level around your plants helps to slow their moisture evaporation. This is good, for when a plant loses water too fast, there is a tendency for the leaves and stems (areas of water loss) to wilt through dehydration. There are several "hows" for interior humidity. The basic, logical ones are:

—*Misting*, a marvelous method! Invest in a small atomizer, making sure it is one which produces a *fine* mist.
—Misting should be a light fog.
—Mist approximately 6″ (150 mm) from plant and around plant.
—Use *only* room-temperature water.
—Mist early in day so that plant can be completely dry by late afternoon.
—Mist with good judgment, moist air means less misting.
Please: no cold water, no soaked foliage.

When your potted plant is set on a gravel- or stone-filled slider, add water to the slider to a level just *below* the top of the gravel or stone. **Don't** allow the pot to stand in water at any time. **Do** keep adding water to the stone bed so that continuous humidity is created for your plant. Eliminate potential of disease by thoroughly cleaning the sliders every 3 or 4 months. Then, too, as mentioned previously, charcoal chips will do a great deal to keep the area sweet and free of odors . . . so place a few on top of the gravel.

If you are already the proud owner of a *humidifier*, naturally, it would be ideal to have it operating in the room where you have your plant.

We know that you know that having a good humidity level in your home is not just good for your plant species but is most beneficial to the human species.

Humidity producer—water level is maintained just below top of pebbles in saucer. Do not allow pot to sit in water.

Washing: The Preventive Wisdom

Ah! Wisdom of the wise—wash . . . wash . . . wash . . . weekly, if you will. And if you won't, wash very well every 2 weeks. Remove your plant to a sink or tub area, when possible, and with vigor do a thorough job.

Why? Off with dust—declogging pores; death to insects and their associated problems; aid in humidity.

How? Always lukewarm water; thoroughly under, over, around leaves, axils, stems; if just water, use forceful spray; preferably, use soap: 1 tablespoon *mild* liquid soap + 1 quart *lukewarm* water = wisdom. *Always* rinse your plant thoroughly with lukewarm water after its soap bath; celebrate with *tonic tea time* (spraying or dipping into a weak, tepid tea solution acts as an antiseptic and deters insect infestation for your plant); it is best to drain and dry your plant out of the sun.

When? Early in the day, as with watering and misting. (Remember, your plant prefers dry leaves at bedtime.)

This chapter is entitled "Washing," yet the word "wisdom" *is* included. I now take a wise liberty and *warn you:* clogged pores, dust retention, and disease can result from the practice of using leaf polish, oil, and wax. These are commercial products available to add shine or gloss to the leaves of your plant.

Point: As we delight in the beauty of the scrubbed, shiny face of a human "cherub," we should also allow the beauty of a plant to remain natural.

Suggestion: If you care more for the "theatrics" of gloss than the welfare of your plant, donate plant to a worthy cause.

Plant Standard—a Coleus developed into standard form by pinching off forming side shoots, retaining but a single stem. When stem has reached desired height, up to 6′ (1.80 m), pinch out tip. Permit branching to occur only at top. To form crown head, continue nipping branches at desired length. This practice also produces the fullness. Note stake needed for stem support.

Espalier—desired shapes are attained by pruning. Remove unwanted material beginning with young plant. Constant attention is necessary to pruning, pinching for desired fullness, and possibly supportive materials.

Bonsai—the Carissa or Natal Plum illustrated has been trained into a graceful form through pruning. Copper wire wound around branches supports and directs growth to a predetermined shape. Bonsai is a rewarding living art form eventuating into a dwarfed mature plant. Success depends upon the application of basic techniques to suitable plant material. Consult a complete Bonsai reference.

Bark-trained plant—the Hoya Bella or small wax flower illustrated is an excellent species for upright training. Supported on a slice of tree bark, available from garden supply outlets, a vining genus can be secured to bark by tying with plastic garden tape. Other genera with ariel rootlets will adhere to bark without supplementary aids.

Topiary—using Hedera or English ivy as living sculpture; chicken wire is shaped into an armature or frame. Moist sphagnum moss is used to fill frame compactly. Strongly rooted cuttings are inserted into the moss, and voila! an all green living bird. Constantly moist moss essential for success. Other methods of approaching topiary culture are gleaned by referring to complete manuals on this topic.

Diet Details of Fertilization

Feeding your plant is not imperative, but it is *very* important. Vegetation will survive in your home without fertilization, if given average culture attention. But is mere survival why you bought this green loving care book?

First, in order that you immediately become acquainted with the simplicity of this "feared" labor, I shall enumerate the steps of fertilization.

Know each plant's name and needs (see *Section I*). Buy commercial fertilizer that meets these needs. Many companies list plant names on container labels. All state the chemical balance of each product. For example, nitrogen (N)—5 (%); potassium (K)—10 (%); phosphorous (P)—5 (%).

Your key to fertilization is: for leaf building (foliage), buy *high* % nitrogen fertilizer; for blossom promoter, buy *high* % potassium fertilizer; for root maker, rely on phosphorous.

Use only water-soluble fertilizer.

Read directions on labels and feed one-half the amount prescribed twice as often.

Water your plant; now add liquid fertilizer till liquid drips from hole in bottom of pot (all liquid must be at room temperature).

Start fertilizing in late winter or early spring when new growth is evident on your plant.

Cease feeding when plant indicates approach of dormant stage in life cycle; generally, when no new growth is evident.

As you absorb the "why" of this cultural phase, you will more thoroughly understand your plant's need for additional nutrition through fertilization. Too, your supply source will offer various nutrient forms such as tablets, stakes, and more. I wish to expound on this area and generalize in several side issues of merit.

Your plant's roots have only a limited amount of soil, as confined by its pot, from which to draw feeding needs. With each watering, a certain portion of these nutritional elements in the soil is washed away. The depletion from normal utilization in plant's growth cannot be restored as it is in the natural habitat by the decomposition of organic materials returned to the soil. Therefore, in addition to beginning with a good potting soil, one can readily understand that eventually chemicals to enrich this soil must be provided on a regular basis.

Fertility is maintained by *scheduled* feeding.

Commence feeding as plant dictates, as in showing signs of young greenery—active growth.

During dormancy period (see specific genus), do not feed, allowing your plant rest and reestablishment time. Shorter days and low light intensity mean slower metabolism of your plant, thus less nurturing.

If your plant is in a state of ill health, *please*, do not feed. There just isn't enough strength for your patient to utilize this energy.

Of course, if the illness is diagnosed as starvation, then implement a program of feeding, starting with a *very*, very mild feeder solution on a weekly basis. As your patient rallies gradually, increase the strength of the solution to *one-half* that recommended by the manufacturer and feed twice as frequently. As soon as full health has been regained, repot with fresh potting mixture.

When transplanting or repotting your greenery with a fresh potting soil, wait approximately one month before starting your feeding program.

If your plant is a new family member, it's good to wait for this one month period before starting to fertilize. However, the true indicator is your plant. Watch for hunger signs: small, stunted leaves—lack of nitrogen; pale leaves—lack of nitrogen; weak stems—lack of potassium; small blossoms—lack of potassium; faded, poor color blossoms—lack of potassium.

Remember: sunlight is your main blossom promoter; *only* use water-soluble products; *only* apply to already moistened soil; *only* use one-half recommended strength fertilizer solution but apply twice as frequently (check specific genus).

In summation, one is fertilizing one's plant when adding to the potting soil mix any chemical elements, organic or inorganic, in concentrated form.

Soils: *Essential Essentials*

Until the near past, the majority of Mr., Mrs., and Ms. General Public wishing to grow a green knew that to so do meant buying a bag or spading a bucket of the good earth, then proceeding with planting plant. The material used, soil, consists of disintegrated rock and humus. These provide the essential chemical elements for plant nurture. Today one can choose to raise certain plants by means of a soilless culture. Regardless of method, we are dealing with the basic establishment of a plant; therefore, it is *essential* that the planting medium contains the proper balance of basic elements needed, for a specific species.

Soilless culture sounds so nonmessy—no mud packs, no aerating. No! No! not as simple as one might assume. The plant grown in artificial soil or a chemical solution needs just as much attention as the plant raised in soil. One process frequently referred to as chemical gardening—you may have heard the terms hydroponics or nutriculture—is when a plant is placed (preferably within a glass receptacle) in a preparation of ready mixed chemicals. A dry mix is used. Following manufacturer's direction precisely, prepare a chemical solution.

If using a metal container or any container with metal parts, it is essential to cover it with two coats of swimming pool or other asphalt paint.

Few plants can be grown in this method without some support to help the plant maintain an upright position:
- —small plants with a spreading leaf that will support themselves on the rim of the container such as the African violet
- —bulb plants that are best grown in special supportive bulb vases
- —small vining (lightweight) plants such as the ivies

For larger plant support, fill the vase with builder's sand (clean, of course). Cover the root system and as much of the stem as necessary with sand to keep plant erect:
- —keep the level of the solution just under the base of the roots
- —solution evaporates, so check daily, adding enough solution to raise to original level
- —roots are in need of aeration; daily blow air into the solution through a straw
- —twice a month pour off all solution and reservice with a fresh mixture
- —monthly wash out sand thoroughly with plain water, then add fresh solution.

Other methods for holding larger plants upright have not proven sufficiently successful for the bother involved. If enticed or challenged by this method of interior plant culture, go to your library or purchase a book on hydroculture for full exposure to cultural process.

Pre-packaged soilless mixes or artificial soils are available at garden supply outlets. These have been formulated to meet the needs of various types of interior plants. Artificial soil is a mixture of materials, other than natural soil, which are conducive to plant life. These materials may be of nature's making.

The following ingredients may be included in a mix:
—sphagnum moss or peat moss—a natural product with factors of acidity and water retention
—vermiculite—a mineral, sterile, water retaining
—perlite—a mineral, sterile, lightweight, and porous, providing aeration factors
—limestone
—superphosphate
—a balanced fertilizer

When using such soilless mixes, check the labels for contents. Some do, some do not contain nutrients. Which brings us to some pros and cons.

Pros

Usually sterile, thus disease- and weed-free:
—lightweight, easy to handle for repotting and potting-on large plants
—provide good drainage
—provide good water-retention, therefore less frequent watering necessary
—provide good aeration, no soil compaction

Cons

May need frequent feeding:
—tendency of soil level to lower through decomposition of organic matter in mix
—wash out of pot easily
—large plant material is "tipsy" because of light weight of mix
—easy to overwater because of water retention qualities

Healthy plants can be grown in soilless mediums. The key to happiness is a human adjustment to the different cultural needs.

And so we return to the *essentials* of the old-fashioned, tried-and-true soil. The specification of a potting mix for a genus in Section I of this manual was determined by referring to the natural habitat of that genus. The balance of elements in the potting mixture should approach as nearly as possible the earth elements provided by Mother Nature for each plant. Because the amount of potting medium in each pot is so small, it must be of the highest quality.

Sterile soil is essential, most packaged soil is sterilized but do check the label. The mixture should be loose and porous for good drainage and aeration.

Perlite. If mix compacts, add perlite—a sterile volcanic rock of neutral pH which will aid in aeration, thus providing oxygenation of roots.

Vermiculite. If mix is too porous, thus allowing too rapid drainage, add vermiculite, an absorptive granular mineral which aids in water retention.

Mix must be of a consistency to keep plant upright.

Add a few pieces of charcoal to absorb excess salts and gases.

Avoid packaged mixes containing fertilizer that breaks down slowly (those said to feed over a long span of time).

A pH rating relates to the quantities of hydrogen available to the soil. The hydrogen quantities present determine the acidity or alkalinity of the soil. Each of these conditions, acid or alkaline, has its own effect on chemicals in the soil, blocking their availability or affecting their structure:
—plants needing neutral conditions (*alkaline*) should have a small amount of *limestone* in their mix.
—standard potting mix has an alkaline balance.
—"hard" water is alkaline.
—plants needing *acidity* should have *sphagnum* or *peat moss* added to the mix.
—sphagnum moss is an acid material.

Note, Peat moss and/or sphagnum moss must be wet when added to mixes.

A standard (neutral) potting mix can be made from:

—2 parts topsoil (good garden soil)

—1 part humus or compost

—1 part *clean* sharp (builder's) sand or perlite

—a few bits of charcoal

An acid potting mix can be made from equal amounts of:

—topsoil (good garden soil)

—humus or compost

—*clean* sharp (builder's) sand or perlite

—peat moss

—a few bits of charcoal

A cactus potting mix can be made from:

—2 parts topsoil (good garden soil)

—2 parts *clean* sharp coarse (builder's) sand or coarse perlite

—1 part humus or compost

—small amount of powdered limestone

—small amount of bone meal

Orchids and bromeliads, air plants or epiphytes, are plants capable of growing with the total plant structure, including root system, exposed to air. In a natural environment, they exist above ground level, in trees or on rocks. It is essential that the planting medium for their interior habitat provides porosity and excellent drainage. Thus, members of these families are potted-up in red-wood bark, sphagnum moss, or osmunda fiber mixed with coarse perlite. The balance is generally 1 part perlite to 3 parts of the combining material. Pot type, humidity, and the species determine porosity needs or quantity of perlite used.

Human nature tends to procrastination when it comes to providing the soil cultural services for a green family member. Time is involved, as well as dirty fingernails or chipped polish, and then all that mess has to be cleaned up! Potting-up, re-potting, or potting-on has got to be. When you have faced and accepted it and finally become involved in the procedure, I'm sure you'll agree it to be a tonic time, not just for your green charge but for yourself. A special something is involved in tending to the needs of and sharing in the cares of Mother Nature. The essentials of proper soil culture seemingly cycle into the essentials of well being in human culture.

Pots: Properties and Potentials

Do please your aesthetic needs in selecting your plant's pot. Being totally visual, the pot is the adornment or complement to your plant.

Perhaps the purpose of this handbook is to add to the thesaurus this synonym. *Plant, n. pleasure.* The plan of this handbook has just that as a goal.

After immersion in prior pages, you are attuned to providing plant care within the dictates of a plant's cultural needs. So it is, too, with selecting the green's container. Now is not the time to ignore any considerations relevant to proper potting. The *size* and relationship of pot and plant are the only factors which should, would, or could deter you from potting a plant in your heart-set-on receptacle.

If the characteristics of the container are not conducive to good cultural function, one should only use it in the double potting method. Your green is planted in a container of the correct dimensions, then set inside the aesthetically gratifying container.

Consider the properties of the various potting containers. The porosity of the pot's material is a consideration of major importance.

UNGLAZED CLAY POT

The porous nature of clay without a sealant (glaze) allows maximum moisture evaporation. This species of housing is the Oscar winner and upstages all other varieties of the pot genus. Condition new porous pots by soaking them in water for 2 hours. The cells of the new pot are air-filled; the saturation in water replaces this air with liquid.

Although any potted vegetation will dry out first on the accessible top level of soil, the clay pot allows for more uniform drying of the contained soil and root ball. One also has less concern about "spotty" watering, which can lead to root rot. The container's porosity allows soil in the root system to dry between thorough waterings—the most healthful, advocated method, in proper plant care.

Remember—particularly with the clay pot—to set it on pebbles (maintain proper water level of pebbles) in a slider to produce a super humidity condition. In environmental conditions of extreme humidity (the rare situation for the interior plant), the porous clay pot is the safest by far. Its use avoids a too constantly moist soil, with its associated problems.

However, because of unglazed clay's porosity, there is an unfavorable aspect: salts and other minerals build up gradually as moisture evaporates on the top rim and exterior walls. You must remain alert and perform housekeeping chores. An accumulation of salts on the moist clay pot is choice for the development of green algae. Note that leaves or petals touching a mineral (salt) crust on the top rim of the pot are in grave danger of being burned. Use a cleanser pad, such as Brillo, to remove this mineral deposit. This is an easy job; so don't procrastinate.

For a tall plant, the clay pot is heavier than plastic or Styrofoam and thus has better balance.

TERRA-COTTA POT

(This is not to be confused with the ordinary clay pot): The consistency of the material in the terra-cotta pot is heavier, not nearly as porous as the standard clay pot, therefore much slower drying. One usually thinks of this pot as a very ornamental container. It is excellent as the outer pot in the double potting method.

GLAZED CLAY POT

This type pot is a great deal less porous because of the sealing character of the glaze. One finds limited moisture evaporation of the soil below the rim; therefore, when using as a direct planting container, make allowance for this factor in your watering program. It is best when used in environment of low humidity.

PLASTIC POT

The outstanding asset here is the vast assortment in style, color, and size at minimum cost. The slowed evaporation of moisture from root system necessitates a careful check of the soil's wetness, in depth, before each watering. Plastic pots are best used in an environment of low humidity. Since plastic is a lightweight material, one must use this type of pot judiciously when considering planting a tall or unbalanced plant. Avoid heartbreak by avoiding plantbreak in a toppled-over friend with broken limbs and in need of amputation.

METAL POT

Skull and crossbones stuff. The metals—copper, brass, zinc—are minerals poisonous to plants. If you insist on planting directly into metal containers, *please* cover the interior of the pot with two coats of swimming pool or aquarium paint.

Metals are nonporous; again, this can cause slow drying out of the ball root of your plant . . . so take care with watering.

STYROFOAM POT

Styrofoam serves a purpose as a planting container and that's about it. Obviously, this container will not enhance the beauty of your green, but I did state, that this part of it, the aesthetics, is strictly your ballgame. Styrofoam is deceiving. Although it looks as though it should have much porosity, there is none. Be careful with the watering program. Careful, too, if contemplating the large or unbalanced plant for this pot. Styrofoam is very lightweight and tragedy prone.

STONEWARE, PORCELAIN, OR GLASS CONTAINERS

These are nonporous but usually attractive. Take care to maintain the moisture level through watering.

Note: The *value* of porous materials is that the soil and root system ball of your plant is kept cooler as the moisture gradually seeps through the walls of the pot and evaporates from the exterior walls. The evaporation then creates a more humid atmosphere for the green.

DRAINAGE

It is difficult to know the precise quantity of water necessary with each watering. You must water the plant thoroughly; therefore, surplus water needs to drain. This excess water must be discharged so that air, essential for proper balance, can penetrate the root system. Also, if the water cannot drain off, we have the oversaturated condition so conducive to root rot. Attempt to pick a pot with drainage.

If a pot does not have drainage, one must provide a substitute condition: fill the container with a minimum of 1″ (25 mm) of gravel. If the pot is of adequate size, fill up to one-third of the unit with gravel, thereby providing greater assurance that the plant's root system will be safe from surplus water. Add a 1″ (25 mm) layer of peat moss atop the gravel to discourage leaching (the lower roots of your plant being tempted into the water layer of the gravel).

Fibremat products (absorptive materials) are available. Place this product in the bottom of pots without drainage. If there is care in watering and surplus water is not overabundant, the fibremat will absorb the surplus and release it as your plant's root system calls for more moisture. This provides a more constant moisture content. The problematic area is gauging the supply of water, since watering should be limited to the quantity only that can be absorbed by the fibremat. Sticky to judge.

Orchid pot—designed with sizable drainage slots to aid proper moisture level of potting medium and root aeration.

DOUBLE POTTING

One plants one's vegetation in a pot with drainage holes. Let's assume this specific pot is of little visual attraction in the eyes of the owner. To enhance and do justice to plant, the proper planting pot is set within an aesthetic container

Double potting—a pot set within a pot. Moist sphagnum moss filling void area between pots is an excellent method of slowing evaporation of moisture from potting mix.

such as the jardiniere. Double potting has the added benefit of insulating roots from extremes in temperatures.

If planter is of porous clay, double potting aids in slowing the moisture evaporation from the ball of your plant. To slow down this drying out of the soil further, one can, in the double potting method, fill space between clay pot and outer container with moist sphagnum moss, coarse perlite, or vermiculite, or even moist (not sopping) peat moss. If the outer container is nonporous, once again you have an asset in the slow evaporation.

Because of the drainage holes in the inner planter, do follow the preceding methods for handling surplus water drainage.

DISEASE-FREE POTS

Clean pots, free of disease, are absolutely essential. Soap and water and elbow grease is one method. To assure yourself that you have destroyed any insects or potential disease, dip the pot (prior to planting in it) into a solution of 1 pint household bleach (such as Clorox) and 1 gallon of water. Rinse the pot thoroughly and allow it to remain exposed to the air in a well-ventilated place for several days to allow toxic fumes to evaporate. *Remember:* The pot's clay pores are now dried out, so soak in water as previously explained before settling in your green.

You have here the properties and potentials of pots; evaluate, compare, and select your pots to serve the plants' needs and your visual pleasures.

Repotting Properly for Plant's Potential

If you discover a root or roots protruding from the drainage holes in your plant's pot, do not automatically take for granted that this root protrusion means the plant is potbound. Your plant could have a few stray roots if the pot is sitting on a moist gravel bed, since its root system is drawn toward this moisture level. However, a checkup is indicated. In order to avoid these worrisome potbound symptoms, schedule semiannual examinations, spring and fall preferably.

Repotting: remove your plant from its pot, adding to or changing the soil, doctoring roots if necessary, and replanting in its original pot or a smaller pot.

Potting-On: remove your plant from its pot, attend to needs and replant your friend in a larger pot.

Now that you are knowledgable in nomenclature, we proceed to the cultural why and when.

Why a semiannual examination? For preventive or corrective care. Problems concealed within the pot may not have advanced to a stage where they can be seen in the above soil-line growth.

When to examine? Semiannually in spring and fall. The spring checkup should occur at least 4 weeks prior to setting your flora outside for its summer vacation; the month is a readjustment period for the handling of shock inherent to the process of repotting or potting-on. Your plant should be in its accustomed environment while regaining its equilibrium.

The cultural attentions you provide in the repotting or potting-on are most beneficial to your plant after a winter of indoor unnatural habitat. This rehabilitation provides a basis for strong summer growth, ensuring health to carry your plant through a home-housed winter.

The second checkup in the fall is more the preventive examination. If your

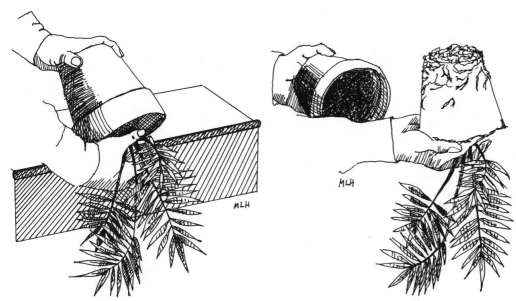

Carefully support plant to avoid damage to top growth while tapping edge of pot against hard surface to aid in removing soil ball.

Plant properly supported with soil ball intact and top growth unharmed.

plant has summered out, the concern is not the nutritional needs, for Mother Nature has fed organically. If your plant family has remained within building confines, nutrition has been satisfied by your spring checkup service and a seasonal fertilization program.

Disease or insect problems are your concern, but all that's needed is a quickie—remove plant from pot and check to assure all's well (removal details below). A problematic area? Good, you can attend to it with ease in its early stage.

In preparation for the actual procedure of potting-on and repotting, gather sterilized soil and clean pot (wash existing pot if it's to be reused). Remember that:

Potting-on is performed when your vegetation is rootbound; therefore, its growth is curtailed. A plant is rootbound if the ball of the plant has more roots than soil or if there is a mass of root system surrounding the ball.

Repotting is performed for all cultural cures other than growth restriction—when pot is outgrown. It provides nutrition with the fresh potting mixture; renovation of damaged roots by pruning of the root system; aeration of compacted soil for proper drainage; eradication of subsoil insects; general renovation of mature plants (those that have reached their growth potential but need periodic maintenance).

To remove plant from pot with least disturbance, run a thin spatula or knife along the inside of the pot. Place your hand over the pot carefully to avoid damaging top growth yet support soil ball on inversion. Invert pot and with hand in place gently tap pot's rim on a hard surface to separate any final particles of root ball still clinging to pot.

Remove upper 1″-1½″ (25-37 mm) of soil from complete ball. Easy—as little root damage as possible, please.

Gingerly force exposed root system apart with fingers, loosening the root mass so that individual roots can benefit from the replanting in fresh soil. This step also loosens soil for better aeration.

By now you can see any root system problems; if necessary, prune the roots as follows:

All soil must be removed from the root system. The easiest method is to hold tenderly but firmly the portion of plant above the soil-line. Remove as

Root ball—over 50% root system, ready for repotting or potting-on for those genera not liking to be pot-bound.

much soil from the root ball as possible by gently shaking. Then rinse root ball under a gentle, tepid stream of water (it is helpful to have spigot flowing beforehand).

Use a sharp pruning shears or scissors to remove all mushy, damaged, and very long roots. Sever these roots at a joint or, if necessary, remove root entirely.

Don't dillydally. Never walk away from an unfinished job, leaving roots exposed to air. It is *imperative* the roots do not dry out. Please—if at any time you must leave either exposed roots or root ball for a length of time (when drying out could occur), moisten the roots or root ball with tepid water and wrap in a plastic bag. Seal the plastic bag at top of root ball, around stem, to exclude air.

Examine soil and roots for insects. If your plant has an infestation, remove all soil from roots as explained above.

When treating a mature plant—one that you estimate to be full grown—proceed as follows for nutritional rehabilitation:

Do not remove all soil, merely 1″-1½″ (25-37 mm), and loosen root mass as previously explained. Prune exposed roots with sharp pruning shears or scissors (certainly no more than one-third of total root system—overpruning can be fatal).

After repotting, prune top growth of your plant an amount equal to that pruned from the root system. This is necessary to maintain plant balance.

Once the potbound plant has had its root mass loosened, pot-on into a container 2″ (50 mm) larger than its previous housing. This increase allows for the next year's growth yet maintains a good balance between your plant and its pot. Using an excessively large pot is dangerous. The oversized soil ball will hold too much water and prevent aeration. This will either drown or suffocate your friend. Some plants prefer being rootbound. Know the characteristics and needs of individual plants.

Heed closely the following steps for potting, to ensure your plant its full potential: sterile soil; clean pot; pot of correct size; place a piece of broken pot over the drainage hole, concave side down, to prevent soil clogging drainage hole.

Take special precautions when planting in a container without drainage. Place at least a 1″ (25 mm) layer of gravel in the bottom of the pot. In larger pots,

Repotting Cattleya labiata
a *Potbound orchid with seven pseudobulbs and roots overflowing.*

b *With sharp, clean instrument, separate pseudobulbs with root system into two clumps.*

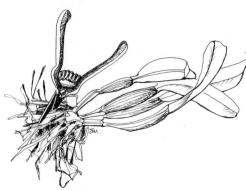

c *Trim and remove all mushy rooting or dead roots.*

d *Place severed end of division against side of pot, near top rim allowing depth of pot for root system. Potting mixture is firmed around positioned division.*

e *Open loops around each pseudobulb and secure to a stake; support division until plant is established in new container.*

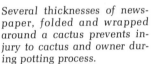

Several thicknesses of newspaper, folded and wrapped around a cactus prevents injury to cactus and owner during potting process.

In handling fern during potting procedures, protect fragile fronds (leaves) by wrapping several layers of substantial paper, folded, around entire foliage near soil level.

When potting-up plant, place a few bits of broken pottery in base of pot to aid good drainage. One piece concave side down covers drainage hole in order to prevent clogging or wash-out of potting mix yet allows drainage of excessive water.

fill up to one-third of the pot with gravel, thereby helping to insulate the plant's root system from surplus water. Add a 1″ (25 mm) layer of peat moss atop the gravel to discourage leaching (the plant's lower roots being tempted into the water in the gravel layer).

Start learning how to estimate the size of the plant in relation to the pot. When planted, the soil line should be 1″ (25 mm) below the pot rim. Add soil to bottom of pot; use a bit more than the amount needed, for the soil depth will decrease with settling.

Place your plant in the center of the pot. Gradually add soil, gently packing it uniformly and thoroughly with your fingertips as you are layering the soil (the feeling is akin to that of touching a bruised spot on your body to determine the degree of soreness). Your aim is to eliminate sizable air spaces. Do not pack hard or tamp the soil, for you then lose the porosity and, thus, aeration. When replanting plant with just a root system (no soil ball), be sure to spread the roots and with tenderness work soil all around and between them. Do not add all the soil in one action or only firm top soil level.

Water by allowing a gentle tepid stream to completely saturate the ball then drain out of the bottom of the pot. (Exercise care in judging quantity of water used in pot without drainage but with gravel.) If the top soil line has dropped below 1″ (25 mm) from the pot's rim level, water a second time with sufficient water to drip through pot's hole. Add enough soil to reestablish this level. Now water again, allowing the water to drain. In a pot without drainage, add just enough water to water-in the new soil.

It is extremely important that a plant be repotted with the proper soil level at the stem, that is, planted at the same level as before. Your plant has an existing soil line on its stem. This is obvious by the color being a shade darker

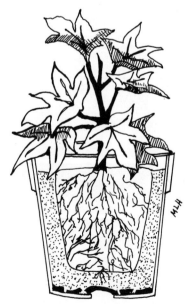

Plant centered in pot; new potting mix added in order that soil line is 1″ (25 mm) below pot rim when potting process is completed.

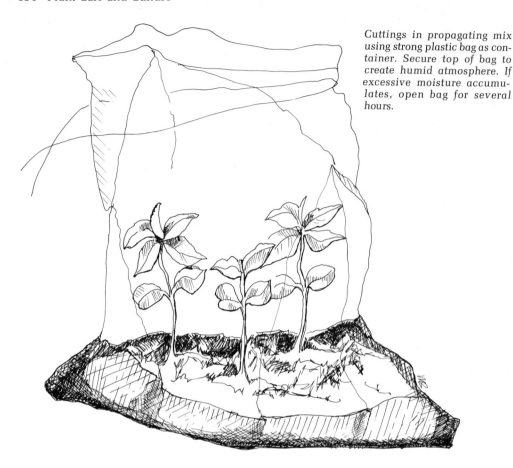

Cuttings in propagating mix using strong plastic bag as container. Secure top of bag to create humid atmosphere. If excessive moisture accumulates, open bag for several hours.

below and lighter above. Ensure that the added soil is level with this line of demarcation, avoiding exposed roots at one extreme or suffocating in the other extreme.

Naturally, you've rinsed the exterior of the pot for good housekeeping. Now set the pot on its gravel-filled slider with proper water level on gravel. (Of course, you have thoroughly washed both the slider and gravel, if previously used.) Keep your lovely out of direct sun and/or wind for a recuperation period of one week. (You'll see, leaves are now firm, and plant is blushing in good health.) Mist your friend at least once each morning to create that healthy humidity . . . it will help enormously.

Side or Top-Dressing In researching a specific plant, you may find it's a genus which likes to be potbound and prefers not to be disturbed. If this be the case, we suggest that semiannually you remove approximately 2″ (50 mm) of soil from the top soil line. Carefully aerate (loosen the soil), disturbing the root system as little as possible. Add new potting mix and lightly cultivate it into the existing earth ball, not necessarily deeply, for the watering processes will carry the nutrients into the subsoil roots. Then water plant thoroughly. This procedure is known as side-dressing or top-dressing.

How very satisfying to be successful in maintaining the vigor of your plant possession. In learning self-repotting and potting-on, you've saved all the way 'round: the cost of having a professional handle the service, or the cost of replacing a plant because you didn't bother to attend to its cultural needs. Too, you saved face conversationally, for now you can compete verbally with the rest of us proud plant-parent do-it-yourselfers. So why not take all this saving and go adopt a new genus to add to your plant family and challenge yourself to a new, stimulating chapter in life?

Parenthood Through Propagation

As with each subject covered in preceding pages, entire books are available on a specific cultural practice. There are simple methods of propagation and very involved, complicated methods of propagation. One can select the seemingly least difficult means if in Section I the procedure is specified for your potentially new parent.

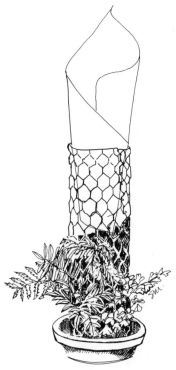

Fern column within antique lantern of leaded glass

a Column made of ½" (12 mm) wire, fixed to slider by plaster of Paris.
  1 place several pieces of horticultural charcoal in base and line base with moist sphagnum moss; pour potting mix through cardboard funnel into cylinder;

  2 firm soil with tamper—should be approximately a 2" (50 mm) depth—and moisten soil; young ferns are inserted through mesh into mixture;

  3 continue layering moist moss, potting mix, watering and inserting ferns. Remove funnel; with potting mix level at top of column, insert fern or ferns vertically on top, leaving fronds (leaves) outside

b Lantern casing is set over column. This casing helps control humidity, mist if moisture level too low, remove casing for several hours if too much moisture accumulates.

Idle fish tank, sterilized and used as convenient propagation container. Removable glass lid controls humid cultural needs.

Propagation is the attempt to reproduce biologically additional plants from an existing plant. Production of plants from seeds or spores is categorized as *sexual reproduction*. All other methods of propagation fall within a second category, *asexual reproduction*, known as vegetative reproduction.

SEXUAL REPRODUCTION

Important: seeds and/or spores must be fresh for assured success.

Seeds can be planted in conveniently available containers. Keep in mind that the containers must be of appropriate size; metal is not suitable, and containers must be disease and pest free.

Purchase and sow two seeds directly into growing blocks, cubes, or pellets. Soak the unit in tepid water, then place in or under secured clear, lightweight plastic; the tent or closed bag method creates a high-humidity environment.

Maintain an average 75°F (23°C) for germination. Heating cables for constant bottom heat are available in various sizes.

Light exposure should be bright but diffused; *never* direct (aside from that for some cacti). Fluorescent grow bulbs—great! Again, buy the technical book on indoor light, for all stages of specific species have differing needs, such as distance to be placed under bulbs and time spans of exposure. (If I were to generalize in foot candles, I would surely get burned.)

Follow instructions on packet for seed sowing.

Planting Mediums and Methods for Sexual Reproduction

Garden soil: must be of totally porous and fine texture and sterile; dampen by light misting prior to sowing seed.

Vermiculite: moisten thoroughly. Place in plastic bag, pour off all excess water, level off in germination receptacle.

Growing in a jiffy pellet, this seedling illustrates the progressive stages of damping-off disease, a fungus attacking at stem base. Seedling weakens, wilts, and passes on.

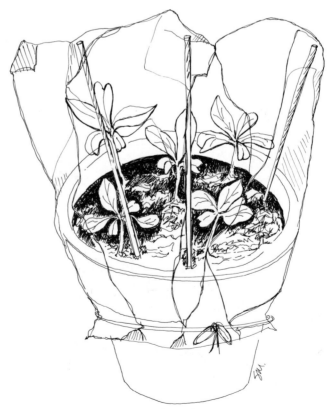

Sprouted seeds in humid atmosphere created by plastic tent.

Sphagnum moss, milled: moisten thoroughly and squeeze out excessive water, level off in sowing container.

Soilless mixes: mixed peat moss and vermiculite, sterile; eliminates possibility of damping off disease, fatal to seedlings, caused by organisms in nonsterile mediums; moisten, removing excessive water, spread evenly in propagation unit.

Fine seed is dusted over the surface of the mix; settle in seed by briefly misting with a very fine and tepid gentle spray; encase in plastic for humidity using one of illustrated methods.

Fern spores are sown as fine seed; maintain high humidity level in plastic enclosure as illustrated; if level lowers obviously, remove plastic and moisten mix with a brief gentle, tepid mist. Spores are generally secured from the underside of the fern frond (leaf). A magnifying glass is needed to determine that the spore case or covering is opening, at which time the frond is cut off to the size convenient for use. Place, underside down, on a piece of paper for a few days until spores fall onto paper and then proceed with method as herein described; or take freshly cut frond and place, underside down, on propagation mix; follow previous cultural advice for ferns in Section I.

Larger seeds are placed in mix, pressing in to approximately ¼" (6 mm) depth; space 2" (50 mm) apart; proceed with misting and plastic coverage.

A few species can have their pits or seeds germinated in water culture.

Sprouted seedlings need stronger light, but do not move into direct sunlight. Procedure prior to and through transplanting will be covered in this section, with rooted cuttings. *Note:* If an excessive amount of moisture accumulates in the plastic humidifying unit, dismantle partially for a few hours allowing free air circulation.

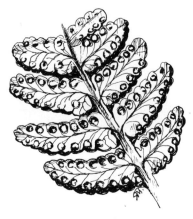

Sori, fern spores, illustrated on underside of leaflets of fronds (leaves) of Dryopteris marginali.

ASEXUAL REPRODUCTION

Vegetative propagation is asexual propagation; either term is correct. The meaning, of no sexual union. This category includes numerous methods of birthing a true plant from the parent plant. All propagation methods described henceforth are of this classification. Refer to Section I for methods for a specific genus. Of interest: Many genera do not produce identically from seed.

Propagation by cuttings is when a piece of a healthy plant is stimulated to root development . . . might well be an accidentally broken off leaf or stem or a

Single cutting in propagating mix; inverted glass jar provides humid atmosphere; asexual reproduction.

Tip growth removal for branching and compactness; nip out new growth with thumb and forefinger at point indicated by black lines.

Double branching has occurred at base of pinched-off new tip growth.

"slip," a portion of the plant removed specifically for propagation. For the plant needing tip growth removal for branching, pinch out new tip growth as it occurs. Double branching will occur at base of removed tip; tip, if large enough, can be used for propagating.

Again, dependent on species, cuttings will root in a number of mediums: water, perlite or vermiculite with medium kept moist (yet not a swimming hole), moist milled sphagnum moss, moist soilless mixes, damp coarse and sterile sand, or any of these mixed with peat moss. Bright diffused light (no direct sunlight) and high humidity are necessary in fostering healthy new plants.

General. Preferably take cuttings in active growth period of parent plant, generally spring to early summer; exceptions follow later.

use young, healthy material

never allow tissue to dry prior to inserting cutting in rooting medium and placing in proper atmosphere

note illustrations for cultural methods

if plant material is not in a regulated humid environment during rooting process, spray frequently with tepid, fine mist around cuttings

maintain constant temperature averaging in 70°F (21°C) range

Leaf Cuttings

For a long-leaved succulent, cut leaf into 2″ (50 mm) lengths; set aside, out of sun, to dry out for 2 days then insert in propagating mix for cacti.

For leaf pieces of species with large, outstanding veins in leaves (as certain begonias), note illustration showing cuts made so that triangle point has vein abutting it; vein point of leaf piece is gently inserted into rooting mix.

For vein cutting—also for large-veined leaves of species of gloxinias and begonias, or relating to gesneriads, note illustration, making short cuts into veins on underside of leaf; settle leaf, underside down on moist propagating mixture, held in place with pebbles or hairpins through leaf; roots develop at cuts.

For leaf stem cutting—as with Saintpaulia (African violet), remove leaf with stem 2½″-3″ (62-76 mm) long; note illustrations; can be propagated in water or stem can be inserted in propagating mix or directly into African violet soil. Much success is also had by inserting small portion of leaf along with stem into mixture; this method stabilizes cutting; see illustration for angle of insertion.

Note All cuts should be made with sharp, sterile instrument; all stems should be cut on angle.

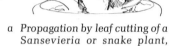
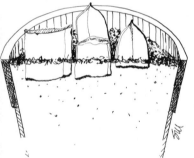

a Propagation by leaf cutting of a Sansevieria or snake plant, using sharp instrument for clean cuts.

b 2″ (50 mm) cutting in propagating mix.

Begonia leaf in vein-cutting propagation. Short cuts are made through veins on underside of leaf; position leaf underside down on moist propagating mix, mix/leaf contact is assured by weighting leaf with pebbles or pinning down in three or four places with hairpins through leaf. Roots develop at cuts with plantlets surfacing from these areas. When good root system has developed, cut plantlet from propagation leaf and pot-up.

Begonia leaf in leaf-section propagation. Cuts are triangular with point and vein abutting.

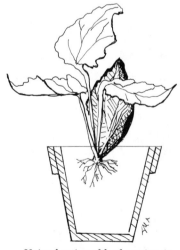

Veined point of leaf section in propagation mix has formed root system and plantlet is now ready for transplanting into proper potting mixture.

Saintpaulia, African violet, leaves rooting in foil-covered clear glass jar. A few pieces of horticultural charcoal aid in keeping water clear and sweet.

Stem cuttings of Plectranthus or Swedish ivy, Saintpaulia or African violet and Pelargonium or geranium, in propagation mix. Corked small clay pot in center contains water. Being porous, it allows moisture to seep through walls gradually, thereby keeping propagating mix at even wetness.

Saintpaulia or African violet leaf stem cutting in propagation mix using method of small leaf portion inserted along with stem. Angle insertion for stabilization.

Stem Cuttings

Cuttings should be 3″-6″ (76-150 mm) for soft-stemmed interior plants and softwood cuttings of shrub-type and tub size plants; note illustration removing flowers and excessive leaves; no more than 3-5 leaves should remain on cutting; cuttings should be of healthy young but well-formed material in active growth, which is usually found in the spring to summer season.

Use 6″-9″ (150-230 mm) length stems for hardwood cuttings; take these cuttings in the fall or winter, after growth, or while plant is in semidormancy to dormancy; stems must have leaf nodes as shown in illustration; wound the cutting by either method illustrated.

Touch stem lightly to rooting hormone, shake off excessive amount; a pencil pushed into propagating mix provides an insertion well for reception of

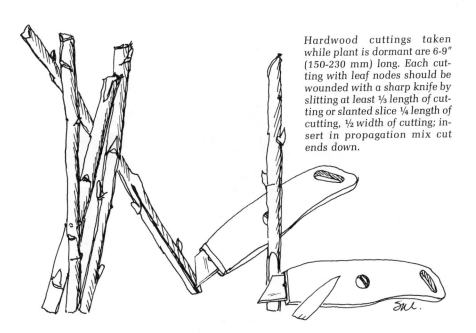

Hardwood cuttings taken while plant is dormant are 6-9″ (150-230 mm) long. Each cutting with leaf nodes should be wounded with a sharp knife by slitting at least ⅓ length of cutting or slanted slice ¼ length of cutting, ½ width of cutting; insert in propagation mix cut ends down.

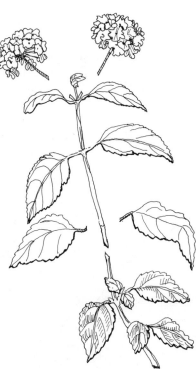

Proper preparation of soft-stemmed genera for stem propagation. Depending on species, stem is cut 3-6″ (76-150 mm) long. Remove flowers and/or buds, and foliage, leaving 3-5 leaves. Note slant of stem cut.

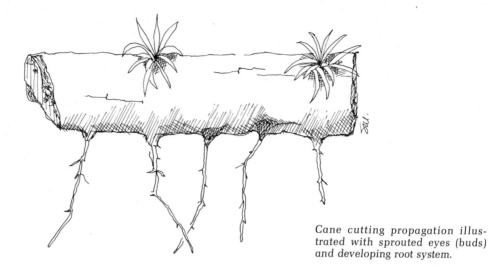

Cane cutting propagation illus-trated with sprouted eyes (buds) and developing root system.

stem; insert cutting in well and firm mix around stem for support; provide humid environment; softwood cuttings are inserted in medium to just below lower leaves, 1"-2" (25-50 mm), making sure a leaf node bud is subsurface; hardwood cuttings are inserted deeply; all nodes must be covered by propagating mix.

Generally, root formation takes far longer for hardwood cuttings. Patience! When leaves sprout, open, remain open and true green, transplanting time has arrived.

A bud or cane cutting can have one or more buds as illustrated; for certain species embed a piece of stem in moist propagating mixture with eyes (buds) exposed, as shown.

TRANSPLANTING

The illustration shows a well-rooted seedling or cutting ready for transplant. Handle tenderly to avoid bruising fragile roots; pot-up in potting medium for

A well-rooted seedling ready for potting.

Propagation by root division—a Sansevieria or snake plant being divided with mature top leaves and root system and ready to be potted.

the parent species. Use a pot relating to the size of the root system, generally a 2"-3" (50-76 mm) pot. Do not over-pot! Water thoroughly, maintain good humidity level, and keep in bright diffused light site up to a week; then move on to light exposure noted for species. Be alert to wilting or shock and adjust light and temperature accordingly.

Root Cutting
Certain species can be propagated by portions of roots being cut then planted separately. Site in propagating environment of bright diffuse light and 70°F (21°C) until surfacing of top growth; when several inches high, site plant in exposure noted for the genus.

Root Division
Separate clumps of certain species by dividing the root system, along with the top growth, into smaller clump. If tender pulling apart of roots cannot master the division without injury, slice through with a sharp knife; pot-up individually into planting medium suggested for genus, water thoroughly, and provide protective environment of muted light and constant temperature until new growth is evident; most genera benefit from increased humidity during this reestablishment stage.

Tuber and Rhizome Division
These are underground stems thickened for food storage; divide so each section to be propagated has an eye; lightly dust cut ends with rooting hormone; pot-up as noted for species; see illustration.

Tuberous Root Division
Roots thickened for food storage; eyes are located at base of parent stem; division must be made so there is a portion of this parent stem with each piece to be propagated; dust cut ends lightly with rooting hormone; pot-up as for genus; note illustration.

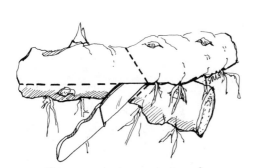

Rhizome, creeping prostrate underground stem utilized as food storage unit. Illustration shows dividing, with sharp instrument, of sections to be propagated. Each must have at least one growth bud or eye to sprout a new plant. Eyes are positioned on top and roots on underside of stems.

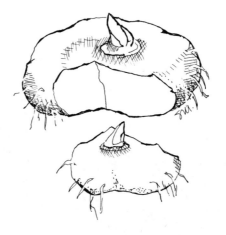

a *A parent tuberous Begonia, to be replanted, from which a section has been correctly removed for propagation, leaving bud or eye on parent plant.*

b *Division with eye from parent bulb ready to be planted for additional Begonia.*

Tuberous rootstock, referred to as rhizome, stores food in thickened ends of slim-type underground stems. Each brand with a bud or eye can be a division for an additional plant. Illustration shows sharp instrument severing into proper divisions at dotted lines.

Tuberous Rootstock (or Rhizome)

An underground stem with end thickened by food storage; rootstock with more than one branch and tuber can be divided; each section to be propagated must have an eye; lightly dust cut ends with rooting hormone and plant as for species; see illustration.

BULB PROPAGATION

Scale (fleshy leaf)—see illustration; the scale is pulled off bulb and planted approximately ½″ (12 mm) deep.

Cormels, bulbils, bulblets (all offsets)—see illustration; remove and plant individually to a depth of three times the size of the offset being planted.

Offsets

Each is a plantlet, actually a side branch growing from the base of the mature plant, each producing its own root system—see illustration; sever with sharp knife as closely as possible to parent plant; kidnap this offspring about half grown (allowing time for development of sturdy root system) and plant as noted in Section I for species.

Runner

A shoot growth of length, running along ground surface, which has buds at intervals, such as the Saxifraga stolonifera (strawberry begonia); roots develop at buds to form new plantlets; each rooted plant can be severed from runner and potted-up individually.

Sucker

A rooted shoot; the shoot begins its growth subsoil; when sturdy foliage has developed and steady growth is evident the shoot or sucker should be well rooted; sever with sharp knife and pot-up individually using method for parent species; common growth habit of palm genera.

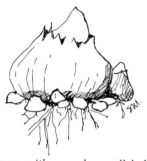

Crocus with cormels, small bulbs, forming at base of bulb and new corm, larger bulb formed to side of bulb. Break off new corm and cormels for propagation. Parent bulb and new corm or corms will bloom following year; cormels need several years to mature to blooming stage.

Narcissus or daffodil illustrating parent bulb with two bulblets or offsets, all with good root system.

Lilium or lily bulb showing fleshy scales (leaves) utilized as reserve food storage units. Single scale in propagation produces new Lilium. Remove only up to ½ of scales from parent bulb if wishing to retain parent for planting.

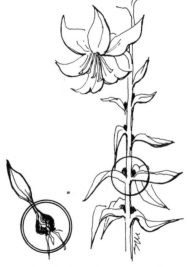

Lilium or lily illustrating bulbils, small bulbs, formed in axils of leaves to stems. Ripe bulbils are pinched out easily. Individual bulbil at stage to be removed from propagation mix and ready for planting.

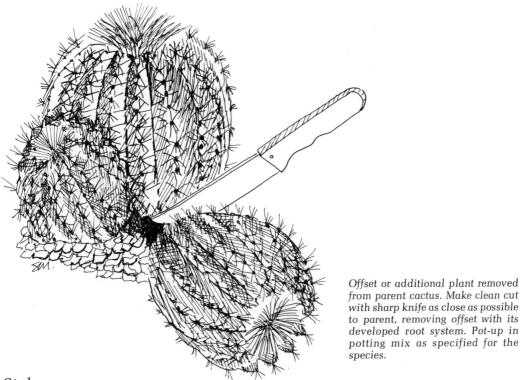

Offset or additional plant removed from parent cactus. Make clean cut with sharp knife as close as possible to parent, removing offset with its developed root system. Pot-up in potting mix as specified for the species.

Stolon

The stolon (a stem or branch of horizontal growth habit) develops a plantlet at its tip which roots when touching soil; see illustration of Chlorophytum, spider plant. Stem is severed when plantlet has adhered to soil. Although many folk remove plantlet from stem and pot-up, propagation is assured when the parent plant is allowed to nourish the babe until it has its own root system established.

LAYERING

Air layering. In this propagation method, used on certain species, a stem is wounded so that roots develop for production of an additional plant; note illustrations. At selected height for new plant, make upward cut into stem with sharp knife—a slanted slit about 1½″ (37 mm) long penetrating the 1/3 of the stem; a matchstick inserted, as shown, will keep cut open. Lightly dust the

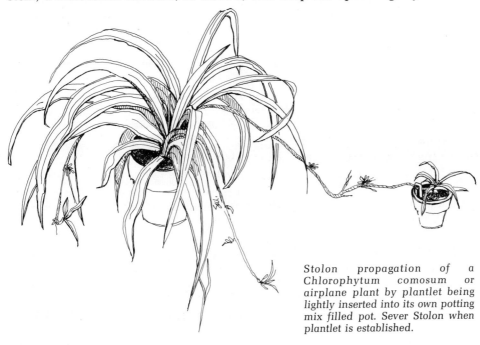

Stolon propagation of a Chlorophytum comosum or airplane plant by plantlet being lightly inserted into its own potting mix filled pot. Sever Stolon when plantlet is established.

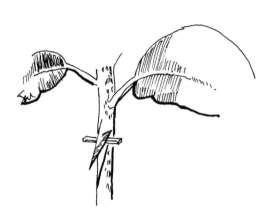

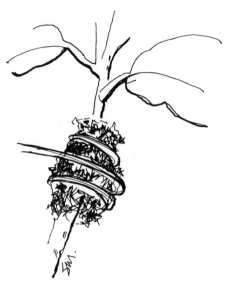

Air layering
a A slanted upward cut 1½" (37 mm) long and into ⅓ depth of stem is made at desired height with sharp knife.

b Insert matchstick to keep cut open.

c Moist sphagnum moss is placed around wound to 2" (50 mm) depth, 3" (76 mm) above and below cut and tied in place.

wound with rooting hormone (air layering kits available at retail garden supply outlets include all necessary materials). Thoroughly water sphagnum moss and squeeze all excess water from it so that it is completely damp; apply a 2" (50 mm) layer of moss over and around wound, extending 3" (76 mm) above and 3" (76 mm) below the cut. Encase the sphagnum moss in polyethylene plastic for moisture retention. Tie or tape to secure, although it is not necessary to have the package 100% airtight; 8-10 weeks of patience should produce the first obvious roots within the plastic housing; have more patience, allow another 2-3 weeks for further root development. The newly rooted section is called a "layer." Sever the layer from the original plant; making the cut several inches below the newly rooted portion is advantageous, for this protruding stem aids in supporting this new layer—which you can now pot-up as noted in Section I for this species.

Ground layering. For certain species; proceed in general manner as with air layering by slitting a young, healthy stem. Wedge wound, keeping it open, dust lightly with rooting hormone, and place wounded area on propagating mix or potting mix. Cover cut thoroughly with mix, weight with pebbles or small rock or pin down with bent wire, provide moderate but constant moisture (barely damp at all times) and good humidity level. When well rooted, proceed with severing layer and potting-up.

Propagation can be fun, exciting, and a super ego builder when successful. The proof of the progeny arrives. Leaving the nursery with its controlled conditions to brave the unnatural interior environment geared to people comforts is the "testy" time for plant; for humans, it should be sympatico time. So, please, be sensitive to "shock" signs. In moving into permanent site, do so gradually.

d *Sphagnum moss is completely encased in polyethylene, tied or taped at ends for moisture retention.*

e *Well-developed root system on layer.*

Adjust cultural attentions to this teenager's needs until totally settled-in:
 —check moisture level daily
 —if a humidity liker—provide a mist an extra time or two daily
 —no drafts
 —no direct sun, except for cacti
 —no temperature extremes
 —a few extra hours with a grow lite is beneficial for most genera

There is more pleasure in store for you and your plant. Now that the new plant is totally established by evidence of constant new healthy growth, present it to a friend; so nice to brighten another little corner of the world.

Disease Symptoms: From Cause to Cure

Whether it is the norm of "be aware care" time or "intensive care" attention, the charts in this chapter should suffice in the Rx area of plant needs. The key word, *care*, means constant concern and good common sense. If you have a splinter in your finger, remove it immediately to avoid serious infection. If you spy a pest, eradicate it immediately to avoid serious infestation. If you have abdominal pains, seek professional attention to determine the cause, then have it treated to deter demise. If you have a wilting plant, give thorough examination to determine the cause, then treat accordingly; yes, to deter demise.

The needs to retain and maintain healthy green friends have been expounded upon in the cultural chapters of this manual. If you *care*, create the correct cultural environment, now. Yet, being cognizant of human frailties, and accepting the inevitable of the microscopic necessarily going undetected, the law of averages dictates that this first-aid section is necessary. There are both unavoidables and avoidables in human control of plant infestations. **Remember:**

- —when handling an ill plant or parts of problematic plant material, the disease can be transferred to healthy parts or plants, so wash hands thoroughly
- —the new green member of an outside source, regardless of how sterile its previous habitat, should be confined to a solitary area until given a clean bill of health
- —when plant is summering outside, realize that constant rain for several days creates conditions prime for disease spores to germinate, thus plant infection.
- —if your greenery is rare, or if you care to cure a common genus but the situation defies you, contact your local agricultural extension service. They will provide you with the most current information on insecticides and fungicides

Please, use *only* products that are biodegradable, those that will decompose in nature:

- —when using spray bomb, keep approximately 18″ (.45 m) from foilage, for gas activating the bomb can burn leaves
- —be aware of chemicals in presence of children and animals
- —set aside an intensive care center for patients

Most Important: follow all directions on chemical products totally, thoroughly, carefully, and completely.

Do not harm the stray ladybug who has honored your interior habitat with her presence. She will be preoccupied with an appetizing aphid or a miserable mite and protecting your plant but not damaging your domain.

Do remember that a pest-ridden plant becomes weakened and therefore disease prone.

Terms to know:

chlorosis—loss of green color

fungicide—substance formulated to aid in fungi prevention

systemic (insecticide)—substance formulated as an insecticide, applied to soil or foliage and absorbed by plant. Toxic to insect partaking of plant material

honeydew—a sweet discharge deposited by aphids, scales, mealybugs, and mites

IF IN ERROR OR NEGLECT, THIS HAPPENS—PROBLEM AND CURE

Cause	Result	Cure
Inadequate light	Wilting—dwarfed new growth; small, few, or no flowers; leggy (thin, tall) plant; chlorosis	Increase length of time and intensity of light
Too much light	Leaf burn; yellowing foliage; dwarfed new leaves; wilting	Decrease light intensity
Site change too rapid from shade to bright light or sun	Brown spots on leaves; brown leaf tips	Resite and increase light intensity gradually; snip off brown tips
Site change too rapid from sun to shade exposure	Leaf drop	Resite and decrease light intensity gradually
Not rotating plant	Unbalanced growth, leaning toward light-source	Rotate plant ¼ turn each watering
Plant sited behind glass exposed to strong sunlight; (window acts as a magnifying glass increasing intensity of light rays)	Leaf burn	Filter light with curtain or move back from glass; cut away burned tissue; dust with ferbam (only until healed)
Compacted soil	Chlorosis; yellow foliage; root rot	Aerate soil, cut off rotted roots to sound tissue; dust with rootone or ferbam; check drain hole in pot
Overwatering	Leaf spot; foliage drop or foliage browning; leads to fungus causing root, stem, and/or crown rot; chlorosis	Check drainage; aerate top soil with fork; water less frequently and/or heavily; read *Watering*
Underwatering	Overall wilting; leaf drop, foliage browning	Check for too porous soil; check moisture level more frequently; water thoroughly each time
Cold water splashing leaves during watering	Yellow or white spots	Avoiding spillage or dripping
Temperature too high	Leaf yellowing, wilting, and/or curling	Lower temperature or resite in cooler temperature
Temperature too low	Wilting; stunted growth; demise of plant	Increase temperature or resite in warmer location
Foliage touching window glass	Brown leaf tips; bleached leaves; brown spots on foliage from sun burn or chill	Resite plants
Drafts	Leaf browning; leaf drop	Resite plant or protect with a barrier

Cause	Result	Cure
Starvation; no fertilizer, no side-dressing or repotting	New growth is dwarfed; leaf drop	Establish feeding program and/or repot or pot-on
Overfertilization	Root burn and/or stem burn causing wilting; distortion (green scum on pot indicative)	Temporarily cease feeding program; immerse pot in warm water for 30 seconds; don't fertilize dormant plants; always apply fertilizer in diluted liquid form; read *Diet Details of Fertilization*
Not enough nitrogen	New leaves are dwarfed; yellowing leaves	Add fertilizer containing nitrogen; check percentages in product being used
Too much fertilizer	Tall, thin, leggy growth	Reduce fertilizer strength and/or frequency of application; check percentages in product being used
Not enough iron	Chlorosis	Apply chelated iron
Build up of salts from fertilizers or watering	White crust appears on soil's surface or pot; leaf burn; leaf drop; wilting	Water plant thoroughly (flush out) to dissolve salts; wash pot; coat rim of pot with wax to prevent salt adherence and thus leaf burn
Poor site planning (object rubbing against leaves)	Browning of leaf tips	Resite plant to non-traffic area
Injury to foliage (cut, scraped or smashed plant tissue)	Curled leaves, susceptable to fungus attack	Dust wounds with fungicide, keep dry until healed
Poor housekeeping (dead flowers and leaves left on plant)	Fungus attack	Remove dead plant parts; mist pot and soil with solution of benomyl fungicide
Low humidity	Foliage yellowing; leaves without luster; foliage with dry, cracked, brown spots; leaf drop; plant wilting	Trays of watered pebbles; misting; humidifiers
No ventilation or air circulation	Fungus causes rotting	Mist with solution of benomyl; use fan, but not directly on plants
Plants subjected to air pollution	Flower buds burst; bud drop; foliage turns brown and/or black	Filter air; if using air conditioners, increase humidity
Potbound	Plant dries out too often; wilting; yellowing foliage; stunted growth	Time to repot or pot-on

IF YOU SITE THIS PEST—EFFECT AND CURE

	Pest	Result	Cure
 Ant	**Ants**—feed on honeydew secreted by insects	Pick up and carry other pests; mealybugs, mites, etc., to other plants	Use any sprays around but not on plants; soak infested soil and pots with a systemic, 40% soluble powder, 1½ teaspoons per gallon of water
 Aphid	**Aphids**—plant lice to ⅛″ (3mm) size; white, red, green, or black soft-bodied insects on undersides of leaves —suck plant juices; carrier of virus and fungus	Foliage deformation—sticky, curled and/or yellowed leaves, and/or sooty mold	For light infestation: remove individual aphids with an alcohol-dipped cotton swab, rinse plant in warm soapy water; follow-up with rinse of lukewarm water; for heavy infestation: spray with pyrethrum, rotenone, or malathion; apply systemic to soil

Aphid on Browallia or sapphire flower

Caterpillar	**Caterpillars**—wormlike immature forms of moths and butterflies	Chewed leaves and flowers	Apply malathion to foliage; hand-pick pests

Caterpillar on Primula or primose

	Pest	Result	Cure

Centipedes—sizable, swift moving, many legged crawler—eat fine hair roots and subsoil plant material

Root rot; stunted young growth; wilt; leaf drop

Repot in sterile potting mix, thoroughly prune affected roots; spray pests with malathion

Centipede

Cockroaches—brownish beetle-type bug—feed on foliage, sometimes flowers

Leaves and/or tender stems chewed-up

Spray with malathion; use roach spray around but not on plant

Cockroach

Crickets—hopping black grasshopper-type insects—eat tender new growth, usually during dark hours

New foliage is eaten or vanishes

Use systemic insecticide on soil; hand-pick pest and destroy

Cricket

Cutworms—wormlike immature stage of moths

Chewed leaves and flowers

Apply malathion solution to soil; hand pick pests

Cutworm

*Cutworm on Primula
or primose*

Earthworms—up to 10″ (254 mm), round segmented worms— tunnel thru soil allowing overabundance of air to roots

Break roots; root rot; clog drainage

Water soil with systemic, ½ tablespoon of 50% soluble powder; apply for all acidic plants limewater, 1 teaspoon per pint; to prepare: stir, let settle, pour off clear liquid on plant

Earthworm

	Pest	Result	Cure
Earwig	**Earwigs**—blackish brown beetle-type insect—eat tender new growth, flower, and foliage	Holes in leaves and flowers	Pick-off and destroy pest; use roach spray around but not on plant; spray plant with malathion
 *Fungus Gnat*	**Fungus Gnats**—very small deep colored flies—hatch in soil, maggot eats the fine root system	Root rot; leading to stunted plant growth, yellowing leaves	Soak soil with malathion; spray gnats with housebug spray
 *Leaf Miner*	**Leaf miners**—the baby insect developed from the egg deposited in the foliage, known as larva, shaped like a small worm or grublike—eat the cellular tissue of the leaf	Tunnellike yellowish brown paths in leaves; leaves dry up, wilt; leaf drop	Destroy infested material, treat soil with systemic granules or liquid; place plant in intensive care ward until controlled

*Leaf Miner on
Sinningia or gloxinia*

| *Leaf Roller* | **Leaf rollers**—caterpillars, immature stage of a moth, known as larva—rolls leaf around itself and munches on foliage | Rolled leaf, holes in leaves | Hand-pick insect; destroy damaged foliage; spray with malathion |

*Leaf Roller
on Begonia*

Pest	Result	Cure

Mealybug

Mealybugs—¼″ (6mm) size white oval adult like small cotton ball—suck plant juices

Pale foliage; leaf drop; stunted growth

Eradicate individual bugs with alcohol on cotton swab; wash plant with soapy water, then rinse with clear water; for heavy infestation spray malathion

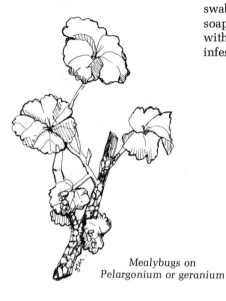

*Mealybugs on
Pelargonium or geranium*

Millipede

Millipedes—fast crawling many legged hard-shelled worm—hiding under pots only to sneak out and eat away on young, tender plant material including subsoil roots

Stem growth, seedlings chewed; root rot; stunted growth

Hand-pick and destroy; spray plant with malathion

Mite

Mites—¹/₃₂″ (.7mm) size; look for webs on undersides of leaves— suck plant juices from new central leaves

Leaf curl; leaf drop; stunted growth; blackened buds; crowns bunched, mottled leaves

Cut away infested parts; destroy severely infested plants; wash with strong water spray then spray with dicofol, repeat in 3 days, repeat in 10 days; alternate with malathion if pest persists

*Mites on Euphorbia
pulcherrima or poinsettia*

Nematodes—microscopic round worms—root sucking disease vectors

Root gall thru root rot to eating away root system

Repot using sterilized soil; or soak soil with nemacide; V-C-13, DBCP, Vapam or formaldehyde

Pest	Result	Cure

a Juniper scale

b Euonymus scale

Scale

Scales—⅛″ (3mm) size; hard-shelled lumps on stems and leaves, obvious along main leaf vein

Foliage yellows

Scrub using soft brush and warm soapy water, then rinse thoroughly; for heavy infestation treat with rotenone, pyrethrum, or malathion

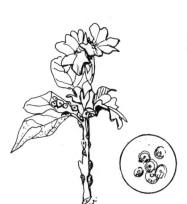

Scale on Crossandra or firecracker flower

Slug

Slugs—gray soft-tissued and slimy shell-less snails

Shredded-type holes in leaves and flowers

Apply insecticide around and near pot; or place saucer of stale beer or grape juice near pot to attract slugs; or apply metaldehyde to soil

Slug on Kalanchoe blossfeldiana or Christmas kalanchoe

Snail

Snails—½″-4″ (12-100mm) yellow to black in color—chew on tender new plant material

Shredded-type holes in leaves and flowers

Apply insecticide around and near pot; or place saucer of stale beer or grape juice near pot to attract snails; or apply metaldehyde to soil

Snail on Kalanchoe blossfeldiana or Christmas kalanchoe

	Pest	Result	Cure

Sowbug

Sowbugs—grayish black small crawling pests —eating young tender plant material, roots, and stems

Root rot; stunted growth

Hand-pick to eradicate; spray soil with malathion or drench with V-C-13; spray around plant but not on it with household bug spray for ants or roaches

Springtail

Springtails—hopping, small pests, deeply colored—drill minute holes through foliage

Pin holes in leaves

Do not overwater; spray around with household bug spray but not on plant; drench soil with water to bring pests to soil surface, or drench soil with malathion or V-C-13

Thrip

Thrips—$1/16''$ (1.60mm) size; slender yellow, green, or black insects suck plant juices

Streaked, deformed leaves; distorted new growth

Spray with malathion

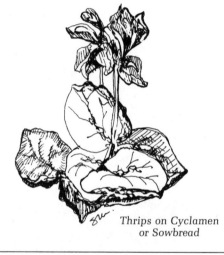

Thrips on Cyclamen or Sowbread

Whitefly

White Flies—$1/16''$ (1.60mm) size; white wedge-shaped wings— suck plant juices

Leaf yellowing; leaf drop

For mild infestation, wash leaves with strong water spray; for heavy infestation spray with rotenone, or malathion; difficult to eradicate so follow up treatment as needed; for ferns use nicotine-sulfate

Whitefly on Lantana or Red Sage

IF DISEASE STRIKES—SYMPTOM AND CURE

Disease	Symptom	Cure
Bacterial Infection	Graying, yellowing leaves, crown rot	Spray with Captan or ferbam
Botrytis Blight	Gray mold on all parts of plant	Avoid overcrowding, over-feeding, overwatering; spray with zineb or ferbam; dispose of infected parts
Edema—plants rapidly absorb water but trans-piration (moisture loss) is slow, moisture backs up, cells burst	Swelling on leaves and corky ridges	Water less, especially on dark humid days, increase temperature; lower hu-midity; allow soil to dry before watering
Fungi Diseases—consisting of mold and galls	Stem and root rot	Dust with sulphur or folpet; increase air circulation; decrease humidity
Powdery Mildew—a fungus	Leaves covered with white powder	Dust with zineb or sul-phur, or spray Karathane or folpet
Virus	Mottle, yellowing; leaf curl; spot-ringed flowers; stunted, dwarfed flowers are anemic	Prompt removal and destruction of infected plant; do not propagate infected plant; control insect vectors—aphids and thrips

IF YOUR PLANT LOOKS LIKE THIS—CAUSE AND CURE

Appearance	Cause	Cure
Flower small, or no bloom	Insufficient light time length and/or intensity	Increase light exposure gradually
Flower buds burst; fall off; petals brown or black	Air pollution	Increase humidity; filter air from air conditioner; remove from polluted environment
Chewed flowers	Slugs and/or beetle-type insects	Apply insecticide around but not on plant; apply metaldehyde to soil; place saucer of stale beer and grape juice near pot to attract slugs
Unbalanced growth of plant, especially toward light source	Not rotating plant	Turn plant ¼ around at each watering

Appearance	Cause	Cure
Plant dries out too frequently	Soil too porous; potbound	Repot or pot-on
Fungus appears on all parts of plant	Plants constantly too wet	Provide better drainage; aerate; water less frequently; decrease humidity
	Poor air circulation	Provide fresh air ventilation
	Honeydew	Check for sucking insects
	Dead flowers and leaves left on plant	Check plant frequently and prune dead or dying parts
Wilt	Under- or overexposure to light	Increase or decrease light exposure in intensity and/or time period
	Low humidity, lack of moisture	Add moisture to atmosphere; set plants on trays of pebbles and water; humidifier; additional misting
	Root rot diseases	Check drainage; water less frequently and/or heavily
	High temperatures	Resite in cooler location
	Potbound	Repot or pot-on
	Root burn, over-fertilization	Flush soil with water to dilute and remove excess salts
Plant covered with gray mold, leaves turn brownish black	Botrytis Blight—gray mold blight	Avoid overcrowding, overfeeding, overwatering; prune infected parts; spray with zineb or ferbam; dispose of badly infected plant
Galls, blights, tumors	Nematodes subsoil	Repot using sterilized soil; soak soil with nemacide-V-C-13, or Vapam
	Insects or disease	Inspect for pests, diagnose and treat
Green scum on sides of clay pot	Excess fertilizer	Wash pot thoroughly; flush out soil several times

Appearance	Cause	Cure
Leafspot	Cold water on leaves	Avoid spillage, dripping; use tepid, room-temperature water
	Overwatering	Check drainage; aerate soil; water less frequently
	Improper potting, thus compacted soil	Aerate soil
	Virus disease or insects	Inspect, diagnose, and treat
Gray mottled leaves; webs on undersides of leaves	Red spider mite	Wash plant with strong spray; if heavily infested treat with dicofol, tetradifon, or malathion
Leaves without luster, crackling	Low humidity	Set pots on trays of pebbles and water; additional misting; use humidifiers
New leaves are dwarfed or misshapen	Lack of fertilizer	Feed plant
	Too much nitrogen	Reduce fertilizer strength and/or frequency of application
	Not enough or too much light	Increase or decrease light intensity and/or length
Curled leaves	Excessive light	Decrease light intensity
	Excessive heat	Lower temperature or move plant to cooler location
	Aphids or virus	Inspect, diagnose, and treat
Brown leaf tips or spots	Draft	Resite or divert heavy air flow
	Object rubbing leaves	Resite plant
	Low humidity	Trays of pebbles and water; additional misting; use humidifier
	Insects	Inspect, diagnose, and treat
	Sunburn	Decrease light intensity
	Insecticide burn	Follow directions for sprays

Appearance	*Cause*	*Cure*
Brown leaf tips or spots, cont'd.	Insufficient water	Water more frequently and/or thoroughly
	Salt build up in soil	Flush soil with water several times
Chlorosis—pale green color in leaves	Insufficient or excessive light	Increase or decrease light intensity; resite
	Improper watering	Adjust water program
	Iron deficiency	Apply chelated iron
	Poor drainage	Check drain hole; aerate soil; repot if necessary
	Root injury	Prune dead roots, dust with rootone, then repot
	Insects or disease	Inspect, diagnose, and treat
Yellowing of foliage	Low humidity	Set pots on trays of pebbles and water; additional mist; use humidifier
	Starvation	Develop fertilizing program
	Potbound	Repot or pot-on
	Root rot; poor drainage	Aerate soil; prune dead or rotting roots, dust with rotenone, then repot
	Severe insect infestation	Inspect, diagnose, and treat
	Excessive light	Decrease intensity
	Old age	That's life! Cremation
	Excessive temperature	Resite to cooler location or lower temperature
Leaf drop	Severe change in temperature; drafts	Site plant in ventilated area; no drafts; subject plant to least amount of change in temperature when moving
	Low humidity	Trays of pebbles and water; additional misting; use humidifier
	Extreme light change	Resite plant gradually
	Insufficient water	Water more frequently and/or thoroughly

Appearance	Cause	Cure
Leaf drop, cont'd	Old age	Dispose of plant
	Insects	Inspect, diagnose, and treat
	Excessive insecticides	Follow label directions
	Starvation	Develop fertilization program
Streaks/rings in leaves; crinkled leaves; yellow spots	Virus	Promptly remove and destroy infected plant material; do not propagate; inspect and control insect vectors
Lumps on leaves—⅛" (3 mm) small hardshelled insects along main leaf vein; honeydew; hard to detect until infestation is severe	Scale insect sucking	Scrub with soft brush or rag using warm soapy water; rinse; if heavily infested treat with rotenone, pyrethrum, or malathion
¼" (6 mm) white powdery masses on leaves and in axils, or around leaves and roots	Mealybug sucking	Eradicate individual adult bugs with alcohol on cotton swabs; wash plant with soapy, tepid water; rinse with clear tepid water; if heavily infested spray with malathion; soil bugs—use systemic granules or liquid dimethoate; wash foliage; discard severely infested plants
Foliage thickened and brittle	Cyclamen mite	Prune parts; destroy severely infested common plants; or spray with dicofol, repeat in 3 days, again in 10 days; alternate with malathion if pest persists
1/16" (1.50 mm) slender yellow, green, or black insects, on foliage and flowers; honeydew present	Thrips	Spray with malathion
Honeydew; white powdered 1/16" flies; fly up when moving foliage; leaves yellow and drop	Whiteflies	Mild cases wash leaves with strong tepid water spray; if heavily infested, treat with rotenone, pyrethrum, or malathion aerosol insecticides—repeat in 8-10 days; for ferns use nicotine-sulfate

Appearance	Cause	Cure
Sticky, curled, yellow leaves; honeydew; foliage becomes deformed; small soft bodied ⅛″ (3 mm) small red, white, green, black insects on leaf undersides	Aphids	Light infestation, remove individual aphids with alcohol-dipped cotton swab; rinse plant in warm soapy tepid water; if heavily infested, spray with pyrethrum, rotenone, or malathion; apply systemic to soil
White powdery covered leaves	Powdery mildew fungus	Dust with zineb or sulphur; or spray Karathane or folpet
Swelling on leaves, and corky ridges	Edema—plants rapidly absorb water, but transpiration (moisture loss) is slow; moisture backs up, cells burst	Reduce quantity of water, especially on dark, humid days; increase temperature; lower humidity; water less frequently; check for potbound or clogged drainage hole, or compacted soil
Stem rot, crown rot—a soft, rotting material, blackish in color	Excessive water	Adjust watering program; check for potbound, or compacted soil; clogged drainage hole
	Fungus	Dust with sulphur or folpet; increase air circulation; decrease humidity
Stem burn	Excessive fertilizer sprinkled on soil	Dilute fertilizer in water; avoid direct stem contact
Tall, thin, leggy stem	Insufficient light	Increase light intensity
	Excessive nitrogen	Flush soil; use lower nitrogen fertilizer
Root rot; dark brown mushy roots	Poor drainage	Check drain hole; aerate soil; if potbound, repot or pot-on
	Excessive watering	Adjust watering program
	Fertilizer burn	Follow label instructions
	Fungus disease	Treat with sulphur dust or folpet
	Nematodes, earthworms	Repot using sterilized soil; soak soil with nemacide-V-C-13, Vapam

Your Vacation

When those vastly varying reasons mean you're absent from home or office for abnormal periods of time, your plants' welfare is the tenacious riddle which you must satisfy.

Please allocate thinking time to the how and who of step parental attention during your sabbatical. Travel and leisure, rest and recuperation, whatever, are preceded by the flurry of packing, hurrying, scurrying 'round, oblivious to faithful green friends till often too late to make adequate arrangements.

There are questions to the problem of substitute care. In deciding, remember that the season, length of time away, and the temperatures and light conditions for your plants' continued good health affect the possibilities. Preplan with common sense for a solution in your absenteeism.

In *Summer Camp for Your Flora*, I urge you to extend to your plants a summer-long vacation by placing them in exterior locations. Once the flora have adjusted to their fiesta condominium, you now face the perplexing problem of seeing to watering needs as you pursue your personal plans. Substitute guardianship in a people-plant relationship is the answer . . . but problematic. Whoever is granted the privilege must check moisture content *at least* once a week.

When you plan to be away for *2 to 3 days*, then:
—if all aspects are normal, leave things status quo
—in summer months, if the house is closed up and abnormally hot, keep plant out of strong light
—in winter months, house closed down and abnormally cold, move plant to warmest spot, in sun if possible
—water plants the day before your departure
—"up" the water level of stones in slider on departing day to retain humidity

If you'll be away *4 days to 2 weeks*, then:
—water plant the day prior to departure
—on departure day, add water to proper level of stones in slider for humidity retention
—place polyethylene bag over plant, pot, and slider on plant of handling size (Be careful not to bruise or harm plant. Use bag larger than plant. Upon enclosure of plant, assure that bag is airtight. The purpose of the bag is to *trap* moisture, change it into humidity)
—keep plant in bright light, no direct sun
—leave shade loving plants in normal location
—move large plants out of direct sun

Going away for *2 weeks or more*? If you are not positive that your plants will receive proper attention while under the protection of a personal friend, by all means, forfeit requesting this favor. In the exception-to-every-rule idiom, it is *not* better to have loved and lost—possibly both friend and plant.

With more frequency one finds advertisements in local newpapers and the yellow pages on the availability of plant-sitting or sitters.

If possible, use an individual or firm recommended by a friend.

Your local garden club is generally more than willing to advise you in selecting the people or places with acknowledged qualifications

Blindfolded selection could so easily raise havoc, with your plants being exposed to disease or pest-ridden new acquaintances while at the caretaker's place.

Remember, automatic waterers answer only emergency needs when all other avenues have dead-ended.

MLH

Select a polyethylene bag large enough not to crowd plant. A moisture retainer when bag is airtight, thus an excellent method of plant care for a people vacation of short duration.

Summer Camp for Your Flora

"Homo sapiens benefits flora with fresh-air fund favor." You merit this headline for bestowing a wealth of health upon your plant. Returning your plants to a natural environment in the appropriate season is the best way to accomplish this.

In fact, you, Homo sapiens, should be so lucky as to have a 4-month-long, no-expense, rest-and-rehabilitation health spa vacation. Properly located in its exterior habitat, your flora will flourish from nitrogen-saturated rain, unfiltered sunlight, and wispy breezes. Of course, you do remember that happiness is humidity; plants will get a daily dose at just the right temperature.

In addition to beneficial aspects for the plants, you will have a respite in daily green care. You have placed your possessions in the hands of Mother Nature. In order for her to perform with perfection, I suggest you preplan this vacation; preparation of plant and selection of site are necessary for proper plant protection.

As vacation time—mid-May—nears, take advantage of windless, cloudy warm days for first outings. Set plants outside in a protected spot for a few hours.

"M-Day!" Moving outside, Mother's Day or toward mid-May. When we are frost-free for another season and the temperatures outside are resembling those of your interior, place your plants in nature's maternal care.

When summering out, most housed plants should be sited in shady areas on the northern to eastern sides of structures.

Most flora receiving full sun within an interior habitat must be protected from that same sun during the hottest part of the day in the exterior environment.

Foliage plants should be settled in for the summer midst exterior plantings where they can have shade protection and the advantage of all possible humidity.

Conceal an inverted saucer in foliage ground cover in exterior summer site for plant. Pot set on bottoms-up saucer deters crawling pests from invasion of potting mix and will not allow roots to penetrate earth.

Fear not high temperatures. Although plants, if they could voice their choice, would nominate day temperatures of 70°-80°F (21°-26°C) and night temperatures of 55°-65°F (12°-18°C) they adjust with ease as long as Mother Nature and you are providing the other cultural necessities: shade, water, and debugging.

The pros and cons of how best to protect your plants with the least need for concern are here exposed:

Take slider and invert on top of soil. Place pot on top of slider. Situate among ground covers, if at all possible, to shelter and aid in maintaining moisture. The purpose of inverted slider is twofold: to eliminate roots growing through pot drainage hole into ground and to eliminate the possibility of your plant sitting in a saucer of accumulated water.

Sink pot into soil to edge of rim. Prior to burying pot, place slider in bottom of hole, again inverted, or layer 2″ (50 mm) of pebbles under pot; either method is to prevent soil rooting. If pebbles are used, lift pot once each week to discourage rooting through their porosity. (If rooting through drainage hole into earth does occur, one must sever these roots when reclaiming one's plant for interior pleasure. When these very active roots are pruned, it causes a setback in growth—just at a time when your pet needs all its energy for the long unnatural enclosure to which it must adjust.)

Remove plant from pot and replant directly into ground. Realize that when plant's vacation is over, it is late summer. One then disturbs the total plant system by digging up and repotting, with no time for your plant to reestablish itself prior to its move back to those four walls, with short days and long nights and all those vitamins.

If you prefer the plant in a specific area, such as porch or patio, where there is no natural growth for plant protection, I suggest you set your pot within another pot to aid in moisture retention. If there is sufficient space between pot walls, place sphagnum moss between these walls as an added insulator. (Do follow previous guidelines for double potting under *Repotting*.)

Naturally, with parental feeling, you will make periodic visits to the campsite to assure all is well: make water, bug, and fungus check; and don't forget *bath* time, about twice a month with 2 tablespoons mild liquid soap in ½ gals (1.9 l) tepid water.

Settling in for the Winter

Along about the beginning of September, around Labor Day, no later than mid-September, is "It's Great to Get Home" time for your plant. Don't chance frost or all is lost. As with moving plants outside for summer camp, be aware of the telltale timing, when temperatures of your interior resemble those outside.

Just as you preplan your family's vacation (after reviewing previous pages, this statement is plant-family inclusive), you preplan to some degree the return home. "To some degree" as it relates to your greens' return can spell *doom*.

Take 2 weeks to delouse before moving plants from camp to house. Follow this procedure before plants' winter housing:

1. Two weeks prior to move, give plants thorough bath with 2 tablespoons mild liquid soap in ½ gals (1.9 l) tepid water.

2. Water soil in pot moderately. When water begins its drip, drip, drip through drainage hole, use soap/water bath solution and drench soil. Drench soil once more with clear tepid water till draining freely. You now undoubtedly have doomed soil's ants, snails, and whatever.

3. One week prior to move, repeat steps 1 and 2.

4. One day prior to move, repeat steps 1 and 2.

5. Rather than placing plants on or near open ground, set them in saucers, right side up this time, in an area thought to be free of crawlers.

6. Re-examine each plant thoroughly in axils and under leaves. If, after all this rub, scrub, tub business, you find even one (1) aphid or other underworld agent, you have not won.

7. Okay, *spray*; you've delayed to wit's end—yours and mine. Use insecticide bomb recommended by manufacturer for interior use (assurance of mildness). Check for specifics of proper spray for foiling particular enemy. Protect your flora and you by following all directions printed on label.

One can use a prepared mixture in pail or tub for immersion of a plant, but I truly prefer you not to mess with this Molotov cocktail; if you must, then see the section, *Washing: the Preventive Wisdom*. The tri-bath treatment should "do in" your plant's enemies, or just about. Their demise will be finalized by the spray bomb.

You now have hale and hardy house plants which in summering in their natural habitat just may have outgrown housing. Your repotting lesson, *Repotting Properly for Plant's Potential*, tells all. Fall is here, so put your mind to the reading matter and your palm to the pot, if necessary. I add: don't procrastinate. Your green will take the repotting now, after its invigorating vacation, with less setback.

Now, gradually settling down for a long winter's nap:
—reset your plant in proper site
—add pebbles to slider and water to pebbles
—mist—daily
—finger-tip touch to test for watering time
—start shampoo sessions
—resume feeding (refer to *Diet Details of Fertilization*)
—note approach of sound slumber period and act accordingly

Seasons will pass from fine fall through a wonderful winter and into a very special spring, as you share in the beauty and pleasure of each plant's progress.

Artificial Light

My apologies, if with enthusiasm you have turned to this chapter eager to absorb a wealth of clues on the precise artificial light cultural method for "a" plant. Section I of this manual refers to supplementary light. Quite a few plants are happy with longer days, so details on how many light hours to approximate before turning off the night light can be found in Section I.

The reason for my backing-off in this last chapter is easily answered; there are just too many variables. Stages of growth of a species, seasons, the conditions of the interior habitat, species and genera, as well as flower color affect the quantity and intensity of light requirements for a species. If I were to generalize, I might be to blame for a plant's demise. Therefore, consider this chapter a brief encounter in the matter of exposure.

Mother Nature does well by her plants, but then, the two have had a good period of time to develop a compatibility. We take of her progeny and resite unnaturally. Supplementary light is just one more cultural service that attempts to aid plant material by supplying a factor beneficial to the biological needs.

Phytoillumination means growing plants by method of artificial light. A *foot-candle* is a unit for measuring illumination. *Light-meters* are the accurate means for measurement determinations. But for the amateur, several good uncomplicated books are available, or one can question an experienced plant owner for the data needed to become involved with artificial light. Trial and error are inevitable. Soon, your reaction to a query on foot-candles will be, "Oh, place those seedlings about 4″ (100 mm) below two 40-watt bulbs."

The cost of bulbs is relatively low compared with their high benefits and length of burning time. Seemingly, each day offers new fixtures. Most demands for space or portability can be met by the use of either portable, expandable, or fixed units.

A reflector is a useful accessory to an artificial lighting system. This can be a commercial unit or something as simple as painting the underside of a shelf or back-up wall white. Of course, the object is the additional illumination from reflection. Then, too, one can add a timer for control and avoid concern about overillumination or electric bill.

The benefits are enormous. Foliage will be more lush; flowers radiate; many species can be made to bloom nearly year round, almost double their normal blooming span. Seedlings are happier, healthier, and grow much more quickly. A plant is formed more evenly, for there is no leaning to a light source: dark corners, previously not usable, are softened with a glowing display of charming flora—all this and more with artificial light.

Remember that:
—artificially lighted plants are very tender, so when moving them to a natural light site do so very gradually
—do not overexpose; plants need resting time
—dusty light tubes emit less light
—aging lights are obvious by darkening ends; these, too, emit less light
—with a fluorescent tube, the greatest light intensity is i the center
—incandescent bulbs throw off more heat than fluorescent bulbs
—sunlamps are not for plant use. They provide ultraviolet rays for tanning; don't sunburn your friend.

Light is of varying colors. Plant growth responds to these colors in differing patterns.
—an incandescent light is richly red; generally, red light causes plants to become leggy or tall
—a fluorescent light is richly blue; blue used alone may cause low, closely growing plant material
—a mixture of these two lights in one unit has proven excellent results

Although certain genera will grow handsomely under only artificial light, most are at their best in combination with normal, natural light. Proven: artificial rays lack the intensity and some life-giving qualities of the sun. Somehow this is a satisfying and reassuring fact.

Botanical Societies

African Violet Society of America, Box 1326, Knoxville, TN 37901.
American Begonia Society, 10934 East Flory St., Whittier, CA 90696.
American Boxwood Society, Box 85, Boyce, VA 22620.
American Camellia Society, P.O. Box 212, Fort Valley, GA 31030.
American Daffodil Society, 89 Chichester Rd., New Canaan, CT 06840.
American Fern Society, The Field Museum, Chicago, IL 60605.
American Fuchsia Society, Hall of Flowers, Garden Center of San Francisco, CA 94122.
American Gesneria Society, P.O. Box 549, Knoxville, TN 37901.
American Gloxinia & Gesneriad Society, Inc., Eastford, CT 06242.
American Hibiscus Society, P.O. Box 98, Eagle Lake, FL 33839.
American Ivy Society, 128 West 58th St., New York, NY 10019.
American Lily Society, North Ferrisburg, VT 05473
American Orchid Society, c/o The Botanical Museum of Harvard University, Cambridge, MA 02138.
American Primrose Society, 14015 84th Avenue, N.E., Bothell, WA 98011.
American Rhododendron Society, 24450 S.W. Graham's Ferry Rd., Sherwood, OR 97140.

Bromeliad Society, Inc., Box 3279, Santa Monica, CA 90403

Cactus and Succulent Society of America, Box 167, Reseda, CA 91335.

International Geranium Society, 11960 Pascal Ave., Colton, CA 92324.

Los Angeles International Fern Society, c/o Wilbur W. Olson, 2423 Burrett Ave., Redondo Beach, CA 90278.

National Chrysanthemum Society, Inc., 8504 Laverne Dr., Adelphi, MD 20783
National Oleander Society, 315 Tremont, Galveston, Texas 77550.

Palm Society, 7229 S.W. 54th Ave., Miami, FL 33145.

Saintpaulia International, Box 10604, Knoxville, TN 37919.

A Selected Bibliography

American Gloxinia and Gesneriad Society. *The Gloxinian*. Old Greenwich, Conn: Monthly magazine.

Askwith, Herbert. *The Complete Guide to Garden Flowers*. New York: A. S. Barnes and Company, 1961.

Atkinson, Robert E. *Spot Gardens*. New York: David McKay Company, Inc., 1973.

Bailey, Ralph, and McDonald, Elvin. *Good Housekeeping Illustrated Encyclopedia of Gardening*. 16 vols. New York: Hearst Magazines, Book Division, 1972.

Baker, Jerry. *Plants Are Like People*. New York: Pocket Books, 1972.

Ballard, Ernesta D. "The Compost Heap." *The Pennsylvania Horticultural Society*, vol. 3, July, 1975.

————. *Garden in Your House*. New York: Harper & Row, 1971.

Banucci, Phyllis Wolff. "Space Age Soils." *Plants Alive*, vol. 3, October, 1975.

Baumgardt, J. P. *How to Prune Almost Anything*. New York: William Morrow and Company, 1968.

Brooklyn Botanic Garden
  A House Plant Primer, 1972.
  Gardening Under Artificial Light, 1960.
  Handbook on Biological Control of Plant Pests, 1960.
  Handbook on Bonsai: Special Technique, 1972.
  Handbook on Dwarfed Potted Trees, 1971.
  Handbook on Flowering Shrubs, 1970.
  Handbook on Flowering Trees, 1967.
  House Plants, 1965.
  Japanese Gardens and Miniature Landscapes, 1961.
  Pruning Handbook, 1966.
  Summer Flowers for Continuing Bloom, 1968.
  Trained and Sculptured Plants, 1961.

Bush-Brown, James and Louise. *America's Garden Book*. New York: Charles Scribner's Sons, 1965.

Chidamian, Claude. *The Book of Cacti and Other Succulents*. The American Garden Guild and Doubleday, 1958.

Crockett, James Underwood.
  Bulbs, 1971.
  Flowering House Plants, 1973.
  Flowering Shrubs, 1973.
  Foliage House Plants, 1973.
  Greenhouse Gardening as a Hobby. Doubleday & Company, 1961.

Perennials, 1973.
New York: Time-Life Books.

Donahue, Roy L. *Soils, An Introduction to Soils and Plant Growth.* New Jersey: Prentice-Hall, Inc., 1958.

Elbert, George and Virginia. *Plants That Really Bloom Indoors.* New York: Simon & Schuster, 1974.

Evans, Charles M., and Pliner, Roberta Lee. New York: *Rx For Ailing House Plants.* Random House, 1974.

Fernald, Merritt Lyndon. *Gray's Manual of Botany.* New York: Van Nostrand Reinhold Company, 1970.

Fitch, Charles Marden. *The Complete Book of Houseplants.* New York: Hawthorne Books, Inc., 1972.

Free, Montague. *Plant Propagation in Pictures.* The American Garden Guild Inc., and Doubleday & Company, Inc., 1957.

Graf, Alfred B. *Exotica 3.* New Jersey: Julius Roehrs Co., 1970.

Hargreaves, Bob and Dorothy.
Tropical Blossoms of the Caribbean, 1960.
Tropical Trees, 1965.
Hargreaves Company, Hawaii.

Haring, Elda. *The Seedling Handbook.* Literary Guild of America, Inc., 1968.

Hay, Roy, and Synge, Patrick M. *The Color Dictionary of Flowers & Plants for Home and Garden.* New York: Crown Publishers, Inc., 1969.

Healey, B. J. *A Gardener's Guide to Plant Names.* New York: Charles Scribner's Sons, 1972.

Henderson, P. *Gardening For Pleasure.* New York: Orange Judd, 1970.

Holtz, Charles. "Less-Grown Fruits For Warm Climates." *Horticulture,* vol. 52, July, 1975.

Ishimoto, Tatsuo and Kiyoko. *Japanese Gardens Today.* New York: Crown Publishers, Inc., 1968.

Kramer, Jack.
Bromeliads, the Colorful House Plants. New York: D. Van Nostrand, Inc., 1965.
Cacti As Decorative Plants. New York: Charles Scribner's Sons, 1974.
Container Gardening Indoors and Out. New York: Doubleday & Company, Inc., 1971.
Ferns and Palms For Interior Decoration. New York: Charles Scribner's Sons, 1972.
Gardening with Stone and Sand. New York: Charles Scribner's Sons, 1972.
Grow Your Own Plants. New York: Charles Scribner's Sons, 1973.
Hanging Gardens. New York: Charles Scribner's Sons, 1971.
How to Grow African Violets. Menlo Park, CA: Sunset Books, Lane Magazine & Book Company, 1972.
How to Grow Orchids. Menlo Park, CA: Sunset Books, Lane Magazine & Book Company, 1971.
1000 Beautiful House Plants and How to Grow Them. New York: William Morrow & Company, Inc., 1969.

Kranz, Frederick H., and Jacqueline L. *Gardening Indoors Under Light.* New York: The Viking Press, 1971.

Kromdijk, G. *200 House Plants in Color.* New York: Herder and Herder, Inc., 1971.

Lamb, Edgar and Brian. *Pocket Encyclopedia of Cacti.* New York: The Macmillan Company, 1970.

Leese, Sir Oliver. *Cacti.* London, England: Triune Books, 1973.

Loewer, Peter. *The Indoor Water Gardener's How-To Handbook.* New York: Walker and Company, 1973.

Mabe, Rex E. *Gardening With Houseplants.* North Carolina: Potpourri Press, 1973.

McDonald, Elvin.
 The Complete Book of Gardening Under Lights. New York: Popular Library, 1965.
 Garden Ideas A to Z. New York: Doubleday & Company, Inc., 1970.
 The World Book of House Plants. New York: The World Publishing Company, 1963.
Milstein, Dr. George. "Bromeliads." *Natural Gardening*, January, 1973.
Moore, Harold E., Jr. *African-Violets, Gloxinias and Their Relatives*. New York: The Macmillan Company, 1957.
Nehrling, Arno and Irene. *The Picture Book of Perennials*. New York: Hearthside Press, Inc., 1964.
Nicolaisen, Age. *The Pocket Encyclopedia of Plants and Flowers*. New York: The Macmillan Publishing Company, 1974.
Novak, F. A. *The Pictorial Encyclopedia of Plants and Flowers*. New York: Crown Publishers, Inc., 1970.
Ortho Books. *House Plants Indoors/Outdoors*. San Francisco: Ortho Book Division, 1974.
Padilla, Victoria. "The Amazing Bromeliads." *Horticulture*, September, 1974.
Rutgers University.
 Care of House Plants, 1968.
 Pruning Shrubs.
Sessler, Gloria Jean. "What to Do With Orchids in Summer." *Horticulture*, June 1974.
Simmons, Adelma G. *Herb Gardens of Delight*. New York: Hawthorn Books, Inc., 1974.
Steffeh, Edwin. *The Pruning Manual*. New York: Van Nostrand Reinhold Company, 1969.
Stowell, Jerald P. *Bonsai: Indoors and Out*. New York: D. Van Nostrand Company, Inc., 1966.
Sunset Books.
 Bonsai, 1969.
 How to Grow Bulbs, 1969.
 How to Grow House Plants, 1969.
 Japanese Gardens, 1970.
 Pruning Handbook, 1973.
 Succulents and Cactus, 1970.
 Menlo Park, California.
Sutcliffe, A. *House Plants For City Dwellers*. New York: Dutton, 1964.
Taloumis, George. *House Plants for Five Exposures*. New York: Abelard-Schuman, 1973.
Taylor, Cathryn S., and Gregg, Edith W., *Winter Flowers in Greenhouse and Sun-Heated Pit*. New York: Charles Scribner's Sons, 1969.
Taylor, Norman. *Taylor's Encyclopedia of Gardening*. Boston: Houghton Mifflin Company, 1961.
Texas A & M University. *Indoor Landscaping With Living Foliage Plants*, 1974.
U.S. Department of Agriculture. *Selecting and Growing House Plants*, 1963.
Westcott, Cynthia. *The Gardener's Bug Book*. New York: Doubleday & Company, Inc., 1964.
Wilson, Helen Van Pelt. *The Joy of Geraniums*. New York: M. Barrows and Company, Inc., 1965.
Wright, Michael. *The Complete Indoor Gardener*. New York: Random House, 1974.
Wyman, Donald. *Dwarf Shrubs*. New York: Macmillan Publishing Company, Inc.
Yang, Linda. *The Terrace Gardener's Handbook*. New York: Doubleday & Company, 1975.

Index of Common Names